The Complete Guide to Illustration and Design Techniques and Materials

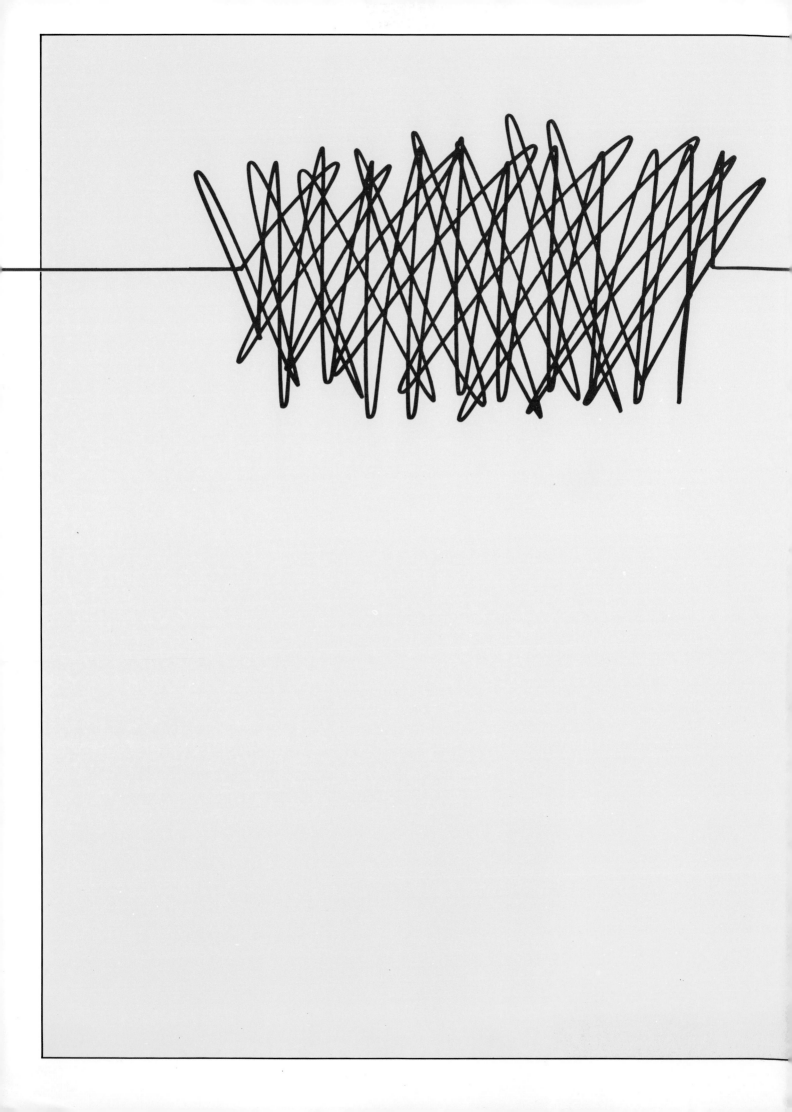

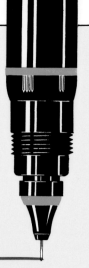

THE COMPLETE GUIDE TO
ILLUSTRATION AND DESIGN
TECHNIQUES AND MATERIALS

Consultant Editor
Terence Dalley

BOOK CLUB ASSOCIATES
LONDON

Consultant editor
Terence Dalley

Contributing editors
Robin Jacques
Ian McLaren
Cecil Misstear
Peter Payne
Brian Perrin
Roger Pring
Brian Sanders
Rufus Segar

A QED BOOK

This edition published 1984 by
Book Club Associates
By arrangement with Phaidon Press Ltd.,
Littlegate House, St Ebbe's Street, Oxford

First published 1980
©Copyright 1980 QED Publishing Ltd.

Filmset in Great Britain by Filmtype Limited, Scarborough and Abettatype Limited, London.
Colour origination in Italy by Starf Photolitho SRL, Rome
Printed in Hong Kong by Leefung Asco Limited

This book was designed and produced by
QED Publishing Ltd.
32 Kingly Court, London W1

Art director Alastair Campbell
Production director Edward Kinsey
Editorial director Jeremy Harwood
Editor Kathy Rooney
Assistant editor Marion Casey
Designers Heather Jackson David Mallott
Marnie Searchwell

Illustrators Edwina Keene Abdul Aziz Khan Elaine
Keenan Tony Lodge John Woodcock Martin
Woodford Perry Taylor Elly King Simon Roulstone

Editorial Jenny Mulherin Derek Prigent Francesca
George Danuta Doroszenko

Photographers Mike Busselle Peter Cogram Jon
Wyand Roger Pring

Picture research Linda Proud

QED would like to thank the many individuals and organizations who have given invaluable help and advice in the preparation of this book: Edward Ardizzone; Archer Press, London; Martin Baker; Leonard Baskin; Edward Bawden; Timothy Benn (Ernest Benn Ltd, Publishers); Pietro Bossi, Benedeto Celsi and staff at Starf Photolitho, Rome; Clement Cheung (Leefung-Asco, Hong Kong); D.S. Colour, London; Clive Crook (Sunday Times); Dartington Cider Press Centre, Totnes, Devon; Tony Dumpleton (Sven-ska Cellulosa Ltd, Sevenoaks, Kent); Fergus Ennis (Leisure Print, London); Ford Motor Company; Michael Freeman; Oscar Friedheim Ltd, London; Milton Glaser; Halco-Sunbury Co Ltd; Jonathon Healé; Octavian von Hofmannsthal of Christies Contemporary Art, London; Paul Hogarth; Jak; Dr Estelle Jussim; Eugene Karlin and Laurie Epstein; Giorgio Keplar; Joyce Kirkland of the Association of Illustrators; Diana Klemin; Robert Lockwood and staff of Langford and Hill Ltd for lending materials for photographic use; Len's Photography; Mitsubishi U-Bix Ltd, Basildon, Essex; Robert Morley; Muller Martini Ltd, Iver, Bucks; William Nash Ltd, Orpington, Kent; Peter Niczewski; Peter Osborne; Michael Peters and Partners, London; Francis Pugh; Purnell and Sons Ltd, Paulton, Bristol; John and Rose Randle (The Whittington Press); Rank Xerox Ltd, Uxbridge; T.R.P. Slavin, London; Ralph Steadman; Summit Photographic; Brian Thomas (Radio Times); Tudor Typesetting; John Ward; George Rowney and Co. Ltd.

CONTENTS

FOREWORD

Illustration and design are two subjects which today have extremely close links as well as traditions dating back hundreds of years. Illustration has served as a narrative aid in manuscripts and books since the earliest known illustrated scrolls – the Egyptian *Books of the Dead* and the *Ramessum Papyrus*; design is, of course, as old as art itself. The term 'composition', for instance, when applied to painting and drawing, means in effect the 'design' of the work.

Illustrators and designers have thus always worked closely together. As Jeanette Collins has put it: 'Illustration, unlike painting, always has to perform a particular function: always has to have a reason for being'. Milton Glaser's definition of the function of design should be a watchword for all designers – 'design conveys information based on the audience's previous understanding'. Thus, the work of the two is intimately linked. This is especially the case today, when most illustration and design has a commercial context. This is a governing factor, even though aesthetic considerations may seem to separate the two disciplines.

Illustration and Design is planned to appeal to the practitioners of both subjects. At first sight, the task might seem to be a daunting one, even taking illustration alone. In his comments on the annual European Illustration exhibition, Philippe Michel commented 'From the rough sketch to the wash drawing, from a caricature to a photograph that has been touched up with an airbrush . . . such different techniques, all of them used by illustrators, simply defy comparison'. Turning to the design field, there are literally hundreds of different roles a designer can fulfil within the broad confines of the discipline. Confronted with this seemingly infinite scope, the authors have adopted a severely practical approach. For convenience, the book has been divided into two sections, entitled respectively Illustration and Graphic Design. In the illustration section, the various media were subdivided into three main areas – materials, equipment and techniques – not only to give a complete a view as possible of the particular subject, but also to make it immediate and relevant to students, teachers, the practising professionals and those whose job it is to commission and reproduce the work of artists and designers.

In other words, this is not just a book of theories. Where and when history is quoted, as it often is, it is in order to acknowledge the origins and show the development of many of the materials, methods and much of the equipment in use today. Similarly, the illustrations have been chosen not as examples of 'fine art' but because they demonstrate certain techniques or ways of working. They are an admirable demonstration of the truism that the art of yesterday is directly relevant to the art of today.

However, the contemporary scene is not neglected. The various contributing editors are all acknowledged experts in their fields and also practising illustrators and designers. Most important of all, many of them are teachers and their writing here has been tempered by their daily experiences. The facts they present and the advice they offer is based upon knowledge gained through many years of experience in their particular fields. Above all, their breadth of vision has enabled them to realize that the various media are inter-related and to apply this fact to colour their views as a whole.

The same basis of practicality was the key factor in planning the design section. As we have seen, the two disciplines are very closely linked, but the designer has to face additional problems, mainly revolving around the mass of modern technology bound up with the subject. During the last thirty years, during which graphic design has emerged as an independent entity, the sheer weight of information the designer needs to know has increased immeasurably. It is no longer sufficient for a designer to be able to commission illustrators; he or she must understand photography, too. Printing, reproduction, typography – these are all subjects the designer must comprehend in order to exploit the possibilities of design to the full. For this reason, the key section here is undoubtedly the chapter on Design Procedures, which takes the reader step-by-step through the various design processes from commissioning to the final printed product.

Having outlined the complexities of the two subjects, let me end with a note of reassurance. Throughout the book, our aim has been to speed both illustrators and designers on their paths through the often complex – even bewildering – range of opportunities now available to them. Our overall purpose has been to demonstrate through example and explanation what is meant by illustration and design, to inform and stimulate and to encourage our readers to form their own judgements and opinions.

Terence Dalley

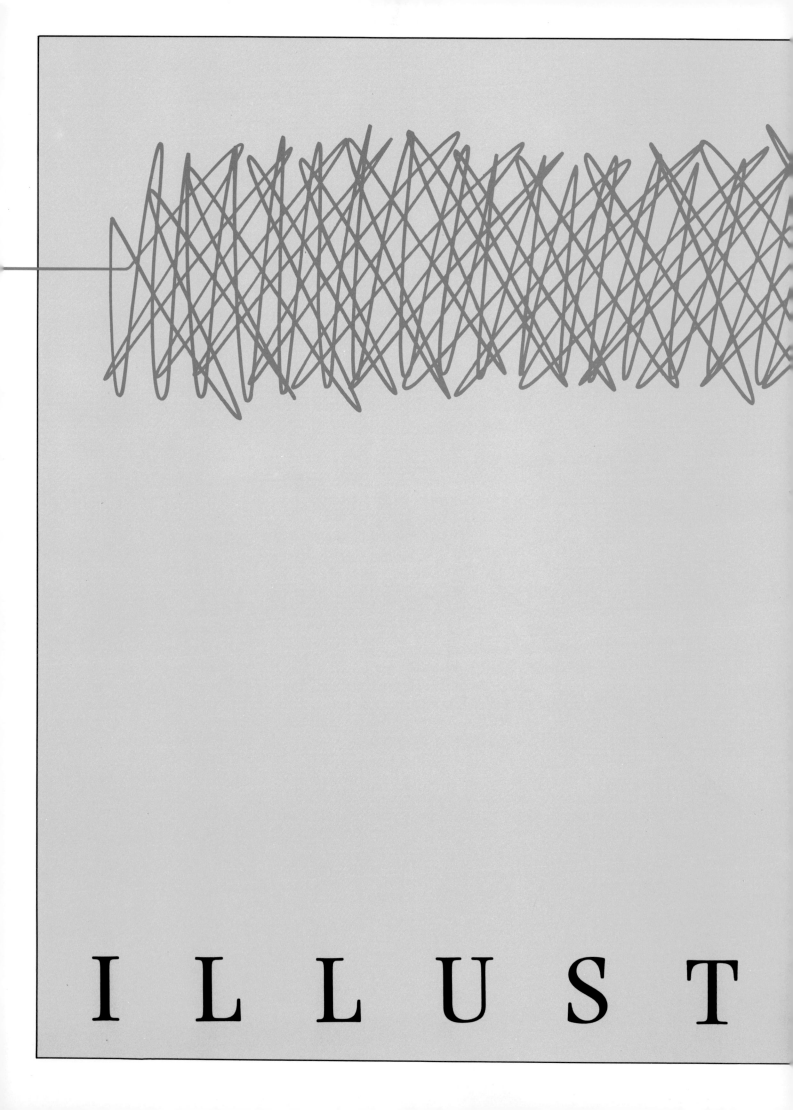

ILLUST

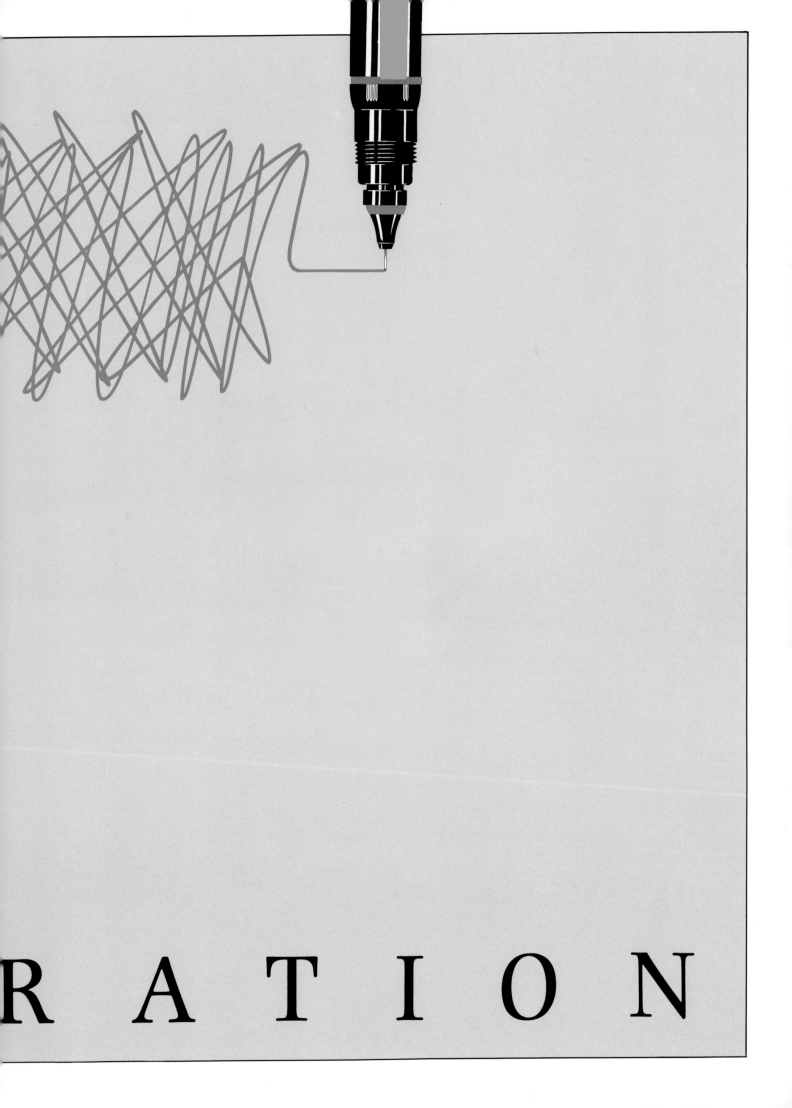

RATION

INTRODUCTION TO ILLUSTRATION

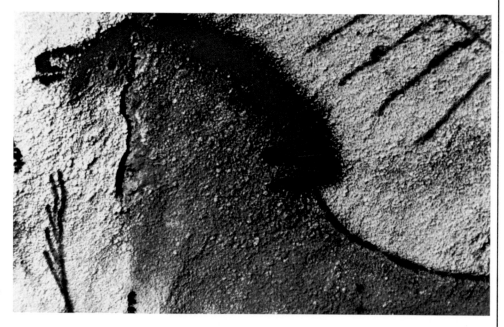

All visual art concerns itself with the production of images. When those images are used for conveying specific information the art form is normally called illustration. However, art and illustration can never be separated entirely; illustration relies heavily on traditional art skills and techniques. Illustration is commonly taken to mean art in a commercial context; and social and economic demands therefore determine the form and content of the illustration.

Illustration has served as a narrative aid in manuscripts and books since the earliest known illustrated scrolls – the Egyptian *Books of the Dead* and the *Ramessum Papyrus* dating from about 1900 BC. The art of medieval manuscript illumination is clearly the forerunner of the later illustration of printed books. The intricate and lavish illumination of books, usually on religious subjects, tended to be done in monasteries. These psalters and *Books of Hours*, of which probably the most celebrated is the *Très Riches Heures* of the Duc de Berry, show a mastery of miniature painting, usually on vellum, using vivid tempera colours as well as gold.

Illustrators have always been eager to grasp the opportunities offered by the development of mechanical aids to improve their skills and widen the scope of their work. In part, this has been because one of the main areas of illustration has always been analytical and descriptive drawing – particularly in the fields of science, topography, medicine and architecture. Greek and Roman artists realized the importance of technical illustration and they also had some idea of perspective. However, it was not until the Renaissance that the secret of how to depict perspective accurately was discovered. The theories of Filippo Brunelleschi helped revolutionize art and transformed the work of the technical illustrator. Artists and illustrators such as Leonardo da Vinci and Albrecht Dürer set a high standard of meticulous observation and clarity of detail in their technical and architectural drawings. The demand for technical illustration of increasing complexity has grown, particularly since the development of industry since the eighteenth century, but even today, in the age of electronics and space travel, the technical illustrator needs the same skills as did his Roman counterpart – the ability to observe and to transform what is seen into an accurate two-dimensional representation of the three-dimensional object.

Book illustration

Book illustration developed from fifteenth century block books, where illustration and text were hand-cut from the same wood block. The earliest surviving printed illustration is the wood-cut frontispiece of the Chinese *Diamond Sutra* of AD 868. Despite this early example it was the invention of printing using movable type, in the late fifteenth century, which gave greater scope for the illustration of texts and for

the reproduction of those illustrations. The early predominance of the woodcut tended to give way in the sixteenth and seventeenth centuries to etchings and engravings on copper plates, although the early master illustrators Holbein and Dürer used both techniques. During the sixteenth and seventeenth centuries the art of illustration moved in different directions in various parts of Europe. Perhaps the most influential illustrator of the period was the Frenchman Geoffroy Tory who concentrated on working with the elements of the page – illustration, text and borders – to create an aesthetic whole. At the same time in Japan the Ukiyo-e

Illuminated medieval manuscripts are a lavish and ornate forerunner of the illustrated book. Some of the most beautiful designs are to be found in the *Book of Hours* (**below**) written and illustrated by monks to the glory of their God and as an aid to their devotions.

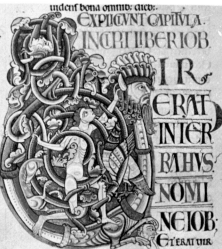

school developed techniques for producing colour woodcuts.

The ornateness which had taken over book illustration during the seventeenth century – demonstrated in the huge architectural, anatomical and equestrian tomes of the period – dwindled during the eighteenth as a lighter touch came to the fore in the works of the Frenchmen Francois Boucher and Jean Baptiste Oudry, for example.

At the end of the eighteenth century the English illustrator and engraver Thomas Bewick developed a technique of engraving the end rather than the plank side of wood which gave results which were both detailed and durable enough to rival the fine engravings then predominant in book illustration.

A major technical breakthrough came in 1796 when the German Alois Senefelder invented lithography. Until then all printing had to be done from a raised surface which was inked and then pressed on to the paper to make the impression. Lithography works on the principle that oil and water do not mix. It was the first planographic printing method meaning that the printing is done from a flat surface. One of the first major books to be illustrated with lithographs was Delacroix's edition of *Faust* which appeared in 1828.

In Britain one of the major illustrative talents early in the nineteenth century was William Blake, although his varied and quixotic talents meant that he stood outside the mainstream of art and illustration. He even developed his own printing surfaces using a method of relief etching. However, this method did not become popular and dwindled after Blake's death. Nevertheless wood engraving remained important particularly in the new industry of magazine production which was getting into its swing in

Opposite One of the masterpieces of prehistoric art and one of the earliest illustrations known to man — this paleolithic painting of a horse from the caves at Lascaux France dates from c. 1400-1350 BC. The significance of these magnificent works of art is unknown though their purpose is thought to have been ritual rather than purely decorative.

Don Quixote and his steed tilting at the windmill **(below)** provide the subject matter of an early poster designed by the Beggar-staffs (the artists William Nicholson and his brother-in-law James Pryde). The simplified line, the areas of flat colour and the integration of the lettering with the illustration combine the three main principles of eye-catching poster design.

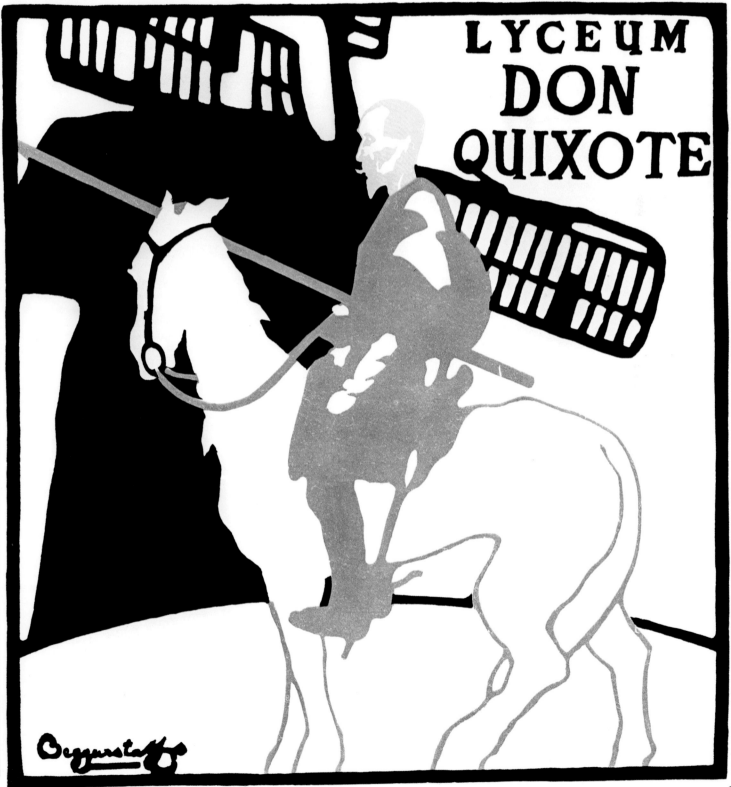

the 1830s and 1840s. It is important to remember that many of the writers of the period such as Charles Dickens and later, in France, Emile Zola, first published their novels as illustrated episodes in periodicals.

The invention of chromolithography in 1851 and the later work of Edmund Evans who printed the 'toy' books illustrated by such artists as Kate Greenaway, brought colour into the realm of the book illustrator, although the process was still time-consuming and expensive. Until then, black and white had been the province of the illustrator. The graphic reconstructions of, for example, the *Charge of the Light Brigade*, which were the hall-mark of magazines such as the *Illustrated London News*, showed the skill of illustrators working in black and white and the illustrator's desire to reproduce reality in graphic form.

The invention of photography thus circumvented much of this type of illustration and it has had an overwhelming impact on twentieth century illustration. The first photographs appeared in printed books around the 1880s. Photography heightened the possibilities of total realism in illustration and this is seen in a divergence between the illustrator who imitates the photograph and strives for greater and greater verisimilitude and the one who moves away from realism into increasing flights of fancy. The feathery and fantastic illustrations by Mervyn Peake of *The Rime of the Ancient Mariner*, for example, show this trend clearly.

In the late nineteenth century the Pre-Raphaelites rekindled interest in the woodcut, which can be seen particularly in the work of Edmund Burne-Jones, such as his *Chaucer* of 1896, and the later work of Aubrey Beardsley and Art Nouveau influenced artists such as Charles Rennie Mackintosh and the developing art of the advertising poster.

On the technical side the nineteenth century saw major developments not only in machinery and printing processes, but also in the colours available to the artist and illustrator, for example the manufacture of cobalt and cadmium. New colours could be added to the spectrum because of the development of more sophisticated dyes and pigments during and after the Industrial Revolution.

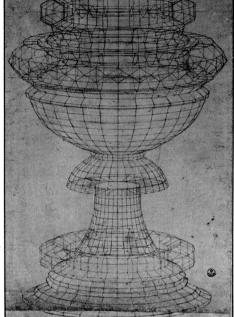

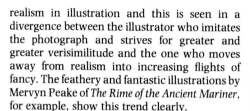

Above This famous fifteenth century illustration of a chalice by Paolo Uccello is an early example of the use of the principles of perspective to create a sense of form and space on a flat surface.

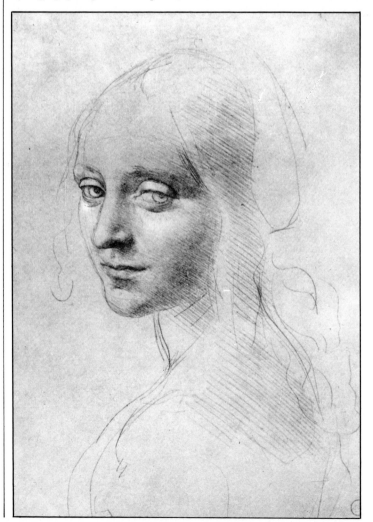

Left A detail of the angel's head from Michaelangelo's *Virgin of the Rocks* executed in metalpoint. Now rarely used, this method is carried out by drawing with a metallic stylus on a specially prepared surface, usually paper or vellum. Limited shading can be created by crosshatching but no amount of pressure on the stylus will create a black line, so it is a style best suited to small-scale drawings where delicacy of line and minute detail are the most important factors.

Another major advance was the development of half-tone reproduction. It became possible to reproduce accurately full colour artwork by overlaying different coloured inks broken down with screen tints to produce tones. Two illustrators who made good use of this technique were Arthur Rackham and Edmund Dulac, who worked mainly in water-colour, a medium well suited to half-tone reproduction. The later introduction of black keyline, which made four-colour printing practical, enabled illustrators to use other types of paint for reproduction, as can be seen in the tempera magazine illustrations by Howard Pyle for *Harpers Magazine*.

Magazines vastly increased the scope of the illustrator. Norman Rockwell used oils as the main medium for his work on magazines such as the *Saturday Evening Post* during the 1920s and 1930s. The extreme realism of his work and of those who followed his lead again shows the influence of photography on illustration.

Advertising and the poster

Advertising is another major expansion in the illustrator's field of activity. Although the *London Gazette* published a separate advertising supplement as early as 1666, it was not until the latter half of the nineteenth century that advertising, particularly in magazines, newspapers and through posters, came into its own. Advertising can be seen as a response to that expansion of commerce and industry stimulated by the Industrial Revoution, which contributed to the growth of competition. In this century the advent of cinema and television has continued to broaden the work of the illustrator.

The visual effectiveness and communicative potential of the poster have made it an effective

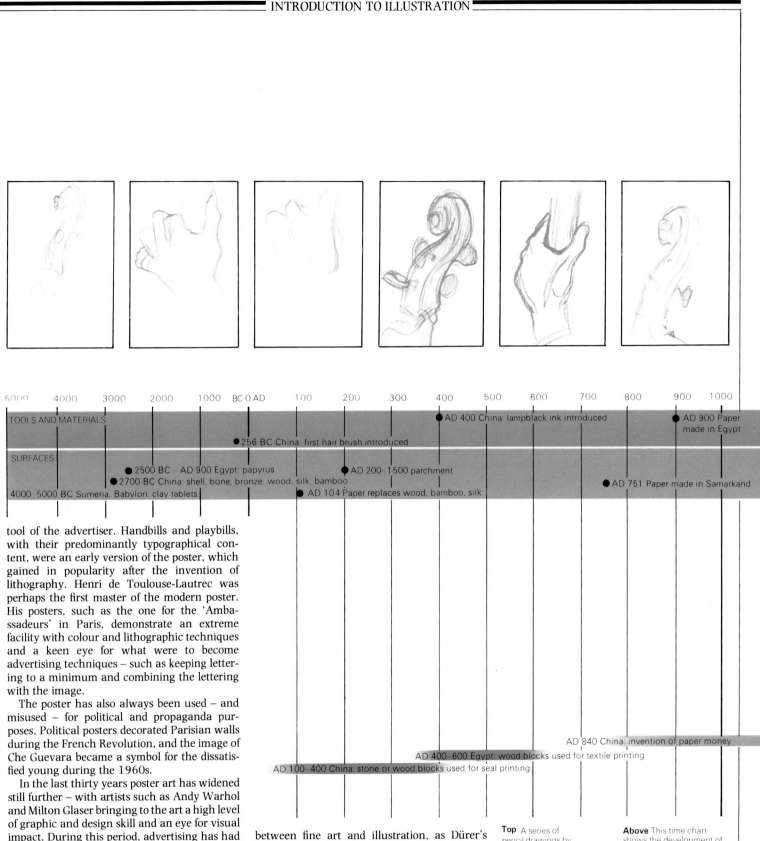

tool of the advertiser. Handbills and playbills, with their predominantly typographical content, were an early version of the poster, which gained in popularity after the invention of lithography. Henri de Toulouse-Lautrec was perhaps the first master of the modern poster. His posters, such as the one for the 'Ambassadeurs' in Paris, demonstrate an extreme facility with colour and lithographic techniques and a keen eye for what were to become advertising techniques – such as keeping lettering to a minimum and combining the lettering with the image.

The poster has also always been used – and misused – for political and propaganda purposes. Political posters decorated Parisian walls during the French Revolution, and the image of Che Guevara became a symbol for the dissatisfied young during the 1960s.

In the last thirty years poster art has widened still further – with artists such as Andy Warhol and Milton Glaser bringing to the art a high level of graphic and design skill and an eye for visual impact. During this period, advertising has had an increasing impact on almost every sphere of life as demand has increased and as technology has made possible more sophisticated – and cheaper – colour reproductive and printing techniques. Full colour reproduction is now cheap enough to be common in newspapers and almost universal in magazines and illustrated books.

Film graphics, especially those evolved for the animated cartoon film, provided another new outlet for the illustrator in this century. This further expanded with the rise of television.

In the early days of the art of illustration it was often impossible to make a clear distinction between fine art and illustration, as Dürer's illustrative work shows. It is interesting that the wheel has now turned full circle, as the poster today is not only an illustration which gives information or advertises a product, but also a work of art in its own right. The non-advertising poster today is a cheap, disposable and almost universally available work of art.

Despite the expansion of the illustrator's field of activity and the increased technological sophistication of available materials and the processes of graphic reproduction, the role of the illustrator has not changed fundamentally. The illustrator still works at the service of a commercial patron and of the media.

Top A series of pencil drawings by Toulouse-Lautrec of the scroll and fingerboard of a violin and the violinist's hands.

Above This time chart shows the development of the artist's tools, materials and surfaces from 5000 BC.

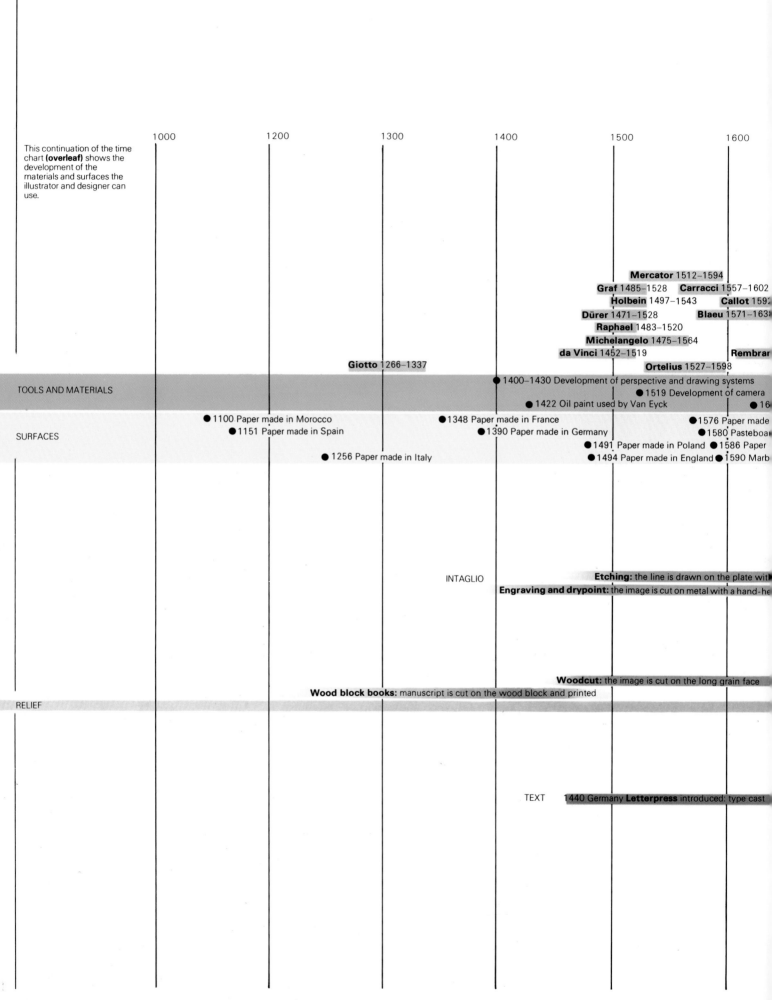

This continuation of the time chart (overleaf) shows the development of the materials and surfaces the illustrator and designer can use.

1000   1200   1300   1400   1500   1600

Mercator 1512–1594
Graf 1485–1528   **Carracci** 1557–1602
Holbein 1497–1543   **Callot** 1592
Dürer 1471–1528   **Blaeu** 1571–163
Raphael 1483–1520
Michelangelo 1475–1564
da Vinci 1452–1519   **Rembran**
Giotto 1266–1337   **Ortelius** 1527–1598

TOOLS AND MATERIALS
● 1400–1430 Development of perspective and drawing systems
● 1519 Development of camera
● 1422 Oil paint used by Van Eyck   ● 16

SURFACES
● 1100 Paper made in Morocco   ● 1348 Paper made in France   ● 1576 Paper made
● 1151 Paper made in Spain   ● 1390 Paper made in Germany   ● 1580 Pasteboar
● 1491 Paper made in Poland   ● 1586 Paper
● 1256 Paper made in Italy   ● 1494 Paper made in England   ● 1590 Marb

INTAGLIO   **Etching:** the line is drawn on the plate with
Engraving and drypoint: the image is cut on metal with a hand-he

Woodcut: the image is cut on the long grain face
Wood block books: manuscript is cut on the wood block and printed
RELIEF

TEXT   1440 Germany **Letterpress** introduced: type cast

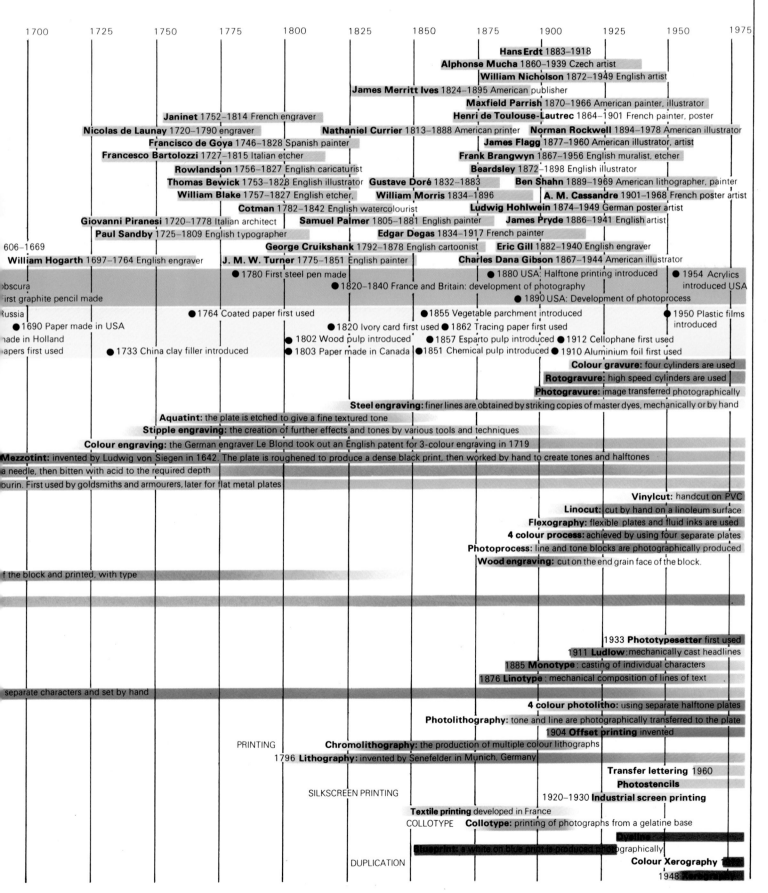

1700   1725   1750   1775   1800   1825   1850   1875   1900   1925   1950   1975

Hans Erdt 1883–1918
Alphonse Mucha 1860–1939 Czech artist
William Nicholson 1872–1949 English artist
James Merritt Ives 1824–1895 American publisher
Maxfield Parrish 1870–1966 American painter, illustrator
Janinet 1752–1814 French engraver
Henri de Toulouse-Lautrec 1864–1901 French painter, poster
Nicolas de Launay 1720–1790 engraver
Nathaniel Currier 1813–1888 American printer
Norman Rockwell 1894–1978 American illustrator
Francisco de Goya 1746–1828 Spanish painter
James Flagg 1877–1960 American illustrator, artist
Francesco Bartolozzi 1727–1815 Italian etcher
Frank Brangwyn 1867–1956 English muralist, etcher
Rowlandson 1756–1827 English caricaturist
Beardsley 1872–1898 English illustrator
Thomas Bewick 1753–1828 English illustrator
Gustave Doré 1832–1883
Ben Shahn 1889–1969 American lithographer, painter
William Blake 1757–1827 English etcher.
William Morris 1834–1896
A. M. Cassandre 1901–1968 French poster artist
Cotman 1782–1842 English watercolourist
Ludwig Hohlwein 1874–1949 German poster artist
Giovanni Piranesi 1720–1778 Italian architect
Samuel Palmer 1805–1881 English painter
James Pryde 1886–1941 English artist
Paul Sandby 1725–1809 English typographer
Edgar Degas 1834–1917 French painter
606–1669
George Cruikshank 1792–1878 English cartoonist
Eric Gill 1882–1940 English engraver
William Hogarth 1697–1764 English engraver
J. M. W. Turner 1775–1851 English painter
Charles Dana Gibson 1867–1944 American illustrator

● 1780 First steel pen made
● 1880 USA: Halftone printing introduced
● 1954 Acrylics introduced USA
obscura
● 1820–1840 France and Britain: development of photography
First graphite pencil made
● 1890 USA: Development of photoprocess
Russia
● 1764 Coated paper first used
●1855 Vegetable parchment introduced
● 1950 Plastic films introduced
● 1690 Paper made in USA
● 1820 Ivory card first used ● 1862 Tracing paper first used
made in Holland
● 1802 Wood pulp introduced ● 1857 Esparto pulp introduced ● 1912 Cellophane first used
apers first used
● 1733 China clay filler introduced
● 1803 Paper made in Canada ●1851 Chemical pulp introduced ● 1910 Aluminium foil first used

Colour gravure: four cylinders are used
Rotogravure: high speed cylinders are used
Photogravure: image transferred photographically
Steel engraving: finer lines are obtained by striking copies of master dyes, mechanically or by hand
Aquatint: the plate is etched to give a fine textured tone
Stipple engraving: the creation of further effects and tones by various tools and techniques
Colour engraving: the German engraver Le Blond took out an English patent for 3-colour engraving in 1719
Mezzotint: invented by Ludwig von Siegen in 1642. The plate is roughened to produce a dense black print, then worked by hand to create tones and halftones
a needle, then bitten with acid to the required depth
burin. First used by goldsmiths and armourers, later for flat metal plates

Vinylcut: handcut on PVC
Linocut: cut by hand on a linoleum surface
Flexography: flexible plates and fluid inks are used
4 colour process: achieved by using four separate plates
Photoprocess: line and tone blocks are photographically produced
Wood engraving: cut on the end grain face of the block.
f the block and printed, with type

1933 **Phototypesetter** first used
1911 **Ludlow:** mechanically cast headlines
1885 **Monotype:** casting of individual characters
1876 **Linotype:** mechanical composition of lines of text
separate characters and set by hand

4 colour photolitho: using separate halftone plates
Photolithography: tone and line are photographically transferred to the plate
1904 **Offset printing** invented
PRINTING   **Chromolithography:** the production of multiple colour lithographs
1796 **Lithography:** invented by Senefelder in Munich, Germany

Transfer lettering 1960
Photostencils
SILKSCREEN PRINTING
1920–1930 **Industrial screen printing**

Textile printing developed in France
COLLOTYPE   **Collotype:** printing of photographs from a gelatine base
Dyeline
Blueprint: a white on blue print is produced photographically
DUPLICATION
Colour Xerography
1948 **Xerography**

15

CHAPTER ONE

PENCILS AND OTHER POINT MEDIA

When charcoal, chalk, pastel, crayon, metal-point and pencil are used – either singly or in combination – to produce drawings, they are referred to as point media. Such drawings have been produced for thousands of years, as surviving prehistoric cave examples demonstrate; and, over this long time span, the style, size, technique and materials used – as well as the reasons for making drawings themselves – have infinitely varied. Largely this is because artists in these media – in common with all others – have produced their work as part of a continuing and developing process from earliest times up to the present day.

Choice of materials and the way in which they are used is naturally a matter of personal preference. However, some knowledge of the characteristic properties of the different media is essential if the artist is to choose the right tools for the task in hand. Many of the point media have characteristics in common and it is not always easy to clearly define the difference between them – when, for instance, is a chalk a pastel? They are also often used in combination with each other, or with other materials, such as oil paints or water colours.

In this chapter, each medium has been seen singly, as far as possible, in order to investigate its individual properties. Illustrations have been selected to show how different artists through the ages have responded to these properties and used them – often to quite different effect.

Surfaces

The range of surfaces suitable for use with these different media is extremely varied – the number of types of paper available, for instance, is vast. For this reason, a separate and detailed account of the various media is given here.

Paper The craft of making paper is said to have originated in China in about AD 104. The first paper was made from vegetable fibres pulped in water and it is thought that it was processed by spreading the pulp on a cloth and leaving it to dry, the fibres naturally knitting themselves together. Later, bamboo trays with a flexible matting of bamboo and silk were dipped into a vat of the pulp; on removal, the water was drained off, the matting removed and the layer of paper laid out to dry.

Knowledge of the process spread from the Chinese to the Moors and it was the latter who introduced paper to Europe around 1200. European paper was made in a similar way to Chinese; the only difference was that the pulp was made from linen rags. These were sorted, washed, and converted into pulp by steeping them in water and pounding in mortars. The pulp was then transferred to a paper vat, diluted with water and passed through strainers made of flat iron wires stretched over a wooden frame.

There the sheet of paper was formed.

After it had been formed in a mould, the wet paper sheet was pressed on to a piece of woollen felt, freeing the mould for re-use. The paper was covered with another layer of felt and the process repeated until a pile of alternating layers was built up. This was pressed in a screw press to remove the water. The sheets were then taken out, laid in a fresh pile and pressed again, after which they were hung up to dry. To make them non-porous to writing ink, the dried sheets were sized in a solution of starch (this was later replaced by animal size). After further pressing and drying, the paper was glazed.

The first paper mill in Italy was established at Fabriano prior to 1283; in France at Troyes in 1338; in Germany at Nürnberg in 1389; and in Austria at Wiener-Neustadt in 1498. In England, the first white printing paper was made by John Tate in 1490. During the Renaissance, it became customary for different towns to develop specialized types of paper; Venice, for instance, specialized in a paper of a particular shade of blue. By the fourteenth century, Italy had become the leading European paper-making centre.

Handmade paper is still produced by the traditional method of dipping a mould into rag pulp and shaking it until a sheet is formed. Size and thickness is determined by a wooden tool called a deckle, which rests on the mould. This deckle gives handmade papers their distinctive edge, known as a deckle-edge. Today, there are various standard surfaces available: these are hot pressed (very smooth), not or not hot pressed (medium) and rough (the natural surface).

The history of machine-made paper dates back to 1799, when the first paper-making machine was patented by Nicholas Roberts, a French inventor. His machine was improved upon by various people, including the Fourdrinier brothers after whom it was eventually named. Today, the majority of papers are made by machine. The ingredients vary according to intended use, but rags, esparto grass, wood pulp, china clay, chalk, size, dyes and water are all included. Wood pulp is probably the most important single ingredient; it was introduced in the middle of the nineteenth century.

The finish given to the paper's surface is usually the last stage in production. There are many possibilities: the surface can be calendered – that is, passed between metal cylinders which compress and smooth the surface; coated with china clay (art and enamelled papers); or given any one of hundreds of different textures.

Paper substance is expressed in pounds per ream (a ream is 500 sheets), or, more usually, in grammes per square metre (gsm). Paper in bulk is sold by weight.

Paper types Certain types of paper suit particular materials more than others. Bristol board, ivory card and smooth paper, for instance, all work well with soft-leaded pencils. Ingres paper, tex-

tured paper, water colour and rough cartridge papers are better suited to hard leads. A leading British manufacturer, Barcham Green, for example, makes a range of handmade papers, which, although they are officially classed as watercolour papers, are also suitable for use with pen, pencil, charcoal and pastel, as well as other media; the papers listed for specific uses also all make good drawing surfaces.

German papers A range of good drawing papers is made by Heinr. Aug. Schoeller Söhne of Düren, West Germany, under the trade name Schoellershammer. The maker claims that the papers are chemically permanent and capable of standing several erasures while still preserving a perfect drawing surface.

The sheet size is $21\frac{1}{2}$in $\times$ $28\frac{1}{2}$in and the type of surface is designated by letters – G (smooth), R (rough), and A, C, and T (different textures). The two colours available are white and antique (a pale cream). The paper comes in a variety of weights, ranging from 150 to 300gsm.

Schoeller also produce a line board and a water colour board.

Japanese papers There are many fine Japanese papers available. They are generally rather lightweight; most, too, are more suitable for use with paints rather than with pencils and chalks. However, they are often particularly beautiful in colour and texture and so are well worth experimenting with.

Kozu shi, Toshi, Tonosawa, Hosho and Gifu Sohji are all laid papers. Hodomura is a heavy white, or cream, wove paper.

Boards These are essential when a rigid support is needed, as in the production of finished artwork for reproduction. There are many types available.

Most boards simply consist of a good cartridge paper mounted on to a pulp, or strawboard, base. Surfaces are graded in the same way as paper into smooth, hot pressed, not and rough. The trade terms for these surfaces vary from manufacturer to manufacturer – line board, fashion board, finished art board and illustration art board are among the common ones used.

Bristol boards are slightly different. They have a particularly smooth drawing surface – excellent for pen and ink work – and come in varying thicknesses of two sheet, three sheet, four sheet and so on. There are two sizes – royal (572mm $\times$ 457mm) and imperial (723mm $\times$ 533mm).

New types of board are continually being introduced. One example of recent additions is the Superline range of boards, manufactured by the Daler Board Company Limited, of Wareham, Dorset, England. This has nine boards, ranging from a fine line surface to a 100 per cent rag mould-made water colour board.

It is vital to use a good quality surface in order to achieve good results. The modern range of paper and boards offers the illustrator a wide choice of good materials suited to specific needs.

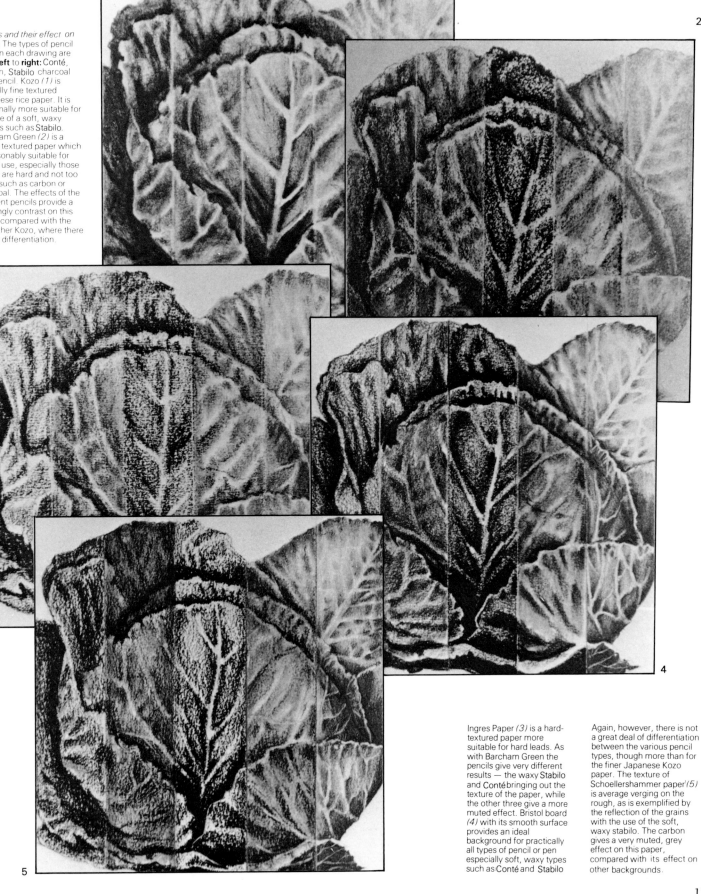

Papers and their effect on media The types of pencil used in each drawing are from **left** to **right:** Conté, carbon, Stabilo, charcoal and pencil. Kozo *(1)* is typically fine textured Japanese rice paper. It is marginally more suitable for the use of a soft, waxy pencils such as Stabilo. Barcham Green *(2)* is a rough textured paper which is reasonably suitable for pencil use, especially those which are hard and not too waxy such as carbon or charcoal. The effects of the different pencils provide a startlingly contrast on this paper compared with the smoother Kozo, where there is little differentiation.

Ingres Paper *(3)* is a hard-textured paper more suitable for hard leads. As with Barcham Green the pencils give very different results — the waxy Stabilo and Conté bringing out the texture of the paper, while the other three give a more muted effect. Bristol board *(4)* with its smooth surface provides an ideal background for practically all types of pencil or pen especially soft, waxy types such as Conté and Stabilo

Again, however, there is not a great deal of differentiation between the various pencil types, though more than for the finer Japanese Kozo paper. The texture of Schoellershammer paper *(5)* is average verging on the rough, as is exemplified by the reflection of the grains with the use of the soft, waxy stabilo. The carbon gives a very muted, grey effect on this paper, compared with its effect on other backgrounds.

Equipment

Specific drawing media are listed under their various individual sections, but erasers and rubbers, which are used with several media, are listed separately here. So, too, are fixatives, knives, blades and sharpeners, and stumps.

Erasers/rubbers For many centuries, artists used bread as an eraser. In 1752, however, it was noted in the proceedings of the French Academy that a man named Magellan had proposed the use of caoutchouc instead of breadcrumbs for erasing pencil marks. The English chemist Joseph Priestley is, in turn, credited with giving the name 'rubber' to caoutchouc in 1770 for the simple reason that it was being used to rub out marks. Until relatively recently, erasers were essentially a mixture of vulcanized vegetable oil, fine pummice and sulphur, bonded with rubber; today, plastic is also extensively used.

Kneaded rubbers, also known as putty rubbers, are one of the illustrator's most useful tools. They are not only non-abrasive but also extremely soft and pliable; this makes them ideal when precision correction is required – in picking out highlights, for example. Soft erasers – coloured white, pink or green – are excellent for use on pencil, as they do not smudge. Art eraser is used on fine artwork.

Plastic erasers come in block shapes of various sizes. Most are made of soft white vinyl, but some are dual purpose; these consist of two-thirds of white vinyl to one-third of blue vinyl. They are used for erasing ink, graphite or type.

Eraser pencils have a round, pencil-like shape and are either encased in wood or in paper, with a pull string for self-sharpening. An eraser core is, as its name implies, a core of eraser that is held in a holder and can be sharpened like a pencil. A fibrasor is for erasing drawing ink.

Electric erasers hold a core or plug of eraser, which can be changed according to the medium being erased. There are a number of different types on the market. There are also special erasers for ink and for removing marks from acetate or drafting film.

Dry cleaning powders and pads are useful tools. The grit-free powder is sprinkled over the drawing surface before work starts. It keeps it clean and free from smudges.

Fixative Fixative is a varnish which is sprayed thinly on to the surface of a drawing or pastel to protect it against rubbing. The best are proprietary brands, which can be bought either as aerosols or in bottles, to be applied with a mouthspray. The latter technique is an easier one to control.

Knives, blades and sharpeners A razor-sharp surgeon's scalpel is one of the most useful knives available, especially since it can be fitted with a variety of differently shaped blades. So, too, can an all-purpose craft knife; the Stanley knife is a well known example. A glasspaper block is useful for sharpening the point of a pencil or a charcoal stick. There are 12 glasspaper surfaces available; the standard size of the block is 83mm × 32mm. An ordinary pencil sharpener is obviously a necessity.

Some clutch pencils incorporate a sharpener for the lead in the button at the end of the holder. Other sharpeners work in a similar way to the ordinary pencil sharpener, but are reduced in diameter to take the 2mm clutch lead. A variety of mechanical sharpeners, both manual and electrically operated, are also on the market.

Some are free standing, while others are designed to be fixed to the working surface.

Stumps A stump is a cigar shaped roll of paper, sharply pointed at each end. It is used to rub charcoal or chalk drawings to obtain delicate transitions of tone. Different sizes are available.

Tortillon stumps are small and round. They come in small, medium and large sizes and are made of thin paper, tightly rolled and pointed at one end. Cotton buds are also extremely useful. They are used in the same way as a stump.

Charcoal

The earliest surviving examples demonstrating the use of charcoal as a drawing medium are the decorations made by primitive man on cave walls in France and Spain. Burnt sticks from domestic fires, together with pigments made from various natural substances, were used by these first artists to produce drawings of amazing quality and size. Many of the drawings at Altamira, for instance, are between five and seven feet wide. For work on such a scale, charcoal is an extremely suitable medium, as it can produce both a broad line and an area of tone.

Over the centuries, charcoal thus became one of the basic artistic tools; its use has been described in almost every manual on drawing. It has been used to define preliminary outlines, which can be easily removed or painted over later. It was – and still is – used in the preparation of large-scale cartoons for murals or frescoes. It has been used in works of such a scale

Equipment The bread rubber *(1)* was one of the earliest rubbers used. Nowadays, various other types are more common, such as the kneadable putty rubber *(2)*, useful where precision is required, the soft rubber *(3)*, and the art rubber *(4)*. This has non-smudging properties. Plastic rubbers *(5)* are suitable for erasing ink, type or graphite while eraser pencils *(6)* and eraser cores *(7)* are ideal where fine-point accuracy is necessary. The fibrasor *(8)* rubs out drawing ink while the electric eraser *(9)* comes with a spare core which can be changed according to the medium. The ink eraser *(10)* removes marks from acetate or drafting film. The fixative *(11)* is necessary to prevent the surface of a drawing from smudging. Both the scalpel *(12)* and general purpose knife *(13)* have a variety of uses, the blades being interchangeable. The glasspaper block *(14)* sharpens charcoal sticks as well as pencils, though ordinary pencil sharpeners *(15, 16)* and clutch ones *(17, 18)* are more often used for this purpose. Table sharpeners *(19)* and *(20)* also serve the same function. Stumps *(21)* are rubbed on chalk or charcoal to acquire a shaded effect as are tortillons *(22)* and cotton buds *(23)* which are finer and therefore they are more suitable for precision work.

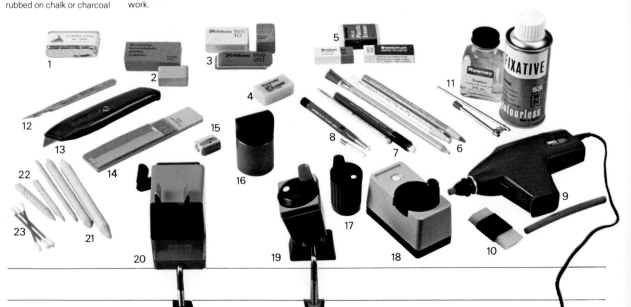

that the piece of charcoal had to be attached to a long stick and manipulated at arm's length.

In the sixteenth century, when artists began to produce individual drawings on a larger scale than their predecessors, charcoal was often used for completed studies in preference to the harder and more compact natural black chalk. Extensive use was made of it in the seventeenth and eighteenth centuries; in the nineteenth century, when high quality natural chalks became harder to obtain, charcoal gradually replaced them. In the art colleges and schools of the Western world, it is still one of the traditional tools for life drawing today.

Types

Charcoal is made by carbonizing wood in airtight chambers. In the past, artists made their own; today, however, not many would consider this worthwhile. For centuries, willow was the preferred wood, but, since the nineteenth century, vine has also been extensively used. This is the finest quality charcoal; it can be easily dusted off the paper if corrections have to be made.

Stick charcoal This is the most commonly available form of charcoal, coming in various grades, sizes and combinations of sizes. Willow charcoal, for instance, is either thick, medium or thin. It is usually sold boxed up in 75mm (3in) or 150mm (6in) lengths; the diameter of the thickest sticks is about 6mm ($\frac{1}{4}$in). With care, these can be sharpened to a point with a blade, though thinner ones should be sharpened with glasspaper.

Sticks of vine charcoal are usually 150mm (6in) long and are sold in regular, soft, medium

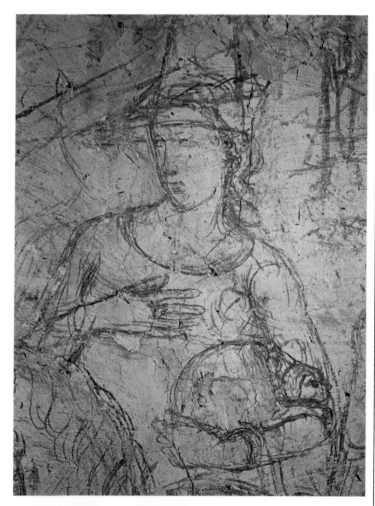

Right A fresco underdrawing showing the use of charcoal in preparatory outlines. Charcoal is an excellent medium for preparatory work on a large scale because it can produce a varied width of line.

Bottom right Albrecht Dürer|*Portrait of a Young Man.* There is a precise and distinct use of charcoal in the foreground, especially for the man's hat and hair, with broad areas of tone in the background. The techniques used in the drawing of this portrait exemplify clearly how both line and tone drawing can be effectively produced with the use of charcoal. A great deal depends upon the pressure applied and the angle at which the crayon is used.

Bottom left This is a blown-up version of a cave painting demonstrating clearly the use of charcoal which gives an effect both of broad line and graduated shading. These techniques are especially important in large drawings.

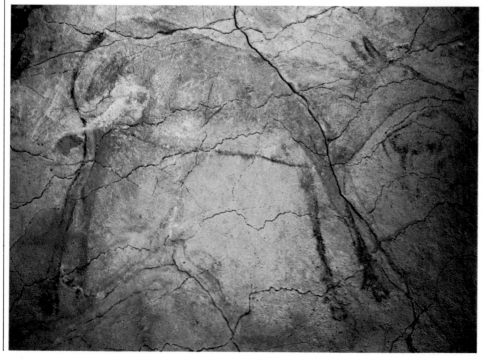

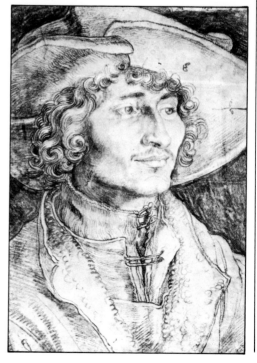

and hard grades. Assorted charcoal is sold in boxes of 75 sticks, with an average stick length of 75mm (3in).

Compressed charcoal Small sticks of compressed charcoal, between 75mm (3in) and 100mm (4in) long and 6mm (¼in) in diameter, are also available. The sticks are made from powder-ground charcoal, compressed into sticks with a binding agent. They do not break as easily as conventional charcoal sticks, but the marks they make are less easy to dust off when making corrections. This makes it less popular with some artists.

Charcoal pencils These are compressed charcoal sticks coated with either wood or rolled paper to form pencils. They are less messy and easier to handle than stick charcoal; this makes them the best form of charcoal for detailed drawings. However, only the point can be used; this means that a broad side stroke cannot be produced.

Charcoal pencils range in degree from extra soft (6B or No 3) to soft (4B or No 2), medium (2B or No 1) and hard (HB or No 0). Three of the best known makes are Royal Sovereign (medium and soft), the General 557 Charcoal Pencil (HB, 2B, 4B, 6B and white) and the Blaisdell

Right *Charcoal* Boxed sticks of willow charcoal are available in a wide range of lengths and thicknesses, for example large *(1)* and small assorted sticks *(2)*. Compressed charcoal is also sold as small sticks *(3)* which are made by compressing powder-ground charcoal with a binding agent. These are stronger than conventional charcoal sticks. Charcoal pencils *(4)* are made from compressed charcoal covered with wood or paper. They are best for detailed drawings, since only the point can be used.

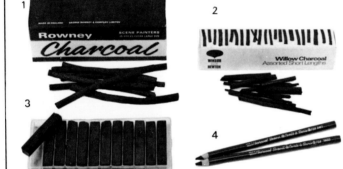

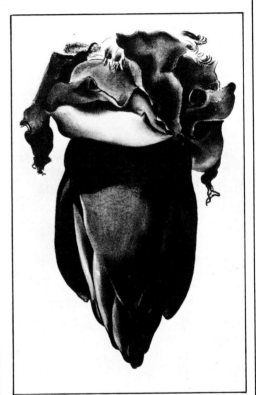

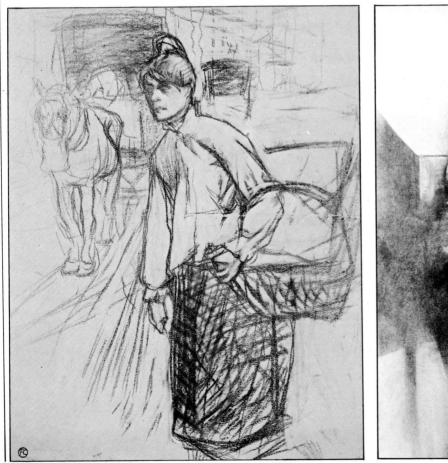

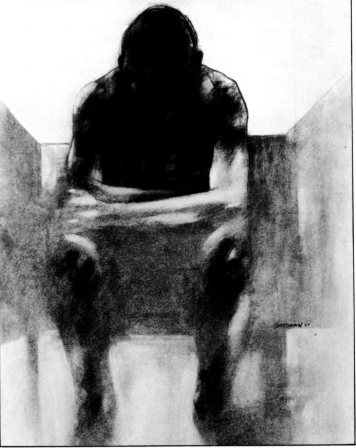

Charcoal Pencil (soft, medium and hard). This last pencil is self sharpening.

Techniques

Charcoal is equally suitable for use in line or tone drawings; it is also an excellent medium for working on a large scale. It has a strong tendency to reflect any grain in the ground – a quality that can be exploited by the artist. Because of its fragile nature, mistakes can be dusted off easily with a chamois cloth or even blown off.

The material, however, does have its disadvantages. It is messy to handle and strokes can be accidentally erased. For this reason it is essential to fix a charcoal drawing if it is to be permanent. This is done by covering the surface with a fine spray of a liquid containing a suitable binding material.

Charcoal has many characteristics in common with chalks and pastels. Large areas can be covered by laying down the charcoal and then spreading it with a stump or by hand. Intermediate grey tones can be obtained by using harder sticks or by applying the stick lightly over the grained surface of the paper. Highlights can be picked out with a putty rubber or bread. Further tone can be added by using a brush dipped in clean water.

Above left Georgia O'Keeffe *Banana Flower* This drawing shows the subtle way in which form and shape can be built up in charcoal. Dark shading gives depth and shadow, while the contrasting highlights define the contours and texture of the flower, giving the effect of light falling on the subject. **Far left** Henri de Toulouse-Lautrec *La Blanchisseuse* In contrast to the deep tones and heavy shading of the flower **(above)** Toulouse-Lautrec's washerwoman illustrates a very light, delicate approach to charcoal drawing. The figure is sketched with fine lines and cross-hatching, with light smudging further softening the outlines. The background becomes hazy and indistinct. **Left** Sidney Goodman *Man Waiting* Here, many charcoal techniques have been used to create a powerfully suggestive study. The outline of a man's bowed head and shoulders is drawn with a fine, clear line. This is filled in with heavy, solid shading, with lighter highlights on the folded arms. In the lower half of his body the charcoal smudging becomes progressively lighter, to merge with the background, and the form of the legs is suggested with slightly darker shading and highlights.

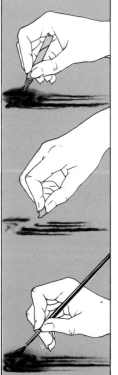

Above Three methods of blending with charcoal are to use a torchon **(top)**, a putty rubber **(middle)** and clean water **(bottom)**.

Chalks, pastels, crayons

The first problem confronting an artist working with chalks is the terminology involved. Words such as chalk, pastel, crayon, Conté and sanguine are frequently used; with some, particularly crayon, there is the possibility of some confusion of meaning. Although not every stick can be comprehensively classified, it is simpler if their main characteristics are defined. This can be done under three headings – natural chalks, fabricated chalks and pastels, and crayons.

Natural chalks are mineral substances shaped as required and used for drawing. Fabricated chalks and pastels are made from dry powdered pigments mixed into a paste with a water-soluble binding medium. The paste is then formed into sticks and dried. Crayons are a sub-category; the powdered pigments are mixed with a medium containing a fatty binder.

Natural chalks The three most common natural chalks were red (varieties of iron oxide), black (carboniferous shale) and white (chalk or gypsum). The reds and blacks were not pure minerals but compositions, in which clay was an important ingredient. This contributed to their softness and texture.

Some forms of natural chalk were used by the Palaeolithic cave dwellers and a few late medieval black chalk drawings have survived. However, it was not until the late fifteenth century that natural chalks came into popular use for drawing. By about 1540, red, black and white chalk were all in use – either singly or combined – often on tinted papers. The chalks could be used in a linear manner or smoothed out to produce tones. The natural red chalks varied in colour from deposit to deposit; in combination with black they produced rich browns. By wetting the chalk immediately before use, artists were able to produce a darker and more solid line. The function of white chalk was to heighten the modelling in drawings.

Natural chalks were the standard drawing material until the eighteenth century, when the supply of quality chalks began to run out and, as a consequence, their popularity began to decline. By the nineteenth century, fabricated drawing sticks with characteristics similar to those of natural chalks were being produced.

A commercial product available today, however, closely resembles the old natural chalks in the results it produces; this is a sanguine Conté crayon. Orange-red in colour, it is slightly less friable than natural chalks.

Fabricated chalks and pastels Fabricated chalks and pastels are made from dry powdered pigments mixed with a binding medium to form a paste (it is from this paste that the word 'pastel' comes). The term could be applied to all fabricated chalks, but it has become particularly associated with the softer, powdery variety and the manner in which they are used. Confusion

can thus be caused when 'pastel' is used to describe the harder varieties of chalks, such as those used for detailed drawings.

Most of the available dry pigments can be used to prepare fabricated chalks and thus, by careful mixing, an enormous range of hues and tones can be produced. This is impossible with natural chalks.

As long as fabricated chalks were used in the same way as charcoal or natural chalks, the same carriers – usually a paper with a slight grain – were used. However, the medium lends itself to many different approaches. In the eighteenth century, for instance, there was a trend towards using pastels to create works possessing the characteristics of paintings. This, in turn, led to the preparation of textured grounds.

Carriers were roughened with pummice, or covered with a coating of glue into which marble dust or pummice powder was sifted. The grain helped to hold the soft, dusty strokes of powder in place. The essentials of this technique survive today; modern pastel drawings are frequently executed on similarly textured grounds.

Relatively hard fabricated chalks are more suited to smaller-scale drawing, the softer pastels allow a much broader treatment and a larger picture size. Whichever material is selected, the resulting drawing must be fixed if it is to be permanent. This is done by spraying the drawing lightly with a liquid containing a binding agent. This, and the manner in which it is applied, can vary according to choice; the two most suitable fixing methods are described in the equipment section.

Supports The colour and texture of the support is an important element in any pastel drawing. Some artists, for instance, often decide to leave some of the support showing as part of the overall colour scheme. The texture must be able to retain the grains of colour.

Ingres-type papers (Fabriano, Tumba, Canson and Arches) are extremely suitable for use with pastel, as they have a defined grain and are available in a wide range of colours. Vellum is a good surface for delicate work. Glasspaper has a good buff mid-tone and a tooth which retains the pigment. Canvas on a stretcher can provide a good ground, as can muslin pasted to cardboard. If canvas is used, it should be protected at the back against the risk of blows or vibrations which may dislodge the pastel particles.

Canvases should not be primed with size containing animal glue, as this can cause mildew. Pastels can be protected against 'foxing' – the growth of fungus – by brushing a ten per cent solution of formalin over the entire support before work begins.

This is by no means the whole range of surfaces available. Experiment is probably the best way of selecting the right support for the particular task in hand.

Right *Supports* Fabriano *(1)* is suitable for a wide variety of styles and subjects, having a defined grain and being mid-tone in shade. Tumba *(2)* comes in light and dark shades. Vellum *(3)*, being smooth, is better suited for delicate work, while glasspaper *(4)*, with its pigment-retaining properties is ideal for blocks of colour. Canvas *(5)* is a versatile chalk support.

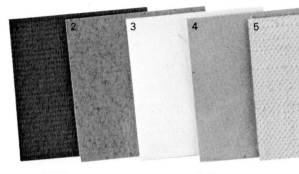

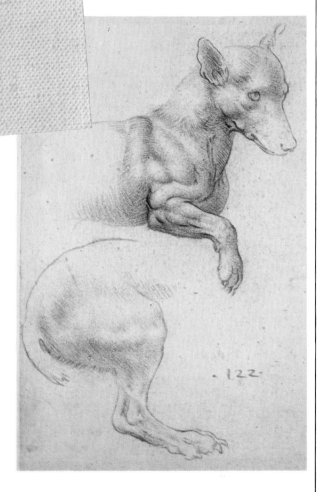

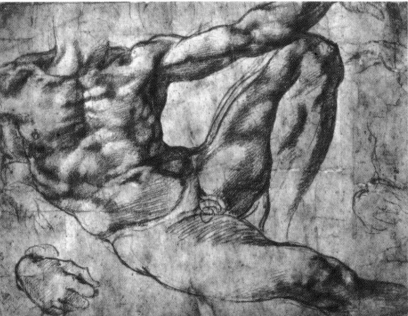

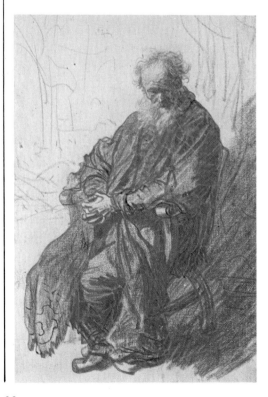

Left Rembrandt van Rijn *Old Man with Clasped Hands, Seated in an Armchair* Both lines and tones are used in this chalk drawing. The quality of light features prominently.

Above left Michelangelo *Study for the Creation of Adam* The chalk is applied linearly with smudged diagonal crosshatching.

Above right Leonardo da Vinci *Studies of the fore-part and hind quarters of a dog* A controlled linear technique was used by Leonardo in this red chalk (sanguine) drawing.

Below This picture of a charging bison was found in a cave in Altimara, Spain. The drawing is completely blocked in with various colours which gives an effect of solidity.

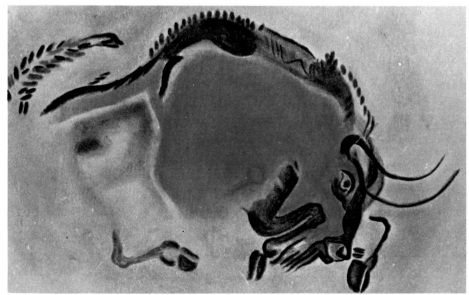

Pastel pictures combine the qualities of drawing and painting. The chalks respond to the surface of the ground; they give the artist the freedom of working in full colour without the disadvantages such as varying drying speeds and sinking colours, that come from using some paints. Good pastel pictures combine delicacy of touch with purity of colour.

Pastel sticks Pastel sticks are classed as soft, medium or hard, according to the quantity of binding media incorporated in the paste. If the proportion is increased to make the stick harder, the brilliance of the pastel is diminished. The most brilliant sticks are therefore the softest and most fragile. The characteristic pale soft pastel shades, particularly the flesh tints, owe their quality to the filler – either clay or whiting – which is added to the pigment to increase its covering power.

With most paints, it is possible to mix two colours on the palette to obtain a third. This is not the case with pastels, so the right colours and tones must be available from the start.

Using a boxed selection is often a good way to begin. In Britain, Rowney make a good range of artists soft pastels, as do Grumbacher in the United States. These are made from the finest pigments ground with a mixture of chalk, clay and other ingredients to control the colour strength. This is defined on a numerical scale from 0 to 8; 0 is the palest tint and 8 the deepest. The colours are permanent. The Dutch firm Talens add decimal points to these numbers to indicate the percentage of white added to the original.

It is not necessary to select the full eight gradations of each colour; a light, middle and dark tone are often sufficient. The colour tint charts produced by the manufacturers are an essential reference; it should be remembered, however, that these are printed on white paper, so it is as well to try out the range on different coloured papers before making a final selection.

Sets of soft round pastels can be built up from either boxes or trays. A typical set might well consist of 144 assorted pastels, 72 selected for landscape and 72 for portrait. This proportion can naturally be varied. For example the Grumbacher tray holds 48 pastels. The trays can be locked together to form a set. Nupastel square pastels are also recommended. They are firmer and stronger than ordinary pastels, but still powder sufficiently to blend. They come in sets of 12, 24, 36, 48, 60, 72 and 96.

Normally, all requirements can be catered for by the manufactured ranges. However, it sometimes happens that a particular hue or colour is not available and, if so, a handmade one must be made up.

Pastel pencils Carb-Othello pastel pencils are highly recommended. They are light-proof, non-toxic and can be mixed and blended. The range is available in 60 colours and sets of 12, 24, 36, 48 and 60 assorted colours are on the market.

Oil pastels and crayons Oil pastels can be blended and mixed directly on the working surface, are light-fast, require little or no fixing and are resistant to rubbing. They come in sets of 12, 24, 36 and 48. Oil crayons are similar, but are usually firmer in consistency than the pastels. They do not smudge and can easily be fixed by rubbing with a soft cloth. They are also free-blending, reasonably light-fast and non-toxic. Sets of 12, 18, 24 and 36 colours are available at good artists' stores.

Crayons Available in sets of 24, 30, 48, 64 and 72, wax crayons are water-resistant, light-resistant and non-toxic. Paper, card, wood and fabric are all suitable drawing surfaces. Ordinary crayons are light-resistant. They can be used on any material. A particularly good water-soluble variety is the Caran d'Ache Neocolor II Aquarelle, which comes in boxes of 30 colours.

Conté crayons can be recognized by their characteristic squareness. Black comes in three degrees – No 1 medium (HB), No 2 soft (B) and No 3 extra soft (BB) – but sepia bistre and red sanguine have one degree only.

Techniques

Pastels are at their best when not overworked. Although a certain amount of blending can be achieved by rubbing, the best way of varying colour and tone is to lay strokes, or areas, of a colour over or alongside another. This builds up the desired effect.

This method naturally means that a number of strokes, with different chalks, have to be applied instead of one. For this reason, it is important to lay the chalks out in a methodical working order and to replace them in their correct positions. Corrugated paper makes a useful palette.

Most artists working with pastels make an outline, or key, drawing in charcoal first. It is wise to make the first pastel strokes tentatively but firmly; too much pressure at the start can overload the grain of the paper and so make the surface smeary. This means that further layers of colour will tend to clog and slip.

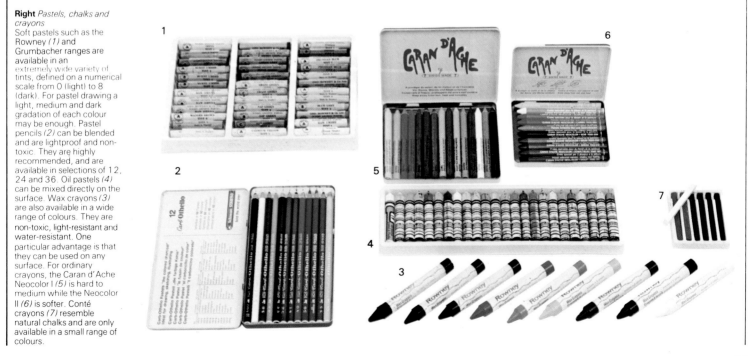

Right *Pastels, chalks and crayons*
Soft pastels such as the Rowney (1) and Grumbacher ranges are available in an extremely wide variety of tints, defined on a numerical scale from 0 (light) to 8 (dark). For pastel drawing a light, medium and dark gradation of each colour may be enough. Pastel pencils (2) can be blended and are lightproof and non-toxic. They are highly recommended, and are available in selections of 12, 24 and 36. Oil pastels (4) can be mixed directly on the surface. Wax crayons (3) are also available in a wide range of colours. They are non-toxic, light-resistant and water-resistant. One particular advantage is that they can be used on any surface. For ordinary crayons, the Caran d'Ache Neocolor I (5) is hard to medium while the Neocolor II (6) is softer. Conté crayons (7) resemble natural chalks and are only available in a small range of colours.

Different results are produced according to the way the sticks are handled and the angle at which they are held. Among the striking effects that can be produced are those achieved by alternating thin and thick strokes; using the sharp edge of the pastel; laying the pastel flat on the paper; using the pastel at varying angles. Applying the right amount of pressure is vital to achieving the different effects. If, say, a great deal of pressure is applied, the pastel will press into the grain of the paper and fill it. This effect can be contrasted with strokes passed lightly over the surface. Cross-hatching and open work are the most practical ways of producing tonal and shading effects. Pastel pencils, such as the Othello, can be sharpened to a point.

Correction and shading need to be done carefully. Too much rubbing in with the finger, stump or torchon in an attempt to blend the colours can destroy the surface and lead to a slick finish. Mistakes can be brushed off with a hog-hair brush or lightly erased with a putty rubber – but this, too, must be done delicately. Otherwise the surface may lose its grain and its ability to hold the colour particles.

Fixing Fixative needs to be applied with care, as it can change the appearance of a pastel, particularly if the picture is over-saturated. In such a case the colour tends to lose its brilliance and darken in tone. The pastel, too, can become thick and heavy; this is because the particles of colour coalesce as they absorb the fixative.

Fixing can be done in a number of ways. The completed picture can be fixed or, alternatively, each layer of pastel can be treated individually. The last layer is left unfixed. This method was frequently used by Degas (1834–1917). It has the effect of building up an impasto quality.

Whichever method is adopted, the fixative

should be applied to the front of the picture. It must be sprayed on as a light mist; otherwise blobs of liquid may run down the paper and cause ridges. Pastels, however, can also be fixed from the back through the combination of the mounting and fixing process. The pastel is pasted to a card and some of the paste is allowed to soak through the paper to fix the powder.

If it is decided to leave a pastel unfixed, it must be mounted, framed and handled with great care to avoid damage. Before mounting some degree of protection can be given by covering the

pastel with a piece of smooth paper, tissue, cellophane or grease-proof paper. This is then covered with a board, to which pressure is applied. This fixes the pastel more firmly into the grain of the paper without affecting the surface.

Oil pastels The effect of oil pastels is altogether different from that of pure pastels. In fact, oil pastels have much more in common with crayons. They give a smooth, intense, rather greasy line, they are not friable, and they do not smudge easily. A good way to use them is to combine them with a turpentine wash, spread-

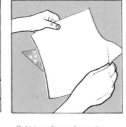
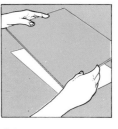
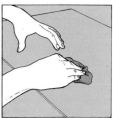
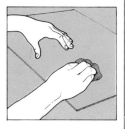

Fixing a pastel drawing 1. To use a mouth spray stand away from the front and spray in a fine mist.

2. When fixing from the back cover the drawing with smooth paper — cellophane, tissue or greaseproof.

3. Cover both the paper and the drawing with a piece of board.

4. Rub down firmly. This presses the pastels into the grain of the paper.

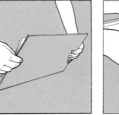
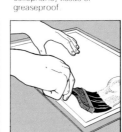
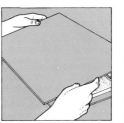
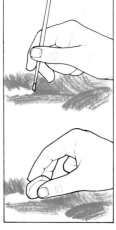

5. For mounting turn everything over so that the pastel is on the top, face downwards.

6. Using a wide brush, apply a thin coat of glue to the back of the drawing.

7. Position the mounting board — usually white mounting card — over the drawing.

8. Press and rub down firmly.

Right J.M.W. Turner *The Jetty* This pastel sketch from Turner's notebooks shows a traditional approach to the medium. Turner used red, black and white chalks on a brown tinted paper. Soft lines and loose shading are combined with muted tones to create a characteristically hazy and romantic seascape. The main structures of the jetty and the ships are suggested with thick, vertical black strokes. The expanse of the sky and the effect of light and cloud is produced by sweeping horizontal strokes, with white smudging bleeding at the horizon. Black, white and red chalks were natural minerals, obtained by mining. They were used extensively until the nineteenth century, when fabricated pastels were introduced.

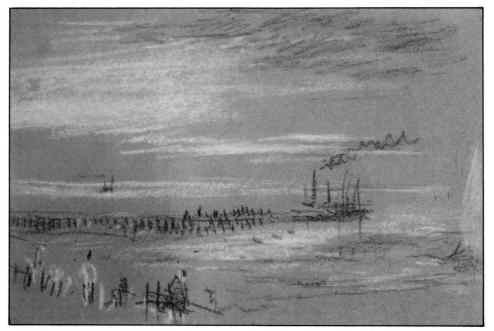

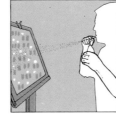

Above *Correcting pastels* Mistakes can be corrected by brushing with a hogshair brush **(top)** or by lightly applying a putty rubber **(below)**. Great care must be taken to avoid damaging the surface by heavy pressure.

ing the colour with a brush dipped in this medium.

Crayons Most crayons are distinguished from natural or fabricated chalks by their viscosity. However, there are exceptions, as some crayons are comparatively dry and friable. This range is achieved by varying the amounts of fatty material present in the binding medium.

The mixing of various fatty substances with dry pigments to make coloured drawing sticks is a practice that has been followed by artists since the sixteenth century. There are references to the manufacture of crayons in early writings on art, but these often relate to the modification of charcoal. By soaking charcoal in oil or wax overnight, for instance, it is possible to produce a crayon-like drawing stick.

True crayons did not come into common use until the late eighteenth century, when the first sustained effort to manufacture them took place. During the 1790s, many people – among them the German Alois Senefelder, the inventor of lithography – were experimenting with different formulae and the type of crayon used by artists today seems to have been developed around this period.

In the nineteenth century, crayons were used extensively. Crayons readily lend themselves to linear drawing, as they produce a rich, smooth stroke and resist smudging.

The lithographic crayon is one of the most widely used and known examples. Not only is it an essential part of the lithographic printing process, but it has also been used to draw direct on to paper to great effect. A further use of the wax crayon is as a resist in resist drawing.

In general, drawings made with crayons do not need fixing.

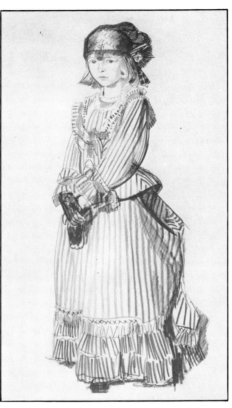

Above George Bellows *Lady Jean* Bellows combined fine line drawing and thicker crayon strokes in the figure; the delicate detail of the girl's face is created with light shading. **Below left** Honoré Daumier *Luigi Filippi* The portraits are drawn with short, tight lines, which build up areas of shade and contrasting highlights in the heavy contours of the face. The texture of the coat is produced by dense cross-hatching. **Below right** Käthe Kollwitz *Death Holding a Girl in his Lap* Broad, sweeping lines are combined with loose shading to create the free, expressive style of this lithograph.

Metalpoint

Metalpoint drawings are produced by drawing with a metallic stylus upon a prepared ground. The drawings so produced are fine in character and linear in treatment, with limited shading created by cross-hatching. No amount of pressure from the artist's hand can produce a black line. This means that metalpoint is best suited to small-scale drawings, where delicacy of line and minute detail are the most important factors. Such drawings are often carried out on a tinted ground.

The history of drawing with a metal stylus is a long one. Medieval scribes used styli to rule the guidelines for texts and in their preparatory drawings for the ornaments in manuscripts. Both Petrarch and Boccaccio mention drawing with a stylus and metalpoints were widely used by artists of the Renaissance.

From the late seventeenth century onwards, metalpoint was used less as a drawing medium in its own right, though it was still used for laying-in preliminary designs for miniatures – particularly those done on ivory, parchment or coated paper. Towards the end of the nineteenth century, there was a great revival of interest in the medium and many leading artists of the time made metalpoint drawings. There was obviously sufficient demand for Winsor and Newton to include silverpoint kits in their catalogues in the 1890s; contemporary artists, though, do not use metalpoint on a large scale.

Surfaces

Grounds The purpose of the ground is to strengthen the mark made by the stylus. Early grounds

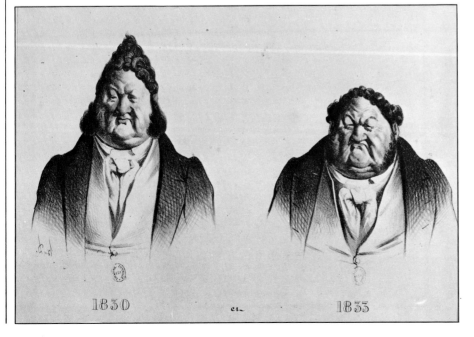

1830   1833

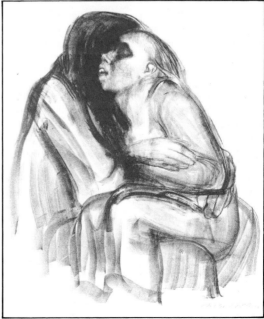

had much in common with the ones used for gesso painting. Old recipes show the main dry ingredients were white lead and bone dust, with the occasional addition of dry pigments for tints. When the white and coloured pigments had been thoroughly ground and mixed, they were added to a liquid binding material, usually glue or gum water. The former was made by soaking skin clippings; the latter was usually prepared from gum arabic.

The liquid ground was then brushed over the carrier one coat at a time until the required surface had been built up. The carrier could be paper, parchment, vellum, wood or cloth.

Today, zinc or titanium white can be used to produce a brilliant white ground. The dry pigments can be mixed with glue water by the artist; alternatively, commercially produced gouache or opaque 'tempera' white, in which the pigment has already been mixed with a gum arabic binder, can be used. Whichever material is chosen, the ground itself must be laid extremely carefully, as rough or coarse surfaces will interfere with the delicacy of line.

A heavy, smooth surface paper, preferably with a matt finish, makes a good carrier. In common with other papers, this should be stretched as for water colour and allowed to dry before the first coat of the ground is applied.

The best way to prepare a ground using dry pigments is to dissolve $\frac{1}{2}$oz of rabbit-skin size in 25 fluid oz of water. This mixture is heated until it is very warm, but it must not be allowed to boil. Four parts of titanium or zinc white dry colour are then added to five parts of the warm glue water. The dry pigments should be very finely ground, as any large fragments may not fully dissolve in the glue.

The ground should be laid over the carrier with a wide brush. To produce a smooth surface, it is better to apply three or four thin coats, allowing each one to dry in turn, rather than one thick one. When the completed ground has finally dried, it can be burnished lightly with a slightly dampened cloth or with fine steel wool. This will smooth the surface and make it more receptive to the stylus.

Metalpoint lines can be removed with either a damp cloth or steel wool, and the clear ground can then be re-used.

Equipment

The stylus To make a metalpoint drawing both a stylus and a prepared ground are needed. Metal-points, except those of lead, or lead alloys, will not mark without the ground. Types of metal and stylus vary; silver, gold, tin, brass, bronze, lead-tin and lead-bismuth have all been used. Only the drawing tip needs to be made of the particular metal; the rest of the tool can be of some other material. Old styli often had highly ornate shafts and the frequent mention of silver in historical references suggests it was the most favoured metal.

Techniques

The quality of stroke depends upon the ground and the metal used. When first made, all metal-point strokes appear grey, regardless of the colour of the metal. Some metals, however, undergo colour changes, becoming lighter or darker when exposed to the air at ordinary temperatures. Silverpoint strokes, for instance, turn brown and become lighter; copperpoint may turn yellowish, while lead and its alloys remain grey. In addition to colour changes, some metals also develop a transparency which creates the effect of delicate light brown or yellowish lines. It is impossible to predict how long it takes for such changes to occur.

The surface should be tested with the stylus before use. If it has been correctly prepared, the weight of the stylus alone should be almost sufficient to produce the line. If too much glue has been added, the stylus will require excessive pressure – if too little has been used, it will score the surface of the ground, leaving ridges of powder on either side of the stroke.

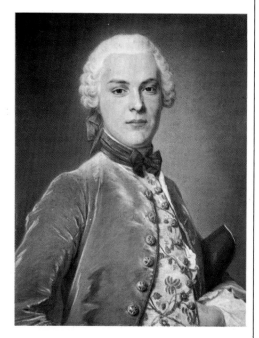

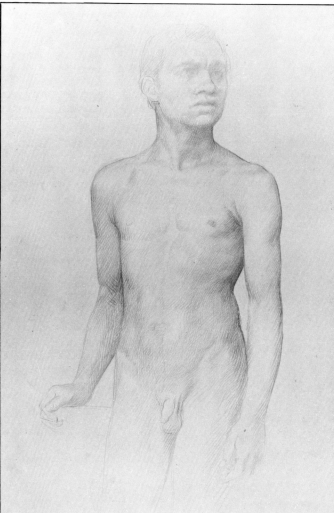

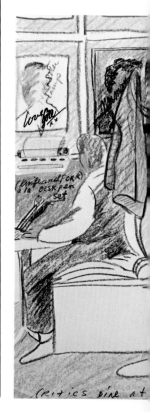

Left Alphonse Legros *Nude Male Youth* This shows the characteristic detail and delicacy of metalpoint work. The figure is drawn with many fine lines and delicate cross-hatching creates light grey shading on the body. Metalpoint was very popular with Renaissance artists, such as Leonardo, but it is rarely used today.

Left This portrait by Maurice de la Tour shows how pastels can imitate the appearance of oil paints. The colours are built up to give an impression of smoothness and density, with no visible strokes. This technique, however, is not typical of the medium.
Right Edgar Degas *Blanchisseuse* Degas was a master of pastel drawing. This picture is typical both of his technique and of pastel work in general. The outline, or key drawing, was done in charcoal, and then filled in with many bold, loose lines in a variety of chalks to build up areas of colour and shadow. **Below right** This pastel drawing by Gary McCarver shows a very different technique. Vivid colours are produced by applying the pastels thickly and using heavy pressure to force them into the grain of the paper. This creates solid, dense areas of colour The tones are produced by smudging, and no individual lines can be seen.
Below This satirical illustration by Donna Muir demonstrates the linear technique of crayon drawing. Here, she uses smooth outlines of varying thickness. Light, rapid strokes create the grey tones in the background, while the areas of rich colour are built up with even, close shading.

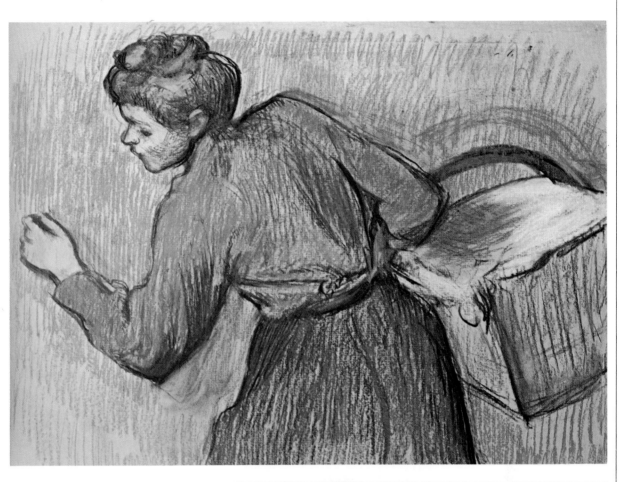

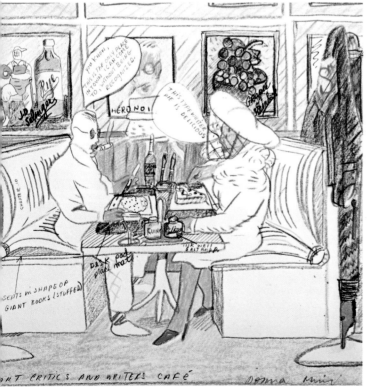

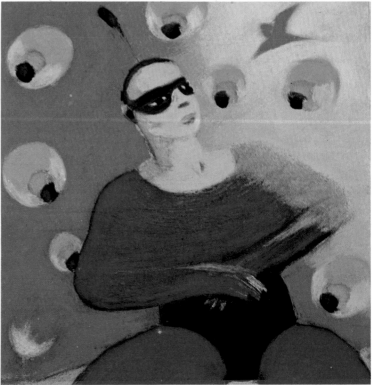

Pencil

The confusion that can arise about the meaning of terms applies just as much to pencil as to pastels and chalks. The description 'lead pencil' is in itself a misleading one; the 'lead' is not lead metal, but a mixture of synthetic graphite and clay, while the word 'pencil' comes from the Latin *pencillus* (little tail) – the name given to the brush used for ink drawings in the Middle Ages. In the artistic parlance of the eighteenth century, pencilling meant 'brushing'. A more accurate description of the familiar instrument we use daily might thus be 'graphite drawing stick'.

The story of pencil began in 1564, when a deposit of pure graphite, at first thought to be lead, was discovered at Borrowdale in Cumberland, England. Mines were opened there to produce graphite as a drawing material (the monopoly in this was held by the Crown) and, until supplies were eventually exhausted in the nineteenth century, they provided Europe with its finest graphite.

Natural graphite was used either as a lump or in holders – porte-crayons similar to those used for silverpoint but adapted to take the heavier graphite stick. However, the scarcity of the natural material made it necessary to look for substitutes and in 1662 the first graphite composition pencil was made in Germany. Kaspar Faber, who established his pencil-making factory near Nürnberg, Germany, in 1761, used a mixture of one part of sulphur to two parts of graphite. In England, T and R Rowney began to manufacture graphite sticks in wooden sheaths in 1789.

The next development took place in France during the Napoleonic Wars, when supplies of English graphite were largely cut off from the Continent. Nicholas-Jacques Conté (1755–1805), an inventor and mechanical genius, was commissioned by Napoleon to begin the search for a substitute for imported pencils. Conté experimented with inferior graphite from European sources and, in 1795, he patented his process, the forerunner of the modern pencil.

Conté prepared a paste-like mixture of graphite and fine clay, which he hardened by baking in a kiln. It was then pressed into grooves in wood, usually cedar. The resulting pencils could be graded for texture, tone and strength, depending on the ingredients, their proportions and the length of firing. Conté was not alone in the field, however; at about the same time, Joseph Hardtmuth was achieving similar results in Vienna.

In the United States, Joseph Dixon started making pencils at Salem, Massachusetts, in 1827. In 1839, Johan Lothar von Faber, a great grandson of Kaspar, improved the Conté process by extruding the paste through a dye and introducing machinery to cut and groove the wooden slats that enclosed the leads. It was

Johan who established branches of the Faber company in New York, London, Paris and Berlin. Another of Kaspar's great grandsons, Eberhard, established a pencil business in his own name in America in 1849.

The way graphite pencils are manufactured makes it possible for various materials to be used in their manufacture, according to the results required; in the past, these materials included waxes, shellac and resins, while lampblack was used to achieve greater blackness. Some of the finer leads available for use in clutch pencils today are made by blending high quality graphite with special polymers.

The quality of pencils depends chiefly on the quality and fineness of the graphites and clays used in their manufacture. The more clay there is in the mixture, the harder the lead will be. Two systems are used to grade hardness – the Conté, based on numbers, and the Brookman, based on letters (BB, B, F, HB and so on). Artists' and drafting pencils range from 8B, the softest, to 10H, the hardest. Hardness in writing pencils is designated by numbers ranging from 1 to 4.

Coloured leads are made from a mixture of colouring materials, filler, lubricant and a binder. The filler is usually clay or talc. The lubricant is a fatty acid and/or wax or a wax-like material, while the binder is either a natural gum, such as gum tragacanth, a man-made gum or a cellulose ether. The colouring materials can either be water soluble or water insoluble pigments, depending on the type of lead required.

Surfaces

The range of surfaces suitable for use with pencil is extremely varied – it includes most types of paper, for instance.

Equipment

A recommended carbon pencil is Wolff's, available in degrees ranging from HH to BBB. Black Conté pencils have three degrees – No 1 medium (HB), No 2 soft (B) and No 3 extra soft (BB). As with the equivalent crayons, red sanguine and sepia bistre have only one degree. So does white. Korn Litho Pencils are excellent for lithographic use. They are paper covered, with a pull string for self-sharpening. Degrees are 1 (soft), 2, 3, 4 and 5.

Drawing pencils An extremely wide range is available. The leads are bonded to prevent breaking and encased in the wood, while the pencils themselves are either round or hexagonal in section. The number of grades is similarly varied; the Mars-Lumograph, for instance, has 19 degrees (EE, EB, 6B to B, HB, F and H to 9H).

Coloured pencils There are three main types of coloured pencil widely available. First come those with thick, comparatively soft leads. They are both waterproof and lightproof and are made in a wide range of colours – Derwent produce 72 shades and Eagle 62 shades. They do

not smudge or erase easily; nor do they need to be fixed.

The Veri-thin variety has, as the name suggests, a thin, non-crumbling lead. These pencils are useful when fine detail is required. They are also waterproof, but, in general, the colour range is more restricted, only 36 to 40 shades being available. They do not smudge or erase easily, although they can be removed with a blade. Venus, however, make a small range of colours which is completely erasable.

A range of coloured pencils with watersoluble leads is also on the market. These can be used in combination with water to produce washes of colour. They are something of a cross between pencils and water colours and are made by various manufacturers with either thick or thin leads in ranges of between 30 and 36 colours.

Pencil holders/extenders These are extremely useful, as they make it easier to draw with partly-used pencils. There are many types available.

Clutch pencils These are a development of the ordinary propelling pencil. They consist of a holder, usually made of metal and/or plastic, inside which is a sleeve. This holds and protects the lead, which is secured in position by a clutch lock. This is released to project the lead forward by pressing a button at the end of the holder.

Some suitable leads for clutch pencils are shown on p. 30.

Techniques

The marks made by the three main types of pencil vary. A graphite composition 'lead' pencil produces grey, shiny marks; a carbon/charcoal pencil matt black marks; while a Conté pencil produces matt black marks that are very slightly greasy in appearance.

All three types are available in varying de-

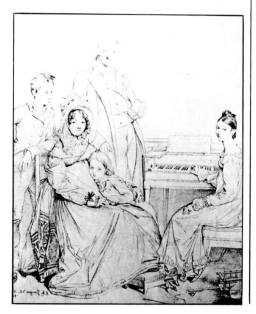

grees of hardness; some vary, too, in the degree of thickness of the lead. The degree of hardness determines whether the pencil is suitable for the particular task in hand. A 6B pencil, for instance, will not retain a sharp point for long, while an 8H is not an ideal pencil for large areas of graduated shading. The amount of pressure applied to the pencil also determines the type of mark made.

Most pencils will make some kind of mark on most of the normal surfaces used for drawing and painting. In general, a slight tooth or grain to the surface means that a more sympathetic mark will be produced. The smoother and shinier the surface, the more restricting it is – on the shiniest surfaces a special pencil, such as a chinagraph, is needed to make a mark at all.

Right John Constable *Cottage and Road, East Bergholt* The use of a soft pencil on a rough texture, which reflects the grain, gives a shimmering, almost Impressionistic effect to this landscape.

Below left Grant Wood *Dinner for Threshers* A soft pencil on smooth paper gives this drawing a regular solid effect. Blocking in is used for tonal contrast.

Below right Terence Dalley *122 King's Cross Road, London WC1* Pencils give both a feeling of solidity and angularity, depending on the pressure used when applying them and the hardness of the pencil.

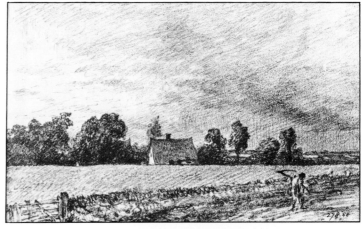

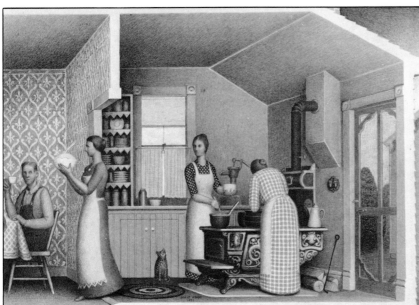

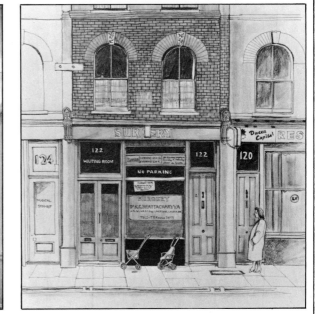

Right Paul Hogarth *Tommy Kelly, Barman at the Bee* To help give the impression of perspective, the artist uses both hard and soft pencils with varying degrees of pressure.

Far right Seurat *Seated Boy With Straw Hat* The shady mysteriousness of this drawing is achieved with the use of Conté pencil which gives a very matt, dark effect. Because of its soft greasy properties, some areas were completely blocked in, resulting in distinctive light and dark contrast.

Left J.A.D. Ingres *La Famille Stamaty* The artist successfully uses stark linear regularity and the absence of shading to convey solidity and feeling in this pencil portrait.

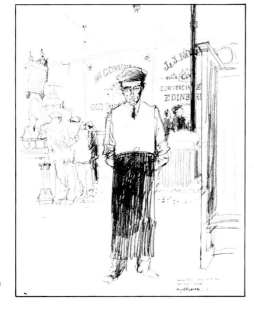

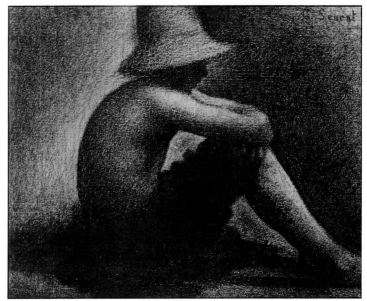

The lines produced by the pencil point can be of a variety of thicknesses and lengths. They may be laid down alongside each other and blended together to make a tone, or they can be laid over each other in any number of cross-hatch techniques. The point itself can be used to create a series of dots which can be varied in strength and distribution.

Most pencil marks can be erased to some extent, but it may not be possible to remove them completely. If a hard pencil has been pressed down firmly, it is more than likely to have created an indent which no amount of rubbing will remove. A very soft pencil will make a mark that may require a soft eraser; too hard a rubber will do more harm than good.

Graphite, carbon/charcoal and Conté pencils all make marks that will smudge. This fact can be utilized in the production of drawings; once such a drawing has been completed, however, it should be fixed. Otherwise further smudging can occur which may well ruin the desired effect.

The information above is intended as a general guide to the use of pencil, as the possibilities open to the illustrator through combinations of types, surfaces and styles are almost infinite. The determining factors are always the skill, knowledge and subjective preferences of the artist. These can only be developed through the willingness to experiment.

Mixed media

Wax resist Various effects can be achieved through the use of this technique. It has been frequently used by Henry Moore (born 1898), particularly in his war-time drawings of figures in the London underground (subway) shelters.

To produce the resist, the basic image is created with a waxy crayon – or even a candle. The image is then covered with a wash; this can be water colour, gouache or ink. The wax acts as a resist, which means that the wash will only 'take' on the uncoated areas of the support. Some pigment may adhere to the surface of the wax, giving a somewhat globular, spotty texture. After the application of the first wash, some of the wax can be scratched away with a blade and another wash laid on.

Rubbings/frottage Brass rubbings are probably the most common examples of the technique, although its potential stretches far beyond this. A sheet of soft paper is laid over a textured surface. By rubbing the surface of the paper with cobbler's wax, a waxy crayon, a pencil or a ballpoint pen, the image of the texture appears on the paper. The higher surfaces of the texture will appear dark in the rubbing, while any indents in the texture will show as unmarked

From 1925 onwards, Max Ernst (1891–1976), the Dada/Surrealist painter, used an adaptation of this technique to create pictures, calling the process 'frottage'. Ernst was extremely fond of the textures of wood and leaves; using a combination of these and other textures,

he created a series of strange beasts to illustrate an *Histoire Naturelle*, published in Paris in 1926.

Transfer This technique produces interesting effects which combine well with other methods and the use of colour. It is a method of working frequently used by the American artist Robert Rauschenberg (born 1925).

The artist takes a printed paper – newspaper half-tones work particularly well – and places it face downwards on a sheet of plain paper. The back of the picture is then rubbed with a pencil or some similar instrument to transfer the image. The marks of the rubbing clearly show on the somewhat ghost-like transferred image.

Negative drawing This technique produces interesting images, though it is not ideally suited to fine detail. It can also be very messy.

Using either charcoal, chalk, or a soft pencil, an area of evenly distributed tone or colour is created on a piece of paper or card. Rubbing with a stump, torchon or cotton bud will help to distribute the granules evenly. The area is worked over until the required depth of tone has been built up.

Drawing is done with a rubber. The result will be a pale image on a dark background; it is, in effect, the reverse of the normal drawing procedure in which the image grows as more lines are added. Here, the image grows as more of the background is removed. The lines will vary in tone according to the amount of rubbing.

With care, and the right choice of eraser, it should be possible to regain the colour of the original surface. Soft rubbers should be used – putty rubbers can be pinched to a point or used broadly. With a pencil eraser, it is possible to exercise considerable control over the line.

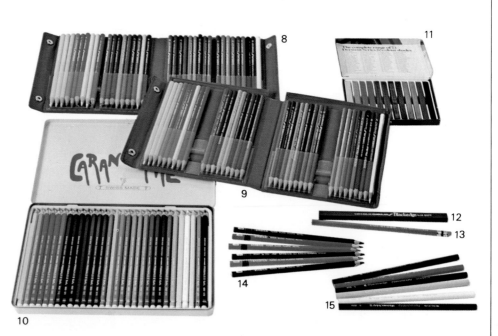

Right In this Glynne Boyd Harte exhibition poster coloured pencils are used loosely to give an effect of lightness and airiness.

Far right The almost photographic effect of this book jacket illustration by Clare Davis is achieved with the fine, tight pencil lines.

Bottom right For this poster, Bush Hollyhead used pencils. Chinagraph pencils were used on rough paper to produce a tonal effect although only line was used. The colours were introduced using silkscreen with a separate overlay for each colour.

Bottom far right This magazine cover by Gareth Williams was drawn using colour pencils to pick out the fine detail. Combined with the use of gouache for the more solid blocks of colour, this produces an almost photographic effect.

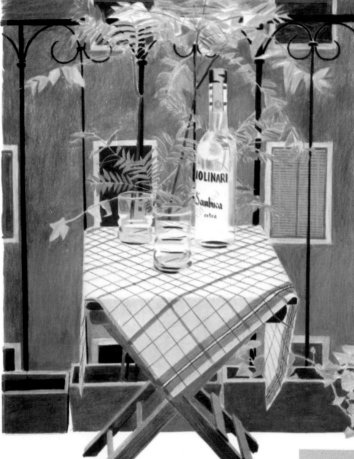

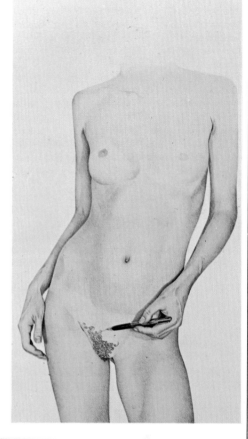

Above left The wide selection of pencils available for the artist's use include carbon pencils (1) ranging from BBB to HH, Conté drawing pencils (2) which come in black, brown, red and white, Steadtler mars lumographs (3) and litho crayons (4). In addition the artist would find use for pencil holders (5), clutch pencils (6) and replacement leads (7).

Left For colouring purposes, Derwent colour pencils (8) and thin lead colour pencils (9) are ideal; the Caran d'Ache (10) is very similar. There are also Derwent colour blocks (11), All-Stabilos (14) and chinagraphs (15), Blackedge (12) is a type of layout pencil; col-erase (13) is a completely erasable colour pencil.

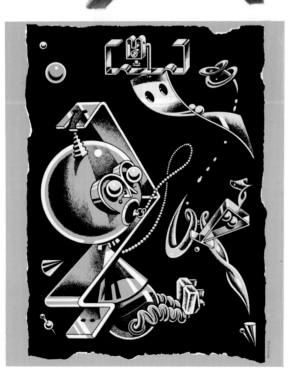

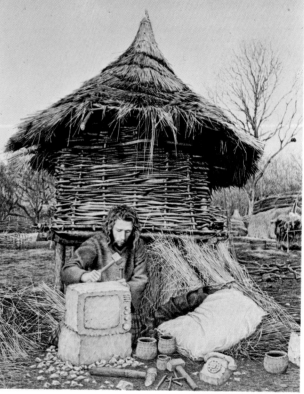

CHAPTER TWO

PEN AND INK

Pen and ink have been tools of illustrators for many centuries. Today, however, their use is inevitably bound up with modern reproductive techniques. No matter how well-executed a drawing may be, or how aptly it is related to its subject, it will have failed in its purpose if it cannot be faithfully printed. This gritty professional truth underpins any discussion of method or technique and is a factor that all artists working in this field must take into account.

Artists working in pen and ink are on the whole particularly fortunate, since their basic requirements are so few. Consider such an artist's advantages. He or she needs only a sheet of paper, a pen and some ink to practise their craft. Like the poet, the illustrator travels light and, like poetry, the medium itself allows an enormous variety of individual expression, whose possibilities can never be exhausted.

One further factor must be taken into account, however, and it is on this that the artist's livelihood depends. Suitable material is needed to inspire illustration just as an actor needs a script from which to work. It is on the liveliness and originality of an artist's response to such material that his or her reputation will be established.

One of the special interests of any study of pen and ink drawing is the contrast between the very different temperaments of the artists who have been attracted to the medium and how, historically, the methods they evolved for themselves were adapted by their successors. Thus, the attack of Salvator Rosa (1616–1673)

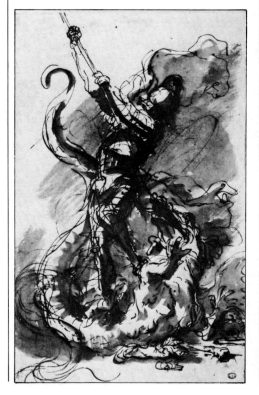

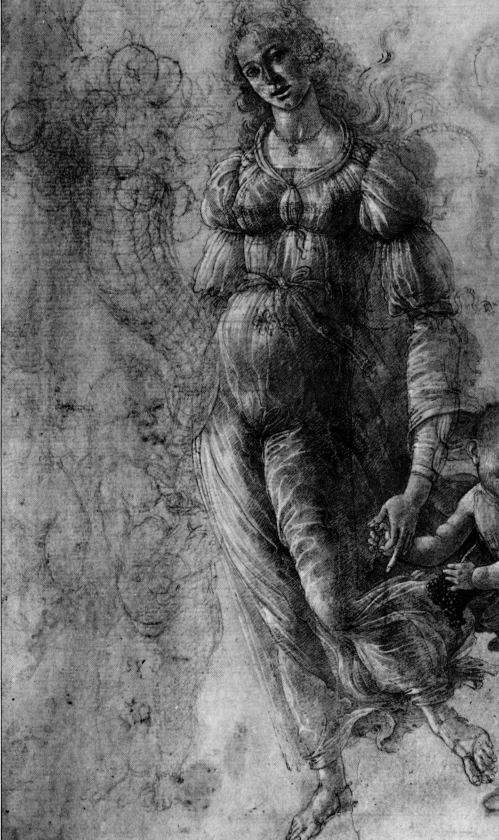

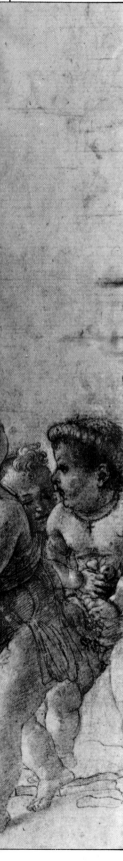

leads through to present-day artists, such as Claes Oldenburg (born 1929) and Ian Ribbons (born 1924) Cooler in feeling, the sensitive and probing penmanship of Leonardo (1452–1519) and Botticelli (1445–1510) is echoed in the work of many modern illustrators. Similarly fascinating is the complete change of style displayed by individual artists over the years. An example is the work of Jules Pascin (1885–1930), whose carefully composed illustrations for *Simplicissimus* in 1905 were transformed into the nervy, sinuous figure studies of twenty years later.

No matter how different their work in style or outlook, the one constant factor in the lives of professional illustrators is the deadline or delivery date. Some regard this as a curse and others as a blessing, though its pressure naturally varies from field to field. These fields are extremely varied; they involve not only books, magazines and advertising, but also sometimes films and television, for pen and ink has proved versatile enough for use in all these media.

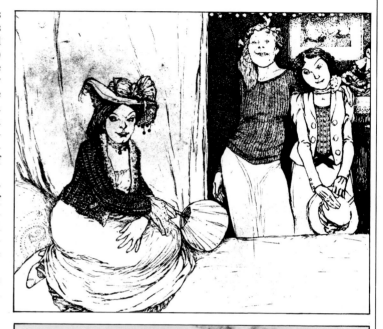

Far left Salvator Rosa *St. George fighting the Dragon* This is a vivid example of his effective use of free, swirling lines.
Left Botticelli *Abundance or Autumn.* The woman's draperies show the delicate effect of fine pen lines combined with wash and white highlights. **Below** Leonardo's anatomical studies also demonstrate the fine texture which can be achieved in pen and ink.

Right These two line drawings by Jules Pascin show how his style and approach changed markedly The earlier drawing *The Three Girlfriends* (1905) **(above)** demonstrates his early use of close, dense lines and varied shading. The later work *Redhead in a Blue Slip* (1926) **(below)** shows his mature style, with its characteristically bold and fluid penwork.

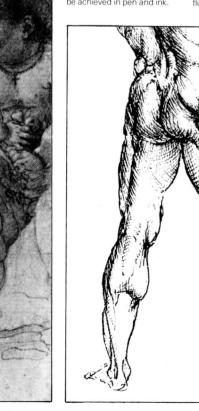

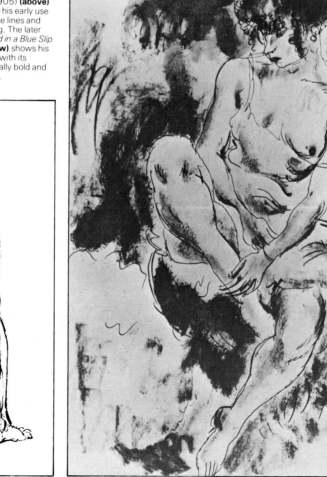

History It was the medieval monks who brought the use of the pen to its first flowering. The highly sophisticated calligraphy and pen drawings which filled their manuscript books grew into the sumptuous illumination and miniatures of the later Middle Ages. The base on which their drawings were made was normally prepared skin – either goat, sheep or the less robust calf, lamb or kid. The quills they used for drawing were usually made from goose feathers, though turkey and swan were also used. Accounts vary as to the nature of the inks employed, but two formulae appear to have been common. The first specified a combination of iron salts and oak-galls, which become dark-brown with age; the second was made from a suspension of carbon, such as lampblack, in a mixture of gum and water.

Such drawings were not the first to utilize quill, but it was more common for artists of previous eras to prefer incision or brush work. It was the patient meditative craftsmen of the cloister who laid down the basic principles for the use of the pen and established the techniques on which the formidable draughtsmen of the fifteenth century built. At about this time, independent artists began to emerge. Some of these were gifted enough to set up on their own,

though, more frequently, they had the backing of one or more patrons. Thus, the idea of the artist as an individual emerged.

With a further increase in independence at the time of the Renaissance, techniques and methods began to be more exploratory, as artists became less tied to the requirements of traditionally-minded patrons. The choice of subject matter broadened and considerable media mixing began. Having thrown off the shackles of early manuscript illustration, the Renaissance artists brought into play crayon, water colour and white highlighting in their twin search for expression and truth. They used a multiplicity of means for the graphic rendering of form and for expressiveness; however, when intellectual considerations dominated, as in Leonardo's anatomical and mechanical studies, the severity of pen and ink alone was used.

This new mood was not confined to Italy. Not only did the Renaissance artists move freely between the courts of Europe, but German and Dutch artists also journeyed south. Dürer (1471–1528) travelled extensively in Italy in 1505, when he created what were probably the first landscape drawings in Europe as well as his animal studies. Half a century later, the Dutch master Brueghel (*c.* 1525–69) followed suit.

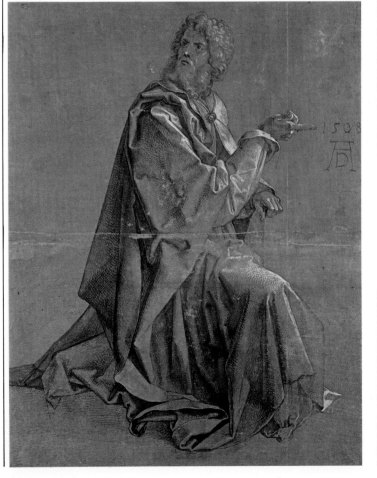

Left Albrecht Dürer *St Paul* Experimentation in techniques and media increased during and after the Renaissance. Here, Dürer achieved various tonal qualities and produced the effect of light and shade by using black ink with white highlights on a background of blue/green paper. These white highlights — on St Paul's hair and the top of his robe — contrast with the darker line shading which gives the effect of the draperies falling to the floor.

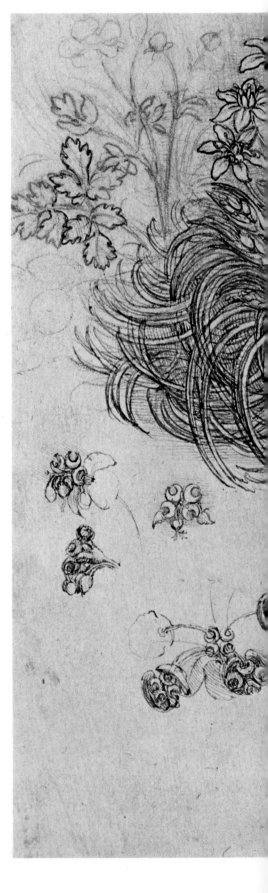

Right Leonardo da Vinci *Flowering Plants* For his mechanical drawings and anatomical sketches, Leonardo favoured the clarity and severity of the pen and ink medium. For his more imaginative subjects and his plant studies, he explored new methods of expression. Here, the swirling pen strokes add vigour and vitality — indeed the pattern of the leaves is almost abstract in quality. The detail of the plant is drawn in pen and ink, over a background sketch in red chalk.

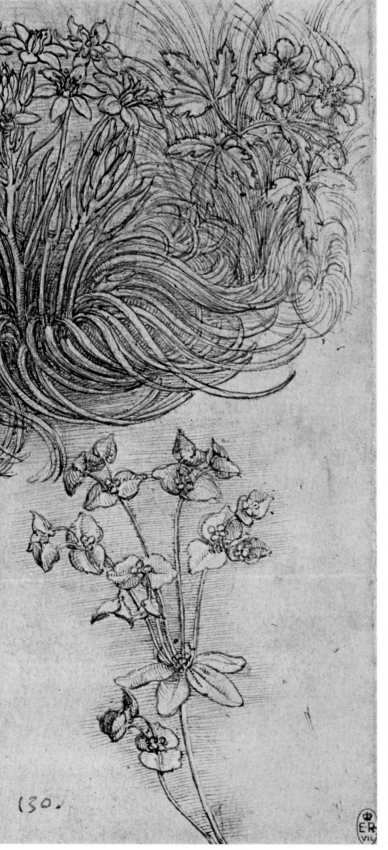

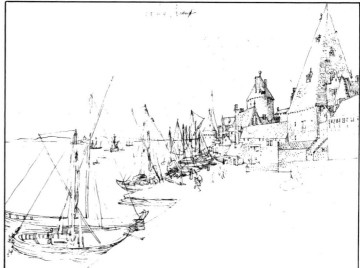

As well as experimenting at home, many Renaissance artists began to travel throughout Europe. Dürer visited Italy in 1505, and produced some of the first landscape drawings in Europe. This demonstrated that the technique of line drawing could be extended to many subject areas. The drawing of the *Harbour on the Scheldt* (above) shows Dürer's fine use of line while the study of *Six Pillows* (below) shows his versatile use of pen and ink in graphic illustration.

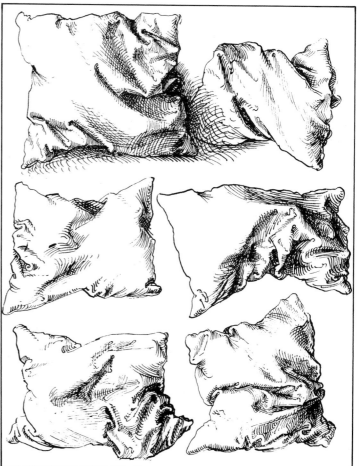

The post-Renaissance period was particularly rich in gifted pen-draughtsmen. This was an age of great self-confidence, the rise of a rich and powerful middle class in northern Europe engendering a similar spirit in art. The formidable talents of Rubens (1577–1640) and Van Dyck (1559–1641) – the latter an extraordinary virtuoso of the pen – make a fascinating counterpoint to the less theatrical, almost intimate, approach of Rembrandt (1606–69), whose drawings in ink and wash are deeply moving. The spirit and majesty of the High Baroque period are nowhere better displayed than in the almost impressionistic drawings of Bernini (1598–1680) and Salvator Rosa, while a similar extravagant spirit permeates the work of Tiepolo (1696–1770) and Piranesi (1720–78).

Further north, the more temperate and rational climate of the Enlightenment created a dual spirit of contemplative calm and sceptical enquiry. The first mood was reflected in the gentle ingratiating charm of the chalk drawings of the period; the second in the wit and attack of Hogarth (1697–1764), a line draughtsman of the first order.

Too impatient and ardent a spirit to spend overlong on preparatory sketches, Hogarth's nervously energetic penmanship carries the viewer straight to the heart of his approach. His style has its echoes in that of the later English satirist Rowlandson (1756–1827), whose boundless wit and invention could not provide a greater contrast to the poetic temperament of his exact contemporary William Blake (1757–1827). Blake epitomizes the interior literary nature of the English graphic genius.

During this period of comparative artistic calm in Britain, the continent of Europe was in turmoil. The French Revolution and the rise of Napoleon had overturned the old order and given rise to almost constant war. The excesses of this were sombrely recorded by Goya (1746–1828) in several series of etchings, for which pen and ink studies were often made.

From Blake's time to the present is very roughly the period of the illustrated book as it exists today. First of all, illustrations took the form of engravings on either wood or metal; they were usually interpreted from ink or pencil sketches made by painter-artists, who were themselves rarely proficient in engraving. Although most of these artists considered their illustrative bookwork as entirely secondary to the more serious business of actual painting, many of them nevertheless developed a quite remarkable affinity for it. Indeed, for quite a few the highly literary content of both was identical.

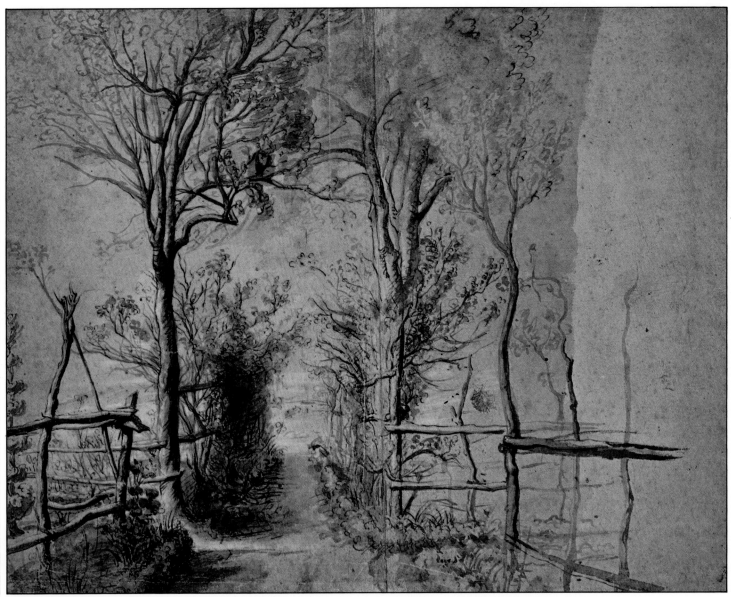

Right The drama and movement in this sketch by Van Dyck are conveyed through the bold, swirling lines. This is a typical example of his spirited approach. His work expresses a feeling of adventure and enterprise shared by many artists of the period. By contrast, the pen and wash drawings of Rembrandt — for example, *Nathan admonishing David* **(far right)** — are more sensitive and restrained in technique. This is in keeping with the more intimate atmosphere of the work.

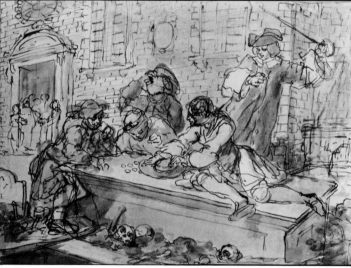

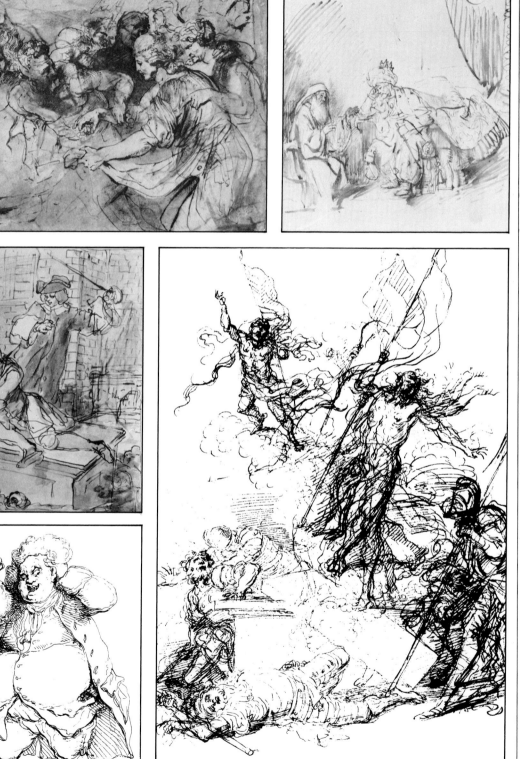

Above William Hogarth *Idle Apprentices at Play in a Churchyard* Hogarth used ink and wash boldly in vivid cartoons which conveyed his satirical purposes.
Right Thomas Rowlandson *An Epicure* The fluid line and spirited humour of Rowlandson's pen and ink sketches epitomize the sometimes cruel wit of late eighteenth century caricature.

Left Rubens *A Path Bordered by Trees* The background and tonal effect effects in the picture were created with brown washes on a brownish paper, using pen and brush. The detail was added with line drawing and stipple. The almost ethereal quality of the drawing comes from the combination of techniques and fineness of line.

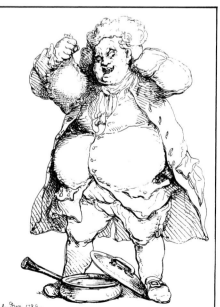

Above Salvator Rosa *Resurrection* Rosa's work is at times almost impressionistic in style and approach, full of a characteristic energy and power. Here, the spirited, free lines — particularly of the figures and banners — vividly express the message of triumph and hope inherent in its subject. They also epitomize the extravagant nature of High Baroque artistic expression.

By the mid-nineteenth century, magazines as well as books had established themselves and provided work for artists such as Charles Keene (1823–91), Arthur Hughes (1832–1915) and A. B. Houghton (1836–1875), who also took his talents to the USA. Another celebrated artist of the period was the brilliant George du Maurier (1834–96). His work was among the last to be engraved from the original on to wood block.

By the turn of the century, the process block had been introduced, which reproduced ink line directly without recourse to an engraver. This new freedom was quickly exploited by very different artists who pressed it to its limits – from the subtly plotted elegance of Beardsley (1872–98) to the earthy wit of Phil May (1864–1903).

In the USA, Charles Dana Gibson (1867–1944) introduced a crisp robustness to the use of the pen which was quite new to the medium. Across the English Channel, the wit and vivacity of Caran d'Ache (1859–1909) and Forain (1852–1931) added a characteristically Gallic flavour to the graphic art of the times. In Britain, inevitably, the literary tradition had, as always, its champions, as in the work of Rackham (1867–1939) and Edmund Sullivan (1869–1933), the latter being an artist of particular force and penetration.

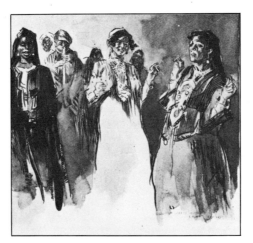

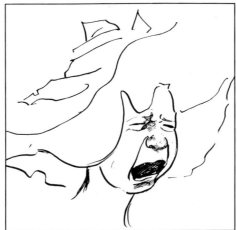

As well as being used for fine art, pen and ink became increasingly popular as a medium for book and magazine illustration in the nineteenth century. These pictures show some of the different styles and techniques employed by various illustrators.
Right Arthur Rackham used a free, loose approach, with heavy dark lines and washes of diluted ink, combined with extremely close attention to detail. The uncompleted area to the right of the picture reveals the preliminary pencil lines on white paper. Rackham's fluid and expressive style was well suited to the imaginative subjects he chose to illustrate, often from Shakespeare, or mythology.
Above left Charles Dana Gibson *In a Coffee House, Cairo.* This is one of Gibson's sketches in Egypt. His combination of rapid incisive linework and wash help create an impression of atmosphere and action.
Left Loose and strong lines in this drawing by Phil May convey an impression of intense emotion.

Below George du Maurier *Art in Excelsis* Du Maurier drew cartoons for *Punch* magazine. The wit of his drawing captures the artistic pretensions of a society family who have invited their friends to admire a newly painted ceiling. Magazine publishing extended and popularized the work of satirical illustrators in the nineteenth century.

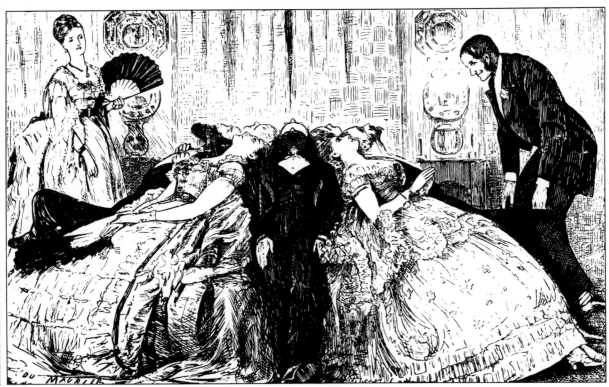

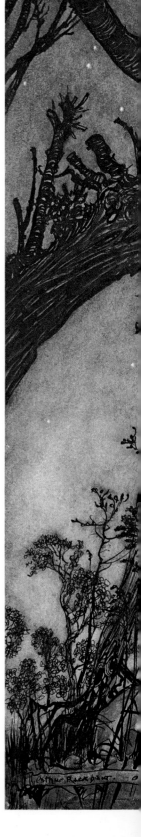

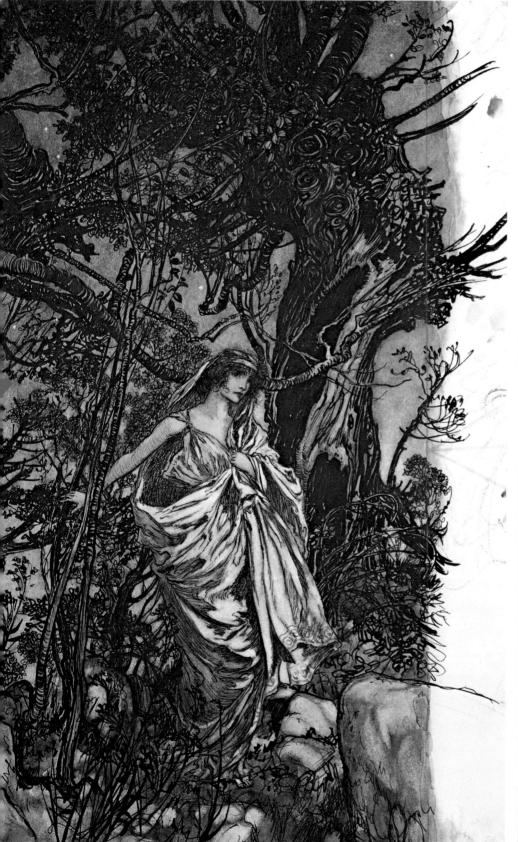

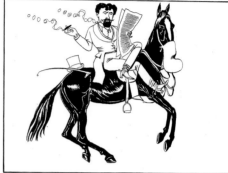

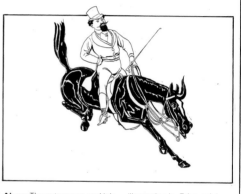

Above These two pen and ink drawings by Caran d'Ache are part of a longer cartoon sequence. The light, stylish drawing, with its bold clear lines and contrasts typifies his wit and style.
In contrast to Caran d'Ache's light touch, this illustration by Edmund J. Sullivan **(below)** uses heavy, dark crosshatching, to create the grotesque faces. This shows the serious side of satirical illustration.

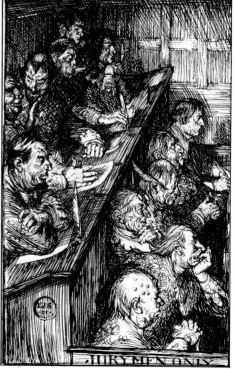

The innovative explosion of the Ecole de Paris, just prior to and following the First World War, was the catalyst for many new departures in the graphic arts. Among other by-products was a new linear clarity and freedom best exemplified in the pen drawings of Matisse (1869–1954), Picasso (1881–1973) and Pascin. Its development in Britain by the short-lived Gaudier-Brzeska (1891–1915) continues to this day in much magazine and fashion illustration. In Germany, the rigours of post-war life created both an introspective and a savagely sardonic graphic style. The line drawings of Käthe Kollwitz (1867–1945) and George Grosz (1893–1959) are typical of both extremes.

The history of the graphic arts since the First World War is a record of constant upheaval and re-discovery. Curious ambiguities are thrown up, as in the case of Salvador Dali (born 1904), whose whole surrealist output is built on a base of carefully academic, almost Victorian, realism. Another surrealist, de Chirico (born 1888), denounced all his own much admired early work. Marcel Duchamp (1887–1968), one of the most revered figures in modern art, abandoned painting for chess.

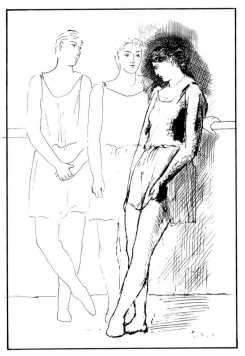

Left Picasso *Three Dancers* The uncluttered simplicity of this pen and ink drawing is typical of Pablo Picasso's work in this medium. The clear, sparse effect is achieved through his use of free, loose lines and light cross-hatching.

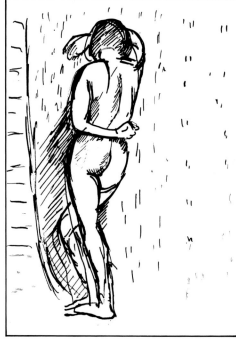

Below The powerful form of this naked figure by Matisse is outlined with thick black ink, with the lines themselves heavily reinforced. The shadows, and the suggestion of texture in the background, are indicated with abrupt, bold pen strokes.

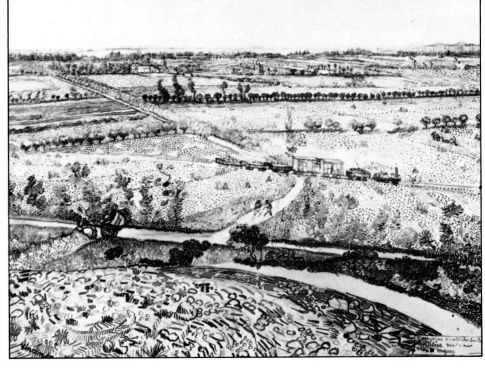

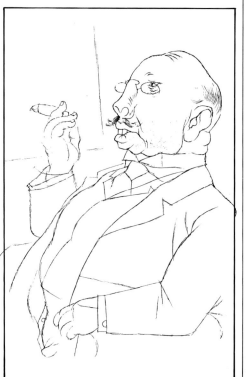

In spite of the dauntingly complex and sometimes self-indulgent excesses that seem to dominate the contemporary art scene, there can be little doubt that, in the smaller-scale world of pen and ink, there is a firm basis for optimism. This is engendered by the excellence of so much contemporary work, as the examples cited in this chapter serve to show.

Above Van Gogh *The Countryside on the Banks of the Rhône* Although best known for his oil painting, Van Gogh was also skilled with pen and ink. Here, he used various techniques with a reed pen to achieve a subtly-textured landscape in brown tones.

Right George Grosz *Face of a Man* The outlines of this satirical caricature are built up with many short, fine pen strokes to give an impression of solid lines. He achieves his effect with a subtle and understated technique of drawing.

Materials and equipment

Pens and nibs

Quills Ready-cured quills can still be bought in art material stores and at law stationers, although the traditional quill-cutting knives are no longer made. A useful alternative is a purpose-built knife, such as the Swann-Morton Craftknife, with its interchangeable blades. Quills can be cut to suit individual needs and are extremely adaptable; however, because of their soft tips, they require constant re-cutting.

Reed-pens Like quills, reed pens can still be bought at specialist art stores. Their use is somewhat limited, since their 'bite' is rather insensitive, but in conjunction with contrasting penwork they can be most effective. The characteristic truncated line they produce acts as an expressive foil to more delicate ink drawing.

Dip pens After the decline of the quill, dip pens became the traditional tool of pen and ink illustrators; they are still in general use, together with the more recent fountain pens, reservoir

pens and fibre tips. Technically, the nib is known as the 'pen' and the holder is known as the 'pen-holder'.

Many varieties of nib are produced for a number of specialized uses. The range now includes heavy-purpose dip nibs, copperplate, script, crow quills, mapping and lithographic nibs. All of these can be used with any kind of ink; they should be cleaned regularly to avoid caking. The more delicate nibs should be replaced as soon as they lose their sensitivity.

Fountain pens These are ideal when an on-site drawing is required. Among the best is the Osmiroid range, now adapted to take black water-proof ink; the Osmiroid Sketchpen, with its flexible steel alloy tip, is a most useful tool. The Rapidograph 3060, with fifteen line widths, is also well-adapted to the needs of the illustrator; it produces a line of uniform and constant width. Both Pelikan and Parker market efficient drawing pens; their disadvantage is they cannot be used with waterproof Indian ink.

Reservoir pens Reservoir pens, in which ink is poured into the reservoir rather than being

sucked up through the nib, are in wide use among draughtsmen and illustrators. Their chief attraction is that the inks made for use with them are waterproof and are available in a wide range of colours. In addition, the inks flow more freely than their drawing counterparts.

The stylo tips provided with the Rapidograph range are available in twelve line widths and are interchangeable. Stylos produce a constant line width which is of use to many types of draughtsmen. Pelikan 'Graphos' pens have a range of 19 nibs – varying from fine to very broad – which are quickly interchangeable and so as useful as the Rapidograph family.

It is essential that reservoir pens are cleaned regularly with warm water and are not left uncovered.

Ballpoints Great improvements have taken place since the early days of ballpoint pens, but they still vary enormously in their sensitivity and dependability. Many illustrators find them antipathetic, since the delivery of ink to the tip is sometimes unreliable and the consequent reworking of the line hard to achieve.

Types of pen The modern graphic artist can choose from a wide range of pens according to his or her technique and the effects desired. Early quill and reed pens were replaced by steel nibs in the nineteenth century. Fountain and reservoir pens followed, and today many sophisticated instruments are available. Some artists, however, still prefer to use traditional equipment.

Right Quills and reeds were the earliest pens, used by the ancient Greeks, Romans and Egyptians. The tip can be cut to exactly the right angle to produce a specific effect, but needs frequent re-cutting.

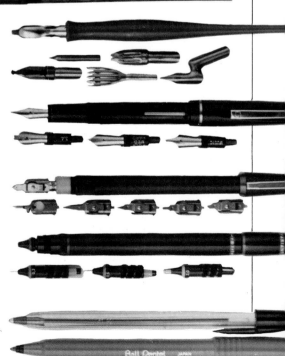

Right The dip pen consists of a main shaft or 'penholder' and a wide variety of interchangeable nibs or 'pens' which are dipped into the ink.

Right The fountain pen has a built-in ink holder which is filled by suction. It can be fitted with a range of nibs; the most common are broad, medium and fine.

Right Reservoir pens have an ink holder which is filled by pouring in the ink. The graphos pen **(top)** can be fitted with several different styles of nib, which are available in a wide range of sizes. The stylo tip pen **(below)** has a tubular nib which gives a constant line width. These nibs range from broad to very fine.

Right In ballpoint pens ink delivery is controlled by a ball in the tip **(top)**. Some types **(below)** have a cushioned plastic tip to give a more even flow.

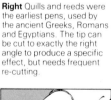

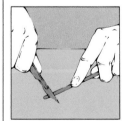

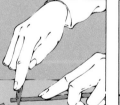

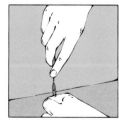

Making a quill pen
1: Cut the end off the quill using, for example, a craft knife.

2. Trim the quill to an appropriate angle.

3. Carefully cut the central slit.

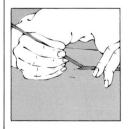

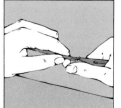

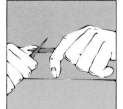

4. Clean out the end of the quill to help prevent blotting.

5. Cut and trim the curved sides.

6. Finally clean up the end. The knife used in making quill pens should always be sharp.

Inks and markers
Waterproof ink is most used for drawing. Its colour density means that it reproduces well. A wide range of colours and types are available — Winsor and Newton *(6)*, FW *(7)*. Special inks are used in stylo tip pens — these are available in bottles or cartridges *(8)*. All these inks are also available in black and white *(9)*. In recent years the marker with a felt or fibre tip has become increasingly popular with illustrators and graphic designers. Markers with felt tips *(5)* give a much broader line than those with fibre tips and have shorter lives. They are mainly used for doing layout work. The range of colours available is extremely wide *(1)*. The fibre tip ranges from very fine *(2)* to medium *(3,4)*. The ink used in felt and fibre tip markers is spirit based and so has a relatively short life. Markers have increasing applications in design work. They are convenient, easy to use and can be utilized at all stages of work from rough to finished artwork.

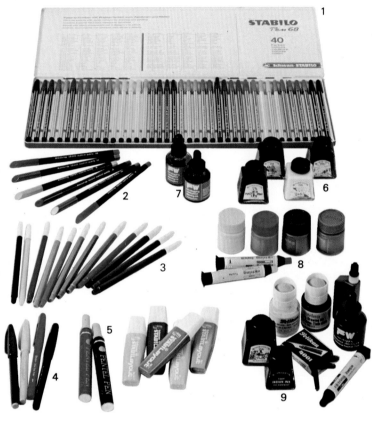

They are almost completely indelible, but the spirit-based ink supply tends to evaporate quickly – especially if the tip is left uncovered.

Inks and papers
Drawing inks Until 1834, when Henry Stephens set up his factory, inks were usually sold by street vendors and varied widely in quality. Stephens' particular claim was that his ink was eminently suited to the new steel pens which were replacing the old quills. Since that time, drawing inks have been refined, made waterproof and produced in an impressive range of colours: Winsor and Newton currently market 22; Pelikan 18; and Grumbacher 17.

The range of black drawing inks, sometimes called Indian, is similarly impressive. Those intended for paper should be carefully distinguished from those made for use on talc or drafting linen, as the consistencies are different.

In general, waterproof ink is the best for drawing, since its density makes it easier to reproduce. Special non-waterproof inks act in a similar way to water colour and are sometimes used in conjunction with waterproof ink. Non-waterproof inks can be washed away with water and are easily diluted.

Other inks in general use are those employed in the ballpoint pen and that used for felt-tipped pens. Ballpoint inks have a glycol base similar to printing inks; felt-tipped ink has a spirit base and hence a short life.

Papers
For illustration work good quality paper is essential. Cartridge paper at 60lbs weight is usually best. With thinner paper there is a danger that, because it is less well sized, the ink will spread unevenly. Paper at 60lbs weight allows for corrections and will also take a water colour or ink wash. The top row **(below)** shows some of the currently

available hard to medium surface papers good for illustration (from **left** to **right**): Bristol board 1 and 2, Kent Hot Pressed (HP), Ivory board, Saunders HP. On the bottom row (from **left** to **right**) are some medium to absorbent papers: cartridge, Kent NHP, Fabriano NHP and Saunders NHP.

Fibre tips These are now produced in great quantity and there are many different makes. The Pentel range, the Flair marker pen, the Tempo series, the Niji Stylist and the Pilot Fineliner all give excellent results.

All these pens come in useful colour ranges. Their essential virtue is that they produce a dependable, flowing and consistent line, while their width sensitivity makes working with them similar to drawing with the tip of a brush.

Paper For illustration, the best quality cartridge paper should be used whenever possible. Paper at 60 lbs weight is usually the most suitable, as this allows for corrections and, where appropriate, for ink and water colour washes. For carefully detailed work with a steel nib, a hard surface works best. However, all artists have their own personal preferences, so the only really satisfactory way to arrive at a choice is through selection and use.

Hard to medium-hard paper surfaces include Bristol board; fashion board; RWS hot pressed; Strathmore Drawing; Kent HP; Ivorex; Arches Special MBM; and Saunders HP. Medium-hard to absorbent surfaces include Daler cartridge paper; Kent NHP; Fabriano NHP; Arches Satine; and Saunders NHP. The chief risk with the softer surfaces is that an ink line can spread unevenly, as they are not so well sized as the heavier ones. In addition, they tend to absorb the ink. In certain cases, this can help the line, but not if a true, sharp line is required. Nibs, too, can catch in them when a quick forceful stroke is made.

Where an ink line drawing is to be augmented by ink wash or water colour, paper suitable to receive both media should be used. In the latter case, it is best to stretch the paper on a drawing board before the wash is applied.

As with all types of equipment and materials it is important to use good quality inks and papers in order to achieve good results.

Techniques

Most pen techniques are derived from two basic elements – the line and the dot. From these simple beginnings, a virtually limitless number of textures can be developed. These, in turn, can be combined with other media, both in black and white and colour. The only limitations are the technical considerations of reproduction.

Subject matter also sometimes influences the choice of technique. When illustrating a story, for instance, the artist may feel that the period in which the tale is set demands a change of style, or that a contemporary pastiche would be appropriate. Whatever the motivation, a wide-ranging knowledge of techniques is helpful, as it helps to extend the range of expression. Certain artists seem to work with enviable self-confidence in several different fields, passing from pen or pencil to water colour and wood block, as if the difficulties of each discipline exist only to be brilliantly surmounted.

Nevertheless, an equally good case can be made out for the illustrator who concentrates on one carefully chosen approach – probably the one most congenial to his or her own temperament – and so probes deeper and further into its expressive potential than a less whole-hearted commitment allows. The work of Edmund Sullivan is a good example; in his hands, the pen medium seems capable of an almost operatic power. The following pages, apart from discussing pen techniques currently in use, also serve to illustrate the work of artists who have consolidated and extended the illustrative use of pen and ink.

Line drawing The line drawing pure and simple, unsupported by textures, is the most direct and in some ways the most exacting of all techniques. Where crosshatching or other tonal additions are eschewed, the outline itself must do the vital job of suggesting form. When successfully used, the pure contour line unfolds as the hand fits the glove; the simplicity of the method allows a freshness and immediacy of response denied to more deliberate approaches to pen drawing.

The best type of pen to use is a fountain pen or a stylo-tip pen. Their use makes it easier to achieve a flowing and uninterrupted line; it also eliminates the need for nib-dipping. Such drawings present few problems to the process engraver or the printer, since there are no tonal areas of crosshatching to clog or close up in the printing. As long as an undiluted dense black ink is used, the line will hold firm for reproduction and the platemaker's camera will capture every twist and turn of the ink.

The paper should be suitably receptive; it should not, for instance, be rough surfaced enough to catch even the lightest pressure of the pen. Nor should it be too porous, or the line will bleed into the surface with an uneven spread.

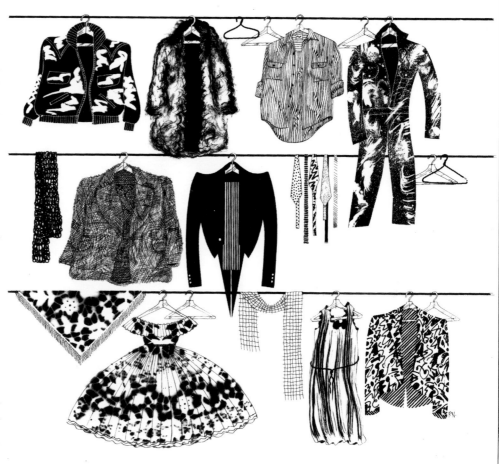

This direct, purely linear approach has attracted artists who like to catch a passing impression or who wish to encapsulate an animated scene in a way impossible for the more deliberate and meditative draughtsman. There are many occasions, too, when a simple instructional drawing in a newspaper, magazine or instructional book is required. Such illustrations are usually some variant of the outline or cartoon approach, in which all extraneous shading is eliminated.

Below Gaudier-Brzeska *Lionesses* This is a vivid example of the clarity and expressive potential of pure line work. The artist relies on the simple fluidity of loose, free drawing to suggest the form and feline power of the lionesses. It shows how effective an apparently simple technique can be.

Above This drawing by Peter Niczewski uses different pen and ink techniques to show the versatility of the medium. On the top row the pattern on the jacket was created by painting on masking fluid and then applying the ink with a paint brush. The furry effect for the coat came from applying the paint with a toothbrush. For the shirt a dip pen with a fine but flexible nib was used, as it was for the dress **(bottom right)**. The boiler suit had masking fluid applied as splatter with the fingers and with a toothbrush. The black ink was then painted over. On the middle row for the crosshatching on the jacket a dip pen was also used. The dinner suit was outlined with rapidograph and filled in with brush. A rapidograph was also used to draw the knitted scarf **(middle left)** and the patterned jacket **(bottom row, right)**. The evening dress **(bottom, left)** was airbrushed using paper doilies as a stencil.

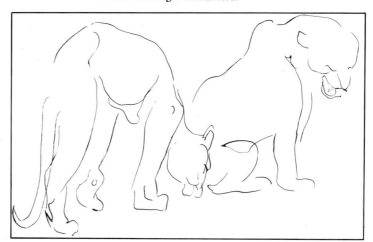

Many artists, however, have introduced further complexities onto this simple basis. In the work of Aubrey Beardsley, for instance, the use of direct outline drawing took a more decorative and dramatic turn. Beardsley aimed for a deliberate and complex design rather than spontaneity, in which subtly assymetrical patterns are built up by the use of areas of solid black played off against linear drawing of the greatest elegance. Tiny patches of stippling are sometimes added, occasionally to suggest form but more often for a purely decorative purpose. Thus, the linear basis to Beardsley's drawing is indisputable, although his stylistic origins are still in the wood block tradition of his immediate predecessors.

Another artist who has made a most striking use of line in conjunction with areas of full black is Eric Fraser (born 1902). Some years ago, he gave an account of his illustrative method, of which the following is a shortened version: 'A small rough visual is first made, based on a careful reading of the story. The sketch was then enlarged to approximately one and a half times reproductive size in pencil on a hard-pressed art board. With a firm pen, such as a Gillot 303 or Hinks Well 303 and waterproof Indian ink, all outlines were drawn in and black areas filled in with a sable brush. Finally with a flexible fine pen and white poster colour thin enough to flow freely, all white lines were put in and edges cleaned up. The basic principle in this type of illustration is the play of movement between white areas broken by black line and black areas by whites.'

These two artists are not alone. There are many examples of artists who have developed a pure-line style in which the planning is all-important, with design having a dominant role in the drawing. In such work, the free-flowing contoured approach is jettisoned in favour of delicacy and detail. Modelling and tonal areas are absent, but are replaced by stylistic elegance. The tool used is either dip pen or stylo-tip.

Line and crosshatch What is loosely termed crosshatching covers a great variety of drawing techniques. Essentially there are two main uses for it in illustration. The first is to act quite simply as shading or to give rounded form to the objects being drawn. The second is to build up the tonal areas of a drawing for dramatic effect or to achieve chiaroscuro – that is, the play of light areas against dark ones. Apart from these directly functional uses, crosshatching is often employed decoratively, as an adjunct to linear outline or contour drawing, or mixed with a modelled treatment of the subject.

The crosshatch method is simply the criss-crossing of pen lines to build up tone and texture. The drawn lines themselves are sometimes mechanically straight or may be broken, wavy and uneven. Successive layers of lateral and diagonal lines are laid on to become progressively denser until solid black is arrived at.

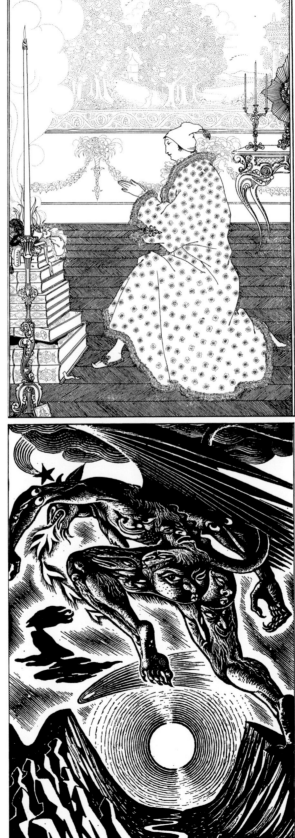

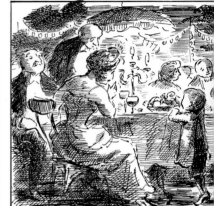

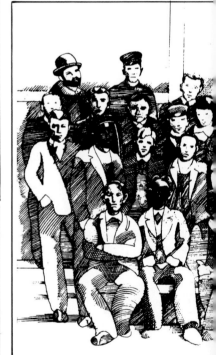

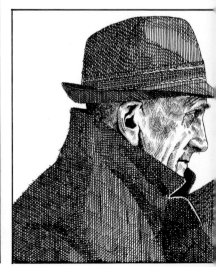

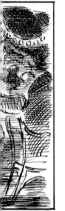

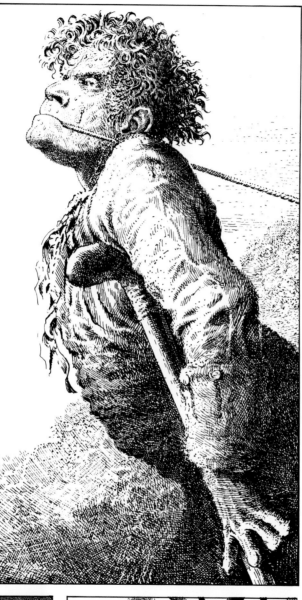

Far left Aubrey Beardsley illustration from *The Rape of the Lock* This shows a stylized use of decorative line work and stippling.
Far left bottom Eric Fraser illustration from *English Legends* Here, line work is combined with blocks of black and white. The remaining pictures show the very different effects which can be produced by various illustrators using a combination of line work and cross-hatching:
left Edward Ardizzone; **below** Milton Glaser; **bottom left** Ron Brown; **bottom centre** Maurice Sendak; **bottom right** Robin Jacques; **right** Mervyn Peake.

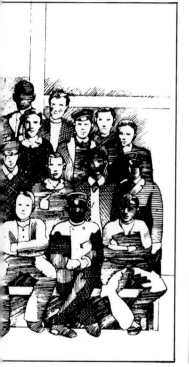

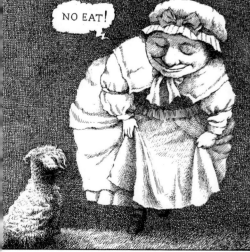

NO EAT!

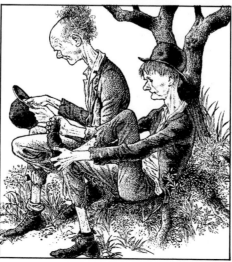

This simple method, however, produces very different results, depending on the personality and intent of the artist concerned. Mervyn Peake (1911–1968), for instance, has described his own very personal approach. On a smooth surface board, a light pencil sketch is laid down as a general basis for the pen and ink work. Inking is then begun, with the hatching being carried out not in a rigid or mechanical way, but with a loose and nervous handling of the pen. There is no contour outline to the figure drawn in except for a carefully controlled profile to the face where the character has to be crystallized. The hatched lines go in every direction but are kept springy and do not settle into a rigid pattern. Beyond the figure itself, a tonal area is built up of lighter textures edged with small clusters of dots. A lively contrast is created between the spiky curls of the hair and the longer inklines over the rest of the figure. Finally, feather strokes of process white are overlaid on parts of the ink hatching – not as corrections, but giving it an added richness of texture.

Edward Ardizzone (1900–1979), too, has his own very personal method. A fairly elaborate drawing in tone is made with a hard pencil. The point of this is that the resulting drawing is grey and will not get in the way of the ink drawing which follows. Then, using the back of the nib, a fairly light and hesitant line is made around the main forms. This is like making a new drawing, as the pencil underneath is not exactly copied; the artist re-draws and extemporizes as he goes along. Next block in all the main areas of shadow with an even horizontal hatch and rub out the underlying pencil. There is then a slight, but complete picture in light and shade.

The third stage is to elaborate the drawing, carrying it into the shadows and to augment them by crosshatching. Finally, by heavier crosshatching – particularly in foregrounds – local colour is suggested, while, by accenting the outlines here and there, an added sense of depth is achieved. Finishing any one part of the whole is avoided; rather, the illustration is built up in stages, just as if a picture were being painted. If a mistake is made, process white is never used to correct it; the offending area is scraped with a knife and then re-drawn. Hence the necessity of using good paper.

Ardizzone's method allows the maximum of freedom to elaborate and modify the drawing as he works. The main danger in the use of crosshatching is that the patient building up of areas of tone runs the risk of becoming mechanical, both in execution and appearance.

Every artist who uses the method will find his or her own answer to this problem, which will depend in the end on their own essential style. Large areas of shading will be shaped, intensified and modelled so that they contribute directly to the composition. They have a job to do and should do it with feeling as well as precision.

Line and wash Line and wash techniques vary enormously, so the best means of approach is to experiment with several until the most congenial one is discovered. As always, reproduction requirements may modify an artist's freedom of choice and it is necessary not to·be too rigid in the chosen method.

In one typical method, a swift and generalized overall pencil sketch is lightly put down to establish the basic composition. This is then worked over in pen, using a waterproof black ink, to produce a more detailed account of the pencil sketch underneath. When the ink is quite dry, all traces of pencil are erased. At this point, the pen is laid aside and a series of washes in brush is laid down over the ink drawing, either in diluted black and coloured inks or in water colour. When this tonal work is complete, the pen is re-employed to build up areas of detail or to strengthen contrast as needed.

If the illustration is to be printed by letterpress, this method should be adapted. This is because, at the plate-making stage, letterpress involves a mechanical screen being laid over the penwork, which may result in the delicacy and bite of the drawing being lost. To overcome this hazard, it is sometimes possible for the platemaker to prepare what is called a combination line and tone plate, in which the line and tonal areas are separately photographed and combined on the plate. From the artist's point of view, it is better to prepare two separate drawings for the platemaker. On the first, all work in pen line appears and on the second, all the colour. The second drawing is registered and keyed to fit directly over or under the first. Initially, this may sound laboured and unspontaneous but, with practice, a freshness of handling can be achieved at both stages.

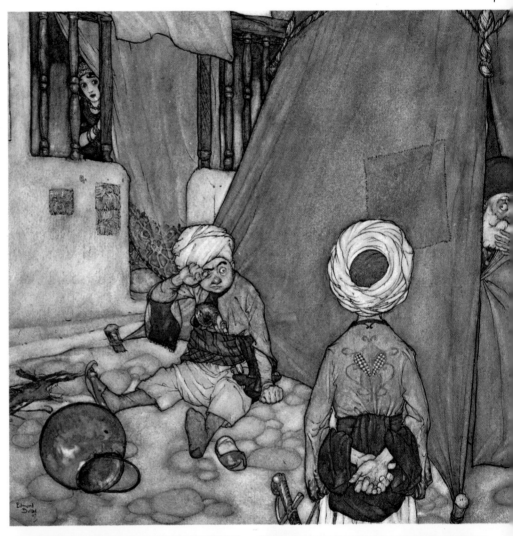

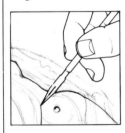
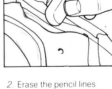

Applying line and wash
1. Draw a pen line over a preliminary pencil sketch.

2. Erase the pencil lines when the ink is completely dry.

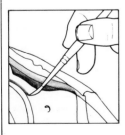
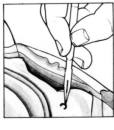

3. Next, washes of diluted and undiluted ink should be applied.

4. Finally the pen lines should be reinforced as appropriate.

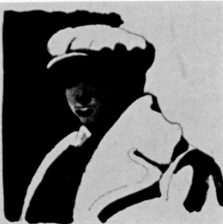
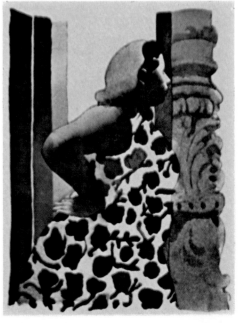

Above and right Milton Glaser: two atmospheric illustrations from a magazine article *Growing up in the Bronx*. These pictures show the loose freedom of Glaser's line and wash technique. Outline and pen work in black ink is combined with broad areas of wash. The tonal effects are created with various dilutions of brown wash.

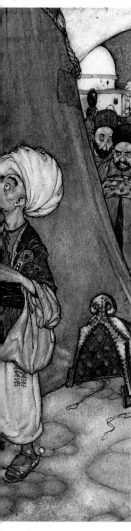

Left Edmund Dulac: illustration from *The Arabian Nights* This is primarily a watercolour illustration, with the fine outlines and detail drawn using a pen and black ink. The washes are created from watercolours in rich shades of blue, brown and yellow. Watercolour washes are the type most often chosen for colour illustration; coloured ink washes are less common.

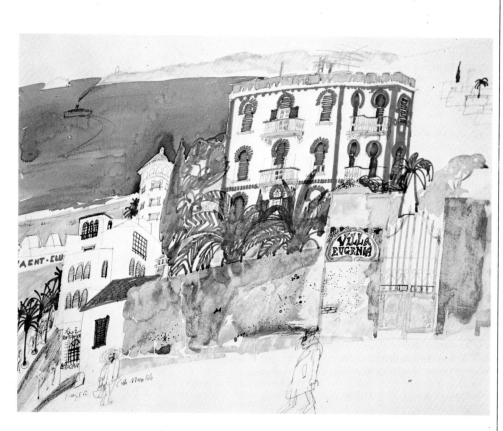

Right Paul Hogarth *Calle Marco Polo, Tangiers, Morocco* Hogarth used a wide variety of media for this picture, including pencil, ink, brush work, marker pens, ballpoint pens and watercolour. He worked from a preliminary pencil outline, building up texture and tone with brush and ink, and filling in the structure of the main building with rough shading marker pen.

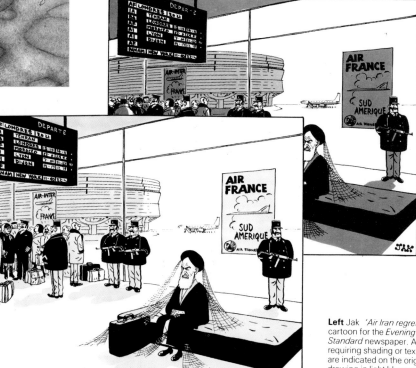

AIR IRAN REGRET TO ANNOUNCE A FURTHER DELAY IN THEIR FLIGHT TO TEHERAN!"

X 4 col WED 31st JAN 79   40% TINT. 20%   ON· PLANE + BACKGROUND BUILDING NOT POSTERS

Left Jak '*Air Iran regret . . .*' cartoon for the *Evening Standard* newspaper. Areas requiring shading or texture are indicated on the original drawing in light blue wash. The tints are then created mechanically by the printer., **Above** How these tinted areas appear in the finished print.

Some artists – multi-media practioners such as Paul Hogarth (born 1917) – often work in any number of variants of pen and wash. Hogarth, for instance, described in his 'Creative Pen Drawing' the development of a North African subject, the Calle Marco Polo in Tangiers. For this, he mixed the use of steel pen, brush, ballpoint and felt-tipped markers with that of pencil and water colour.

A further interesting variant is the use of chalk or crayon with pen work. Here again, the approach varies widely from artist to artist, but, most commonly, the pen drawing is carried out first in waterproof ink on a paper chosen for its receptivity to both media. This is then over-drawn with chalk or crayon; finally, the whole drawing is treated with fixative to prevent smudging. The attraction of this method lies in the contrast between the crisp, incisive pen line and the soft expressiveness of the chalk textures.

Line and tint This form of drawing is frequently practised by artists whose professional lives mean that they have to meet constant and pressing deadlines. Such an artist is the British cartoonist Jak, whose work frequently has to be prepared in a matter of hours. Not for him the patient crosshatching needed to achieve areas of tone or texture. These are produced instead by the judicious use of mechanical tints. These he indicates on his drawings by washing on areas of pale blue ink or water colour. From them, the photo-engraver can determine just where the tint is to be laid in and at what strength.

The artists who work for the weekly *Time* are not quite as rushed as Jak, but their work in line and tint similarly calls for accuracy and balanced judgement. Explanatory diagrams drawn in both black and white and colour are used to simplify and summarize highly-complex information. This means that mechanical tints have to be used carefully and fastidiously.

A further use of tints – this time of adhesive ones – has been given by the illustrator Dodie Masterman. She never considers how she is going to use zippatone tints until she has finished a drawing without them. Then she likes to freely dramatize with the tints, applying them like a wash. This adds some new function to the drawing with a character of its own, but it does not neutralize the feeling behind the part played by the pen. Her approach is creative, impulsive and entirely unmechanical.

Stippling and splattering The progressive building-up of areas of tone by the use of drawn dots is called stippling. It involves fine judgement – once again because of the possible limitations of the reproductive method employed – as to how far the detail can be taken. A combination of poor paper and indifferent printing can cause fine dot work to close up or clot on the page. Therefore very exact calculations are called for to decide exactly just how open or how fine the stippling is going to be. At its best, the technique

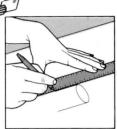
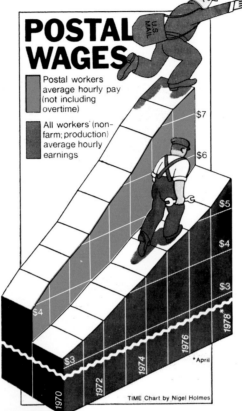

POSTAL WAGES

■ Postal workers average hourly pay (not including overtime)

■ All workers' (non-farm; production) average hourly earnings

$7
$6
$5
$4
$3
$4
$3
1970 1972 1974 1976 1978*
*April

TIME Chart by Nigel Holmes

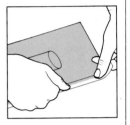

Preparing a drawing for a mechanical tint 1. Draw the image.

2. Stick a sheet of Amberlith paper over the image by taping along one side.

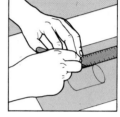
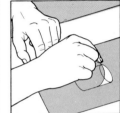

3. Cut away the film from the area which does not require tinting.

4. Peel off the excess film. Each tint will need its own overlay so one drawing may have several overlays.

Mechanical tints provide professional illustrators with a speedy alternative to cross-hatching as a method of applying tone and texture to a drawing or diagram. A diagram by Nigel Holmes for *Time* magazine **(above)** uses tinting as a method of shading. In this fashion illustration by Dodie Masterman **(right)** tints have been used like a wash. In complete contrast is Lyn Gray's very precise use of tinting for her illustration **(below)** which appeared in a *Sunday Times* article about body cosmetics.

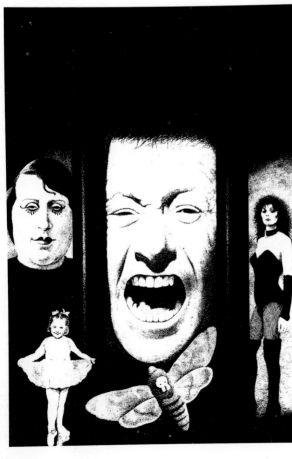

Martin Baker's design for a Penguin book jacket **(left)** illustrates another method of adding tone and texture through a series of dots or stippling.

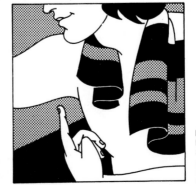

Right Stippling has also been used to build up the areas of tone on this drawing of a French horn showing how this technique can be used in different ways.

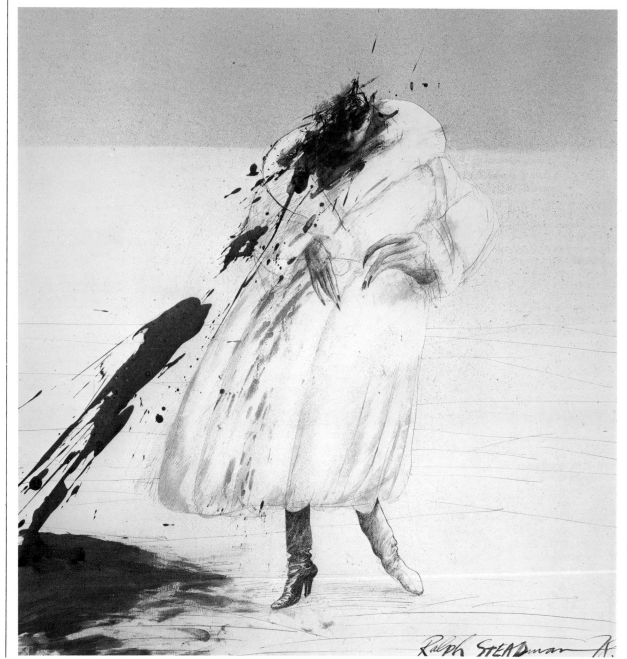

Ralph STEADman

Left Ralph Steadman has used a mouthspray to create splatter in his design entitled 'I wouldn't be seen dead in a seal fur coat'.

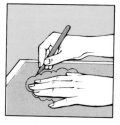

Splatter 1. Cut a mask from tracing paper or clear plastic film to cover the area which is to be kept clean.

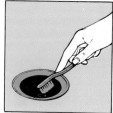

2. Dip a brush — a toothbrush or nailbrush will do — in the paint.

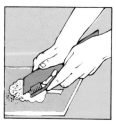

3. Run the bristles along a straight flat surface, such as a ruler, over the area to be splattered.

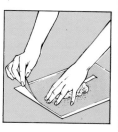

4. Peel off the masking paper or film.

allows the greatest tonal subtleties to be employed.

A modified use of stippling is often employed with other techniques – sometimes to render form within ink outline drawing and sometimes to indicate distant or indistinct objects. Its application and appropriateness for purely decorative areas of texture and patterning is self-evident.

Splatter technique is one of several textural devices employed to complement an existing base drawing. Depending on how it is applied, it can convey effects as different as the graininess of a stone surface and an explosive upheaval.

Splattering is carried out by applying a layer of ink to a tooth or nail brush and then running a straight-edge along the hairs of the brush to achieve a controlled flicking of the ink onto the paper.

Confident use of the method requires experiment and it may be necessary to mask off any areas of the drawing which are not to receive the splatter effect. In general, the method seems to work best with drawings of a bold and vigorous nature, rather than a delicate one. This is because the somewhat haphazard spraying of the splatter may distort carefully judged fine-line work.

Scraper board The first step in scraperboard is to assemble the requisite materials. These, with the exception of Indian ink, are entirely different from those used for pen drawing. Paper is replaced by a prepared white or black board with an egg-shell finish surface. This may be cut into or incised. The process is related to the craft of wood engraving and the procedure is quite similar. The essential differences are that the metal tools for scraperwork are cheap and easy to maintain or replace, the prepared board is simpler to use than the box wood block, and the scraperwork prints facsimile.

The drawing must be planned carefully in advance, since hours of patient engraving can be ruined by ill-considered design work. The nature of the medium precludes loose sketching so that effects must be carefully judged from the start.

Techniques vary, depending on the use to which the work is to be put. Most often, a detailed preliminary drawing is made on tracing paper, with dominant areas of tone carefully indicated. These will form the basis of the scraperwork. The drawing is then traced through on to the prepared board – great care being taken not to damage the delicate surface. Assuming that a black board is used, a general scraping away of the pencil outline is started, followed by the removal of whatever will print as white. What remains are the general areas of black, out of which will be built the tonal contrasts that become the drawing itself. These areas of tone are achieved by scraping, stippling and hatching with the appropriate tools.

If a white board is chosen, the black areas are brushed in with Indian ink. leaving the white masses free. The black areas are then scraped and the tonal effects in line arrived at.

Blotting and frottage Apart from the everyday use of blotting paper to protect and dry off ink work, it sometimes has a more directly creative function. As with the line and wash method, many variants of blotting are used, though the essential aim is the same. This is to achieve rich tonalities through successive washes of inks, exploiting the natural qualities of the medium and the paper itself.

In general, the procedure is first to lay down a wash of diluted ink with a large brush. The wash is then blotted. A second wash – this time of undiluted ink – is then laid over the first, so that the two separate tonal textures are played off against each other. For success, much depends on the quality of the paper, which has to sustain not only separate washes but also may have to accommodate ink line work with a nib.

Other methods of arriving at expressive textures include the sponging on of diluted and undiluted ink. Naturally, this again needs controlled handling and, once more, the use of blotting paper is called for to achieve this. Successive spongings of diluted and undiluted ink are made and these are judiciously blotted at

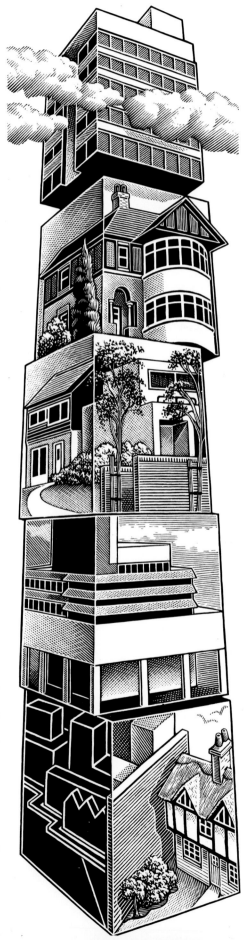

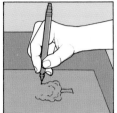

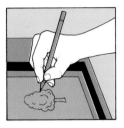

Scraperboard
1. Make a detailed preliminary drawing on tracing paper, indicating tones.

2. Trace the drawing in rough on to the prepared board, taking care not to damage the surface.

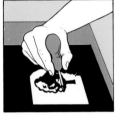

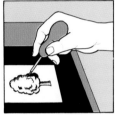

3. Scrape away the pencil outline with a metal tool and remove areas which are to appear as white when printed.

4. Create areas of tone by scraping, stippling and hatching with the appropriate tools.

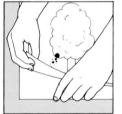

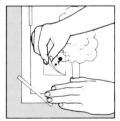

Corrections
1. Place the same kind of paper under the drawing.

2. Tape it lightly at the edges and corners to hold it in position.

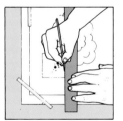

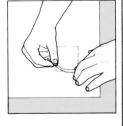

3. Cut a panel through both sheets of paper with a very sharp scalpel.

4. Lift out top section, revealing the clean section below.

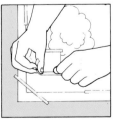

5. Stick down lightly from the top using masking tape.

6. Turn sheet over, tape underside firmly, remove tape from top.

Far left This illustration by Bill Sanderson shows the clear outlines and sharp black and white contrast achieved with scraperboard. Tone and texture are created by many different techniques — dots, crosshatching, lines and stippling.

Below In this illustration Paul Allen used airbrushing to create an almost-photographic impression. Rounded contours and delicately graded shadows are combined with the effect of light shining on the glossy surfaces.

Below far right Paul Hogarth is a master of pen and ink and mixed media drawing. In this illustration he combines pen work with blotting. The detail is drawn in fine ink lines, with a broader fluid outline for the bar. These outlines are filled in by blotting in a variety of darker tones and mottling. Blotting is particularly suitable for this type of rapid, witty sketch; it combines precision and crisp contrast with subtle effects of light and shade.

carefully-judged stages. A fine sponge will give the best results; it should be thoroughly washed each time before re-use.

Still more varieties of texture may be obtained by frottage. In this method, medium to light-weight paper is laid over wood, stone or brass and the surfaces rubbed to obtain relief impressions on the paper. This is more usually done with pencil or chalk, but careful rubbing by ballpoint can also be employed.

Corrections and erasing When making corrections to pen drawings or removing blots, the following methods are useful. When the ink is dry, a razor blade or glass fibre eraser can be used to deal with small areas effectively, while a gentle blowing away of any black paper particles that have been scraped off will prevent these being ground back into the paper by the pressure of the erasion. If the ink blot is still wet, apply a damp section of blotting paper to the centre of the blot. This should be repeated several times – each time with fresh paper – laying the paper over the blot and applying as much pressure as is necessary to soak up the maximum amount of ink. Clean water on a brush should absorb most of the remaining stain, but whatever is left can be removed when dry with a soft, clean rubber.

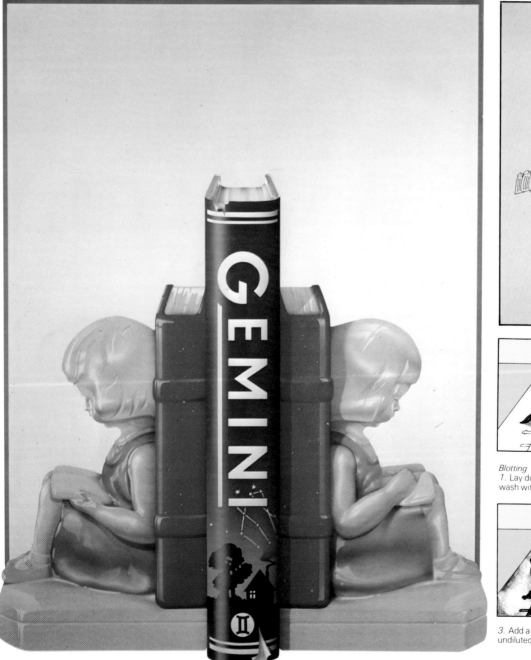

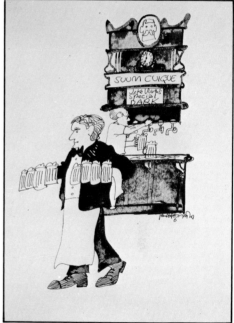

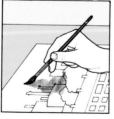

Blotting
1. Lay down a diluted ink wash with a large brush.

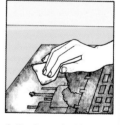

2. Blot the wash with a piece of blotting paper.

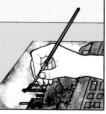

3. Add a second wash of undiluted ink over the first.

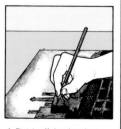

4. Finish off the drawing with line work in pen and ink.

CHAPTER THREE

OILS AND OTHER PAINT MEDIA

Throughout history illustrators have played a major role in pictorial art and continue to do so today, when the dividing line between illustration and fine art is once more becoming blurred.

The greatest changes in picture making have been brought about by the workings of market forces, together with the materials available to, or created by, artists of any given era. Artists have also always, been quick to grasp at the invention of mechanical aids in order to improve their skills; the exploration of the rules of perspective by Brunelleschi (1377–1446) and Uccello (1397–1475) bears witness to this.

History The technique of encaustic (hot wax) painting was known to the ancient Egyptians, together with the use of a form of watercolour made by mixing ground pigments with gum arabic or tragacanth. However, until the end of the Middle Ages, the majority of illustrative techniques were carried out in distemper or tempera. The most common medium used in Romanesque illuminated manuscripts and the medieval Books of Hours was egg tempera. Egg white, or 'glair', on vellum or parchment was the standard base used in such works. The white was beaten and left to settle to a clear, smooth-flowing liquid which was easy to handle and mixed well with the ground pigments then available.

The Books of Hours were so-called because, before any mechanical means for recording time had been invented, canonical hours established rules for the recital of prayers at certain times of the day. Lay people, wishing to follow the example of the religious classes, commissioned prayer books to follow this pattern and so the Book of Hours came into being. They were executed by the equivalent teaming of today's designer/typographer and illustrator. The scribe who wrote the text and the artist who executed initials, borders and miniatures, worked in close collaboration.

Books of Hours were often produced by several groups of artists working together in a workshop. The books gradually became not only prayer books, but also status symbols of established wealth, including in them family portraits and visual records of the possessions of their owners. Artists also used them as an excuse to fulfil their own creativity by such devices as including nudes. The most common excuse for this was to depict a naked man and woman clasping each other to illustrate Gemini in the astrological section of the book.

Before this, the palette of colours available was somewhat limited. The ancient Egyptians produced seven colours – Azurite, Malachite, Orpiment, Realgar, Cinnabar, Blue frit and White lead. The Romans expanded on this by adding Indigo, Tyrian purple and Verdigris to the list, and, by the end of the thirteenth century, Lead tin yellow, Madder, Ultramarine and Vermillion were also in use.

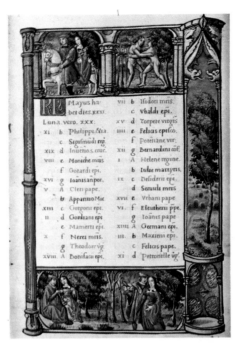

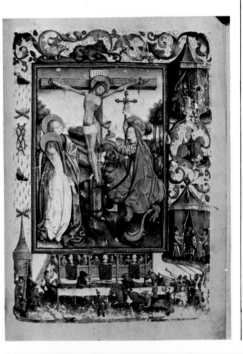

In the second quarter of the fourteenth century, illustration broke free from text illumination to become panel painting. The church, state and laity continued to commission both well into the fifteenth century. Artists even acted as propagandists – Uccello, for example, painting for Cosimo de Medici a somewhat one-sided version of the 'Rout of San Romano'.

The mid-fifteenth century brought new discoveries in oil painting techniques. Vasari (1511–74), the Italian artist and biographer of painters, credits the brothers Van Eyck with many of them, but it is now known that they were in existence centuries before. The earliest oil painting extant today comes from thirteenth-century Norway. Jan Van Eyck (active 1422, d.1441) perfected an oil medium which revolutionized Flemish painting. It was later taken up by the Italians.

With the invention of movable type and the development of the printing press, illustration moved in two directions – namely works for reproduction and narrative painting. From about 1660, there was an increasing middle-class demand for both.

Scientific progress in glass and lens making during the sixteenth century also influenced artistic developments. The construction of the Camera Obscura by Erasmus Reinhold (1511–1553) for use in solar observation is one major example, for artists later took to the use of the invention to study and more closely observe the subjects of some of their drawings. Both Vermeer (1632–75) and Canaletto (1697–1768) used it to produce closer-to-life paintings. Vermeer's 'Lady with a Guitar' for instance, clearly shows the effect of such study in contour drawing around the folds of her dress.

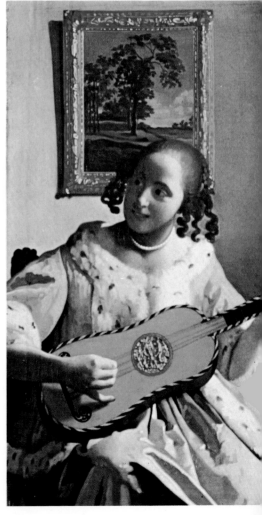

Far left *Book of Hours* This sixteenth century French manuscript, illustrating the month of May, uses the common medium of that period — egg-white tempera.

Left This medieval manuscript, with its Crucifixion centrepiece, is typical of the illustrative style used in *Books of Hours.*

Right Jan van Eyck *Giovanni Arnolfini* Van Eyck perfected the use of an oil medium and varnish. The brilliant, glass-like finish of his colour greatly influenced contemporary artists.

Below Jan Vermeer *The Lady with a Guitar* The realistic detail in the folds of the girl's dress in this oil painting are especially noteworthy.

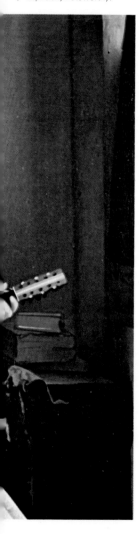

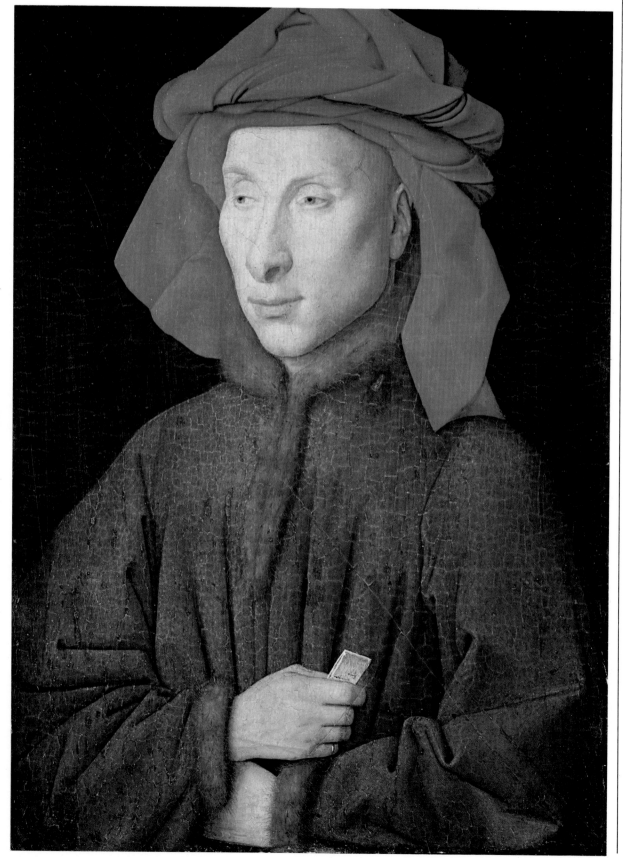

By the mid-sixteenth century, copper engraving rivalled woodcut as a means of artistic reproduction and in the seventeenth century came the final break with the traditions of Gothic and Renaissance in pictorial art. The new style of Baroque began in book illustrations. On the painting front, oils reigned supreme. The decorative title page became a vehicle for engravers, who produced emblematic and allegorical designs, and this attracted many painters to the field. For example, Francis Barlow (1626–1702) engraved his own 'Barlow's Natural History'.

One of the greatest illustrators of the period was William Blake (1757–1827), who developed a process which he termed 'illuminated printing'. The text and design were etched in relief, printed in one colour and hand tinted afterwards. Then came the major advance of the development of aquatint engraving. Together with this, the establishment of the English style of watercolour painting led to the production of great colour plate books. Notable are the 'History of the River Thames' with plates by Farington, engraved by Stadler, and the 'Microcosm of London' by Thomas Rowlandson (1756–1827) and A. C. Pugin (1762–1832).

During this period, excellent colour plates of flower illustrations were also produced, such as in John Thornton's 'Temple of Flora'. Cruickshank (1792–1878), whose life spanned both the Regency and the Victorian eras, expanded the genre of book illustration further by illustrating works by Dickens, such as 'Oliver Twist'

The booming industrial nineteenth century brought new and exciting inventions which were quickly adopted as tools by the artists of the period. Chemical 'spin-offs' from the Industrial Revolution greatly boosted the palette of colours available to the artist. These included Chromes, Cadmiums and Cobalts. Photography may have seemed frightening to some artists, but others readily grasped its possibilities. The Impressionists, for instance, not only occasionally worked from photographic prints but their compositions were also dramatically affected by them. Figures and objects were treated as they had never been treated before; photographic imagery here showed artists a new way to crop the figures and objects at the edges of paintings. There are many examples, but 'Carriage at the Races' by Degas (1834–1917) clearly demonstrates the application of this approach. Artists of all kinds have used photography ever since.

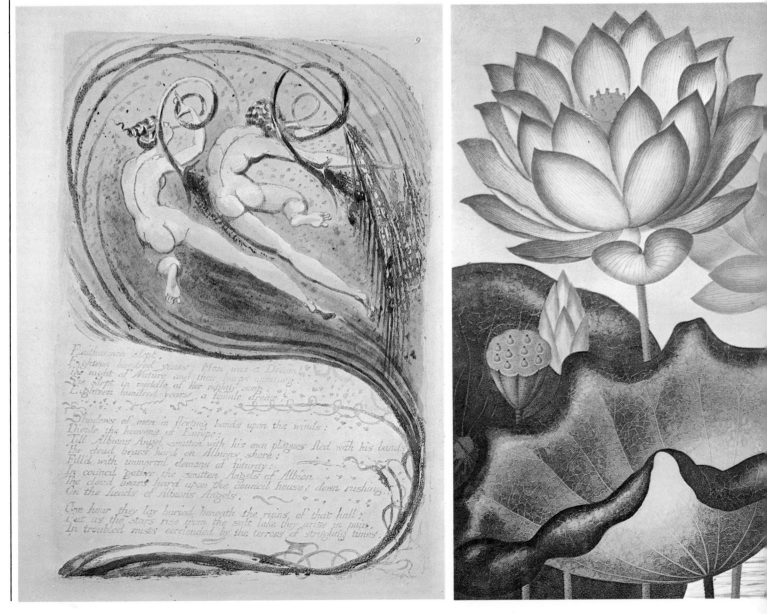

Eighteenth and nineteenth century illustrative techniques **Below left** This example of Blake's 'illuminated printing' involved the engraving of the text and the design, which was then hand coloured. **Below centre** This splendid colour plate from John Thornton's *Temple of Flora* typifies the accuracy of both design and colour found in books on natural history during this period. **Below right** This aquatint by Rowlandson and Pugin demonstrates the skilled use of this technique. **Right** The composition of Degas's painting *Rehearsal* shows the influence of photography, particularly in capturing movement.

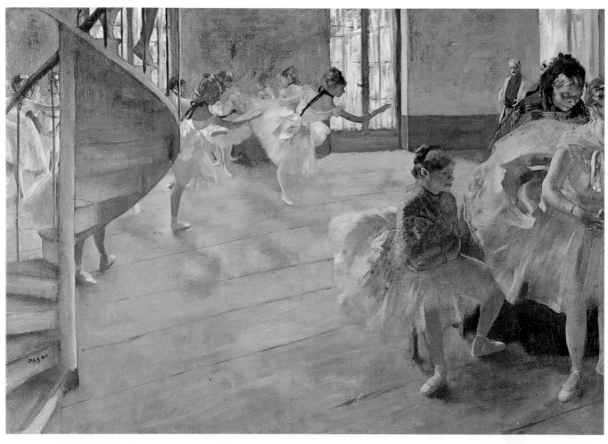

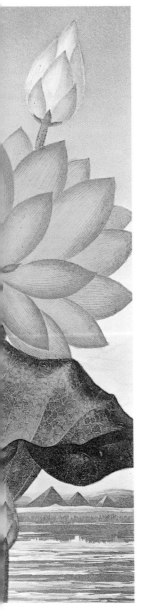

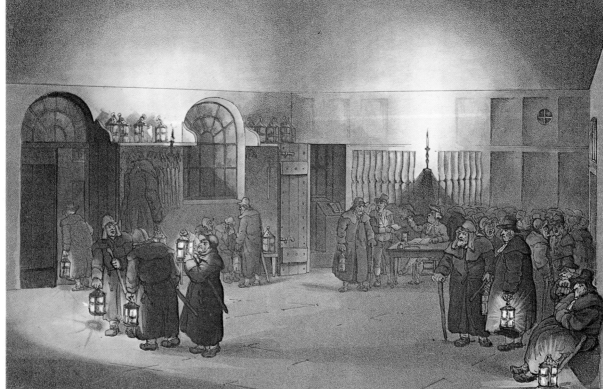

Another major advance in the nineteenth century was the advent of half-tone reproduction. The overlaying of red, yellow and blue inks, broken down with screen tints to produce many tones, made it possible to reproduce full colour artwork accurately. The process was quickly exploited to provide reasonably priced illustrated books for the masses. A golden age of illustration brought forth many fine artist illustrators such as Carl Larsson (1853–1919), Arthur Rackham (1867–1939) and Edmund Dulac (1882–1953). All worked in watercolour, the ideal medium for the process, which still, however, had the drawback of lacking black, though black could be made by overlaying all three colours at full strength. To help overcome this lack, Dulac, in particular, outlined and pointed up many of his drawings with black Indian ink. This, when printed, softened and enhanced the succulent watercolour washes and textures which they surrounded.

The introduction of black keyline to make four-colour printing possible enabled illustrators to make use of more solid forms of painting for reproduction. To the fore came great names of illustration such as Howard Pyle (1853–1911), and N. C. Wyeth (1882–1944), followed by the supreme exponent of illustration using oil – Norman Rockwell (1894–1978).

Rockwell understood clearly the advantage of working large, in order to gain tightness and clarity when his work was reduced in size for reproduction purposes. His works are very broadly painted, as any examination of an original shows. Coincidentally, it is unfortunate that because of his prolific output and the speed at which he worked, many of his originals are deteriorating. Oil paintings cannot be abused by taking short cuts at the drying stage if they are to last for posterity.

The influence of contemporary painters such as Andrew Wyeth (born 1917) and Alex Colville (born 1920) have led many current illustrators to explore the areas of hyper-realism further. At the same time, the variety of materials available to the artist make present-day forms of illustration more varied than at any time in history. For example, photography and other sophisticated visual aids are now established as everyday tools through which an artist can speed up the illustrative process. This is vital when working to a demanding deadline for, say, print, film and television media.

Fine works are still produced in watercolour, oils, tempera and gouache, however. In addition the introduction of acrylics to the range of media available has further increased and expanded the illustrator/designer's scope. Artists, too, are now working with computer graphics. This represents yet another challenge, but the lessons of history show that the skills of the artist and his or her ability to utilize available materials to the full are rarely discarded, once discovered. They are continually in use century after century.

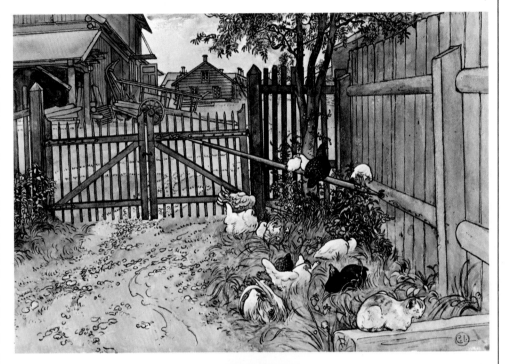

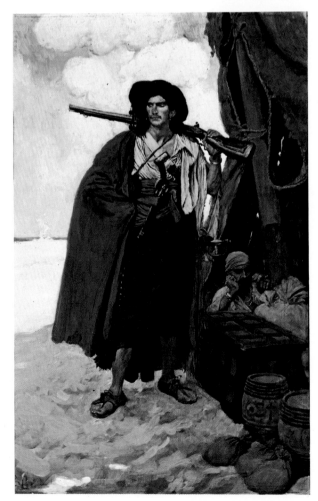

Above Carl Larsson *Gate* This watercolour illustration was suitable for reproducing using the half-tone method. One disadvantage of this technique was that it was difficult to reproduce black except by overlaying all the colours. It was also difficult to ensure that both fit and register were correct. To help avoid any lack of clarity in the finished picture Larsson has outlined the components in the picture with black Indian ink.

Left Howard Pyle *The Buccaneer was a Picturesque Fellow* This painting, executed in oil, was specifically produced to illustrate a feature called 'The Fate of a Treasure Town', published in the American magazine, *Harpers,* in 1905. The development of four-colour printing at the beginning of this century made accurate reproduction from oil paintings possible.

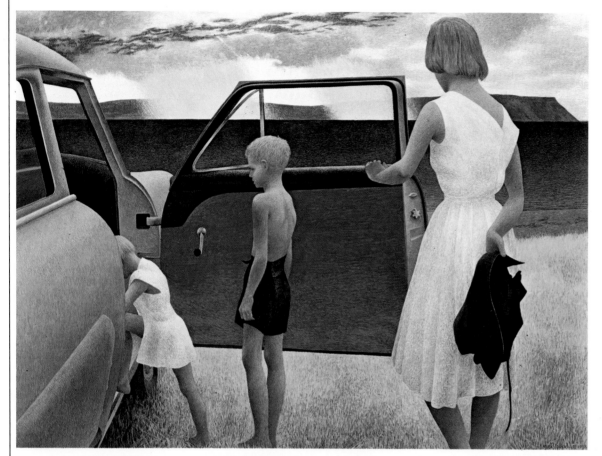

Left David Alexander Colville *Family and Rainstorm* Despite the wide variety of materials now available to the present-day artist, traditional techniques, as in this super-realistic painting using tempera on board, can still produce highly original results.

Below Norman Rockwell *The County Agricultural Agent* One of the most prolific of modern illustrators and familiar to millions through his work for *The Saturday Evening Post,* Rockwell perfected the use of oil techniques for reproduction. By working on relatively large surfaces, the almost photographic clarity of his work could be retained in reproduction when it was considerably reduced in size.

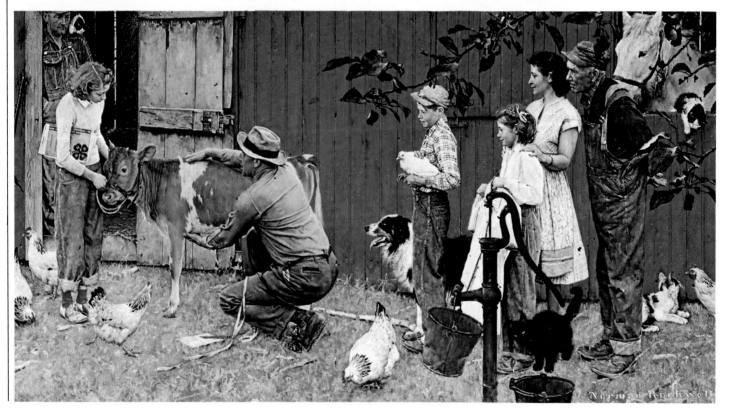

Tools and materials

A number of tools, including brushes, are suitable for use in several different painting disciplines. They are therefore listed here as a whole, independently of the sections of this chapter dealing with the different painting media.

Brushes It is important to have available a wide selection of good quality brushes. Buying and using cheap ones is a false economy; good brushes, with proper care, will last longer and improve the quality of the work.

The best hog hair brushes are made from bleached hog bristles, and there are five basic shapes. Brights are short, with squared ends, and are used for laying on thick paint. Rounds are round-ended, used for detailed work and the application of thin paints. Filberts are broader than rounds, gently curved towards the pointed end, and excellent for drawing strokes. Flats are similar to brights, but have longer bristles and hold more paint. Chisel-ended brushes are no longer in common use but are good for drawing straight lines and edges.

Blenders are usually made of badger hair. They look not unlike a shaving brush at the head, and are used for blending wet paint. Fan brushes are usually made of sable and are also used for the gentle blending of wet paint. Wide brushes are used to lay grounds – a good decorator's brush is suitable for this. Sable brushes are very expensive, but essential for good watercolour work. They come as rounds or are chisel-ended. The largest sizes of both varieties are used for washes; the smallest for detailed work. For beginners, it is a good idea to start a sable brush collection with numbers 2, 4, 8 and 12 quality rounds.

Fitch and camel brushes are not as good as sable ones, but are, however, less expensive. The term camel is, in fact, a misnomer; the brushes are made from squirrel hair, and are now often termed squirrel.

Hog hair, blender, fan, wide, sable, fitch and camel brushes, from sizes 1–12, are suitable for painting in oils, acrylics and tempera. Sable, fitch and camel brushes in sizes 00–12, are used in watercolour and gouache.

Choice and care Choosing the right brush is vital. One test for suitability is to wet the brush, shake it to remove surplus water and then roll it in the palm of the hand. If the point is sparse and lacks body, the brush will have only a short life.

After using oils, the brushes should be cleaned with petrol, rather than turpentine, washed with soap and water, and thoroughly rinsed. The hairs can be laid in olive oil, to keep them supple. After using water-based media, the brushes should be thoroughly washed with soap and water. It is vital to rinse well – making sure all the pigments are removed, because some are poisonous – before re-shaping by mouth or with the fingers. The brushes should be stored upright, but, if they are to be kept for a long period without being used, they should be laid flat or kept in a brush tube with a moth-ball.

Palette and painting knives Palette knives are used for mixing colour on the palette and for

Types of brush
Good quality brushes are essential. The best quality — and the most expensive bristle — is hogshair. Sable, fitch and camel (or squirrel) are also used. The five main types of brush are brights, rounds, filberts, flats and the less common chisel ended. Blenders and fans are used for blending wet colours. In the selection **(below)** the size of the brush is shown in brackets.

Knives
Palette knives **(left, top)** are for mixing paints or applying paint to the support. They are made of smooth flexible steel. *Painting knives* **(left, below)** available in several shapes are used for applying paint. *Cutting knives* **(right)** A utility knife **(top)** is extremely useful for general cutting, while a surgeon's scalpel **(below)** should be used for finer work. Both come with a range of interchangeable blades.

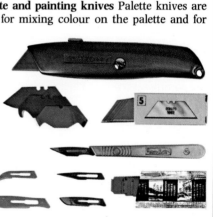

Hogshair bright (2)

Hogshair round (1)

Hogshair filbert (2)

Hogshair flat (1)

Sable flat (1/8)

Sable fan (2)

Squirrel round (16)

Blender (6)

Oxhair wide (7/8)

cleaning paint from it. They are made of steel and are long, smooth and flexible. Painting knives are used for applying paint to the surface. They come in a range of small, trowel shapes; the best are French-made.

Cutting knives A knife such as a craft knife is a good, all-purpose tool. For safety reasons this is fitted with a retractable blade, which is changeable. A surgeon's scalpel is useful for finer work, such as stencil or mask cutting. A Swan-Morton handle and a 10a blade is one of the most common combinations, and most artists' stores stock them.

Projectors There are now several projectors on the market, specifically designed for use by the illustrator and designer. They should be regarded as capital investments, because they tend to be very expensive, and fall into two categories, for front and back projection respectively.

Front projection is frequently used by artists to draw or paint direct on to the painting surface from a photograph, or by enlarging a drawing. There are several ready-made systems available;

two of the best are the Optiskop, made in Switzerland, and the Liesegang, a West German projector. Both are episcopes and project flat prints or drawings. With special attachments, they can be converted to epidiascopes, to project large transparencies.

The Lucidagraph is a very useful tool for drawing still life objects. It is a prism with lens attachments mounted on an adjustable column. The instrument is attached to a flat table or drawing board and, when the eye looks through the lens, the image is seen projected on to the surface on which the hand is drawing or painting. The simplest, and probably the cheapest method, however, is to use an ordinary slide projector and work from 35mm transparencies, projected horizontally on to a vertical surface.

Back projection The Grant and the Copyscanner are the most popular back projectors. As far as illustration is concerned, their main drawback is that the image can be projected only through thin paper, which usually means that the drawn image has to be traced again on to the painting

surface. However, back projectors are extremely useful tools for designers who want to enlarge artwork and type to fit layouts.

Colours Coloured pigments are the same for all paints, whether they are oil, watercolour, tempera, gouache or acrylic. Only the medium in which they are suspended changes. Since the illustrator or designer usually needs to work at speed, and since there is a wide range of ready-made paints on the market, it is unusual for paints to be individually prepared, although this is possible if special effects are desired. The quality of ready-made paints is also extremely high. This further obviates any necessity to prepare one's own colours.

Most brands of paints come in two qualities – artists' and students'. It is much better to use the former rather than the latter. Artists' paints are more permanent, the texture of the material is better, and less 'filler' is used. It is therefore more sensible to use a small budget to buy a limited range of good quality paints than a larger range of indifferent ones.

Brush sizes **(below, left)**
Brush sizes are standardized internationally. Sizes 1-12 are suitable for working in oils, acrylics and tempera while the finer range 000-12 is used for watercolour and gouache. For large scale work extra large brushes come in sizes up to 36. A reasonable collection of brushes would include at least three or four of each of the brush shapes. The hogshair brushes **(left)** show a good range for oil painting while the sable brushes **(below)** are for watercolours. The size of the brush is as important as its quality. Brushes should never be cut back or trimmed. The painting ends are carefully shaped by the brushmaker who arranges the individual bristles or hairs. Any adjustment should be made at the non-painting end.

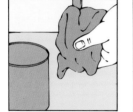

Cleaning brushes
1. After using oil paint the brush should be cleaned with petrol not turpentine and then wiped with a rag.

2. Then wash with soap and water, work on the palm and rinse well. To keep hairs supple lay them in olive oil.

3. After using water-based paints rinse the brush thoroughly in water, then wash in soap and water.

4. Having rinsed the brush well, re-shape it using the fingers or the mouth. This is important for the brush to retain its shape.

5. After cleaning, brushes should be stored upright. For longer storage lay the brush flat in a brush tube.

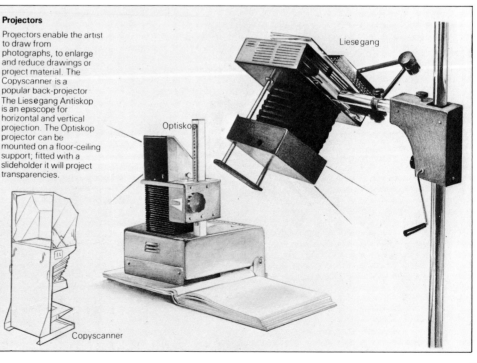

Projectors

Projectors enable the artist to draw from photographs, to enlarge and reduce drawings or project material. The Copyscanner is a popular back-projector The Liesegang Antiskop is an episcope for horizontal and vertical projection. The Optiskop projector can be mounted on a floor-ceiling support; fitted with a slideholder it will project transparencies.

Liesegang

Optiskop

Copyscanner

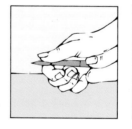

Oil painting

Surfaces and materials

Canvas The most common surface used in oil painting is canvas. Linen is best, but cotton, a linen-cotton mixture, or hessian can all be used. However, stretched canvas is easily damaged in transit, so it is not always the best support for illustration.

Wood Mahogany is the best available wooden surface; in common with all wood, it must be seasoned to counter a tendency to warp and crack as it dries. Panels should be 25mm (1in) thick. Plywood 8-ply is a good working material, but it should be cradled against warp by having two struts battened, parallel to each other, on the back.

Hardboard This can be an excellent surface if properly cradled. Cradling, however, is not necessary for small-scale work.

Cardboard Only the thickest qualities should be used, and both sides must be sized.

Prepared board Commercially-prepared boards can be bought from most art stores. Their disadvantage is that they often have unsympathetic grains, are indifferently primed and are expensive.

Underpriming If a picture is to last, its base must be sized before the ground is applied. Sizing prevents the ground from rotting the support. One of the best sizes is leather-waste, more commonly known as rabbit-skin glue, but bone glue or casein size can both be used.

Grounds After sizing, the support must be coated with a ground. This serves both to protect the support from the oil in the paint and provide a good surface to work on.

There are four basic types of ground – oil, gesso, emulsion and acrylic. Oil grounds take up to six weeks to dry after application, so it is best for the illustrator who is working at speed to use the acrylic variety. Acrylic grounds can be used for oil or acrylic painting, and on any support. Not only do they dry quickly but they can also be applied to any surface without the need for priming.

Gesso can be used on rigid supports. It is not ideal for oil painting, if a long life is expected from the original, as the slow drying time of the oil can produce cracking. Emulsion is the quickest ground to use on any support. It can be tinted before application.

Paints Illustrators and designers usually work to a commission, which means that artwork must be completed by the designated deadline. For this reason, most illustrators buy ready-mixed, branded, tube paints, rather than blending their own. However, it is, of course, possible for artists to mix their own paints, using ground paints from artists' stores and binding them with selected oils.

Binders Suitable binders for ground paints include linseed, poppy or walnut oils. The selected oil can be blended on a piece of plate glass with the ground paint, using a palette knife. Once bound, the paint is ready to be brushed on to the painting surface. In drying, it absorbs oxygen and seals the pigment to the surface.

Linseed oil is the most commonly used binder. Cold, pressed linseed is the most suitable, but refined linseed oil, bleached to produce a clear, thin binder, is also very good. Raw linseed oil is more durable but darker in colour, and so its use is not recommended for illustration. Stand oil is linseed oil treated to make it darker; it dries to an enamel-like finish when mixed with pigment.

Poppy oil is less acidic than linseed. It dries slowly, is less yellow when dry, but cracks more readily. Walnut oil is very pale and thin.

Artificial drying agents can be added to speed up the drying process. One such agent is manganese oxide, one part of which can be added to three parts linseed oil.

Painting media These are used to apply paint to the support, to thin paint, and to speed its drying. The most common mixture is 60 per cent of linseed oil to 40 per cent of turpentine.

Other media include beeswax (see wax painting, p.62); gels, which combine oil with a synthetic resin, for thick application; and Maroger's, an emulsion of boiled linseed oil, mastic varnish, gum arabic and water. Many artists find this last mixture a particularly pleasant one to use.

Diluents Oil paint can be thinned for glazing by the addition of spirit or varnish to the medium. Turpentine is used most frequently, but mastic or damar varnish are just as good if they are available.

Oil supports
Canvas is the most common surface used in oil painting, although one can use any inert support which will allow paint to adhere. The best type of canvas is linen, which is, however, expensive. Canvas comes in various forms and colours — for example white unprimed calico (1), brown unprimed linen (6), coarse primed canvas (8). Hessian with its coarser weave is also suitable but it requires much priming. It too comes primed (3) or unprimed. Wood is more difficult to use for oil painting. It neither absorbs oil paint nor dries out evenly. Mahogany is the best surface available (4) but it should be well seasoned to prevent warping. Plywood (5) must be cradled to prevent warping. Hardboard (2) is a good surface. For large scale work it needs cradling. Only thick cardboard (7) can be used for oil painting, it should be sized on both sides.

Materials and equipment
below The first stage in preparing a canvas for painting is applying the size. Rabbit size (1) is made from leather waste. Size prevents the ground from rotting the support. The ground is applied next. This helps protect the support from the oil in the paint and provides a good working surface. Three types of ground are gesso (3), which should be used on a rigid support such as wood, acrylic (2) and emulsion (4). Acrylic grounds dry quickly and can be used on any surface without priming. Emulsion ground dries quickly and can be applied to canvas or

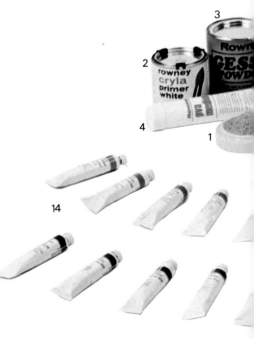

14

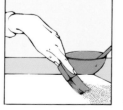 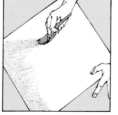 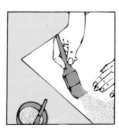 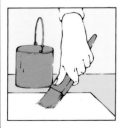

Applying size and grounds
1. Brush on size when hot. Make sure that it penetrates the weave. Allow to dry thoroughly. Repeat.

2. Allow the size to dry for 12 hours. Prepare the ground. When the size is dry, brush the ground on.

3. Brush on the ground thickly and work into the weave. Make sure there are no brush marks. Leave to dry for 24 hours.

4. Apply another coat of paint on it. For quicker drying use an acrylic ground.

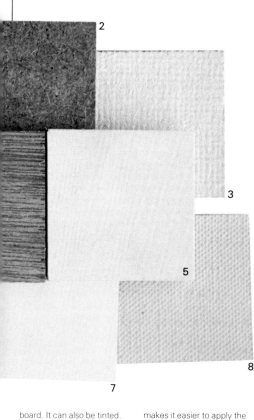

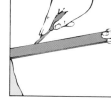

1. Cradling board Cut two battens as shown. Chamfer the ends, drill holes, screw to the board.

2. Stretching canvas Place the corners of the stretcher together firmly, tap with a hammer to secure.

3. Check the stretcher is square by measuring the diagonals.

4. Using a ruler and knife cut the canvas to size, leaving 1 ½ in overlap.

5. Put the stretcher on the canvas, fold over at one end and staple the outer edge.

6. With pliers pull the canvas tight at the opposite end and staple. Repeat on the other sides.

7. Staple at 3in intervals all round, except for the corners. Fold in the first corner tightly.

8. Fasten each corner with two staples. Wedges can be inserted to stretch the canvas further.

board. It can also be tinted. However, it does not last as well as oil, which takes a long time to dry.
Oil paints are either bought ready prepared or made up by the artist. Ground pigment is mixed with a binder, a type of oil — mainly linseed (5, 7) or poppy oil (6, 8). A medium makes it easier to apply the paint. The most common medium is a 40/60 mixture of turpentine (9) and linseed oil. Palettes are another essential for the artist. The traditional wooden, kidney-shaped version with a thumb hole (10) is still preferred by some artists. Disposable paper palettes (12) are useful if a clean palette is preferred. Other types of palette include a plastic model (13) and a metal one with recesses (11). A wide range of ready prepared oil colours (14) are available today. Prepared canvas (15) and board (16) is all the artist needs now before starting to paint, apart from a mahl stick (17) on which to rest his or her arm while painting. Mahl sticks can be bought or made by wrapping rags around a garden cane.

Equipment
For the range of brushes, knives and projectors suitable for painting in oils, see pp. 58–59.

Palettes The commonest type of palette associated with art by the non-technical is wooden, has a thumb-hole, and can be held in one hand. However, few professionals in fact use it, most preferring a large sheet of glass, marble or a similar non-absorbent material. Disposable paper palettes are available to save the effort of cleaning, while sheets of greaseproof paper can also be used.

Dippers These hold the oil/turpentine medium. Ready-made dippers can be bought, but it is easier and cheaper to re-use small plastic pots or glass jars.

Mahl Sticks These are used to support the painter's hand while work is in progress. They are propped against the support or nearby supports. Again, they can be bought, but can be quickly improvised by padding rags over the ends of lengths of cane or dowelling.

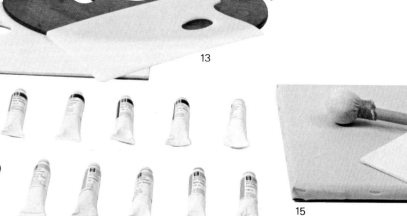

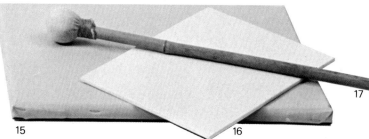

Easels Oil painting is best done on a near-vertical surface, so the usual studio drawing table may well not be suitable. There are a great many oil painting easels on the market, ranging from the 'donkey' type, through collapsibles, to the larger studio models. The obvious type to choose is one which suits both the needs of the artist and the space in which the work will be done. Many artists mount battens on a wall – choosing this carefully to ensure the best possible light – and use them as props for their paintings.

Techniques

Staining the surface If an acrylic-prepared surface or canvas is to be used, acrylic colour can be mixed either with matt white emulsion paint or gesso to produce the exact tint of colour required. An oil-primed canvas or board can also be stained with oil paint to produce a neutral or a tonal ground. The canvas should be covered with small dabs of paint. Then a little turpentine should be poured over it and the surface wiped with a clean rag, using a circular motion, until the paint is evenly spread across it. To finish off, the surface should be wiped with the cloth in parallel strokes, until an even tone is produced with the desired colour density.

Underpainting Once the drawing has been made on the canvas, or surface, and lightly fixed, the next stage is the tonal underpainting.

In order to save time at this stage, acrylic paint can be used because it dries quickly. It should be used in thin washes, mixed with water, to block in the whole canvas and to establish the tonal values of the picture. Raw umber is a good colour to use.

Purists sometimes prefer to use oil paints throughout. In this case, the paint should be used very thinly, diluted with turpentine and a little linseed oil. Again, umber is a good colour, but some artists prefer a range of greys. Such an underpainting can be completed by glazing over with colours.

Palette The range of colours used is always a matter of personal choice, but for most purposes a basic palette should consist of the following: Flake or Titanium white; Cadmium red; Alizarin; Cadmium yellow; Golden ochre; Viridian; Raw umber; Burnt umber; Ultramarine; Cobalt blue; Cerulean blue; and Black.

Black is optional; it should be used as little as possible as, when mixed with white, it easily produces a 'sootiness' which is very unpleasant to the eye. It is quite possible to produce a tonally satisfactory painting without using black at all, while the depth of colour rarely depends on the amount of black added.

Laying-out colours on the palette is a matter for individual decision, the most important criterion being convenience. It is worth laying them out amply; any paint left unused can be easily scraped off and stored in a jar of water for later use.

The painting It is very important to use the right amount of the chosen medium when building up the painting, as tube paints do not all have the same consistency. If turpentine is used alone, cracking will inevitably result. The most commonly used medium is a mixture of 40 per cent of turpentine to 60 per cent of linseed oil.

The thin underpainting should be built up gradually with solid colour. The basic rule is to start thin and finish fat to produce the most lasting results. Alterations can be made at any stage by removing paint with a palette knife and wiping the area carefully with a cloth dampened with turpentine.

Glazing is achieved by laying transparent colour over the underpainting. The essence of this technique is to ensure that the correct amount of light is reflected from the underpainting through the clear glaze; consequently, it is important that the underpainting is not too dark. An oil and turpentine mix is thus not a suitable medium – 'thixatropic' medium must be used, preferably one like Ruben's Medium, which contains beeswax.

Drying oils Artificial drying oils speed up the process of naturally-drying oils through the addition of a catalyst. The recipe for a good, strong drying oil has already been given.

Alla prima Alla prima is the most direct method of painting in oils and possibly the freshest one. It is not, however, the easiest, as it requires considerable practice to produce satisfactory results.

Paint is applied direct to the canvas or surface without underpainting, often leaving brush marks and areas of the base showing through. This direct method generally produces looser work, and is best used when working from life, or in landscape painting, where speed dictates the choice of technique. Most Impressionist paintings are alla prima.

Wax and oil painting The great advantage of wax painting is that the paint dries perfectly matt overall. The resulting pictures have a beautiful depth of colour and, furthermore, it is difficult to make them muddy. It is simplest to use a ready-made medium such as Feigenmilch, produced by the Weimar Paint Company. Winsor and Newton's 'Ceroline' colours are also made from a wax and oil medium.

Wax painting Oil colours can be combined with beeswax to produce a jelly. The beeswax must first be bleached and then dissolved either in turpentine or spiked lavender to form a paste. It

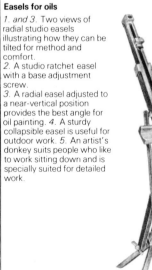

Easels for oils

1. and 3. Two views of radial studio easels illustrating how they can be tilted for method and comfort. *2.* A studio ratchet easel with a base adjustment screw. *3.* A radial easel adjusted to a near-vertical position provides the best angle for oil painting. *4.* A sturdy collapsible easel is useful for outdoor work. *5.* An artist's donkey suits people who like to work sitting down and is specially suited for detailed work.

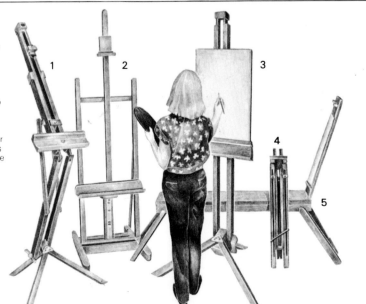

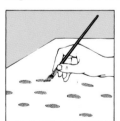

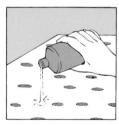

Staining the surface
1. Cover the flat canvas with small dots of paint.

2. Pour on a little turpentine.

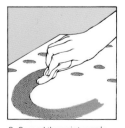

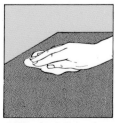

3. Spread the paint evenly by wiping with a clean rag using a circular motion.

4. Wipe the cloth over the surface with steady strokes to produce an even tone.

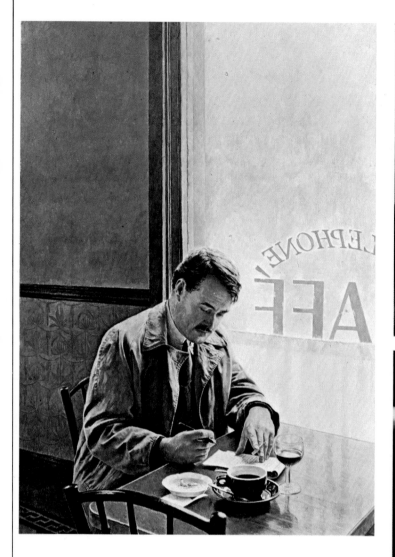

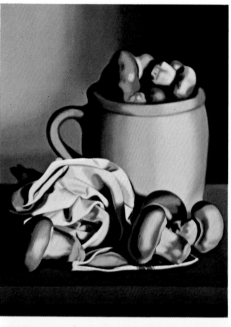

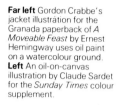

Far left Gordon Crabbe's jacket illustration for the Granada paperback of *A Moveable Feast* by Ernest Hemingway uses oil paint on a watercolour ground.
Left An oil-on-canvas illustration by Claude Sardet for the *Sunday Times* colour supplement.

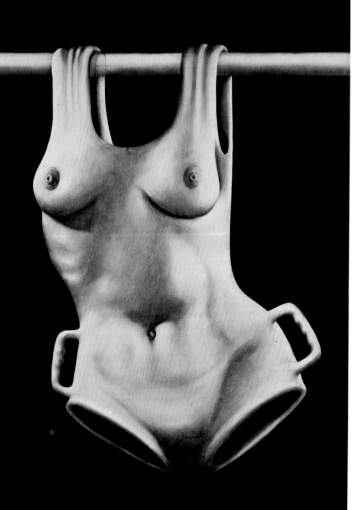

is important to use the right amount of wax; if too much is used, the paste will not cover the surface well, but if too little is used, the matt finish will be lost. It is also important to make sure that ground used is semi-absorbent, because the colours will peel from sealed or non-absorbent surfaces. A rigid surface is most suitable, but stretched canvas may be used.

To bleach beeswax, pure beeswax should be melted in a suitable container. To each pint (0.56 litre), ten grammes of sodium nitrate should be added, with twenty grammes of sulphuric acid, diluted in the proportions of one part of concentrated acid to ten parts of water. The melted wax should be kept hot while the sodium nitrate and sulphuric acid are stirred in.

The mixture is left to stand for several minutes. The container is next topped up with very hot water and then allowed to cool. The resulting bleached beeswax must be washed thoroughly under running water to remove all traces of acid. It is then dried re-melted and allowed to solidify again to increase its hardness.

Right John Holmes's striking illustration for the Panther paperback of Germaine Greer's *The Female Eunuch*. To achieve the matt effect the artist used oil and wax paste on gesso coated board building up the shades by successive layers of colour from light to dark.

Watercolour

Surfaces Paper is without question the best support for watercolour. The range available is extremely wide and it is up to the individual artist to choose the one he or she considers most suitable for the job in hand. Basically there are three types of watercolour paper – hot pressed, or HP, not and rough.

Hot pressed, or HP, paper has a smooth surface best suited to line and wash work. Many artists find it too shiny for pure watercolour use. Not means not hot pressed – cold pressed, in other words. It is a medium-rough paper, suitable for both wash and fine detail. It is probably the best paper for beginners to use. Rough paper, as its name implies, has a very positive raised tooth which breaks down wash to produce a speckled effect. This is because the pinnacles retain less pigment than the cavities. It is more suited for use by a practised water-colourist than an inexperienced one.

Hand-made papers In terms of quality, hand-made papers are the best, because they have a high linen-rag content. In addition, they are usually sized on the correct side – the one on which the watermark appears the right way round when the paper is held up to the light. Recommended papers include: Barcham Green R.W.S.; Arches; Fabriano; Green's Pasteless; Saunders; Kent Rough Turkeymill; Michallet; Creswick; and David Cox.

Rice papers are very fragile and extremely absorbent. However, they are well worth trying, as the work of the Japanese painter Hokusai (1760–1849) demonstrates. Among the kinds readily available are Kozo, Mitsumata and Gambi. Of these, Kozo is the toughest.

Paper weights are judged by the weight of the ream (480 sheets). A paper referred to as 70 pounds is fairly thin because 480 sheets weigh only 70 pounds, whereas a 140 pound paper will be thick.

Stretching It is always desirable to stretch lighter-weight papers, although some of the heavier papers do not require it. The paper is first soaked for a few minutes under water, then laid out on a drawing board with the edges taped around with wetted brown paper sticky tape.

It is not advisable to stretch paper merely by pinning it to the board around the edges, as this often results in the paper tearing. Nor should large sheets of paper be stretched on too thin a board, such as hardboard, because the pull of the paper will warp the board as it dries. It is also worth noting that more than one sheet of paper can be stretched over another.

After the painting has been completed, the sheet should be carefully removed by cutting through one layer of sticky tape, to expose the next sheet for use. There is no need to worry if the paper bubbles when wet because it will dry down tightly to the board.

Stretching frames similar to canvas stretchers can be bought, but the resulting drum-head quality produced makes paper stretched on them extremely susceptible to damage.

Dry mounting Papers may be dry-mounted to produce boards, using a dry-mounting press. In all but the roughest grades, this produces a kind of hot pressed surface.

Prepared boards There are many on the market, and, of course, they do not require stretching. Alternatively, boards can be prepared from the thinner papers by firmly gluing them to mounting cards. To prevent warping, a paper thinner than the one being used as the surface paper should be glued to the other side.

Paints

Watercolours are made up from very finely ground pigments and gum arabic. The gum dissolves readily in water, and the resulting mixture adheres to paper when dry.

Only artists' quality paints should be bought: among the most reliable are those from Winsor and Newton; Rowney; Reeves; and Grumbacher. They come in pans, half-pans and tubes. Half-pans are the most convenient for general use; it is better to reserve tube paints for really dense washes. A mixture of the two can be used, if the artist so desires, but it is worth remembering that tube paints cannot be used to top up pans, as they have a different consistency.

Pigments Water colour pigments fall into three main categories – earth colours, organic, and chemical dyes. The last named usually stain more than the others. To test for this, blobs of wet colour should be laid out on to paper and allowed to dry. Then they should be worked over gently with a brush and water, rinsed under a tap and allowed to dry again. The varying densities of colour left will indicate which colours stain.

Palette colours There is a very large range of ready-made pan and tube colours available and most effects can be obtained from the following: Yellow ochre; Gamboge; Raw umber; Indian red; Sepia; Cadmium red; Crimson lake; Prussian green; Cerulean; French ultramarine; Prussian blue; and Paynes grey. With experience and the consequent desire to produce a greater variety of colours, the palette will naturally expand.

As with oil painting, the use of black should be avoided, unless the artist is very experienced. In any case, it is rarely necessary to use black when working in colour, as Paynes grey – used alone or mixed with sepia – is quite sufficient. White, too, is never used if a clear, vibrant picture is desired.

Bottled water colours These are used to boost the palette colours and are especially valuable if a really startling colour is required. Again, there is a wide range available. It should be noted, however, that many of the colours are fugitive – that is, they fade quickly when exposed to light. Two good brands are Luma colour and Dr Martin's.

Equipment

General equipment The full range of brushes, knives and projectors required by watercolourists is described on pp. 58–59.

Paint boxes The most common boxes are made of lacquered metal, usually designed with indentations on the inside of the lid which act as wash

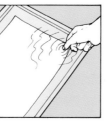
Stretching paper
1. Soak a sheet of lightweight paper in water for a few minutes. Keep it flat.

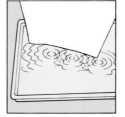
2. When the paper is well soaked, pick up by one edge, remove from water and shake off excess.

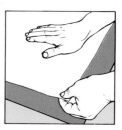
3. Place the wet paper on the drawing board. It should be at least 2in larger than the paper.

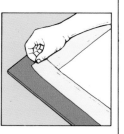
4. Attach one side to the board with gum strip. Keep the paper flat, repeat for the other sides.

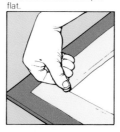
5. To fix the paper more firmly and prevent wrinkling, fix drawing pins to the corners of the paper.

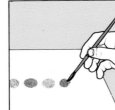
Watercolour staining test
1. To test how colours will stain put a blob of each colour on some paper.

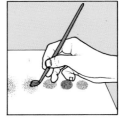
2. When the blobs are dry work over each colour with a wet brush.

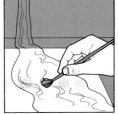
3. Rinse the paper under running water and allow to dry. The resulting colour will be the stain.

Papers
Five examples of the range of papers which can be used for watercolour painting show the very different effects which can be achieved on varying surfaces. Hotpressed or HP paper *(1)* is compacted to a hard smooth surface by machine. It is best suited to line and wash work and many artists find it too shiny for pure watercolour painting.RWS Rough *(2)* is a hand made paper and noticeably less smooth than the hotpressed machine-made paper used for the previous watercolour. The centre picture has been painted on a prepared board *(3)* — this is simply thin paper mounted on card and is very convenient as it requires no stretching. Rice paper *(4)* provides a delicate, fragile surface for watercolours, it tends to soak up paint and absorb the colour. Green's pasteless paper *(5)* can be used without stretching and provides a strong rough surface for the watercolour paints.

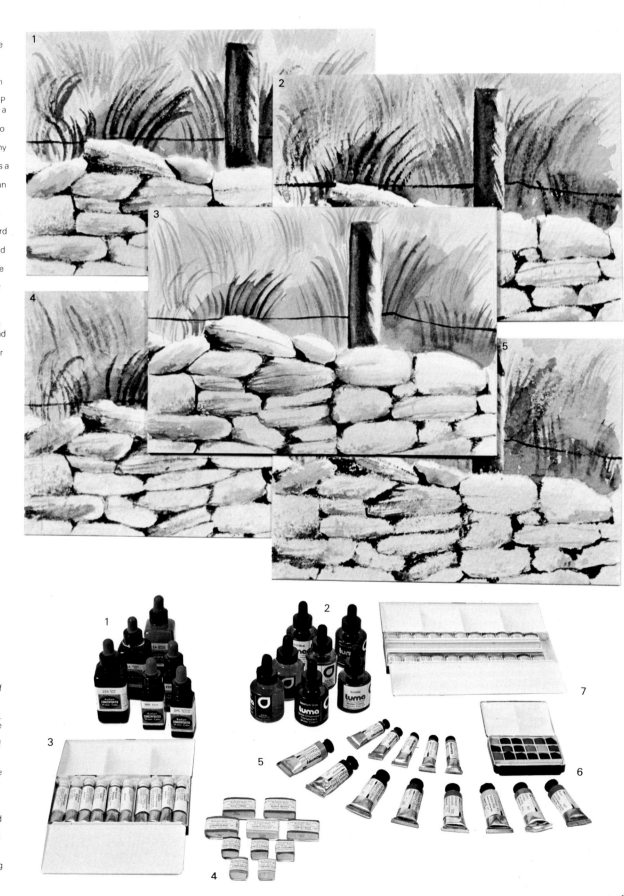

Watercolour paints
There are many qualities of watercolour paints on sale but, unfortunately, price does tend to reflect quality. Manufactured paint can be bought dry in cake form; semi-moist in whole or half pans *(4,6,7)*; as liquid colours in tubes *(3,5)* or bottles *(1,2)*. Half pans are the most commonly used because their size and cheapness have obvious advantages; tubes tend to be slightly more messy and are best used for obtaining really dense washes; while bottled watercolours are used to boost palette colours and when a striking shade is required.

pans when the box is open. The best have an extra metal flap which provides a mixing palette. On the bottom, there is often a thumb ring to make the box easier to hold while the artist uses it. Paint boxes come in a number of sizes, depending on the number of pans each contains.

Water containers It is always best to use distilled water, if possible, since this is absolutely pure and so will not cause chemical reactions with the paint. Any type of screw-top bottle with a wide neck is suitable for carrying water into the field. Large jam jars are ideal for the studio.

Easels There are many purpose-built easels on the market, designed to provide changeable angles of board, but any table against which a drawing board can be propped can be used. The normal adjustable draughtsman's desk is excellent. A drawing board with a strap is good for work outdoors, for painting both sitting and standing.

Techniques

The wash From the purist's standpoint, the basis of true watercolour is the transparent wash. It is important not to overlay more than three washes; the result of additional applications will be a dirty colour and a dry surface. Nor is it a good idea to lay a weak wash over a stronger one. Unless a particular, loose, wet effect is desired, one wash should always be allowed to dry before a further one is applied.

The surface having been chosen – if paper is selected rather than board it must be suitably stretched first before the wash can be applied. If pan colours are used, they should first be damped with plain water. Then the wash should be mixed thoroughly to the required depth of colour. It is sensible to overestimate the amount of pigment required, because watercolour dries to a much lighter shade than its wet colour would suggest. Blotting paper should be kept close at hand in order to mop up any runs.

The drawing board should be placed on the knees, or propped against a table or desk. The board should be angled to approximately 30 degrees – the exact angle will vary according to whether rough or smooth paper is used. By holding the board in this manner it is possible to change the angle either to speed or retard the running wash.

Two points must be kept constantly in mind.

First, the brush must be kept fully charged with mixed colour. Second, because watercolour paint is sedimentary, it is vital to keep mixing it as the wash is applied. The first stroke of the wash should be applied horizontally across the paper. The wash is brought back across the paper. The brush must then be recharged with mixed colour, and the next stroke applied like the first, so that the previous one runs into it. This process continues down the paper until the end result – a continuous flat colour – is obtained. Any excess at the bottom can be soaked up with a squeezed brush or a corner of blotting paper.

If the paper has been properly stretched, there is no need to worry if it has bubbled or risen; it will go flat again when dry. With some papers, it may be necessary to lay a wash of pure water before using colour. This avoids streakiness. A separate, clean brush must be used for this purpose.

This basic wash can be used to draw around any shape, and practice enables the artist to draw with the brush whilst working.

Shading a wash The principle is the same as that for a plain wash, but it is better to damp the paper first with a sponge and water. Having blotted off excess water, the paper must be allowed to dry until it is only slightly damp.

The brush should be charged with a mixed colour wash, and used in the same way as for a plain wash; water, however, is added to the colour in the palette as the work progresses. In other words, the work starts from dark and works towards lighter shades.

Shaded washes can be applied in various shapes, such as circles, triangles, vertical and horizontal columns. Because it is impossible to alter a graded wash once it is completed, it is important to gain experience through experiment before applying it to finished artwork.

Dry brush and splatter Dry brush is often used for the final details of pictures but can also be used overall. The basic principle is to apply the paint with as little water in the brush as possible. The brush is lightly charged with pigment, dissolved in water as for a wash, and then wiped on a spare piece of paper until almost dry.

By using the point of a fine brush either to cross-hatch or dot, form can be built-up. The brush can also be dragged lightly over rougher papers to produce texture or flicked wet to produce splatter effects. However, the more the pigment is piled on, the more the colour is reduced and so the danger of deadness in the finished work is increased.

Alterations Watercolours are extremely difficult to alter. With a very good paper or board, it is

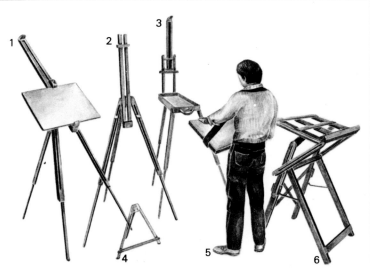

Easels for watercolours
Easels are available in various forms, sizes and weights to suit the requirements of the individual artist — sketching easels (1, 2) are light, collapsible and adjustable for angle. The combined colour box and easel (3) is practical for holding paints as well. For those who prefer to sit while painting the aluminium table top model (4) is particularly useful, as is the drawing board with strap (5) for painting out of doors or moving objects. The combination easel (6) can be converted easily from a studio easel to a drawing board.

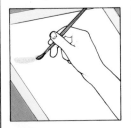

Applying a wash
1. Draw the fully loaded brush across the paper.

2. Draw the brush back across the paper.

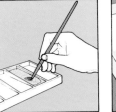

3. Recharge the brush after every stroke to ensure uniformity of colour.

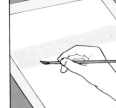

4. Apply a second stroke of colour merging it into the first.

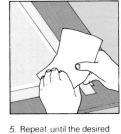

5. Repeat until the desired area is covered and soak up excess paint with blotting paper.

Applying a shaded wash
The principles of application are similar to those described **left** for a plain wash except the paper must first be washed with a sponge and water, the excess blotted off and the paper allowed to dry out until just slightly damp. The paint is applied in the same manner except the brush is dipped in water instead of paint between strokes to achieve the shaded effect.

possible to sponge most of the pigment from the surface; but this will affect the surface, which will no longer receive wash in the same way. An alternative method of correction is to make changes with body colour, either manufactured gouache (see pp. 68 – 70) or watercolour mixed with white. However, this is never a very satisfactory solution, as the glow of the paper showing through will be lost.

It is possible to recover lost highlights by scraping a good paper with a razor blade or scalpel, but this again damages the surface and it cannot be washed over again. For this reason it is best to mask out any small highlight which is to be retained before starting work. A very good masking agent is Copydex, which can be diluted, if necessary, with ammonia. It is waterproof when dry, leaves no stain, and, when the picture itself is completely dry, it can be rolled off gently.

Ox gall Ox gall can be used to remove any stubborn greasy areas from the paper surface. A few drops should be mixed into a wash of clean water and worked gently over the surface which is to be cleaned.

Glycerine A teaspoon of glycerine added to a cup of water will reduce drying time. It is particularly useful when working out of doors on a hot day.

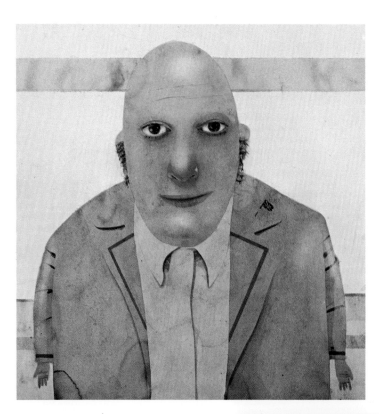

Left Ian Pollock's book jacket design for *Brothers of the Head* by Brian Aldiss uses watercolours over a wash. The glistening highlights are achieved by scrubbing off areas of paint with a toothbrush.

Below A card designed by Dan Fern using watercolour inks applied with an airbrush.

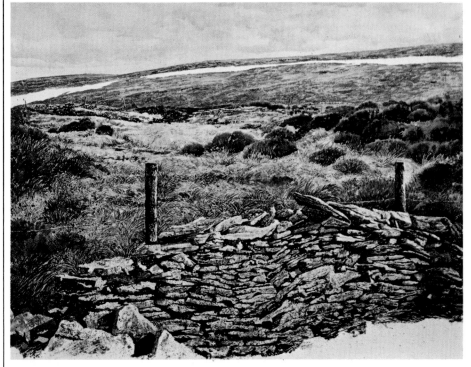

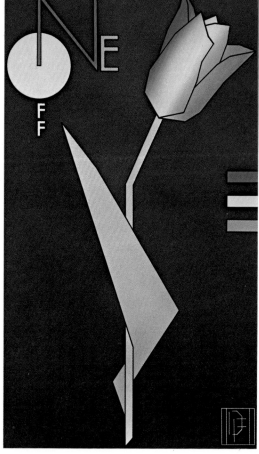

Above Brian Sanders *Dry Stone Wall* exhibits many of the basic techniques of water-colour painting — note the highlighting achieved by masking with Copydex glue; the basic washes used to create the bracken on the right and the splatter and dry brushwork used for the grasses and stone wall.

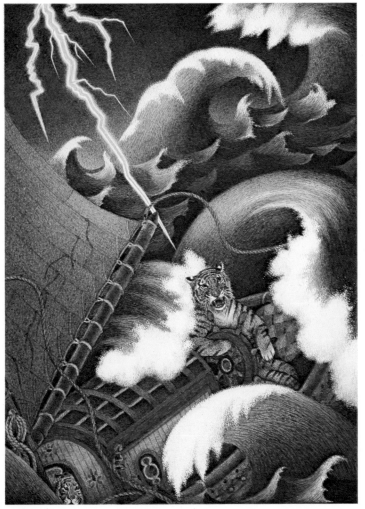

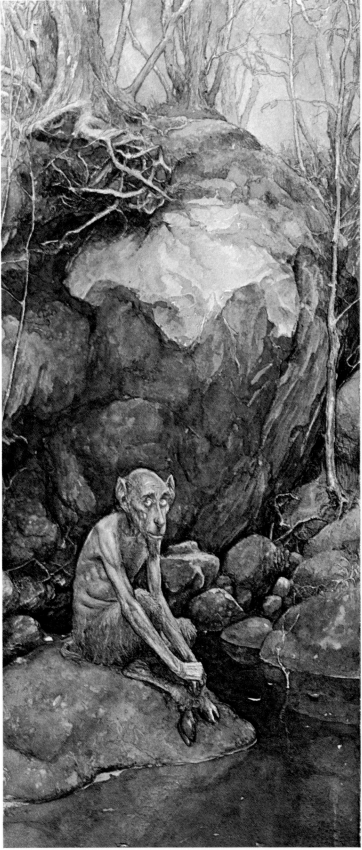

Above This illustration from *The Tyger Voyage* by Nicola Bayley uses water colour to good effect almost creating an impression of airbrushing in the swirl of the waves. The illustration was first drawn up completely. Then a thin wash was applied. The artist achieves the unusual texture by dotting on the colour using a thick brush with a fine point.

Below This picture of fish by Norman Weaver demonstrates the photographic quality which can be achieved with water colours, particularly in the clarity of the scales of the fish.

Right The use of water colour in this Alan Lee illustration shows the fine detail which can be achieved in this medium. The outlines were first drawn on in charcoal pencil, which gives a darker outline than graphite, and then the colour was washed on.

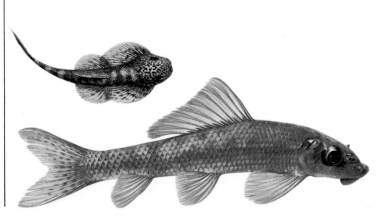

Gouache

Surfaces and materials

Papers With the exception of heavy, rough-surfaced papers, all papers used in water colour are suitable for gouache. Tinted and coloured papers can also be used to good effect.

Boards The same types of prepared board used for watercolour are also suitable for gouache, but the ideal surface for fine work is a slightly abraded one. Recommended boards include Geliot and Whitman No. 2; Arteko 3; and Colyer and Southey cs 2. Very smooth boards are not suitable.

Paints

Binders and colours As with watercolour, the binder for gouache is gum arabic. Unlike watercolour, however, all colours contain white, so gouache can be worked from dark to light or light to dark. Some gouache colours also contain a plastic emulsion, and so are waterproof when dry.

Colours come in tubes or bottles, both usually labelled 'designers' colours'. A range of excellent quality is provided by Winsor and Newton. Powder and poster paints are not suitable for professional use, and should be avoided.

Palette It is almost impossible to recommend a standard colour palette for gouache; it can change completely according to the demands of the work. Warm colours will be selected for a warm-looking picture; cool colours for a cool one. It is sometimes easier to use a number of different reds, greens, and other colours rather than mix them. Because tube colours have a relatively short shelf life, they should be bought as they are needed.

Watercolour paints can be mixed with white gouache and water to which a small amount of gum arabic has been added. If this is done, the normal watercolour range can be used. If watercolours are used for gouache work, it is very

Right *Boards for gouache*
The type of board used for water colours is equally suitable for gouache. Especially good results can be obtained on rough unsized cardboard. Suitable manufactured varieties include T.V. Gray, Crescent and Schoellershammer, as well as Geliot Whitman No. 2 *(1)*, Arteko 3 *(2)* and Colyer and Southey CS2

important to make sure that they have been thoroughly cleansed of gouache before they are used again for watercolour.

Equipment

Brushes A full range is listed on pp. 58–59.

Palettes, Easels and Sponges Any glazed surface can be used as a palette; china plates and small dishes are perfect. See the section on watercolour (pp. 64 – 68) for easels, and other suitable equipment.

Techniques

Gouache is watercolour with white added, but, apart from using the same kind of brushes, the similarity between the two ends there. Gouache is a solid body colour; unlike watercolour, it does not rely for its effect on the glow of the paper showing through.

Because all colours other than black contain some white, they dry very much lighter than when first applied. The final surface produced is matt and slightly chalky in appearance. The advantage of gouache is that it is possible to produce an absolutely flat finished surface, but it takes considerable experience to acquire this ability.

The wash As with watercolour, the wash should be applied from the top and worked downwards. Unlike watercolour work, the drawing board surface should be flat – that is, parallel to the ground. The wash can also be flooded into areas in pools of colour.

Tube colours should be mixed with water to the consistency of very thin cream before being flooded on. This will ensure maximum coverage with no brush marks showing through. If a second coat is needed, the first must be allowed to dry before it is applied. A second coat always leaves a 'tide-mark', so, if perfection of surface is required, it is always necessary to re-coat the whole area.

The dry surface is very easily marked or damaged, so areas which have been worked on should be covered with blotting paper for protection.

Modelling can be built on to washes with a fine brush. Because the painted surfaces are rather absorbent and thus take up water, drag will result if the paint is too dry. Because of the thickness of the medium, it is extremely easy to produce a contouring effect, making the surface even more susceptible to damage. The superb English artist-craftsman Norman Weaver once told a young illustrator, who had been applying gouache extremely liberally, that his final white highlights were in literal danger of

Right *Paints and Palette*
Although any glazed surface can be used as a palette, a special palette(**centre**) is still useful. Tube colours are efficient, but owing to their short shelf life, it is best to buy them as they are required. The selection of colours gives some idea of the range available.

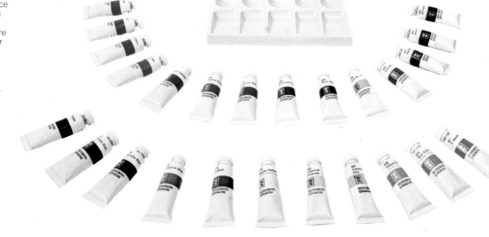

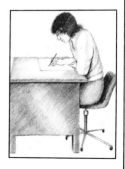

Applying a wash
For a gouache wash the drawing board should be kept flat so that the paint does not run

'falling off' on the way to the client.

Texture, Splattering and Scratching The splattering techniques used in watercolour and acrylic painting can easily be utilized with gouache as well. To produce texture, the painting surface can also be scratched with a razor blade, knife or scalpel point. Texture paste, too, can be mixed with the paint and brush-marked or dragged with a hair-comb across the surface to produce wood texture, whorls, and other effects.

Alterations Because gouache is an extremely flexible medium, small alterations can be made quite easily by painting over the existing paint-work. In addition, two other methods can be used. The first involves soaking the area carefully with a sponge and mopping up excess water with blotting paper. The area should then be coated again with a brush charged with clean water, and mopped again with blotting paper. The process is repeated until the desired amount of the pigment has been removed. When the surface is dry, it can be repainted. The second method involves gently scraping away paint from the area with a razor blade or scalpel, then reworking the surface.

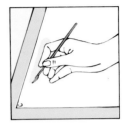

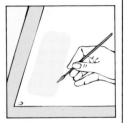

Laying a wash
1. Lay down as with a water colour, taking care that the paint is of the right consistency.

2. Lay further stripes parallel with the first to merge them together before they dry.

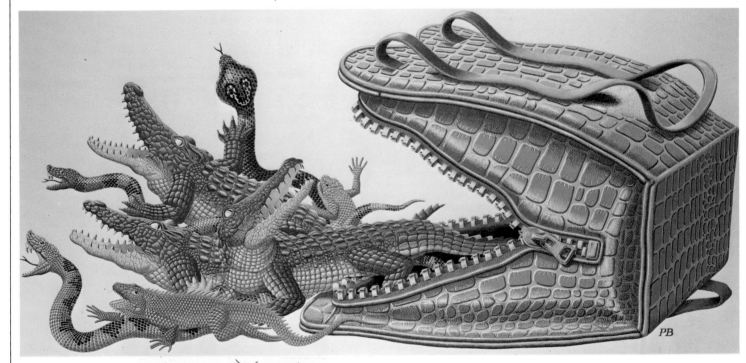

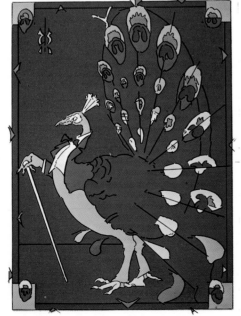

Right Brian Grimwood *Pride* To create the clear flat colour areas in this picture the artist laid a gouache wash and then used a dip pen to emphasize the outline.

Far right Terence Dalley's use of gouache in this picture shows another way in which the medium can be used — gouache can be blended subtly. The colour is painted on, left to dry and then blended with a wet brush.

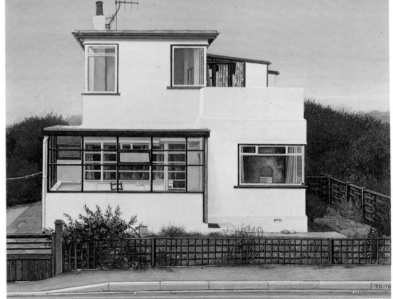

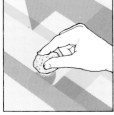

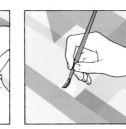

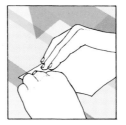

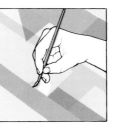

Corrections
1. Apply clean, preferably distilled, water with a sponge.

2. Soak up the paint with some fresh blotting paper.

3. Coat the area with water applied with a clean brush.

4. Mop it up with blotting paper again.

5. When dry the area can be repainted with fresh colour.

Left Peter Brookes *Beauty and the Beast*. The artist used fashion board for this illustration for a *Sunday Times* article on endangered species. Using a number of very small brushes and fairly thick paint, the artist worked from the top left-hand corner to the bottom right-hand corner, crosshatching to build up the colour. This was the technique employed by medieval miniaturists. Mistakes can be corrected by hatching in new colour.

Right George Hardie's design for a business card for a firm of garden designers uses gouache as the main medium together with coloured pencil, and pen and ink.

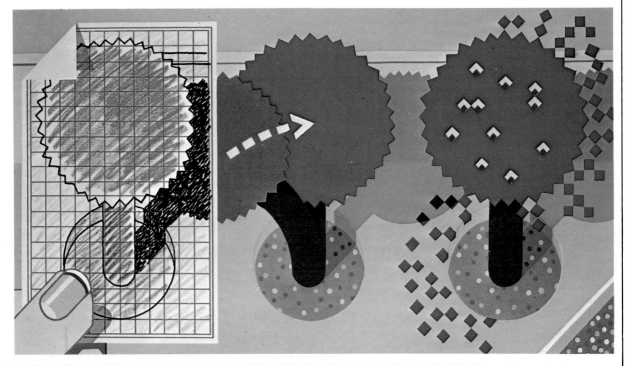

Once employed only for retouching, airbrushing is now widely used when colours have to merge gradually into one another giving one gradated tone. As can be seen on the record sleeve by Bob Norrington **(left)**, this technique can produce extremely fine lines as well as areas of even colour, all with almost photographic precision. The example shown here is in gouache. This is also suitable for areas of flat colour or for work which will have additional drawing on top of it.

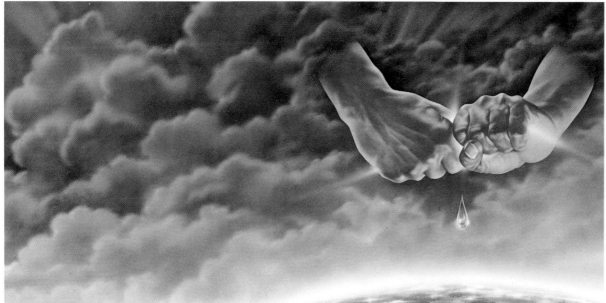

71

Tempera

Surfaces and materials

Canvas One of the best surfaces for working with tempera is finest quality canvas. This is best used glued to a panel, but it can be stretched, as in oil painting.

Panels Panels are also excellent for tempera. Hardboard, masonite and chipboard are all good, but plywood and block-board are less suitable, because they tend to split

Paper and prepared boards These may be used unprimed if speed is the chief requirement, but the result will not be permanent.

Grounds Painters and illustrators in tempera adopt different attitudes to grounds. To a painter, the preparation of the ground is probably all-important; to the illustrator, working at speed, the preparation matters less. For this reason, illustrators more frequently buy gesso grounds suitable for use with tempera rather than make them up themselves. Excellent results, too, have been obtained from white emulsion painted on to heavy mounting board, with no signs of deterioration apparent years after the painting was completed.

Experts in tempera recommend that supports be sized before the ground is applied. Again for speed, this stage is often omitted by illustrators, but it is always best to do it if time allows. Gelatine size is the most convenient medium. Five leaves of gelatine – powder cannot be used – should be soaked in a pint of water until they swell. This will take about ten minutes. Then the mixture should be heated very gently until the gelatine dissolves. The solution can then be applied to both sides of the surface. It should be left to dry overnight.

Paints There are many branded kinds of tempera available on the market. Among other companies, Rowneys make excellent ready-to-use prepared colours, all of which are suitable for illustration. A simple method for preparing paints is described in the section dealing with tempera techniques and ground colours can be bought from good artists' colour stores.

A basic range of colours similar to those used for watercolour painting will be adequate for the beginner. The colours in the palette will obviously be increased in number as required.

Equipment

Any type of brush can be used for tempera, but water-colour brushes are the most suitable.

The palette must be made of a non-absorbent material. Deep saucers are ideal because they can be covered by raffia table mats which have been soaked in water. This keeps the colour moist between painting sessions, but it will be necessary to lay out more colour on the following day.

Techniques

Tempera has now come to mean any kind of paint which contains oils in emulsion, and which can be used with water as a medium. It is without doubt the most durable of all the painting media; if it is correctly used on a suitable surface, it will not react either to humidity or temperature changes when dry. Its fast drying time can sometimes prove a drawback because, unlike oil paints, tempera cannot be softened for blending. When dry, however, it hardens like no other painting material, and protects the surface on which it is painted, rather than reacting against it.

As previously stated, the time factor involved in working to a deadline means that illustrators and designers normally buy good, ready-to-use, tempera colours rather than prepare them from scratch. However, there are occasions when grinding and mixing colours may be necessary. The simplest way of doing this is as follows.

The colour is ground in distilled water and then mixed with the desired quantity of egg yolk. This can be used pure, or with a little vinegar added to prevent mould. A further refinement is to bleach the egg yolk by mixing it with pure alcohol and exposing it on a saucer, placed on a window ledge.

Painting It is unnecessary to prime absorbent surfaces, such as paper or wood; tempera will seal once the first coat has been applied. The beauty of the medium lies in its richness and depth of colour. It should be built up in washes or glazes of colour and fine brushwork; it can also be worked over a tonal underpainting.

It is a mistake to load the brush too heavily, or to use tempera in an impasto fashion – that is, laid on very thickly – since heavy paint will almost certainly crack from the surface. If a textured surface is required, one can be prepared by rough brushing or stippling with gesso. Most of the tempera works of the celebrated American artist, Andrew Wyeth – a master of the medium – were created on such a surface.

Finishing When completely dry, the painting can be given a pleasant finish simply by rubbing it with a cloth. A piece of silk is ideal.

There are branded varnishes on the market but the paint must be allowed to dry really hard before such a varnish is applied; this usually means waiting for six months once the painting has been completed.

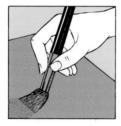

Preparing a panel for tempera
1. Paint the previously sized panel with glue. This must be free of lumps.

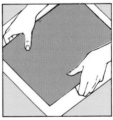

2. Having smoothed out the canvas place the sticky side of the panel on the canvas.

3. Turn the panel over, put a sheet of paper over it and rub the canvas through to ensure it is stuck.

4. Apply glue to the edges of the panel at the back and stick down the canvas edges.

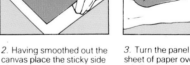

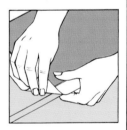

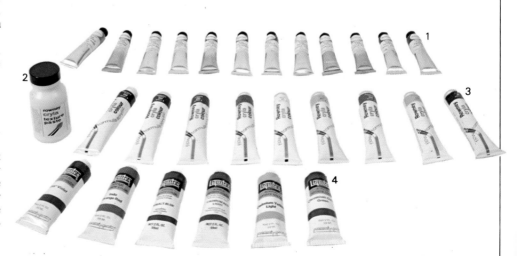

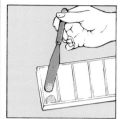

Making tempera paint
1. Put a little pigment on a mixing palette using a palette knife.

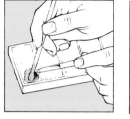

2. With an eye dropper add some distilled water. Mix using a glass rod.

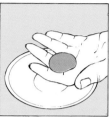

3. To make the egg yolk binder, separate it from the white by draining the white through the fingers.

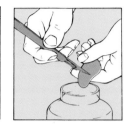

4. Dry the yolk. Hold it, cut the sac and let the liquid run into a glass jar.

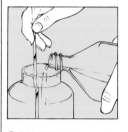

5. Add distilled water and stir. When the mixture is the consistency of thin cream, strain into a glass jar.

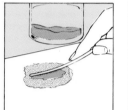

6. Mix the pigment paste and the binder with a palette knife. A paper palette is recommended.

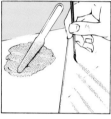

7. To make sure that the paint will bind properly paint a little on to a piece of glass.

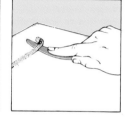

8. When the paint is dry, peel it off. If it crumbles, add more egg.

Right Roger Coleman *The Boxers* This tempera painting shows the effectiveness of large blocks of tempera colour.

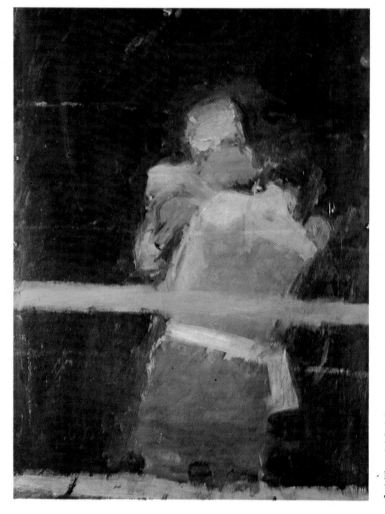

Left *Tempera and acrylic paints* There is a wide variety of tempera and acrylic paint available today: for example Rowney Tempera paints *(1)*, Rowney Cryla colours *(3)*, and Liquitex acrylic paint *(4)*. Rowney Cryla texture paste *(2)* is used as an extender to build up heavy impasto textures. Similar paints are manufactured by Grumbacher and Winsor & Newton.

Acrylics

Surfaces and materials
Surfaces Acrylics can be used on a wider variety of surfaces – primed or unprimed – than any other painting medium. The only unsuitable surface is an oil-primed one, though some experts argue that emulsion is also unsuitable as a base. However, since acrylic paintings based on emulsion have lasted in many instances for a good ten years without any signs of deterioration, this belief is increasingly open to question.

Canvas All kinds of canvas are suitable, but those used for oil painting are best (see pp. 60–61). Canvases should first be primed with acrylic.

Papers, cards and prepared boards All of these are suitable for use primed or unprimed, according to the effect required. If paper is the chosen surface, it should first be stretched, especially if a lightweight type has been selected. Otherwise it may buckle if the surface is flooded with colour wash.

Fashion and art boards of all varieties can also be used, whether primed or unprimed. An excellent prepared surface can be made merely by coating heavy mounting card either with acrylic primer or emulsion paint, leaving the brush marks to give the surface bite.

An excellent cheap canvas board may be prepared from butter muslin, scrim, or even old, clean linen sheets, pasted directly on to thick mounting card or smooth hardboard. The material should be about 15mm ($\frac{1}{2}$in) smaller all round than the board to which it will be applied. The cloth should be wetted, and gently wrung out. Then the cloth should be laid on to the board and pasted to the surface, using a 3in brush and matt white emulsion paint. It is a good idea to start at one end and work towards the other, stretching the material slightly as the work continues. The emulsion paint is worked through the fabric, and sticks it firmly to the board.

The board should be pinned down and allowed to dry. When dry, it should be rubbed down slightly with fine sandpaper and then re-coated.

If the artist does not trust emulsion paint, an acrylic primer can be used. Two or three coats should be applied, each being allowed to dry before the next. This will produce a greasier surface, but is much more expensive.

Paints Many of the pigments in acrylic paints are similar to those used in more traditional paints, but a number of new chemical pigments have been added. An entirely new range of colours, such as Napthols, Dioxazines and Pthalocyanines, have thus been developed.

The paints are available in tube form or in plastic containers. The latter are more convenient when large quantities are required. They come in two categories – polyvinyl acetates and acrylic polymers. The acrylic range is the better. Two of the best paints are Rowneys Flow Formula Cryla and the Liquitex range. Both have a large variety of colours, but the Liquitex modular colours are particularly impressive. These are ranged in tonal values, making them extremely useful both to the designer and the 'hard-edge' painter.

Rowneys, too, have produced gouache colours suitable for use with acrylic media. These have the advantage of not picking up the colour from the previous layer when they are superimposed on to it.

The palette The following colours make a good working palette, which can be augmented according to personal taste; White; Cadmium yellow; Yellow oxide; Golden oxide; Chromium oxide of green; Pthalocyanine green; Raw umber; Burnt umber; Ultramarine blue; Cerulean blue; Cobalt blue; Acra violet; Cadmium red; Red oxide; Paynes grey; Black.

Any glazed surface, such as a sheet of glass or an old plate, can be used as a palette. An old, enamelled butcher's tray has proved very effective. Plastic, however, is not suitable. Dried paint can be soaked off with hot water.

Media There are several kinds of media suitable for use in acrylic painting, all of which can be added to the paint on the palette. Gloss provides a shiny finish; matt a semi-flat one.

Brushes The same brushes used in other media are also used in acrylic painting. Brushes should be washed in water immediately after use. Hard dried paint may be removed with methylated spirits.

Texture paste This is used to build impastos and to create rough grounds. It is readily obtainable at good artists' stores.

Techniques

The first acrylic and polyvinyl acetate paints brought on to the market were not of a very high standard, but, over the past few years, the former have been greatly improved. They now provide the artist with an extremely flexible and comprehensive painting medium.

Painting solidly As previously stated, acrylic paints can be used on almost any surface, with the exception of an oil-primed material. Canvas, board, paper and wood are all good surfaces on which to work; they can be toned with tinted matt emulsion paints or acrylic primers before painting commences.

The paints themselves can be used alla prima, or, as in oil painting, be underpainted in monochrome and built up with glazes or solid paint. If building with solid paint, a branded retarder or pure glycerine can be used to slow down the drying time. The latter is much cheaper. For fast drying the paints may be mixed to the required consistency with water or water to which a little retarder has been added.

The covering power of acrylics, however, is not their best quality and two thin applications

of paint are often better than one thick one. By mixing colours with white they will cover better, but dry lighter. Conversely, colours used straight from the tube invariably dry darker when applied thickly. Experimenting to find the drying qualities of colours will help the illustrator to produce the tonal values required in the finished painting.

Impasto Acrylics are very suitable for all types of impasto – either applied with a palette knife, or straight from the tube – but it is not advisable to build them up too thickly. If high reliefs are required, a branded texture paste – or any flexible household filler – can be used to build up the impasto before the acrylics are applied. The process does not impose any great delay as the paste dries very quickly at normal temperatures. The built-up surface should be primed with white and glazed over with paint.

Texture pastes can also be used to good effect by stippling on areas to give the impression of walls, broken ground, grass and so on. The paste should be applied to the area required, and painted over when dry.

Acrylic 'watercolours' Acrylics can also be used in a similar manner to watercolours, though

there is one disadvantage to this. Once dry, edges cannot be softened as with watercolours, and the spectacular watery washes of true watercolour cannot be easily achieved. Their advantage, however, is that many washes can be applied, one over another, without producing the dirtiness that would result if true watercolours were used. There is very little difference in tone between the wet wash and the dry one, thus making it far easier for the artist to judge tonal values.

Paper can be dampened before use to produce a softness of edge, but professionals use watercolour pencils. These are applied around the edges of the wash area, either before the wash is applied or while the wash is still wet.

Dry brush, stippling and spatter Washes can be built on with dry brush – that is, the brush is kept dry with its bristles slightly parted – just as in watercolour techniques.

The advantage of acrylics is that a painting can be 'worked up' without producing sootiness or loss of colour. Using this technique with this medium, it is easier to produce highly finished 'photographic' styles, than with any other medium, the sole exception being the airbrush.

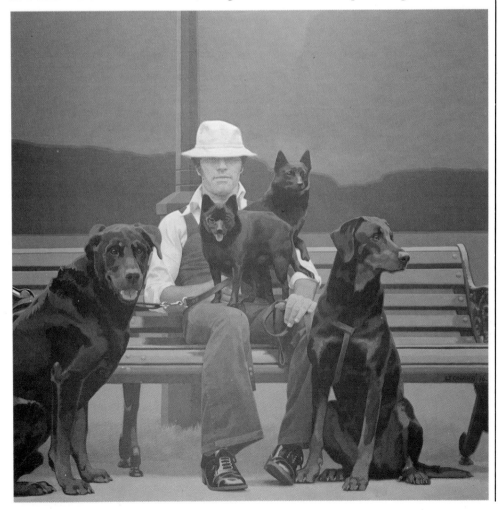

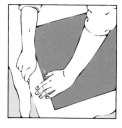

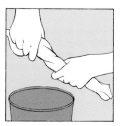

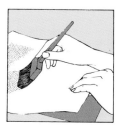

Preparing a panel
1. Cut a piece of fabric about 15mm (½ in) smaller all round than the board.

2. Wet the cloth — muslin, scrim or linen can be used — and wring it out gently.

3. Lay the cloth on the board and paste it down with matt white emulsion paint and a wide paint brush.

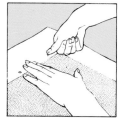

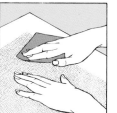

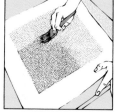

4. Pin the board down and leave it to dry.

5. When it is dry, rub the surface down slightly with fine sandpaper.

6. Recoat the board with emulsion. Alternatively, two or three coats of acrylic primer can be used.

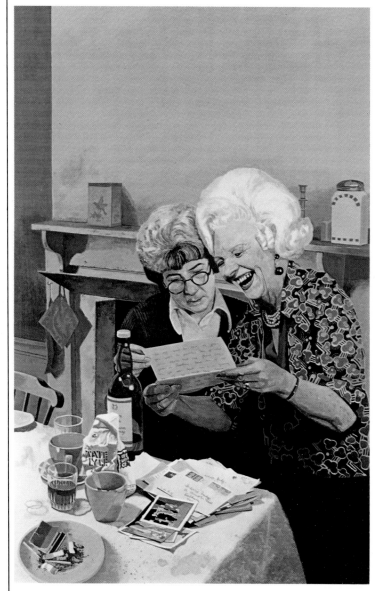

Acrylic is a very versatile medium. Michael Leonard's *Dogs and Overcast* **(far left)** uses acrylics on cotton duck canvas to create an almost photographic image. Alan Manham **(left)** achieves a grotesque and heightened realism using gouache with an acrylic medium on board. Brian Sanders **(below)** also used acrylic for the effects varying from the wash in the background to stipple in the foreground.

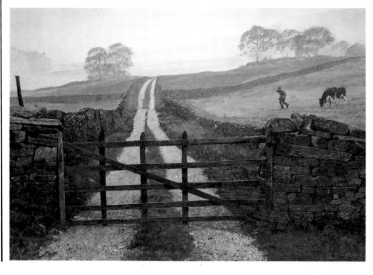

A dry brush can also be dragged across rough papers to produce broken effects, while the paint may be stippled with the point of the brush to produce dotting, in the pointillist manner. With practice, controlled spatter can be used to good effect. The paint should be flicked from a hogs-hair brush with the thumb, or alternatively, a toothbrush can be charged with paint and the bristles scraped with a knife. It is naturally vital to ensure that areas which are not to be spattered are masked off with spare paper, held securely in position with masking tape.

Mixed media Acrylics can be used to paste down other materials, such as cloth or paper, to make collages. These can then be painted over using any of the acrylic techniques. Acrylic gloss or matt media can also be mixed with coloured inks and used to produce startling colour glazes. Inks can additionally be used with a gell medium to make textured or brush-marked scumbles.

Such techniques should be used with care, however. There was a time when many illus-trators were using gell media on glazed surfaces to produce an overall textural effect nicknamed 'bubble and squeak'. It is now very much out of fashion.

Alterations Alterations can easily be made when using solid acrylics. The area to be changed should be whited out with white acrylic, emul-sion paint or gesso, and the work started again. Paint should never be removed with methylated spirits, as the result will be a sticky mess.

Varnishes Gloss and matt varnishes are avail-able for finishing acrylic paintings. They are both useful for 'bringing together' a painting which may have both gloss and matt sections, and where varying techniques have been employed.

CHAPTER FOUR

PRINTMAKING

Though the general term printmaking is used to describe a variety of different methods, the basic process is always the same – to create an impression through contact with an inked plate, stone block or screen. The end product, however, is not merely a reproduction; it is a work of art, even when many prints are taken from one block. It is this facility, in fact, that attracts many artists to the medium.

When many proofs are produced, the printmaking process can be extremely complex, often involving the employment of skilled technicians and elaborate equipment. At the other end of the scale comes the individual artist who conducts his or her own experiments and innovates techniques in order to obtain individual effects for each individual image. In both cases, the potential and possibilities are almost limitless.

Today, the rigid distinctions that differentiated the various printmaking processes in the past have largely disappeared – indeed, many modern methods defy formal classification. Some prints, for example, now combine etching, lithography, and silk screen printing with photomechanical processes and vacuum images. In practice, however, there are four main methods of producing prints, which are used to identify the type of image produced. These are: relief (woodcuts, wood engraving, linocuts); intaglio (etching, engraving); planographic (lithography); and stencil (silkscreen).

History Of the many methods of printmaking, relief, or raised surface printing, is probably the oldest. It has been practised in Europe for about 500 years, but its origins go back much further – to China, where it was first developed between AD 600 and 900. The first relief prints took the form of rubbings, but the technique of cutting images into woodblocks and printing from them speedily developed.

The woodcut is the simplest form of relief printing. Examples of its use vary widely; in the sixth and seventh centuries AD, it was used to print patterns and repeat designs on cloth, while in Europe the earliest woodcut prints consisted of crude and broad outlines, which were sometimes coloured in by hand.

When paper became widely available in Europe in the late Middle Ages, printmaking, too, began to expand. One important step forward was the development of printing, following the invention of type by the German Johann Gutenberg. This created a demand for woodcuts as accompanying illustrations to printed text, and they speedily became the standard method of book illustration.

During the fifteenth century, many goldsmiths and armourers adapted their engraving skills in response to the demand from the print industry. One of the earliest and most famous artists in this field was Albrecht Dürer (1471–1528), who was himself originally an apprentice goldsmith. He used the relief method to illustrate a wide range of subjects, ranging from Biblical themes to scenes from nature.

The next important step forward was the development of etching. This began to flower in the seventeenth century, when acids were introduced into the print process. The innovation gave engravers greater flexibility, and allowed them to achieve a more sensitive and delicate finish in their work. This, in turn, was followed by the invention of lithography, at the end of the eighteenth century.

Meanwhile the techniques of woodcut illustration were being refined and perfected in Japan. A school of woodcut artists was founded there in the mid-seventeenth century, and it continued to grow in importance over the next two hundred years. The Ukiyo-e, as the members of this school were called, specialized in prints illustrating scenes from daily life and the theatre.

Relief Printing

Relief printing is the most direct and least expensive method of printmaking. It includes woodcuts, wood engraving and linocuts. The artist starts with a blank, smooth-surfaced block, then cuts away those lines and areas which are to come out white in the finished print. The remaining 'islands' of relief are then inked and printed.

Woodcut

Materials, tools, techniques Woodcut is the simplest and oldest method of relief printing. Almost any well-seasoned wood can be used for the block, including plywood, block-board and hardwood. Simple plankwood – wood cut in the direction of the grain – is particularly suitable because of the natural grained surface this provides for the artist.

The image to be printed is either drawn directly on to the surface of the wood, or traced on with carbon paper. The block is then firmly clamped to a bench or table top, and the artist begins to cut out the outline of the design, working with a craft knife or a traditional Japanese woodcut knife. The knife is held tightly in the fist and the blade drawn back in the direction of the grain. Once the contours of the design have been cut, the wood is carved away

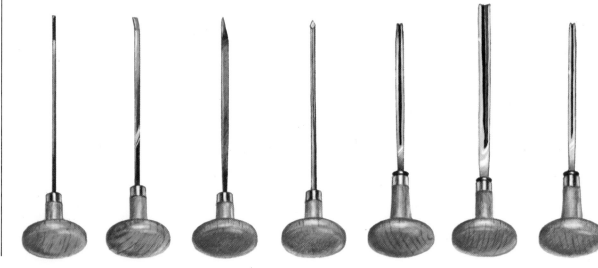

Right Hiroshige I *Autumn Moon at Ishiyama* This delicate woodcut by the nineteenth century Japanese artist Hiroshige demonstrates how highly refined the woodcut technique had become in Japanese art over a two hundred year period. The blended colours used here on a single block were known as 'rainbow inking'.

Left Tools for wood cutting include (from **left** to **right**) engravers — flat, round and lozenge — and a burin, as well as cutters — large, small and 'U' shaped.

from the line with a tool known as a gouge, leaving the parts to be printed standing up in relief.

The gouge should be pushed from behind, and held at a low angle (20°–30°), so that it does not cut into the wood too deeply. Different types of gouge will create a different texture in the finished image, a wide gouge giving a broader and coarser effect than a thin one. Almost any tool – a chisel, wire brush or even a power tool – can be used, provided it will incise the block.

Wood Engraving

Materials, tools, techniques Unlike the woodcut, where the image is cut with a gouge on the plank or long grain of the wood, a wood engraving is normally incised on the end grain of the block. It is cut with fine, sharp graving tools which produce a delicate, precise line. The process was developed and made popular in England by Thomas Bewick (1757–1828) with his fine illustrations of nature and rural scenes. From this time onwards the wood engraving became the most common method of cheap illustration until it was superceded by photo-reproduction in the twentieth century.

The most suitable woods for engraving blocks are hardwoods such as boxwood, maple or pear; they are usually supplied to the artist in type-high blocks. Gravers are generally made of steel and are available in a very wide range of shapes and sizes. They must be held at a flat angle to the surface of the block, so that they do not dig too deeply into the surface. As the work progresses, the artist can check the development of the design by rubbing chalk into the cut lines.

Linocut

Materials, tools, techniques The basic principles involved in making linocuts are those of the woodcut, and the same tools can be used. Lino, however, has no grain, which means that, unlike wood, it can be cut in any direction. Marks and scratches can be easily removed by scraping with a sharp razor blade, or fine sandpaper. These qualities, combined with its cheapness, make lino a very popular and widely-used medium for all levels of printmaking – from the simple prints made by schoolchildren, to the advanced art of practitioners such as Pablo Picasso (1881–1973) and Henri Matisse (1869–1954).

The most suitable lino for blockcutting is medium soft and at least 6.5mm (0.25in) thick. If the material used is thinner than this, it should be mounted on hardboard for added support. Lino is also ideal for flat colour printing because of its smooth surface, and it is often used in combination with intaglio plates for this reason.

Printing Wood engravings, lino cuts and wood-cut prints are all printed in the same way. The process can be carried out by hand or mechanically, using a printing press. Once the design has been cut on the block, ink is applied evenly over the surface with a roller – usually made of rubber or composition. Most oil-based inks, including those employed in letterpress and lithography, can be used. When the relief areas are sufficiently coated, the paper can then be placed on the inked surface.

If the printing is to be done by hand, the artist next rubs the back of the paper evenly with a rounded object, such as a tablespoon; alter-

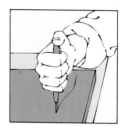

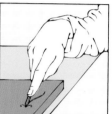

Linocut
1. Thin lino may first be mounted on hardboard for added support. Cut the outline and detail of the design with a fine gouge.

2. Cut out broader lines and large areas with a medium gouge, working away from the line. A craft knife can also be used for large patches.

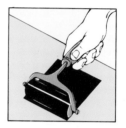

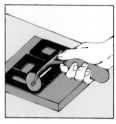

3. Ink the roller on an inking pad. Most oil based inks are suitable for lino cuts, including those used for letterpress and lithography.

4. Apply the ink evenly over the surface of the block with the roller.

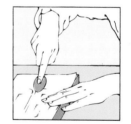

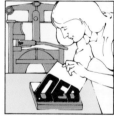

5. Place a sheet of paper on the block and rub the back smoothly with a baren — the back of a tablespoon or any rounded object can be used instead.

6. Remove the paper carefully from the block and allow the ink to dry.

Below Tools for lino cutting include a roller **(left)** and a handle fitted with a cutter head **(right)**.

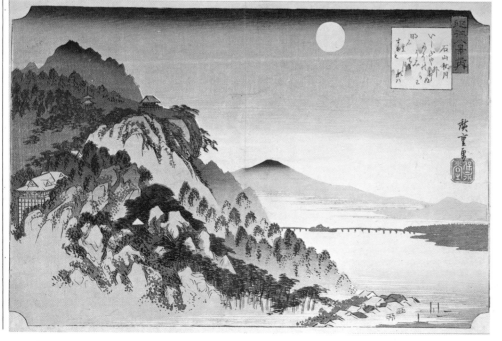

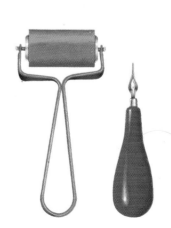

natively, a special tool, called a baren, can be used. Hand printing using a circular baren was the standard method of the Japanese Ukiyo-e school, while the Norwegian artist Edvard Münch (1863–1944) and some members of the German Expressionist group *Die Brücke* (1905)

also produced prints by hand. Large blocks, however, are normally printed mechanically. Platen presses, such as the Albion or Columbia, are usually used.

Correct registration is vital if the end result is to be satisfactory, so it is essential to ensure that

the block and paper are accurately positioned before the image is transferred. One easy way to make sure of this is to use a sheet of stiff paper or cardboard, on which raised marks are glued. These correspond to the edges of the block and the paper, which can then be positioned.

Right This linocut by the modern British artist Ian Cooke shows the skill and artistry that can be achieved by this method of printing. The clear lines of the trees and branches demonstrate the artist's considerable draughtsmanship. The linocut reveals how finely such detailing can be reproduced.

Below Jonathan Heale *An Alphabet* This splendid series of woodcuts which runs through the next pages, uses aspects of country life — farmyard animals and crops — to illustrate the alphabet. These, executed in 1978, and so spare and simple in design, show how effective the modern woodcut can be in producing a graphic image which is not only original but also in perfect harmony with its subject matter.

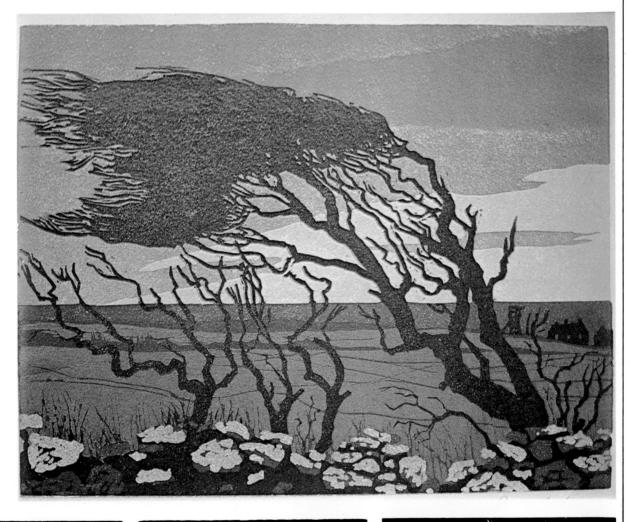

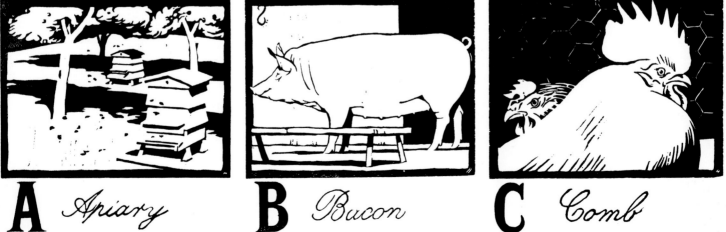

A *Apiary*

B *Bacon*

C *Comb*

Intaglio

Etching and engraving are the two chief components of intaglio. In this, the image is first cut into the metal plate so that the lines lie beneath the flat surface. This is done either by incising the plate by hand – engraving – or by using acids which bite into the surface – etching. The plate is then coated with ink, and finally the surface of the plate is wiped clean, so that the ink remains only in the crevices.

Line Engraving

Materials, tools, techniques The most simple and direct way of making intaglio plates is by line engraving. In this method the design is cut or incised on the plate rather than being bitten on chemically. It is the oldest intaglio process, used in the Middle Ages to decorate armour.

Line engraving is fundamentally a linear technique producing fine hard lines. The method of drawing is not the same as with a pen or pencil. The tool, known as an engraver or burin, is held at a low angle, resting in the palm of the hand. As it is pushed forward over the plate it digs into the surface and raises a strip of metal, which leaves a furrow to hold the ink.

Drypoint

The difference between drypoint and engraving is that in the latter the metal is completely removed from the line; in drypoint, a ridge, known as the burr, is thrown up on each side of the cut. This holds the ink when the plate is printed, with the result that a soft, velvety line is produced. This delicate, blurred quality has appealed to many artists; leading practitioners of drypoint include Rembrandt van Rijn and

Jacques Villon (1875–1963). The method, however, has one major disadvantage. The burr wears under the pressure of printing, so only a limited number of proofs can be produced.

Materials, tools, techniques To make a drypoint engraving, a line is scratched into the metal with a very sharp point, such as a diamond head, or a toughened steel needle. The pressure and angle of the needle determine and control the depth and thickness of line. Copper is the ideal medium for engraving, but today it is so expensive that zinc, steel or aluminium are generally substituted.

Mezzotint

Mezzotint was first developed in the seventeenth century, and remained popular for the next 200 years. Its rich half-tone effects made it particularly suitable for reproducing painting but an increasing number of artists are now returning to the medium, despite the laborious preparation involved in making a plate.

Materials, tools, techniques The first stage in the process is to scour the metal until it will produce a uniformly black print. The surface is roughened with an instrument known as a rocker, which consists of a curved blade with a serrated cutting edge. This is applied to the plate with a rocking movement; it bites into the copper, or whatever the metal used, to make a series of indentations and raise a burr on the surface. A burnisher (a highly-polished and smooth steel tool), and a scraper (a hollow, three-sided knife made of ground steel) are then used to polish the image gradually so that it emerges in lighter tones from the black ground.

Etching

Etching is the term used to describe the process of biting lines and textures into metal, using various acids. Though it is a simple technique in itself, it is capable of a wide range of applications.

Materials, tools, techniques The plate to be etched is prepared by being thoroughly cleaned and de-greased. This is usually done with a paste of powdered whiting and diluted ammonia. It is then covered with an acid-resistant coating. When dry, the surface is coated with ground – standard hard etching ground consists of beeswax, bitumen and resin, prepared in the form of a small ball or cake. The plate is heated and the ground is then applied by dabbing with a leather-covered pad or with a hard roller of leather or rubber. Next, the plate is usually smoked by passing the waxed face over a flame; this produces a shiny black surface which makes the drawn lines easier to see.

The design is drawn freely through the hardened ground, the artist using any instrument capable of penetrating the wax mixture and exposing the metal underneath. Specialized etching needles are available; alternatively these can be improvised from nails, pins, or even old dentists' tools.

When the design has been drawn through the ground, the prepared plate is submerged in a bath of acid solution. The acid acts only on the unprotected areas exposed by the drawing needles. Before this, however, the back and edges of the plate must be coated with a protective varnish (some ready-treated plates are now available). The acid bath is normally made of plastic or fibre-glass, and, for reasons of safety, should only be used in a well-ventilated room.

The plate is kept immersed in the solution until the lines of the design are sufficiently bitten. The time for this varies from minutes to hours. Finally, the plate is removed and washed clean.

The most commonly used metals for etching

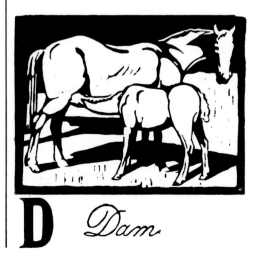

D *Dam*

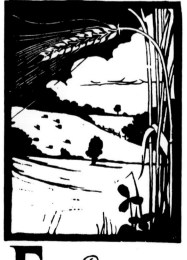

E *Ear*

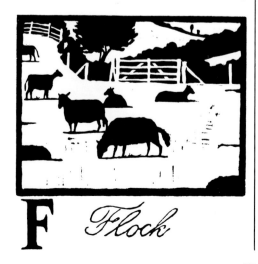

F *Flock*

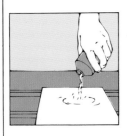

Making an etching
1. The etching plate is cleaned with ammonia which is rubbed over the plate and then rinsed and wiped off.

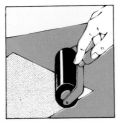

2. The clean plate is placed on a hot surface and wax is applied with a roller to the centre of the plate and rolled evenly over the surface.

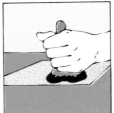

3. The wax, which should be applied as thinly as possible, is further smoothed over the surface with a rounded pad to cover any tiny holes.

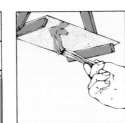

4. The plate is then hung waxed side down in a holder and smoked with tallow tapers. This hardens the surface, making it acid-resistant.

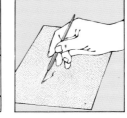

5. The waxed side of the plate is laid on a work-top and the design is drawn into the wax with an etching needle or sharp instrument.

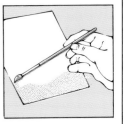

6. The plate is then propped up to prevent dirt settling on the etched side and the back is varnished to protect it from the acid.

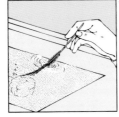

7. The plate is now put in an acid bath image side up and kept immersed in the solution until the lines of the design are sufficiently bitten.

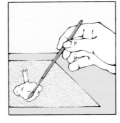

8. As the acid bites, the bubbles which form should be wiped off with a feather. The plate is then removed, washed and dried with blotting paper.

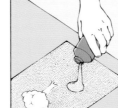

To make a lift ground
1. The design is drawn on the plate using a mixture of sugar, water and any water soluble paint for colouring.

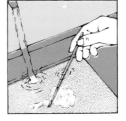

2. The plate is then spread with a solution of varnish thinned out with turpentine. This should be spread evenly and then allowed to dry.

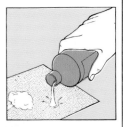

3. The plate is now immersed in warm water and brushed so that the varnish coating flakes away. This area is then aquatinted.

4. After putting the plate in an acid bath, it is taken out after the required length of time. The varnish is then removed with turpentine.

are copper, zinc and steel, usually in sixteen or eighteen gauge. Copper bites slowly giving a precise line, and is especially suitable for fine work. It can also be used for engraving. Zinc bites quickly and deeply; it is a soft metal, so corrections can be easily made with a burnisher or scraper, but very delicate tones wear down quickly. It is, however, much cheaper than copper and particularly suitable for making colour prints.

There are three principal mordants or etching solutions – nitric acid, hydrochloric acid and perchloride of iron. The strength of the acid solution is varied according to the process and metal involved. For example, copper is etched in a solution comprising one part acid to two parts water and zinc in one part acid to eight parts water.

Nitric acid is used for copper, zinc and steel etching. It is a 'rough' acid that eats wide and deep, and, unless care is taken, often bites in a fine, ragged line. This is because, as it acts, the acid causes small gas bubbles to collect on the exposed lines. These must be regularly removed with a feather to ensure that the biting is even.

When mixed with a small saturated solution of potassium chlorate, hydrochloric acid is known as Dutch mordant. This is mainly used on copper. Dutch mordant has a slow, accurate action, biting straight down to produce a fine, precise line. This makes it ideal for delicate work. Perchloride of iron has a similar effect, but, during etching, it leaves a deposit of iron in the lines. To avoid this, the plate should be placed face-downwards on small blocks in the acid bath so that the sediment will fall out.

Some printmakers prefer to draw the darker lines of the design first and etch them for a period before adding the lighter lines and biting both together. Others draw the entire design before

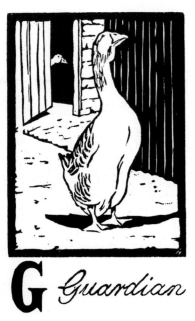

G *Guardian*

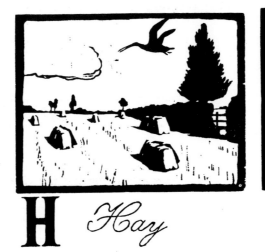

H *Hay*

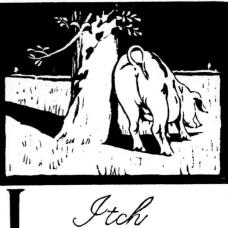

I *Itch*

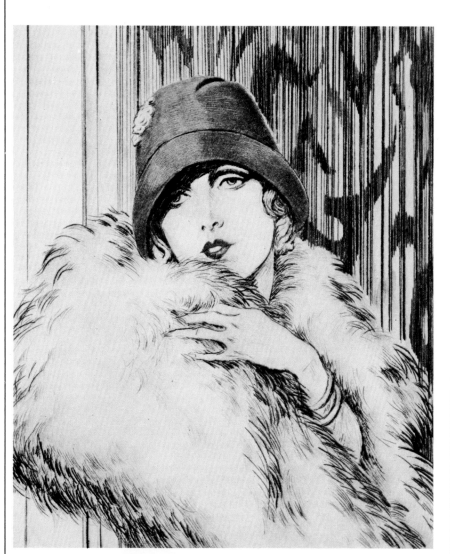

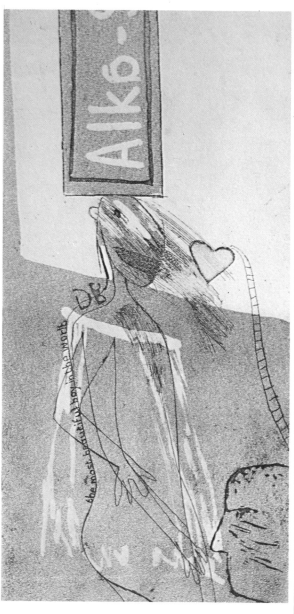

Above Frank Martin *Vilma Banky* This drypoint engraving produced on one plate did not use acid.

Right This etching by David Hockney shows a modern use of this technique. In etching acids give varying effects as they 'bite' differently.

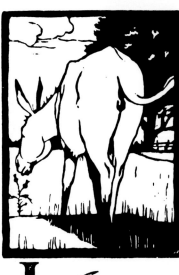

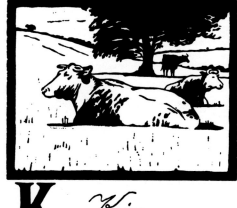

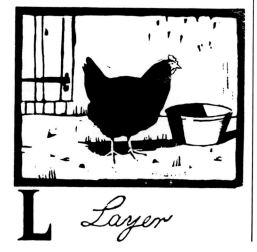

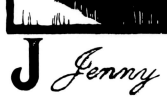 **J** *Jenny*

K *Kine*

L *Layer*

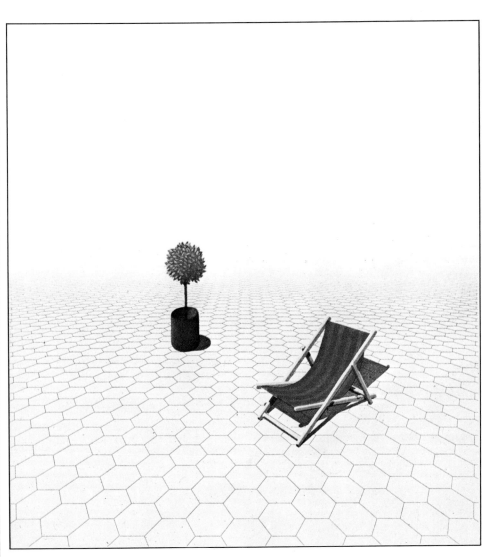

Above Phillip Solly *Endless Summer* This aquatint by a contemporary British artist illustrates the way in which fine detail and simple design can be given dramatic quality through the tonal effects that aquatinting can produce. To achieve this stark but subtle and evocative image the artist used three plates and three colours

submerging the plate. After the first biting, the finer lines are stopped out with varnish. The process is then repeated several times, the strongest lines being etched for the longest time. When the plate is finally removed from the bath; it is washed in water to remove all acid.

Soft ground

Materials, tools, techniques The technique of soft ground etching is similar to that of hard ground. The chief difference is in the nature of the ground itself – soft ground contains beeswax and grease and never hardens. When various textures are pressed into this they leave a corresponding impression exposed on the metal. The textural possibilities of soft ground etching are virtually infinite. Soft, chalky lines can be created by drawing on the plate in the conventional way, using a hard pencil on soft paper. Rubbings, textiles, string or crushed paper can all produce very interesting effects. They are pressed into the soft ground by being placed on a prepared plate, then passed through the press under reduced pressure. The plate is then etched in the same way as used in hard ground etching.

Aquatint

Aquatint is the most common way of creating tonal qualities in a print. It can produce a wide range of effects, from the fineness of a wash drawing to the coarse texture of sandpaper. **Materials, tools, techniques** To prepare an aquatint, the plate is first dusted with powdered resin. This is done either with an aquatint box, in which the resin is circulated by a fan or bellows, or by shaking a cloth bag filled with resin over the entire plate, or certain areas of the surface. The plate is then heated on a hot plate until the resin becomes transparent and melts into mi-

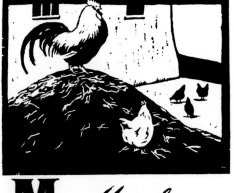

M *Much*

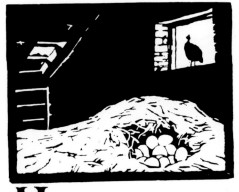

N *Nest*

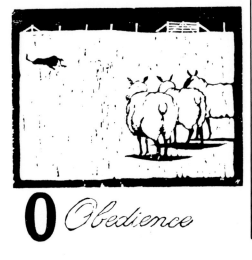

O *Obedience*

nute drops; alternatively a wire rack and gas can be used. When the plate is immersed in the acid bath, the acid bites in the unprotected spaces between the melted resin. Different effects of texture and tone can be achieved by controlling the amount of resin and the time allowed for etching.

Sugar aquatint

Unlike ordinary aquatint, where the negative areas are stopped out, the sugar lift ground technique enables the positive image of a brush stroke to be etched into the plate. The commonest mixture used for the lift medium is a saturated sugar solution dissolved in an equal quantity of poster paint. The plate is prepared with a resin ground before drawing with the solution. Then a diluted stop-out varnish is thinly painted over the plate, which when dry, is placed in water. The sugar dissolves and lifts off the varnish, leaving the metal exposed in the drawn areas. Alternatively the solution can be drawn directly on to the bare plate, and the resin ground is laid only after the lift ground is dissolved.

Printing In the printing process, dampened paper is placed on the engraved plate. It is then covered with specially made resilient blankets and rolled through the press. Here it is subjected to heavy, even pressure, which forces the damp paper into the crevices to transfer the image.

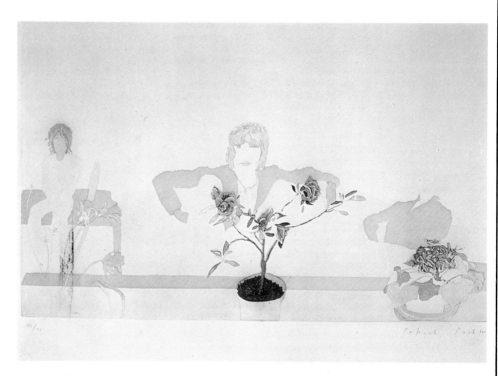

Below Fine detail, as in this Stanley Spencer monochrome lithograph, is one of the varied effects lithography can produce

Above right The remarkable delicacy of this aquatint by Patrick Procktor demonstrates the technique's versatility

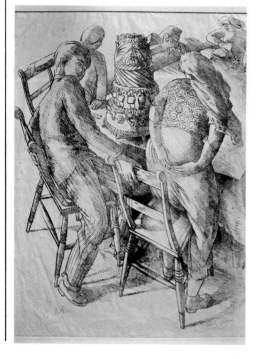

Lithography

Lithography is the name given to the process of printing chemically from stone plates to produce planographic or flat-surface images. The first experiments in lithography took place in the early 1780s, but the perfection of the technique is usually attributed to the German Alois Senefelder, in 1798. At first, the discovery was used mainly for ordinary printing purposes, but its potential for original art work soon became apparent, as the prepared surface is sensitive to a variety of crayons, inks and washes, making it an ideal artistic medium. The first artists to discover these qualities were Goya (1746–1828) and Honoré Daumier (1808–1897); other famous practitioners include Toulouse-Lautrec (1864–1901), Edouard Vuillard (1868–1940), and Pierre Bonnard (1867–1947). Their developments, in turn, prepared the way for many modern artists such as Matisse, Braque and Picasso.

Materials, tools, techniques The lithographic process operates on the principle that grease and water do not mix. The image is drawn with a grease-based material on the flat surface of the plate or stone. Bavarian limestone is traditionally used because it is hard but porous, so the surface retains moisture for long periods. Lithographs can also be made on zinc and aluminium plates; this method is now more commonly used than stone, particularly for commercial printing, because it is cheaper and more convenient.

When the design has been drawn, the surface is lightly etched, so that only the drawing will attract the printing ink. The etch is not used to bite the plate, as in intaglio, but to fix the drawn and undrawn areas of the surface chemically.

Because of the reliance on the controlled rejection of water by grease, it is essential that the working area should be clean and not too hot. The artist must also take care no to touch the surface with the hands; a simple precaution is to protect the margins with gum arabic.

To prepare the surface, the stone must first be ground. Either a levigator (a flat metal disc with an upright handle) is used, or another stone; the fine drawing surface is obtained by working upwards from coarse grades of carborundum or grit to finer textured grades. Preliminary drawings can be made on the stone with a red Conté pencil, which will not print; or they can be traced through paper coated with red oxide.

Almost any greasy product can be used for drawing as long as it will reject water. The most common are lithographic pencils, crayons – various grades are available ranging from very soft to very hard – and ink. The best results are achieved by slowly building up the tone, starting with a hard crayon, and gradually progressing to the softer grades.

Ink can be obtained in both liquid and solid form. Solid, stick ink is mixed by rubbing the stick against a warmed dish or saucer until it is soft. It can then be mixed with distilled water to the consistency initially required and further diluted to create very fine washes. Mixing the ink with turpentine causes it to break into particles; the result is a mottled texture. The finest tones are created with an airbrush, while cruder splatter work can be done with a tooth-brush. Pen drawing is best if done with ready-mixed ink on a fine ground stone; the nib must be cleaned frequently to avoid clogging.

When the image is completed, it is dusted with French chalk to make it acid-resistant. It is then etched by applying a mixture of gum arabic and acid to the stone. The gum will fix the drawing and de-sensitize the clean surface. The strength of the etch solution depends on the type of image required – the more greasy the drawing medium the stronger the etch solution will need to be. A weak solution consists of ten drops of Nitric acid to one ounce of gum arabic; at the other end of the scale, the strongest solution is made in proportions of thirty to one.

When the coating of etch and gum is ab-solutely dry, the mixture is washed from the stone with a wet sponge. While the stone is still wet, the drawing is washed out with turpentine, the untouched gum acting as a protective covering. The grease image remains clearly visible on the clean stone.

Printing A simple cast-iron press is traditionally used to print lithographs directly from plates or stones. The first stage in printing is to place the stone on the bed of the press, ready for inking. The image must be regularly and evenly spon-ged during this part of the process so that it stays damp. If it is allowed to dry out, the ink will form a scum on the drawing when the stone is rolled. The inking roller consists of a padded wooden cylinder covered with leather or plastic, which is loaded with stiff ink and rolled lightly, but briskly, over the stone. The process of inking the roller, damping the stone and rolling up is repeated several times, until the image develops to the strength of the original drawing. When the stone has been inked a sheet of dampened printing paper is laid on it. The best paper for lithographic printing is soft-surfaced but robust; four recommended all-purpose papers are Rives, Arches, Crisbrook and Barcham Green.

Before the actual printing begins, the paper is covered with a protective padding of newsprint.

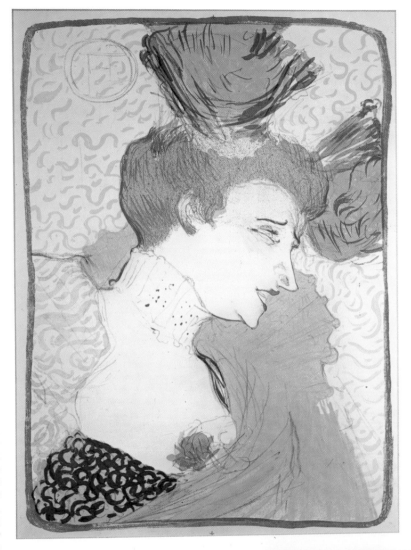

Above Henri de Toulouse-Lautrec *Aux Ambassadeurs* This coloured lithograph, like so many of Lautrec's lithographic poster designs, is notable for its areas of flat, often vibrant colour and its dramatic but simplified line.

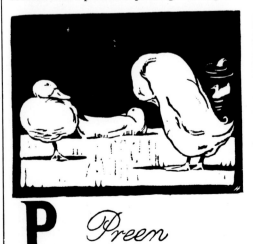

P *Preen*

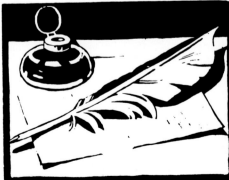

Q *Quill*

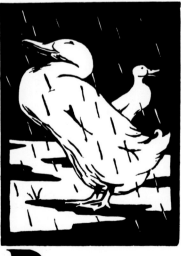

R *Rain*

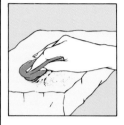

Making a lithograph
1. The lithographic stone, which is a porous stone with a flat smooth surface which will retain a fine grain, is first wiped with French chalk.

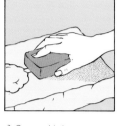

2. Gum arabic is then applied to the stone with a sponge, after which the stone is wiped with a rag and allowed to dry. The gum fixes the drawing on the clean surface.

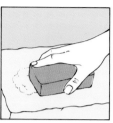

3. The stone is next washed with water and turpentine so that chalk and ink are removed. The greasy image is clearly visible and will pick up the printing ink.

4. While the stone is still damp the ink is applied with a roller, which is loaded with stiff ink, and rolled lightly but briskly over the stone. The ink adheres to the grease.

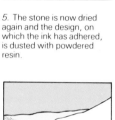

5. The stone is now dried again and the design, on which the ink has adhered, is dusted with powdered resin.

6. The stone is again dusted over with French chalk, as in step 1. This makes the image acid-resistant.

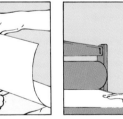

7. For erasing use a snakestone — a stick made of pumice and rubber — with some water. Another method is to scrape errors out with a scalpel.

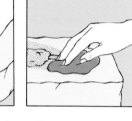

8. The gum is then washed off and the old ink removed with turpentine. The stone is then washed clean.

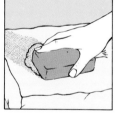

9. The process of applying gum arabic to the stone with a sponge is repeated, as in step 2.

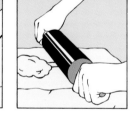

10. Wash the gum off, remove the old ink with turpentine, wash the stone clean. Apply fresh ink with the roller while the stone is still damp.

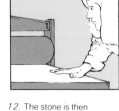

11. Printing paper — soft surfaced is most suitable — is then placed on the inked-up stone, on top of which packing is laid.

12. The stone is then placed on the bed of the press and a print taken. The weight of the press should obviously not damage the stone.

Resting on its bed, the stone is cranked under the scraper, which consists of a strong piece of wood covered in leather. This produces the necessary pressure and movement to transfer the image to the paper. The stone must be dampened between each printing. After the preliminary proofing, it is dried, dusted with French chalk and resin, and gummed again. When dry the work is washed out and the edition can be printed.

Accurate registration is ensured by marking the plate and then positioning the edge of the print accordingly. Alternatively, pins can be used to pierce corresponding marks on the print and the stone.

Colour lithographs are produced by the same printing method as monochrome ones. An impression is first taken on transfer paper so that the design can be reproduced on several separate stones, according to the number of colours required – although, in practice, it is not always necessary to use a new stone for each colour. Inked impressions from other surfaces, such as engraved plates, wood blocks, and rubbings, can be transferred for printing in the same way.

Metal plate lithography The principles of metal plate lithography are the same as those for stone printing, but the processing procedure is different. The drawing is processed with a variety of special commercial plate etches, such as Victory etch. The chief materials used for the metal plate process are zinc and aluminium. The main advantages are that the plates are light and easily stored, but the metal surface is very sensitive and susceptible to damage and scratching. Metal plates can be printed by a hand press, like stone, or by offset press. Offset is a commercial method of lithography, in which the image is first transferred from the plate to a rubber roller, and then applied to the paper.

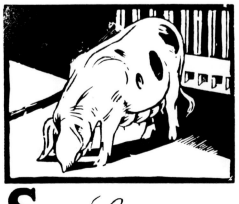

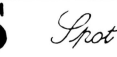
S *Spot*

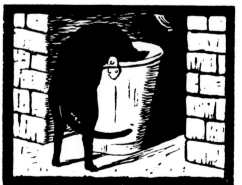
T *Thief*

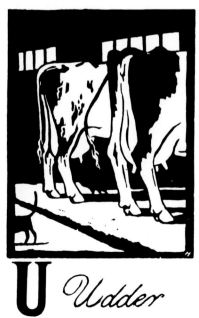
U *Udder*

Screenprinting

In its present form, silkscreen is the most recent development among the main printmaking processes. Although stencil printing was used as an art form by the Chinese and Japanese centuries ago, its later use in the West was largely as a commercial process; the first patents for it were taken out in England in 1907.

Silkscreen is a versatile technique. It is suitable for almost any surface, including metal, ceramics and many types of plastic. The first recognition of its potential, which was to culminate in the development of the stencil process into a fine art medium, probably came in the USA in the 1930s. This was the period of the Great Depression, when the relative cheapness of equipment and materials required for silkscreen gave it an advantage over other, more costly forms of printing. Many contemporary artists, such as Andy Warhol (born 1930), Robert Rauschenberg (born 1925), and Roy Lichtenstein (born 1923), have experimented with elements of silkscreen in their work. New concepts and techniques have evolved with the advent of the photostencil process and the development of new materials.

Materials, tools, techniques Screenprinting operates on the principle of forcing ink through a stencil, which is fixed to a mesh screen, tightly stretched on a frame. The frame can be made of hardwood or metal, but it must be strong enough not to bend or warp under pressure. Several different fabrics can be used for the screen, including silk, nylon and Terylene; artificial fibres have now largely replaced natural ones. The type of image eventually produced depends on the fabric chosen – the finer the mesh, the finer the image.

The stencil, which is the 'pattern' for the finished print, can be of paper or any other ink-resistant material. Paper stencils are the easiest and cheapest to make. They can consist simply

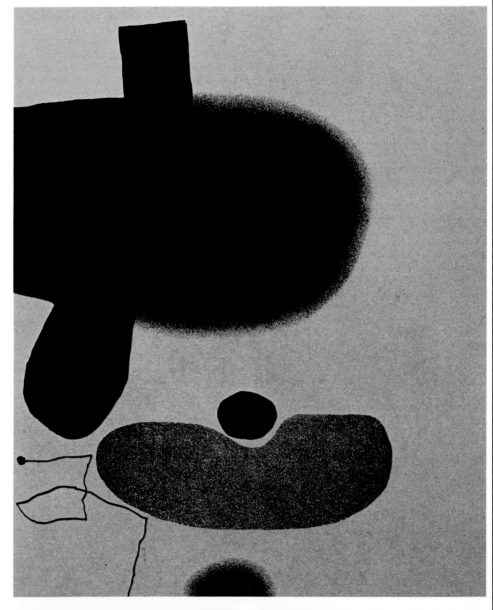

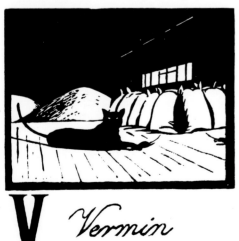

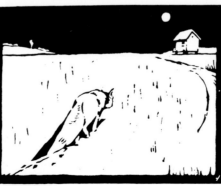

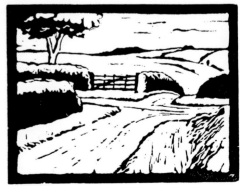

V *Vermin*

W *Wicked*

X *Cross-road*

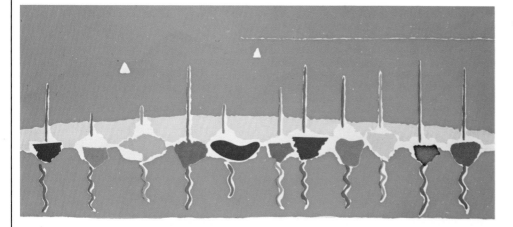

Left Victor Pasmore *Points of Contact — No. 20* This screenprint by one of Britain's leading abstract artists illustrates the subtle but seemingly simple juxtaposition of design and colour that can be achieved by the use of this printing process. Most leading modern artists have experimented with this technique in one or other of its forms.

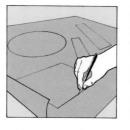

Making a screenprint
1. Place the stencil film (autocut) over the design and cut through the top layer with a scalpel.

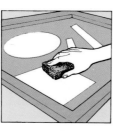

2. A screen is then laid on top of the cut film and wiped with a damp sponge so that the film sticks to the mesh.

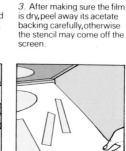

3. After making sure the film is dry, peel away its acetate backing carefully, otherwise the stencil may come off the screen.

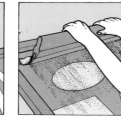

4. To make a print the paper is placed under the screen and printing ink is poured over an area at the edge of the screen.

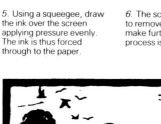

5. Using a squeegee, draw the ink over the screen applying pressure evenly. The ink is thus forced through to the paper.

6. The screen is then raised to remove the print. To make further prints the process is repeated.

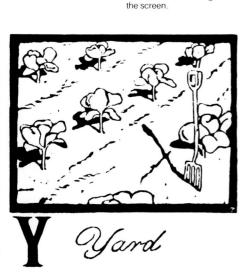

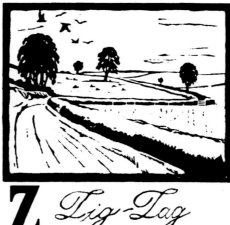

of torn or cut paper fixed beneath the screen, though manufactured hand cut pre-coated stencils, such as Hydro amber, can be used if more precise edges are required. The stencil is cut with a very sharp stencil knife, extreme care being taken not to penetrate the acetate backing. As soon as it is cut, those areas through which the ink will pass are peeled off. The cut stencil is then attached to the underside of the screen.

Another simple stencil can be produced by using gum arabic. Here the image is drawn directly on to the mesh with a wax or oil-based crayon. Otherwise stop-out varnish or lithographic ink can be applied with a brush. The screen is then coated with gum arabic. When this is dry, the drawing can be washed out with universal screen wash or turpentine, leaving a clear image through which the ink can pass.

Printing To print silkscreen, printing ink is forced through the mesh by the action of a rubber-bladed squeegee – or similar tool – which is loaded with ink and drawn across the screen. The stencil blocks the ink from certain areas, and so the image is transferred to the paper. It is important that the mesh does not touch the paper on the table until the squeegee presses down to make the print. To ensure precise registration, a piece of acetate is fixed to the table, and a proof taken on to this. Then the printing paper is placed under the acetate beneath the image, and its position is marked with masking tape.

After the proofing of each print, the squeegee is pushed back over the screen and flooded with fresh ink. This prevents ink drying in the mesh. Both matt and gloss inks can be used; a wide variety is avilable, and the final effects produced can range from opaque to highly transparent.

Photostencils The introduction of the photo-stencil method has even further extended the possibilities of contemporary screen printing. The artist first makes a film positive by printing on to film instead of paper. Otherwise a drawing on drafting film can be used. This is then transferred to the photostencil film by exposure to ultraviolet light in an exposure frame. This method operates by using light-hardened gelatine.

In direct stencil printing, the film positive or drawing is transferred directly to the pre-sensitized screen. This is done by exposing the film, image or drawing, in direct contact with the mesh in an exposure frame.

CHAPTER FIVE

TECHNICAL ILLUSTRATION

Skilled technical illustration has developed into a precise art largely through the immense demands that advancing technology has made on it over the centuries. Nothing speaks so clearly as a detailed and accurate drawing. It transcends the barriers of language; it can explain at a glance, or in a few moments' study, far more than literally pages of words.

Both the Romans and the ancient Greeks used carefully calculated drawings to guide the masons who built their precisely engineered palaces and temples. Bas-reliefs, carved into the tombs and pyramids of the ancient Egyptians, are also a kind of technical illustration – a stone record of how these famous monuments were built.

The Renaissance and the Industrial Revolution put new premiums on the skills of the technical artist. Deft use of the pencil and thoroughly competent ability to sketch are vital. The technical artist must also confine his or her talents within much stricter disciplines than the landscape painter – he or she must draw only what can be seen and they must both be able to see it accurately in the first place. This skill of observation, the power to see something exactly as it is, is as vital to the technical artist as the skill to draw.

These two characteristics dominate each of the three standard classifications of technical drawing. These are on-site recording; studio reference; and orthographic reference – the three-dimensional drawing of an object within a cube.

On-site recording demands a high degree of quick observation. The artist must make a clear sketch with sufficient, adequate measurements. Ambiguity and omission must be avoided – they can lead to a costly, and possibly embarrassing, return visit.

These difficulties are greatly diminished in the studio. There, technical illustration can make use of the camera. Accurate pictures can be taken of both complete and dismantled assemblies to give a total and an exploded view of a subject. This can be done by positioning the component parts on clear glass and holding them in position with plasticene on the blind side of the camera. The resulting photographs can be used for illustrative reference to obtain a perfected technical drawing.

Orthographic projection, one of the techniques used in technical illustration, demands some skill from the artist. A complete under-

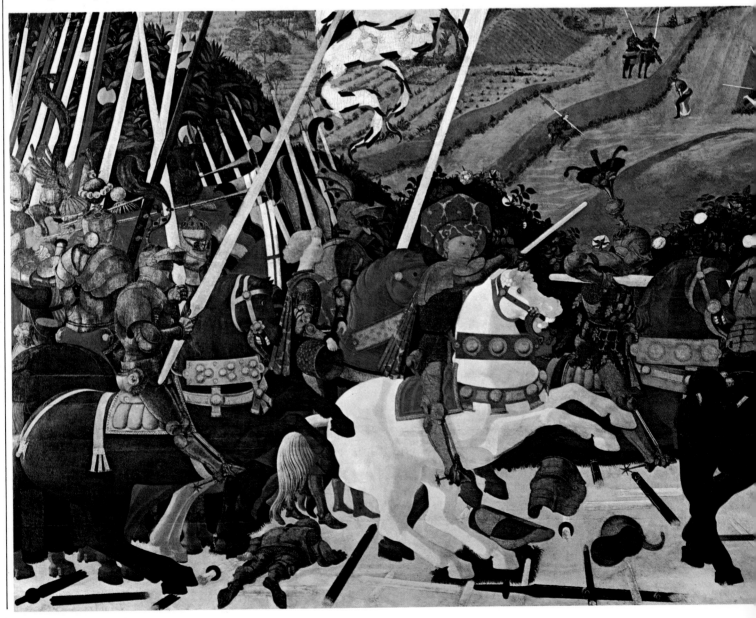

standing of angles and horizontal and vertical planes is critical. The artist must develop an ability to visualize the subject in advance as a three-dimensional projection. This can be done only by someone thoroughly familiar with projections in both first and third angles. To achieve this familiarity requires both application and experience.

Early engineering and architectural drawing
The Greeks and the artists and architects of the Classical age certainly knew the values and the problems of technical illustration. The precise 'order' of the columns in their buildings was based on exact mathematical calculation and certainly required some form of written or drawn instruction. They also knew about perspective and the truth that objects in the distance

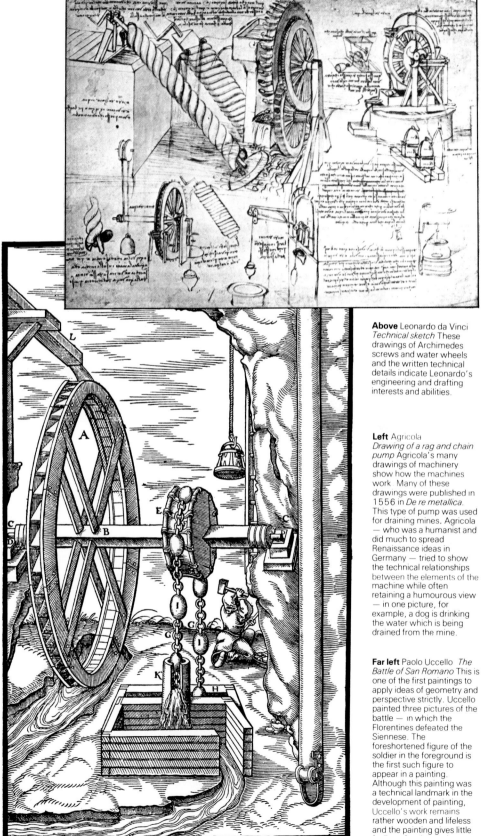

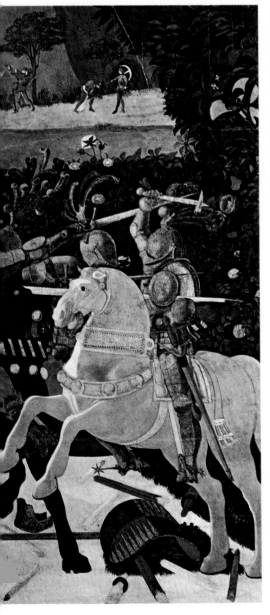

Above Leonardo da Vinci *Technical sketch* These drawings of Archimedes screws and water wheels and the written technical details indicate Leonardo's engineering and drafting interests and abilities.

Left Agricola *Drawing of a rag and chain pump* Agricola's many drawings of machinery show how the machines work. Many of these drawings were published in 1556 in *De re metallica*. This type of pump was used for draining mines. Agricola — who was a humanist and did much to spread Renaissance ideas in Germany — tried to show the technical relationships between the elements of the machine while often retaining a humourous view — in one picture, for example, a dog is drinking the water which is being drained from the mine.

Far left Paolo Uccello *The Battle of San Romano* This is one of the first paintings to apply ideas of geometry and perspective strictly. Uccello painted three pictures of the battle — in which the Florentines defeated the Siennese. The foreshortened figure of the soldier in the foreground is the first such figure to appear in a painting. Although this painting was a technical landmark in the development of painting, Uccello's work remains rather wooden and lifeless and the painting gives little feeling of action or drama.

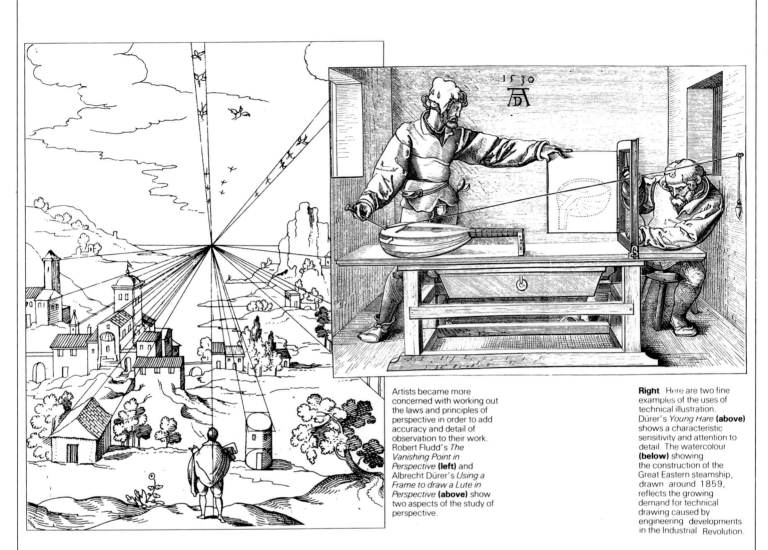

Artists became more concerned with working out the laws and principles of perspective in order to add accuracy and detail of observation to their work. Robert Fludd's *The Vanishing Point in Perspective* (**left**) and Albrecht Dürer's *Using a Frame to draw a Lute in Perspective* (**above**) show two aspects of the study of perspective.

Right Here are two fine examples of the uses of technical illustration. Dürer's *Young Hare* (**above**) shows a characteristic sensitivity and attention to detail. The watercolour (**below**) showing the construction of the Great Eastern steamship, drawn around 1859, reflects the growing demand for technical drawing caused by engineering developments in the Industrial Revolution.

should be drawn smaller than objects in the foreground. Vitruvius, writing in about 46 BC in the only Latin treatise on architecture to survive, bears witness to this, as he mentions that perspective was well understood at an early date. But the mathematical rules that govern perspective were not, for there was no rational order in the diminishing size of such distant objects.

Artists had to wait another 1400 years to find the secret of perspective. Its discovery was to revolutionize art and transform the work of the technical illustrator. The mathematical means to work out the ratio at which objects decrease in size as they recede into the background was discovered by Filippo Brunelleschi (1377–1446), one of the great Florentine architects of the Renaissance period. One artist instantly influenced by Brunelleschi's theories was Paolo Uccello (1397–1475). In his famous battle scene – the Battle of S. Romano – painted in about 1450, Uccello applied geometry to his design. In the foreground, he painted a dead soldier, the first foreshortened body to appear in a painting. However, there is something wooden about Uccello's work: he had not mastered

another vital technique of the technical artist – the use of light and shade, which is so important in emphasizing depth and space.

Leonardo da Vinci (1452–1519) was not only an artistic genius but probably the most prolific technical illustrator of the Renaissance. He left volumes of notes and sketches, including a detailed exploded drawing of a weight-driven motor, one of the earliest surviving examples of this device. It spells out its message and detail clearly and simply in a way that is still used today and is far easier to follow than Georgius Agricola's sectional breakdown of the parts of a chain and dipper pump which appeared in *De re metallica* in 1556.

Albrecht Dürer (1471–1528) meticulously used the new technique of perspective to add detail and accuracy of observation to his work. His explicit portrayal of a hare, painted in 1502, is an object lesson to the on-site technical illustrator. Nothing has been missed. Not even a camera could have been more truthful.

In the Low Countries, Jan Vredeman de Vries (1527–1604) built up architectural drawings following the lines of perspective to the ultimate

vanishing point, tracing in cross-hatches of horizontal and diagonal lines. But it was Samuel Marolois in his book on perspective in 1629, who first put forward the idea of perspective grids and set technical artists on the exciting trail that led to modern perspective drawing.

These ideas, brilliantly developed by the architects of the European Renaissance, were to find new expression in the Industrial Revolution. The development of metal engraving created a new medium for fine line reproduction. The improved skills and knowledge of the artist were quickly used to feed the growing demands for technical illustration in the eighteenth century. The growth of increasingly complex and diverse engineering requirements called for more and more technical drawings; these meant that artists had to look inside their subjects as well as around them – as Leonardo had done two centuries earlier with human anatomy.

The technical complexities demanded of the illustrator have never been greater than they are today in this age of the space machine and electronics. The skills required, however, are still the basic trademarks of the past masters – the ability to observe and to sketch accurately.

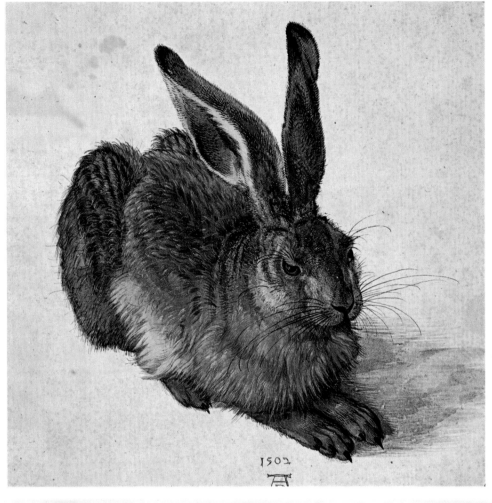

Equipment

Even the most skilful technician needs the proper tools to do the job. An extensive variety of equipment is available, though not all of it is essential. Always choose the best tools you can afford and look after them carefully.

Pencils These are essential. For most technical work the artist will need at least the following grades – 2B, HB, 2H, 4H, 6H and 9H – though individual needs will naturally vary. Test your own work using the various grades to see which suit you best. Many people are quite happy with the traditional wooden, graphite pencils, but these need constant sharpening and get shorter and shorter. Some artists prefer the mechanical type, consisting of a holder, with a chuck or claw to grip the lead. These do, at least, keep constant height.

Always keep the point of a pencil correctly sharpened. There are two types of point – needle and wedge. A needle point is created by rubbing on a sanding block or sanding pad holder, keeping the shaft and holder rotating between the fingers while rubbing. A wedge is made by holding the shaft or holder at the required angle and rubbing along the sander to form a chisel edge on one side. The lead is then rotated through 180 degrees and the rubbing is continued until that side meets the other to form the wedge shape.

It is a good idea to keep the surface graphite powder left as a deposit on a sander after pencils have been sharpened. This can be tapped off into a small container with a lid and can be used later with cotton wool to apply a tonal effect.

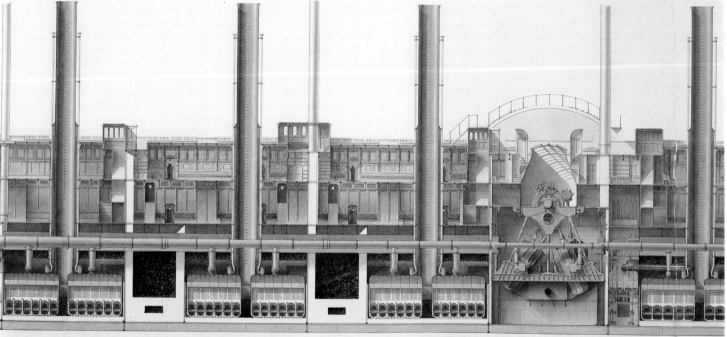

Set squares (triangles) The best set squares are made from clear flexible plastic. One should have angles of 45°–45°–90°; the other, angles of 30°–60°–90°. The largest side should not measure less than 40cm.

For convenience, accuracy and speed, the following modification can be made. Using geometric construction, draw two straight lines at 90° to each other, making sure that they cross, to give an accurate angle. Place the longest side of the set square edge to align exactly along one of the straight lines, at approximately two-thirds of the total distance. Secure the set square firmly with masking tape. Take a metal type scale, or some other suitable straight edge, and carefully align it along one edge of the other line at right angles and tape this firmly in place, too.

Take a stylus needle or another suitable scribing tool and score a groove, taking care not to make it too deep, into the surface of the set square. Remove the masking tape to release the set square and fill the groove by cross-rubbing with a red pencil crayon. Clean the set square by removing any smears left on the surface by cross-rubbing with a cleaning pad.

Compass and dividers Choose a compass with a pencil or pen attachment for drawing arcs and circles. Some compasses have a second point to enable them to be used as dividers. For work on a larger scale, a beam compass is essential. This has two points that can be moved, then screwed tight to any point of a beam. This instrument can give much wider arcs and circles than the simple bow-type compass.

Scales Measuring scales are invaluable to a technical artist. They have two basic functions, the first being the measurement of distances and the second the translation of dimensional units to a required drawing size.

Metal scales are more durable, but high quality cardboard scales, carefully handled, are adequate. Diagonal scales are essential when divisions prove minute. It is normal practice to dispense with the isometric scale.

Trimetric scales, however, are essential for trimetric projection. Apart from perspective, the use of this technique produces a closer resemblance to the visual form than any other. It also has the following technical advantages. Firstly, the choice of view can be varied by rotating and mirroring the vectors. Secondly, all dimensions are to scale. Thirdly integrated, cutaway and exploded views can be produced from a single preparation.

Drafting machines These are standard equipment in most drawing offices. Design details vary from make to make, but basically they all function in the same way. The drafting head can be moved to any part of the drawing board surface either by swing-arm movement, or horizontal and vertical motion. The head, or central control unit, has two scales at right angles to each other. They can be set at any degree between zero of either vertical or horizontal.

The Perspect-o-metric, produced in the USA, is a conversion attachment, designed to fit any standard drafting head. The centre scale remains constant, and at right angles to the horizontal. The other two scales (left and right) remain in line with their vanishing points.

The Centrolinead is a machine for drawing vanishing lines of perspective when these are too distant to fit into the drawing board surface. The machine consists of a ruler with two adjustable arms fixed to it. It is operated by placing two pins on one side of the board – one above the horizon line, one below. The adjustable lines are placed against the pins, so that the whole machine forms a shape like the letter Y. The inside edges of both arms can be moved against the pins, producing along the edge of the ruler radiating lines to a distant vanishing point. The position of the pins and the angles of the two arms will determine the degree of divergence of the vanishing lines.

Scalloped (perspective) drawing board Devised by three Californian technical artists, this board has three centrolinead arcs or scallops cut into it. Printed or mounted on the board are the three co-ordinates, each with scaled, diminishing perspective increments.

The Medigraph This works on the same principle as the Perspect-o-metric, but it does not need the support of a drafting head or parallel motion. Two spools are mounted on pivots at the end of two adjustable horizontal arms. The pivot pins act as perspective vanishing points, and each spool contains a spring-loaded steel ribbon, which keeps the foreshortening scales under tension.

Perspector Universal Drafting Machine This machine, still in use but no longer manufactured, provides isometric views at a scale of 0.816. The machine uses a double pantograph mechanism attached to two drawing boards. One is fixed and has orthographic views positioned on it; the other has an isometric trace.

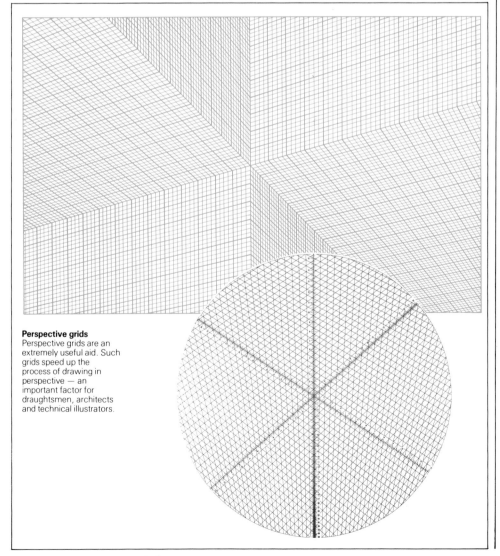

Perspective grids
Perspective grids are an extremely useful aid. Such grids speed up the process of drawing in perspective — an important factor for draughtsmen, architects and technical illustrators.

Techniques

Every artist must master the two basic techniques of technical illustration. These are firstly the expression of form by line and, secondly, shading and the use of tone to amplify lines where necessary.

Line is elemental to technical illustration; the artist must therefore have a complete grasp of this technique before embarking on the nuances of shading. It is often said, with some truth, that shading is an excuse to cover up bad drawing. It can certainly do that, but it is no substitute for an accurate line.

Isometric drawing It is easier to compare various line techniques by studying isometric drawings, since these are symmetrical without perspective, all angles are equal, and all lines are on the same scale. In isometric drawing, shape cannot be expressed through the use of perspective but only by the use of light or dark lines.

One of the fundamental exercises in isometric drawing is to draw a cube so that three intersecting edges make equal angles with the projection plane. The symmetry of the projection will make all the angles 120° with each other. All profiles are equally foreshortened. The drawing appears distorted because the parallel lines do not recede to converge upon one another.

The nine drawings of a cube shown as illustrations - right - demonstrate the following points. In the first, each line has a constant weight and this makes the drawing ambiguous. It depends on the viewer's reactions as to whether the object is seen as a hexagonal pyramid or as a geometrical solid. In the second, ambiguity is eliminated by making some lines heavier than others. This is a geometrical solid, and the line of horizon is clearly above. In the third, the lines have been tapered, which, depending on the attitude of the viewer, may make them even more expressive of the real form. Once again the line of horizon is above. In the

Isometric drawing In isometric drawing shape is expressed only through the use of lines not through perspective shading. The nine cubes **(right)** show different ways of making an ambiguous drawing *(1, 6)* clear using weighted lines to clarify the perspective from which the cube is being viewed.

Isometric scale **(left)** A cube is placed so that three intersecting edges make equal 30° angles with a projection plane. All profiles of the cube are equally foreshortened. To use the isometric scale, draw a full size scale at 45° to a base line and the isometric scale at 30°. Drop a perpendicular from the full size scale to the bottom line. The correct point on the isometric scale is where the perpendicular intersects the 30° line.

Oblique perspective **(far left)** This uses the 45° angle. The front face of the cube remains in full scale, the side dimension is foreshortened by reducing it by half. This is done by dropping a perpendicular from the hypotenuse of the triangle, which meets the base line at 45°.

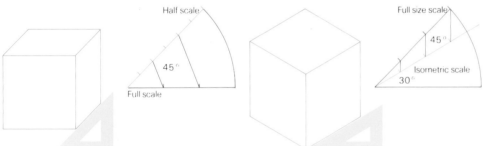

Half scale
45°
Full scale

Full size scale
45°
Isometric scale
30°

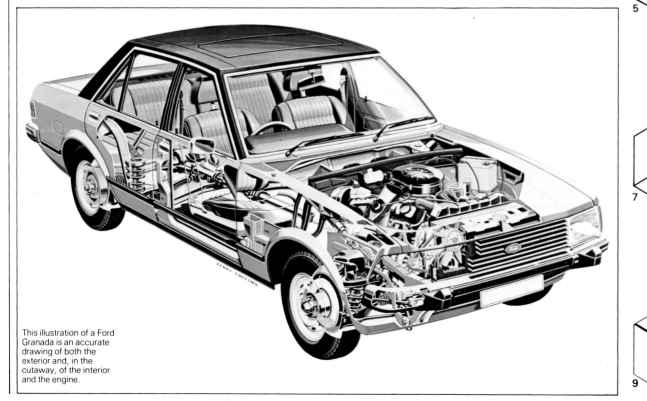

This illustration of a Ford Granada is an accurate drawing of both the exterior and, in the cutaway, of the interior and the engine.

fourth, the line treatment is the same as in the second drawing, but the line of horizon is below. In the fifth, the line treatment is the same as in the third drawing, but the line of horizon is below.

The sixth cube is again ambiguous, as all lines have the same weight value. It is therefore not clear whether you are looking down on something, or up at a ceiling. So, too, is the seventh cube. It is now impossible for the viewer to tell whether he or she is looking up at the underside of a cube or down at the floor. In the eighth cube, the drawing is transformed by the different values of line thickness – the light source is clearly from the left – while in the ninth the heavy lines give the clear impression of looking down into a box.

Circles in isometric All drawings, whether in perspective or isometric, rely on accuracy in interpretation and neatness of the finished line for acceptability. A normal circle, must always be seen as a true ellipse. Because arcs, curves and circles constitute a major part of any technical drawing, it is thus important that they should be constructed correctly.

Isometric circles differ from normal ones because, though they appear elliptical, they are not really true ellipses at all. This is because they are constructed around four centres, as opposed to the normal circle's one. In the true ellipse, the major axis is slightly longer and the minor axis slightly shorter than in the isometric one.

Constructing an ellipse Ellipses can be constructed in various ways. Either purpose-built

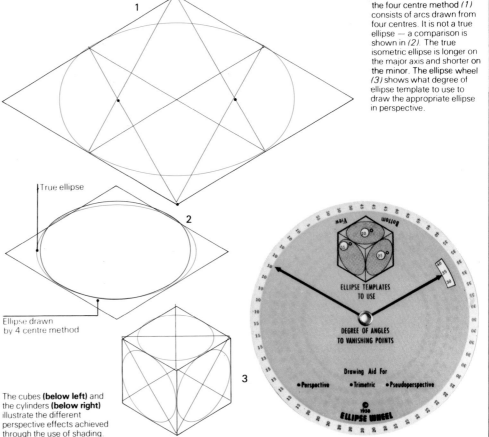

1

True ellipse

2

Ellipse drawn by 4 centre method

3

The cubes **(below left)** and the cylinders **(below right)** illustrate the different perspective effects achieved through the use of shading.

Left A circle constructed by the four centre method *(1)* consists of arcs drawn from four centres. It is not a true ellipse — a comparison is shown in *(2)*. The true isometric ellipse is longer on the major axis and shorter on the minor. The ellipse wheel *(3)* shows what degree of ellipse template to use to draw the appropriate ellipse in perspective.

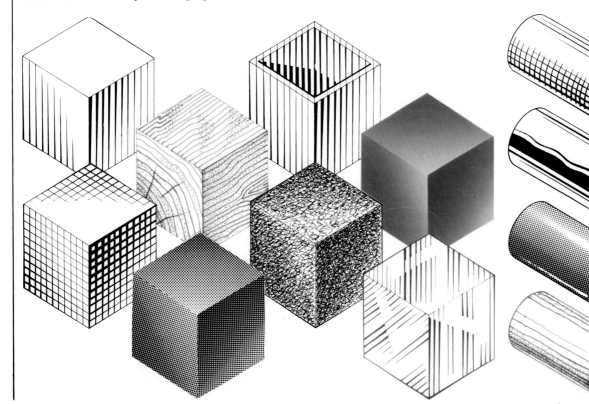

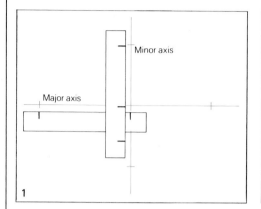

Major axis

Minor axis

1

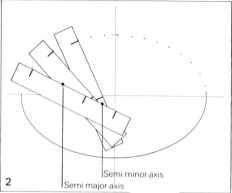

Semi minor axis

Semi major axis

2

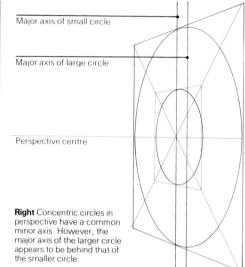

Major axis of small circle

Major axis of large circle

Perspective centre

Right Concentric circles in perspective have a common minor axis. However, the major axis of the larger circle appears to be behind that of the smaller circle.

Constructing a circle using the trammel method.
First construct a trammel — it is best to use the edge of a piece of paper. Then work out and mark the length of the major axis and the minor axis *(1)*. To construct the ellipse move the strip of paper keeping the inner mark in register with the major axis and the outer mark in register with the minor axis. Draw a series of points *(2)*.

instruments, such as Ellipsograph, Ruleipse or Ellipse Guide Templet (template) can be used, or, alternatively, a paper trammel. The last is by far the most convenient method, since the trammel can be made from the edge of a strip of paper.

The diagram above outlines how this is done. First establish the lengths of the major and minor axes. Then mark on the paper strip the distance equal to the semi-major axis, making sure that one of the marks on the paper coincides with the measure point of the semi-minor axis. Make a mark on the edge of the paper strip where the two axes intersect.

The ellipse is now constructed by moving the strip of paper, keeping the inner mark constantly in register with the line of the major axis and at the same time keeping the outer mark in register with the minor axis. Carefully plot a series of points as the edge of the paper is circumscribed. The more plots you make around the ends of the major axis, the greater will be the accuracy of the finished drawing.

A simple way of finding the proportionate ratios of large and smaller ellipses is to place the edge of a set square across the points of the major and minor axes. Place a straight edge or a metal scale against one of the other edges of the set square, preferably the longer edge. Hold the straight edge firmly between the fingers of one hand and slide the set square along it until it registers with the known axis. Draw a line along the edge of the set square to bisect the other axis line. You can then draw an ellipse in exact proportion to the one you started with.

Templates can also be used to draw ellipses in proportion. However, since these are usually supplied with increments of five degrees, artists are tempted to use this ratio alone. This makes the drawing suit the template, rather than the other way around. It may be easier to use a template than a trammel, but it is not always as flexible a tool. As always in drawing, accuracy is

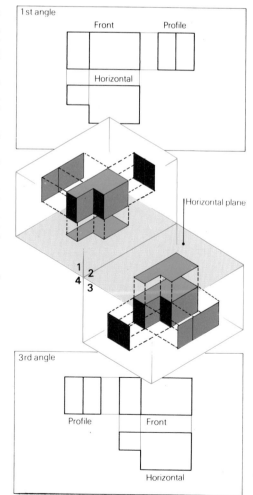

1st angle

Front

Profile

Horizontal

Horizontal plane

1 2
4 3

3rd angle

Profile

Front

Horizontal

Orthographic projection
This is a way of showing an exact shape by extending a series of rays from the object on their respective planes of vision — usually profile, front and horizontal. The planes divide space into four quadrants (1st to 4th angle).

the chief concern. Whether using a template or a trammel the ellipse values must be correct.

Orthographic Projection This is a method of representing an exact shape by dropping and extending a series of rays or projectors from the object on to their respective planes of vision. Because the point of vision is taken as being finite, all the projectors are parallel. Three planes are usually projected – front, horizontal and profile. These are generally enough to give an accurate presentation. In cases of complex subjects, the object being drawn can be surrounded by six planes as shown in the diagrams on the left.

Orthographic projection was first developed by Gaspard Monge, who was born at Beaune, France, in 1746. He was apprenticed as a draughtsman and later became a mathematics scholar.

The projection planes are indefinite and divide space into four quadrants, identified as 1st angle, 2nd angle, 3rd angle and 4th angle. All the perpendicular projections are of true length. First angle is the traditional method of orthographic projection and the one used by Monge. The projection is cast upwards from the horizontal plane. The view of the object appears as a shadow cast behind it, so that the object appears between the observer and the projectors.

Third angle is the one most commonly used in orthographic projection. In this, lines are dropped from the horizontal plane and the object is placed in the third quadrant. All the planes fall between the observer and the object.

Illustrators can produce views and diagrams in perspective solely from orthographic projections. It is essential to understand the projections and to read the angles correctly. Draughtsmen are not infallible and information can be inaccurately recorded in a mixture of first and third angles that can be totally confusing to the artist.

Airbrushing

The very first perfected airbrush was patented by the British artist Charles Burdick in 1893. Since that time, many technical improvements have been made and the airbrush of today is an extremely refined instrument. As such, it is a vital part of the technical illustrator's equipment.

With adequate practice, a skilled artist can produce a remarkable variety of light, shade and tones that fade into each other with a precision that matches the results produced by the camera. Through the use of the numerous techniques available, such as filling in and shading, comprehensive illustrations – both cutaway and exploded – can be produced.

There are many types of airbrush available, varying in type and design according to purpose and price. However, they all operate in the same way and contain the same basic parts. The principle of operation is that compressed air (at an average pressure of 30 pounds per square

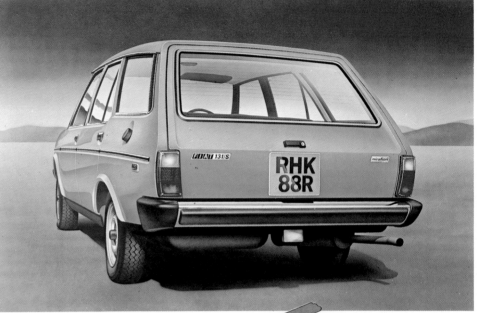

Below Ben Johnson *Bicycle* This painting by the modern British artist Ben Johnson shows the application of techniques used in technical illustration in a painting.
Right *The airbrush* All airbrushes work in very similar ways and have broadly the same construction. An airbrush for precise, intricate work has an open reservoir and small nozzle while one for larger scale work has a bigger nozzle and reservoir. The size of the nozzle is related to the rate at which air is expelled. The paint in the reservoir is at normal pressure and is mixed with the pressurized air flowing through the channel and the mixture is expelled as an atomized spray.

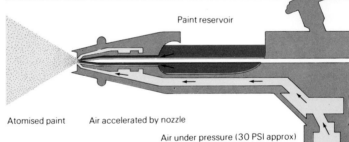

Paint reservoir

Atomised paint   Air accelerated by nozzle

Air under pressure (30 PSI approx)

Above This example of commercial air-brushing by Penny Black demonstrates the skills of the technical illustrator. The crispness of the colours could not be obtained using photography.

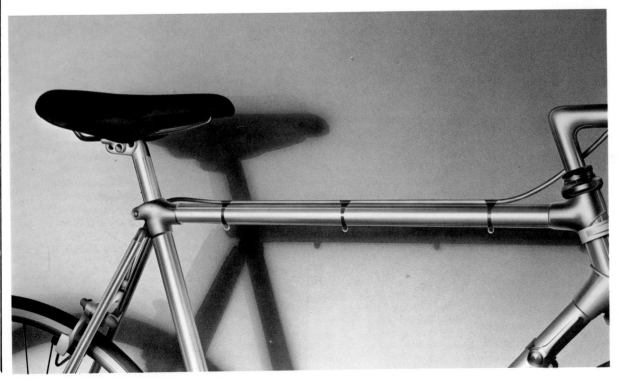

1

inch) is passed through a narrow passage, called the venturi. This opens out into a wider one, where expansion takes place to create a partial vacuum. Paint under normal atmospheric pressure flows from the reservoir to mix with the air stream and be atomized. The resultant spray is directed through a conical air cap as either a cone or a fan on to the subject being painted.

Methods of supplying the compressed air vary. Air can be obtained from an aerosol can, a foot pump, a refillable canister of the type used by divers, or an electric compressor. Though the last is expensive, it is probably the best method for the serious artist. The best compressors have a reservoir, which overcomes the problem of varying air pressures.

Airbrushes themselves are expensive to buy and therefore it is important to take care of them properly. They should be cleaned thoroughly after use. Any distortion of the shape of the air cap will alter the effect of the atomized spray. Never allow paint to congeal in the cap, reservoir, channel or orifice, as this will similarly cause malfunction. It is essential, therefore, to

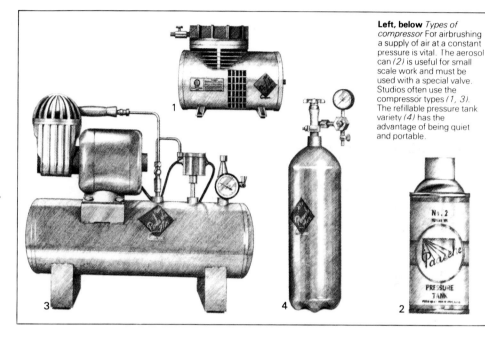

Left, below *Types of compressor* For airbrushing a supply of air at a constant pressure is vital. The aerosol can (2) is useful for small scale work and must be used with a special valve. Studios often use the compressor types (1, 3). The refillable pressure tank variety (4) has the advantage of being quiet and portable.

Airbrushing equipment Film (1) is used for masking. The can of compressed air (2) acts as the propellant for the airbrush (6). Use water (3), a bristle brush (9), tissues (5) and a special fluid (4) for cleaning. Concentrated water colours (7) can be used. A palette (8), steel rule (10) and scalpel are (11) also useful.

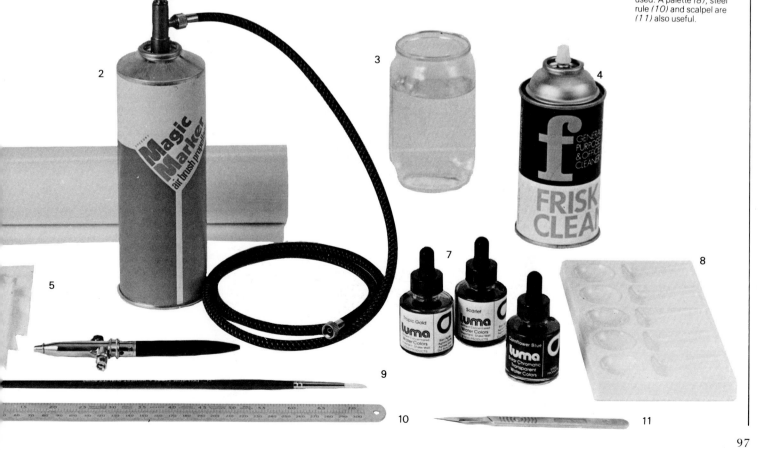

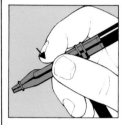
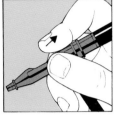
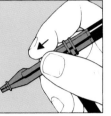

Holding the airbrush
1. To release the air, press the button with the index finger.

2. To release the paint, pull the button back.

3. To stop the flow of paint push the finger back.

4. To stop the flow of air, remove the index finger from the brush.

clean and maintain the brush according to the manufacturer's instructions, if it is to function properly.

Operating mechanisms Airbrushes operate in one of two ways – single action lever and double action lever. Single action is the simplest form of airbrush, in which the pattern of spray cannot be directly altered except by lessening or increasing the distance between the brush and the surface being sprayed. When the lever is depressed, the brush fires a mixture of air and paint in a fixed ratio; this cannot be altered except by the use of a separate adjuster. This can be fitted to the end of the airbrush to change the spray to either fine or coarse.

Though simple to maintain, this type of airbrush is only adequate for general background work. It cannot achieve the precision of detail required in more specialized artwork.

The great advantage of the double action lever is that it gives the artist the ability to control the proportions of paint to air. As the lever is depressed, it releases air, not paint, through the brush. When it is pulled backwards, paint meets the airstream; the further the lever is retracted, the greater the amount of paint that flows.

With this system, it is far easier to control and vary paint density. This makes the double action brush essential for the precision and detail required in much technical illustration.

Types Of the many types of airbrush on the market today, the following are among the best available. The Aerograph Super 63 A–504 is a double action lever model, giving precision control. It is suitable for all types of work. The Super 63 E–504 is similar to the A–504, but has a larger reservoir, so allowing a greater area to be covered in a shorter time. The Sprite is a simpler double action type and, as a consequence, is less precise if used for fine line work. The Conograph is a single action lever brush with detachable cups allowing rapid change of colour.

The Wold A1 is a double action lever brush with two air caps – one coned and one flared. It can be used successfully for work ranging from fine line rendering to broad wash tones. The Wold A2 is similar to the A1, but has an improved air cap assembly. The M type has double the capacity of the A series Wolds. It is fitted with a 1oz or 2oz jar and has interchangeable cups for quick colour changes. The K–M is single action with wheel control that predetermines spray volume. It handles large quantities of colour in a short time.

The Thayer and Chandler models AA and A are both double lever brushes. They produce fine lines and broad coverage of tones. The C type's 2oz colour capacity makes it ideal for large areas, while the E and G1 models are ideal for display artists.

The Paasche AB is a fine arts airbrush, capable of producing the finest hairline thickness or dots. It is ideally suited for freehand drawing and is also excellent for photographic retouching. The Paasche H1, H2 and H3 types are single action control lever brushes with separate controls which can be pre-adjusted for colour and air. Air caps and colour nozzles are interchangeable to provide a range from fineline to broad spray. The Paasche V1 and V2 are double action; the V1 is suitable for finer work and the V2 for medium rendering. They are both good brushes for vignetting. Each has a micrometer line adjuster giving rapid setting from very fine to broad.

The Paasche air eraser holds an abrasive instead of paint. Its fine-controlled spray can erase ink, paint and colour without smudging or streaking. It can also be used for blending highlights and shadows.

Preparing colour It is vital that the colours used in an airbrush are prepared correctly. Make sure that the pigment is not too thick and that it has been properly diluted; failure to ensure this can lead to a grainy or stippled effect on the artwork. It can also lead to the nozzle clogging; this can distort the needle action and even bend the tip – a matched nozzle set and needle is an expensive replacement. In general, the mixed paint for an

Types of airbrush
The Aerograph 63 *(1)* is a high quality medium speed instrument. The Aerograph Super E *(2)* is high speed for covering large areas. The Aerograph Sprite *(3)* is an economy model. The Thayer and Chandler Model A *(4)* is for all purpose uses. The Paasche AB *(5)* is for photo-retouching. The Paasche VL and H models *(6, 7)* have a selection of nozzles. The Paasche VI *(8)* is good for finer work. The air eraser *(9)* is also made by Paasche.

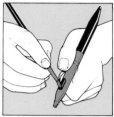

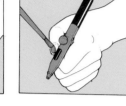

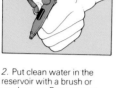

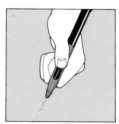

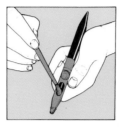

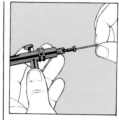

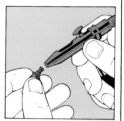

Cleaning the airbrush
1. To remove the excess paint from the reservoir, brush with a paint brush or eyedropper. Spray through what remains.

2. Put clean water in the reservoir with a brush or eyedropper. Remove any remaining paint from the side with a brush bristle.

3. Spray clean water through the airbrush. Repeat the process until all the paint has been removed.

4. Use a dry clean brush to remove excess moisture from the reservoir.

Removing the air-cap
1. Unscrew the handle, loosen the nut which locks the needle in position. Take the needle out about 25mm (1in).

2. Unscrew the air-cap and remove the nozzle.

Airbrushing effects
From **left** to **right** *fine lines* — use a ruler for this; *graded tones; blending* — for grading and blending it is best to work from lightest tone to darkest; *splatter* — a special cap can be used.

Above The airbrush A cross-section of the Aerograph Super 63 shows: *(1)* air cap guard; *(2)* air cap; *(3)* nozzle; *(4)* nozzle washer; *(5)* fluid needle; *(6)* model body assembly; *(7)* needle gland washer; *(8)* needle packing gland; *(9)* lever assembly; *(10)* cam ring; *(11)* cam; *(12)* fixing screw; *(13)* square piece; *(14)* needle spring; *(15)* needle spring box; *(16)* needle locking nut; *(17)* handle; *(18)* diaphragm nut; *(19)* diaphragm assembly; *(20)* air valve washer; *(21)* air valve stem; *(22)* air valve spring; *(23)* air valve box; *(24)* air valve spring retainer.

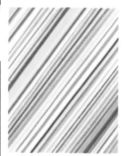

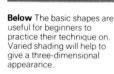

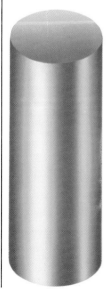

Below The basic shapes are useful for beginners to practice their technique on. Varied shading will help to give a three-dimensional appearance.

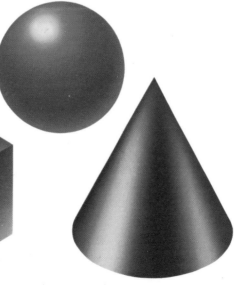

airbrush should be about the same consistency as milk.

It is sound practice to clean out the paint reservoir with a solvent every time the pigment is changed or the reservoir emptied. It is a good idea at times to hold the finger over the end of the air cap – making sure the needle is pulled back first – to help in cleaning the air cap and air cap guard. By following these simple procedures an airbrush will operate without trouble for years. Neglect, however, can cause the brush to become clogged and to malfunction very quickly.

Filling Use an eye dropper or a syringe to fill the reservoir or cup of an airbrush. Either method is suitable, but a paint brush can be used as an alternative. If a brush is chosen, make sure that the hairs are bristle or some other coarse substance – a sable brush or anything similar should not be used. This is because fine hairs can easily become detached and so block the nozzle.

After charging a brush, always wipe the outer surface dry with a clean cloth or piece of paper tissue to remove any paint on the outside. If this precaution is not followed, the paint could run down the outside of the brush, damaging the art-work.

Techniques It is sound practice for beginners to familiarize themselves with an airbrush by experimenting on basic forms prepared from orthographic planes. These are: flat plan; spherical (convex and concave); cube; pyramid (convex and concave); cylindrical (convex and concave);

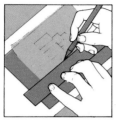

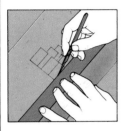

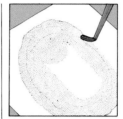

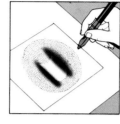

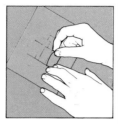

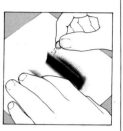

Cutting a mask
1. Put the film on the board, place a sheet of artists' carbon paper between the image and the film and trace down the image on to the film.

2. Cut the masking film using a scalpel. If the cut is too deep the surface will be scored.

3. Peel off the mask and replace it carefully on the tracing.

Using liquid mask
1. Apply masking fluid to the desired area with a brush. It is possible to draw fine lines through the fluid.

2. When the mask is dry, spray over the area and the fluid keeping the air-brush 15 to 20cm above the paper.

3. To remove the mask rub it gently and peel it off. Be careful to do this only when the paint is perfectly dry.

and conic (convex and concave). Produce as many visual variations as you can from one basic shape. This will help achieve skill and dexterity in the use of the brush.

Beginners should start by producing straight lines of varying width and vignetting. Examine artwork to see how often this technique is used.
Straight line vignetting Apply maximum air and minimum colour mixture and spray off the edge of a mask from right to left, keeping the airbrush as near right angles to the working board as possible. For thin lines, hold the brush close to the work surface; for broad ones, hold the brush away from it. You will soon learn how to control the width of line by raising or lowering the brush.

Hold the brush at about 10cms from the working surface and in one constant movement, working from the shoulder, move in a straight direction across the board. Turn the spray upwards by rolling the wrist without releasing or relaxing the finger pressure on the lever. Bring the spray down again by reversing the wrist action. Guide the spray back by retracting the line over the mask.

Repeat the movement, reducing the length on each occasion, so that the number of spray coats applied to the work surface will be greatest nearest to the mask. Left-handed artists should work left to right.
Spraying Cut a rectangle about 4cm by 12cm out of a scrap of litho negative film, a piece of Permatrace or a similar material, to make a mask. Place the mask on the paper surface, anchoring it down with weights – strips of metal bar are ideal – or lay lengths of printer's rule along the edges of the mask to stop it blowing up under the air pressure. Then start the following sequence of experiments.

Hold the airbrush about 15cm to 20cm above the masked paper and spray an even tone over the whole area. Start the spray on the mask and carry it evenly across the surface, applying one covering coat over the complete area. Change direction and spray up and down in the same manner. Apply a third layer diagonally from left to right and a final coat at right angles to that. Remove the mask and examine the result for evenness of tone and density. Density can be

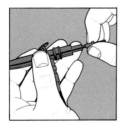

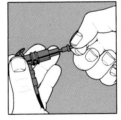

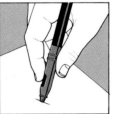

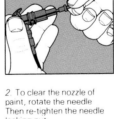

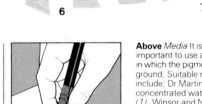

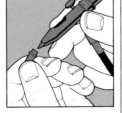

3

1

2

4

5

6

7

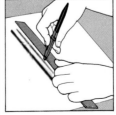

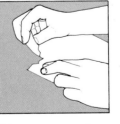

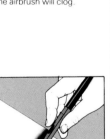

Clearing a blocked nozzle
1. Unscrew the handle and then loosen the needle locking nut.

2. To clear the nozzle of paint, rotate the needle. Then re-tighten the needle locking nut.

Clearing the air-cap To clear any build up of paint, hold the airbrush vertically on a flat surface and spray a quick burst of air.

Above *Media* It is important to use a medium in which the pigment is finely ground. Suitable media include: Dr Martin's concentrated water colours *(1)*, Winsor and Newton inks *(2)*, FW inks *(3)*, Vallejo concentrated water colours *(4)*, Grumbacher acrylics *(5)*, Pelikan gouaches *(6, 7)*. If too coarse a medium is used, the airbrush will clog.

Putting on the spatter cap
Unscrew the handle, loosen the needle, then remove the air-cap. Fit the spatter-cap, leaving the nozzle in place. Finally reset the needle.

Spraying straight lines Raise one edge of a steel ruler above the surface of the paper and hold it steady. Spray while sliding the nozzle along the raised edge of the ruler.

Using a torn paper mask
1. Tear a strip of paper to produce a jagged edge. Hold the paper above the area to be sprayed — the further above the surface the softer the line will be.

2. Hold the airbrush above the paper and spray. The edge can be made harder or softer by varying the angle of the airbrush.

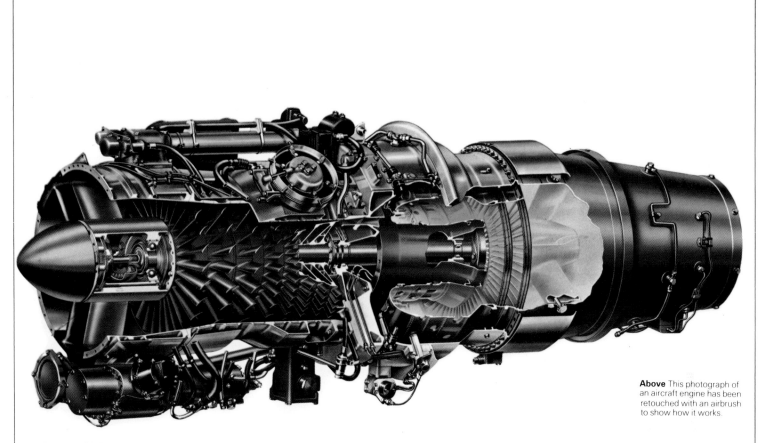

Above This photograph of an aircraft engine has been retouched with an airbrush to show how it works.

easily controlled simply by spraying either more or fewer coats as required.

Make sure that the mask is dry. You can do this by going over the surface with the brush adjusted for air only. Place the mask in a new position and graduate the colour tone from top to bottom by applying a greater number of coats as you move towards the top of the mask.

Use the same mask to produce a convex form. Re-position the mask and make a concave form.

Cut around the perimeter of an isometric cube and, with the help of two straight edge templates, practice spraying the three different planes in different densities to express form. Position the mask carefully. If it is slightly out of register it will leave highlights along each edge of plane.

Cut out a circle with a 6cm diagonal and airbrush on to it a variety of visual forms. The best way to get the basic spherical shape is to hold the airbrush at right angles away from the

work surface and spray very lightly on the mask around the perimeter of the circle. Add more tone to the side which is away from the light and leave the area of highlight as white as possible. As you paint in, away from the light source, hold the airbrush nearer to the surface and lay on a denser tone. Arc the airbrush both to left and right to give a fading effect within the crescent shape you have produced. Take care to see that this is done away from the unmasked edge, so that reflected light extends more than halfway around the circumference of the circle.

Use loose mask templates for expediency. Any fuzzy edge left at the perimeter of the artwork can be sharpened by painting white with a brush to the edge of the work before it is photographed. As an alternative, commercially produced self-adhesive masking, such as Frisk film and Frisket, can be used. Lay it on top of art–work and simply cut out with a sharp knife the area you intend to work in. Masking liquid

can also be used with a brush to allow exposed areas to be retouched. The dried masking can quickly be removed by plucking at the protected surface with low-tack transparent sticking tape.

Computers

The task of the technical illustrator is becoming much more simple with the use of computers applied to interactive design. Computers can store thousands of completed engineering drawings together with complex calculations.

Using visual display units capable of drawing intricate lines, stored drawings can be called up on the screen and modified, extended and even re-assembled by the use of sophisticated electronic devices. Isometric and perspective views of components and assemblies can be rapidly lined up on the screen. There are still developments to be made in the field of computers in design, but these will offer the technical illustrator a new dimension in speed and accuracy.

Left A computer can be programmed with the dimensions of an object and it can then produce an image of the object indicating all its dimesions from any angle.

FRONT VIEW

GRAPHIC

D E S I G N

INTRODUCTION TO GRAPHIC DESIGN

Graphic design has only emerged as an independent discipline in the last thirty years. Design itself, which can be defined in general terms as the arrangement, composition and combination of shapes and forms, is, of course, as old as art itself. The term 'composition' used with reference, for example, to painting and drawing, means in effect the 'design' of the work.

Craftsmen throughout the ages have also been designers – creating an object, whether in gold or silver, wood or metal, involves working out the relationship between the elements of the object, its design. However, towards the end of the last century and to a much greater extent during this century, the functions of designer and creator have tended to diverge, and the design aspect has become more independent.

Art, illustration and graphic design

There.is a close resemblance between the work of the graphic designer and that of the illustrator. Like the illustrator, the graphic designer is artist as servant to those who commission his or her work and the graphic designer's scope of activity has also expanded enormously as technical reproduction processes have increased in sophistication.

The aims of the artist and the graphic designer differ considerably. The renowned contemporary American designer Milton Glaser has pinpointed the difference clearly: 'In design there is a given body of information that must be conveyed if the audience is to experience the information. That objective is primary in most design activities. On the other hand, the essential function of art is to change and intensify one's perception of reality.'

As advertising and the media have expanded so has the work of the graphic designer. Some designs, such as the shell-shaped motif for Shell petrol or the package design for Coca Cola bottles and cans, have become almost synonymous with the products themselves. Today virtually everything one can buy – from a new car to a packet of soap powder – has been designed, and the graphic designer will have been involved at some point in the design process whether working out the promotion material for the new car or the package design and format for the soap.

History of graphic design

Much of the history of graphic design runs parallel to the histories of art and illustration. The sixteenth century illustrator, Geoffroy Tory can perhaps be seen as one of the first graphic designers as he was one of the first to design books and pages by manipulating text, illustration and borders with regard to their visual impact.

During and since the nineteenth century, as it has become more practical to reproduce illustration and as commercial competition between products made packaging and presentation more important, so the art of graphic design has

increased in importance. In a parallel development the importance of all other fields of design – whether in industry, architecture, technology or commerce – has also increased in a similar way.

Much design today involves bringing together elements of art and of industry and commerce, but the two fields have not always worked together in harmony. The nineteenth century British artist, craftsman, illustrator, designer and writer, William Morris, can be seen as one of the founding fathers of modern design. Morris,

in his practical work and his writings, sought to reassert the importance of crafts and craft skills in the face of what he saw as the shoddy quality of design and manufacture in mass-produced goods.

William Morris's contribution to design reflects his multi-faceted talents. The firm he founded in 1861 produced fine quality furniture, fabrics and tapestries as well as stained glass, while the Kelmscott Press founded in 1890 produced books which revived the art of fine book production in their layouts, typog-

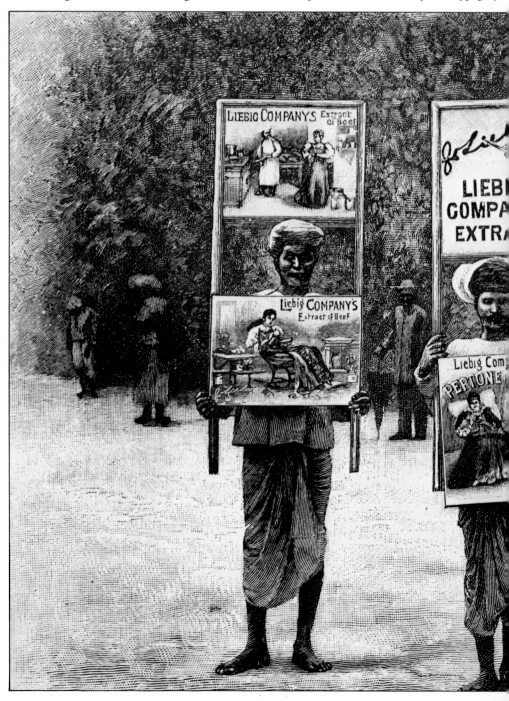

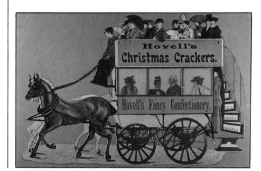

Early advertising mainly took the form of posters. Public transport, today still an important area of advertising, was one of the first to be exploited by advertisers for example the bus promoting Hovell's Christmas crackers around 1890 (left). Europe was not the only area to take to advertising as is seen in this engraving of sandwich board carriers in Bombay (below). Although the sandwich board has dwindled in popularity, this early example shows the use of image and lettering in combination. An interesting cultural and political sidelight is cast by the illustration of wall posters in French and German displayed in Paris during the Prussian occupation of 1870-1871 (right).

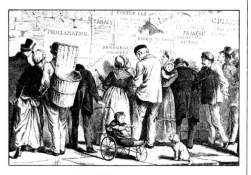

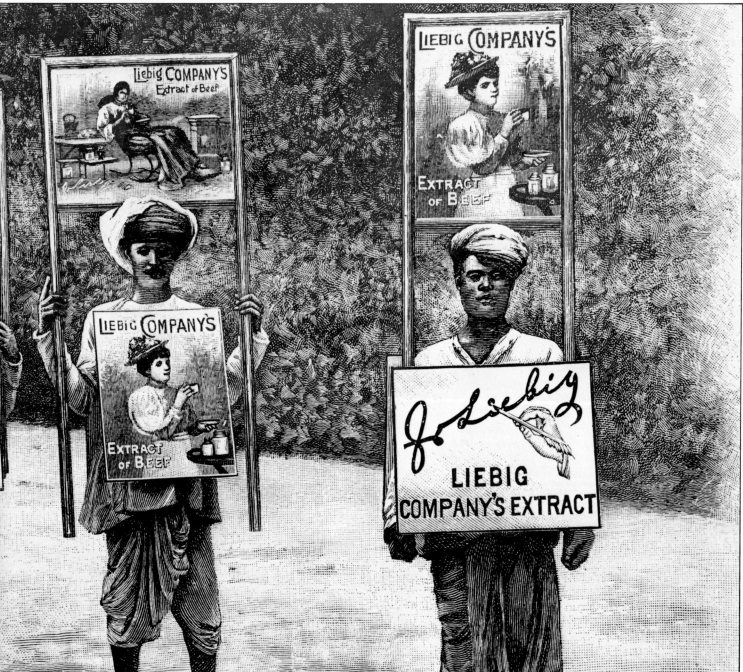

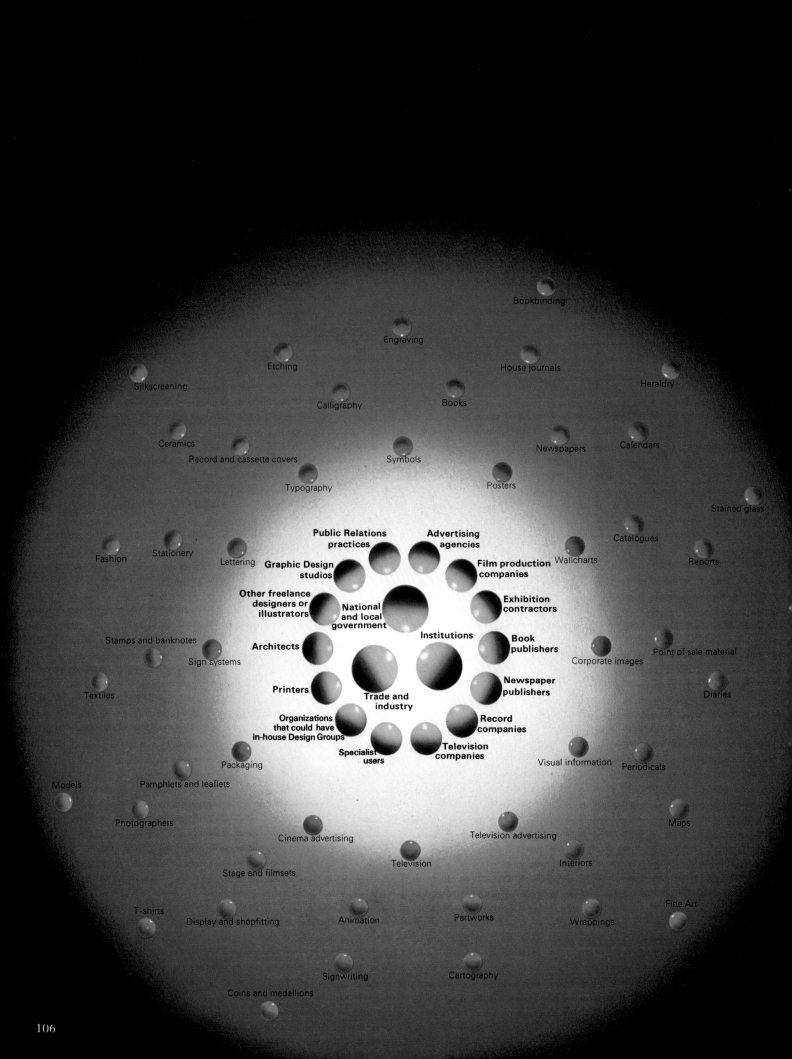

Bookbinding

Engraving

Etching

House journals

Silkscreening

Heraldry

Calligraphy Books

Ceramics

Newspapers Calendars

Record and cassette covers Symbols

Typography Posters

Stained glass

Public Relations practices **Advertising agencies** Catalogues

Fashion Stationery **Graphic Design studios** **Film production companies** Wallcharts Reports

Lettering

Other freelance designers or illustrators **National and local government** **Exhibition contractors**

Stamps and banknotes **Architects** Institutions **Book publishers**

Sign systems Corporate images Point of sale material

Printers **Newspaper publishers**

Textiles **Trade and industry** Diaries

Organizations that could have in-house Design Groups **Record companies**

Packaging **Specialist users** **Television companies**

Models Pamphlets and leaflets Visual information Periodicals

Photographers Maps

Cinema advertising Television advertising

Stage and filmsets Television Interiors

T-shirts Fine Art

Display and shopfitting Animation Partworks Wrappings

Signwriting Cartography

Coins and medallions

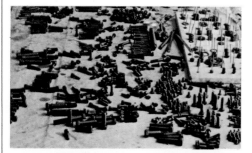

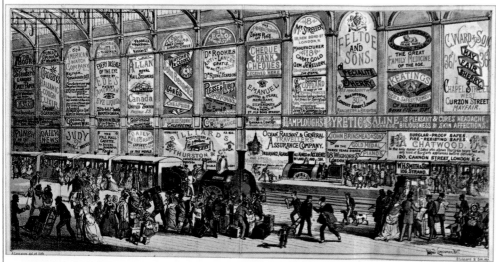

raphy and illustrations. His use of colour and the craftsmanship of his designs together with the quality of their execution formed a challenge to the poor quality of design and manufacture of many mass-produced goods. Morris's practical abilities were linked to his feeling that art should be made 'by the people, for the people as a joy to the maker and user'. Morris's views and his work increased awareness of the importance of design and quality and, in this sense, his work is the general foundation on which today's designers still work.

If Morris appeared to widen the rift between industry and art then the work of the German architect and teacher Walter Gropius in the 'Bauhaus' at Weimar and then Dessau after the First World War attempted to bring the two together. Gropius and his followers were extremely important not only in the Functionalist style of design which they developed and which has remained influential, but also in their views on the education of artists and designers and the relationship between art and industry.

The 'Bauhaus' was a school of design which sought to train students to be equally adept and skilled in art and craft, as well as in industrially orientated, functional craftsmanship. Practical instruction, where emphasis was placed on the industrial problems of mass production, took place in workshops and the quality of the teaching in the 'Bauhaus' contributed greatly to its impact. Gropius outlined their aims: 'our object was to eliminate the drawbacks of the machine without sacrificing any one of its real advantages. ... Our ambition was to rouse the creative artist from his other-worldliness and to reintegrate him into the workaday world of realities and, at the same time, to broaden and humanize the rigid, almost exclusively material mind of the businessman.' With the later work in the USA of many of those involved in the 'Bauhaus', such as the Dutch architect Mies van der Rohe, its impact spread far beyond the boundaries of Germany.

In areas of graphic design where typography is of extreme importance two main influences in the period between the First and Second World Wars were the letterers and typographers Stanley Morison and Eric Gill. Morison expanded the range of type faces commercially available particularly when he worked for the Monotype Corporation, while Gill designed, among others, the Gill Sans and Perpetua type faces. Typography as a purely functional discipline is perhaps seen at its best in the neat and highly legible books produced in the 1920s and 1930s whose main characteristics were calm anonymity and quality without ostentation. However, at the same time style and fashion were provided by the development of display type faces and families which were used in the ever increasing industry of advertising.

The current explosion in graphic design began in Europe in the 1960s and earlier in the USA. It was brought about by consumer prosperity which fuelled a massive increase in advertising, journalism and book publishing, as well as the spread of television and radio. Graphic design and its potential has been further stimulated by developments in printing technology, particularly affecting the quality and economic viability of colour reproduction.

The design process
Each design has to go through several different

Left *Careers in graphic design* This diagram shows some of the very wide range of careers open to the graphic designer today
Top The nuts and bolts of a Roland 6 four-colour printing press may seem a far-cry from artistic inspiration but an understanding of the techniques of colour reproduction and printing is an essential part of the graphic designer's trade if he or she is to achieve good results.

Above An English railway station in 1874. Like so many public places railway stations have long provided a natural showplace for graphic design.

Bottom The fifteenth-century *Books of Hours* provide an early example of book design which integrated text and pictures.

stages in order to realize the original idea in graphic form. The factors in a design obviously vary according to the object of the proposed piece of work. The first stage is the commission – choosing the designer who – in the eyes of those commissioning the work – is most suited to carrying out the work. It is unusual for a designer to work without a commission. The first stage is the briefing session between the designer and the client. At this stage the outline of what is wanted from the designer must be worked out in conjunction with other questions such as the budget and schedule. Once the initial details have been thrashed out the designer prepares a rough version of the design. The rough may vary from just an outline of the basic components of the design to a finished rough. The rough must show the placing of the type (if any) and the layout of the graphic elements. The designer works with a language of signs and images and in all cases the designer is trying to communicate information (which may not be new or exciting) in a way which is both new and exciting to its audience.

The designer may now have to supply estimates of reproduction and printing costs, so he or she must be well acquainted with all aspects of reproduction and printing processes. It may

be up to the designer also to commission photographs or illustrations for the design, and so he or she must be able to brief the photographer or illustrator as well as to budget fully for such work.

When the designer has all the copy, photographs and illustration he or she can begin to prepare the design for reproduction and printing. Once the artwork has been prepared it is sent to be reproduced. When the proofs are returned to the designer all the colours should be checked and corrected and blemishes should be dealt with. The final stage before printing is the paste-up, for which all details should have been finalized and printing instructions specified.

Final checks, particularly of colour, should be made when the job is 'on machine', that is, ready to be printed. Alterations at this stage are expensive and difficult to make. These are the main stages in any graphic design job, although jobs differ in what is required – for example several roughs are frequently needed before the design is finalized; while designs for books and magazines tend to necessitate close collaboration between designer and editor.

Graphic design today

A graphic designer today can work in any

number of fields from the more obvious ones such as advertising and posters to designing maps, stamps and coins or T-shirts and construction kits. He or she could work in fields as varied as textiles, ceramics, heraldry, signwriting and photography, or in the expanding areas of public relations in, for example, national or local government, tourist organizations, and charities. Major areas of activity which have come to the fore recently are book jacket and record sleeve design. It has now long been accepted that the design of cornflakes or soap packages can play an important role in selling the goods, but with the expansion of book publishing – especially in the paperback area – and the record industry, the 'packaging' of these products has become an increasingly important element in the sale of the product.

Graphic design has been defined as 'the making of the possible' and what is possible changes according to the state of techniques of printing and reproduction, and the social or economic constraints placed on the designer. The designer must know how to use the vast range of materials and resources available and how to exploit them economically and aesthetically in his or her manipulation of the language of signs and images.

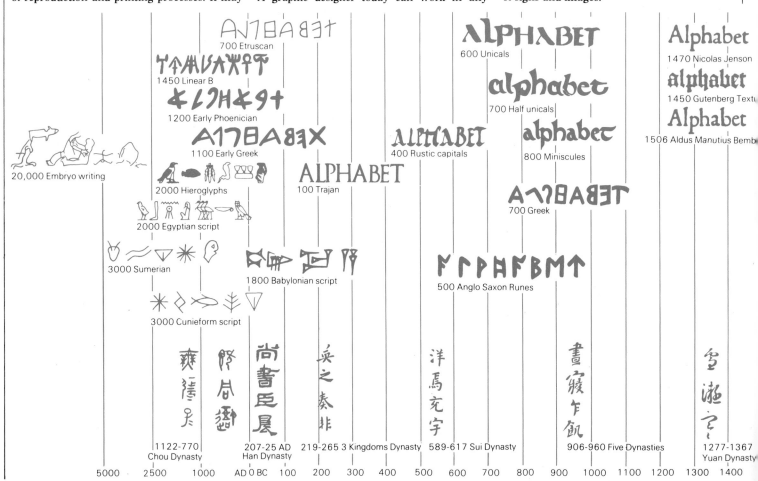

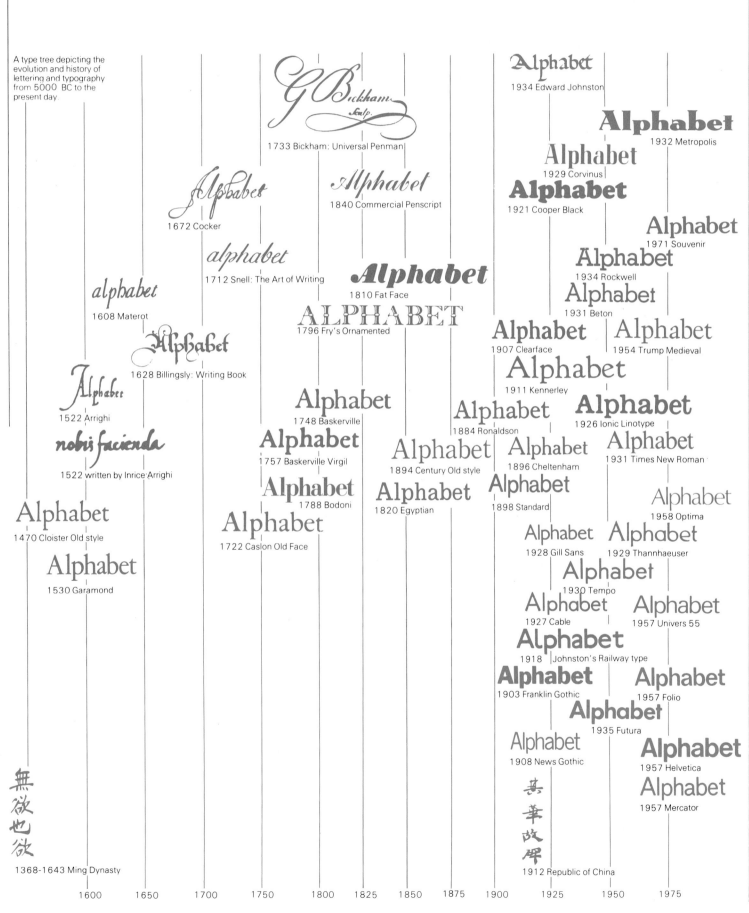

A type tree depicting the evolution and history of lettering and typography from 5000 BC to the present day.

CHAPTER SIX

DESIGN EQUIPMENT

All graphic designers need a wide range of equipment to enable them to work to the deadlines and to the high standards demanded today in the still expanding sphere of graphic design.

This equipment ranges from tools which have changed little through the ages to those which have only been developed recently using the latest technology. For example, the wood-cased pencil first manufactured commercially during the eighteenth century has changed little while precision engineering has improved the reliability of clutch and propelling pencils. These will maintain an even line and can be used with varying thicknesses of lead. Erasers also show such improvements. While simple forms retain their usefulness different types of eraser have been developed to erase not only pencil but also many inks.

Precision engineered instruments are vital for exact and accurate drawing. Today there is a wide variety of extremely high quality instrumentation available. These instruments are an essential for any graphic designer. Pens and inks are also today of a very high quality. Since the Industrial Revolution the range of pigments and paints has widened and improved. For example, special inks have been developed for use in the stylo-tip pen, an instrument which produces an even line which is therefore indispensable for design work. The wide range of available nibs makes this pen particularly versatile. Continuing refinements ensure that the quality of the instrument and therefore of the work which it can produce, continue to improve. At the other end of the range of pens needed by the graphic designer are the recently developed felt and fibre tip markers. These have many applications in all areas of graphic design from outlining roughs to preparing camera-ready artwork.

Other basic equipment for the graphic designer includes a good drawing board, good light, a selection of scalpels and other cutting tools. With deadlines to meet, the graphic designer must be able to work quickly and accurately – and so any device which can speed up work is valuable. Frequently used are templates, stencils and curves for drawing, fixatives for different substances and dry transfer lettering. This recent development is now invaluable for both roughs and finished artwork.

The selection of equipment on the following pages covers the vast range which a graphic designer should have – or at least have access to – in order to do his or her job efficiently, competently and to the high standard demanded.

For all types of graphic design it is important for the designer to obtain the best possible quality of material and equipment. The quality of the finished design will be greatly enhanced if the equipment used is also of a high quality. In all aspects of graphic design today quality is paramount.

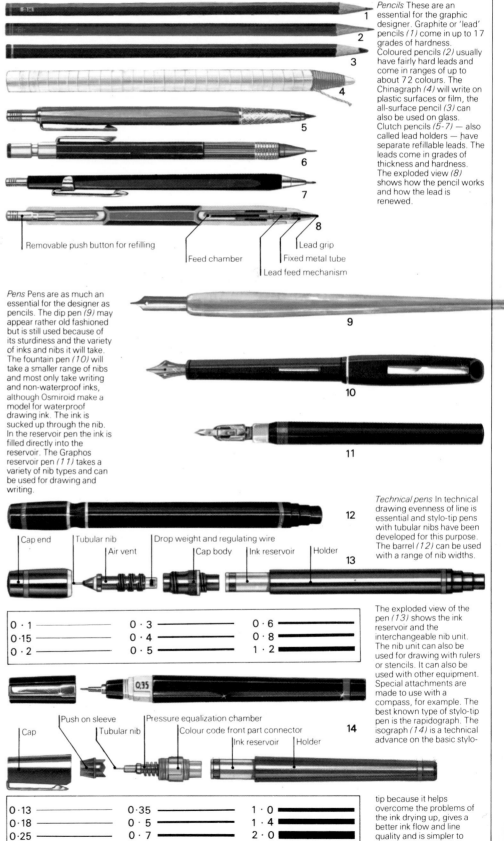

Pencils These are an essential for the graphic designer. Graphite or 'lead' pencils (1) come in up to 17 grades of hardness. Coloured pencils (2) usually have fairly hard leads and come in ranges of up to about 72 colours. The Chinagraph (4) will write on plastic surfaces or film, the all-surface pencil (3) can also be used on glass. Clutch pencils (5-7) — also called lead holders — have separate refillable leads. The leads come in grades of thickness and hardness. The exploded view (8) shows how the pencil works and how the lead is renewed.

Removable push button for refilling
Feed chamber
Lead feed mechanism
Lead grip
Fixed metal tube

Pens Pens are as much an essential for the designer as pencils. The dip pen (9) may appear rather old fashioned but is still used because of its sturdiness and the variety of inks and nibs it will take. The fountain pen (10) will take a smaller range of nibs and most only take writing and non-waterproof inks, although Osmiroid make a model for waterproof drawing ink. The ink is sucked up through the nib. In the reservoir pen the ink is filled directly into the reservoir. The Graphos reservoir pen (11) takes a variety of nib types and can be used for drawing and writing.

Technical pens In technical drawing evenness of line is essential and stylo-tip pens with tubular nibs have been developed for this purpose. The barrel (12) can be used with a range of nib widths.

Cap end
Tubular nib
Air vent
Drop weight and regulating wire
Cap body
Ink reservoir
Holder

0·1	0·3	0·6
0·15	0·4	0·8
0·2	0·5	1·2

The exploded view of the pen (13) shows the ink reservoir and the interchangeable nib unit. The nib unit can also be used for drawing with rulers or stencils. It can also be used with other equipment. Special attachments are made to use with a compass, for example. The best known type of stylo-tip pen is the rapidograph. The isograph (14) is a technical advance on the basic stylo-

Cap
Push on sleeve
Tubular nib
Pressure equalization chamber
Colour code front part connector
Ink reservoir
Holder

0·13	0·35	1·0
0·18	0·5	1·4
0·25	0·7	2·0

tip because it helps overcome the problems of the ink drying up, gives a better ink flow and line quality and is simpler to maintain.

Inks Ink is an essential medium for the graphic designer. It gives a sharp, dense and constant line and reproduces well. Among the wide variety available are: coloured drawing inks for use in fountain and stylo-tip pens *(1)*, 'T' ink for use in drafting and on film *(2)*, varieties of black Indian ink for drawing *(3)*, coloured Indian inks *(4)*, fountain pen ink *(5)*, drawing inks *(6)*. Process colours *(7)* are used for correcting film and for work to be photographically reproduced.

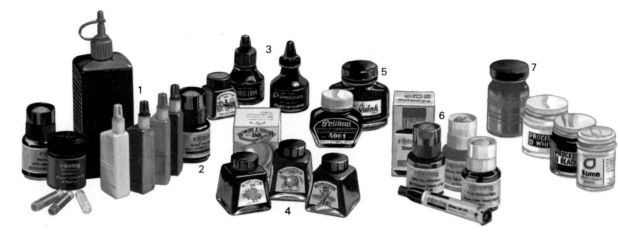

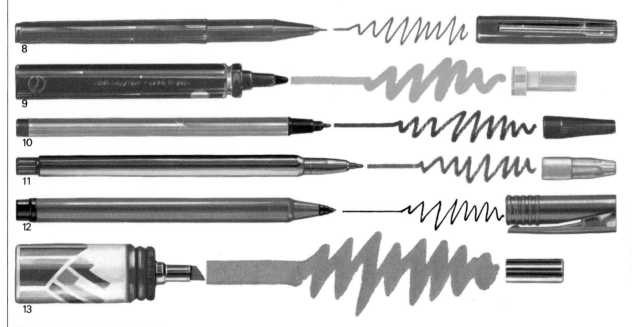

Markers A recent development in equipment for the graphic designer has been the felt and fibre tip marker. The felt tip gives a thicker line and is less hard wearing than the fibre tip which is made from thousands of tiny fibres. The inks in the pens can be either spirit or water based, the former is not water-soluble. This selection shows varying thicknesses of spirit based fibre tips *(8, 10)*, spirit based felt tips *(9, 13)*, and a water based felt tip *(11)*. A newer development still is the 'rolling writer' ball pen *(12)* which has the features of the conventional ball-point pen but which is filled with a water-based ink which flows evenly and smoothly. Markers are very versatile and can be used both for rough and precise design work.

Pantone

Pantone is a range of products for selecting and matching colours. It allows the designer to control and match colours in all stages of the design, printing and reproduction from the initial roughs to the finished print. There is a range of over 500 colours, each of which has a reference number. The system is used internationally.

The colour/tint overlays *(1)* give a large area of consistent colour and the overlay can be repositioned. This also comes in a smaller format *(2)*. Every sheet of the colour paper — available in 505 colours — *(3)* has a printing guide. The colour markers *(4)* come in fine and wide points. Colour selectors *(5, 6)* for paper and overlays help the designer choose and match colours. The paper pickers *(7)* shows all colours in numerical

order, the printer's edition *(8)* shows them on coated and uncoated paper. The colour and black selector *(10)* gives different amounts of black in combination with 90 of the colours. The colour specifier *(9)* can be used to specify inks.

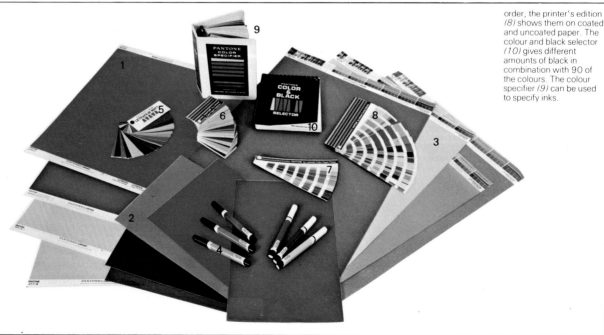

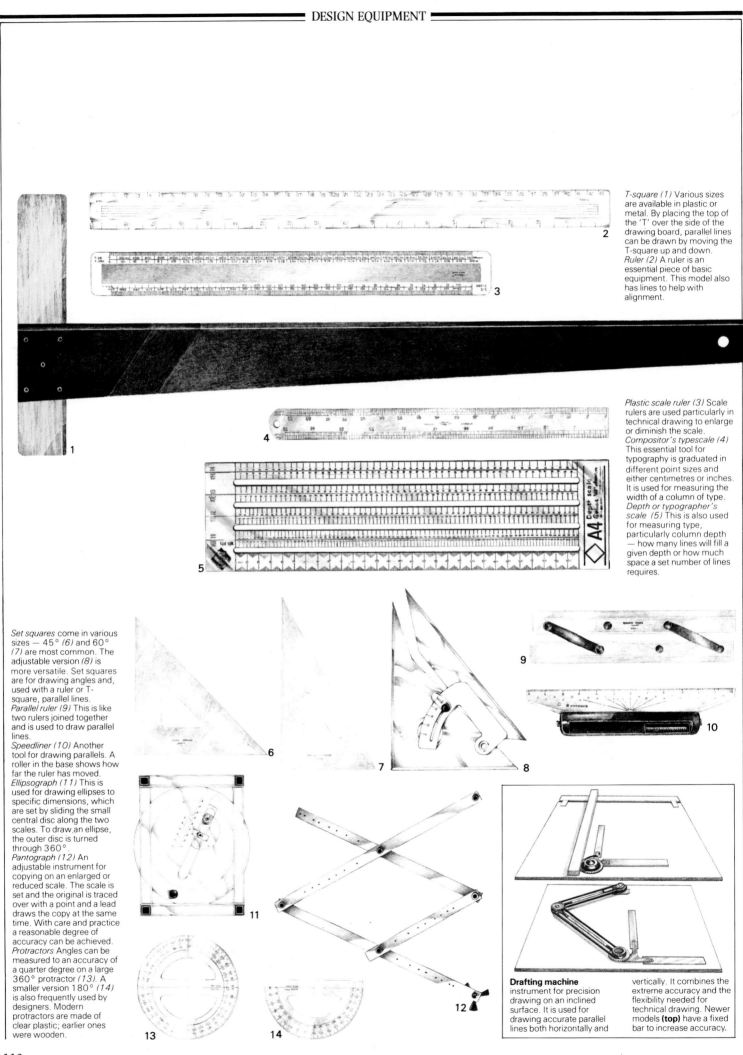

T-square (1) Various sizes are available in plastic or metal. By placing the top of the 'T' over the side of the drawing board, parallel lines can be drawn by moving the T-square up and down.

Ruler (2) A ruler is an essential piece of basic equipment. This model also has lines to help with alignment.

Plastic scale ruler (3) Scale rulers are used particularly in technical drawing to enlarge or diminish the scale.

Compositor's typescale (4) This essential tool for typography is graduated in different point sizes and either centimetres or inches. It is used for measuring the width of a column of type.

Depth or typographer's scale (5) This is also used for measuring type, particularly column depth — how many lines will fill a given depth or how much space a set number of lines requires.

Set squares come in various sizes — 45° *(6)* and 60° *(7)* are most common. The adjustable version *(8)* is more versatile. Set squares are for drawing angles and, used with a ruler or T-square, parallel lines.

Parallel ruler (9) This is like two rulers joined together and is used to draw parallel lines.

Speedliner (10) Another tool for drawing parallels. A roller in the base shows how far the ruler has moved.

Ellipsograph (11) This is used for drawing ellipses to specific dimensions, which are set by sliding the small central disc along the two scales. To draw an ellipse, the outer disc is turned through 360°.

Pantograph (12) An adjustable instrument for copying on an enlarged or reduced scale. The scale is set and the original is traced over with a point and a lead draws the copy at the same time. With care and practice a reasonable degree of accuracy can be achieved.

Protractors Angles can be measured to an accuracy of a quarter degree on a large 360° protractor *(13)*. A smaller version 180° *(14)* is also frequently used by designers. Modern protractors are made of clear plastic; earlier ones were wooden.

Drafting machine instrument for precision drawing on an inclined surface. It is used for drawing accurate parallel lines both horizontally and vertically. It combines the extreme accuracy and the flexibility needed for technical drawing. Newer models **(top)** have a fixed bar to increase accuracy.

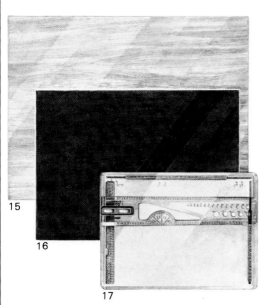

15

16

17

Drawing boards Designers use drawing boards to provide a smooth surface for their work. Boards come in a variety of sizes and are made of different materials. It is often necessary to use a backing sheet with a wooden board (15) while the formica covered board (16) can be wiped clean. The adjustable model (17) has a drafting head which can be fixed in any position on the board.

Adjustable drawing boards Drawing boards (18, 19) can also be adjusted to various angles. Some can be clamped to a surface and adjusted for any angle, while others adjust to a set number of positions. The drawing stand (20) offers the same flexibility. It also has counterweights and a straight edge to help ensure accurate measurement and positioning. The Rotoboard (21) is highly adjustable and is used for work requiring mutliple ruling.

18

19

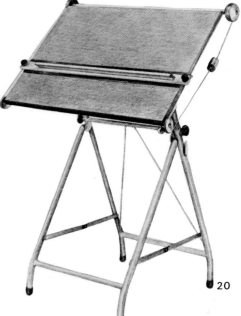

20

21

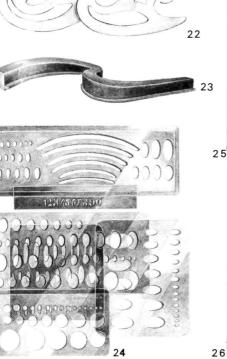

22

23

24

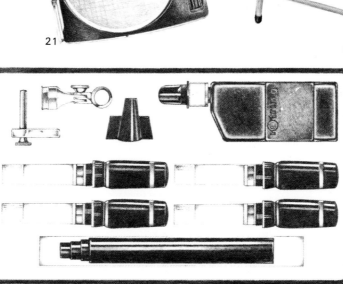

25

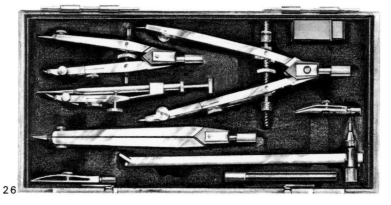

26

French curves (22) These clear plastic line-guides are designed to provide as many degrees of curve as possible. *Flexible curve (23)* This is also used for drawing curves and can be bent to any angle. *Templates (24)* Plastic templates come in many shapes. Those used most by graphic designers are ellipses which enable the designer to draw circular shapes accurately and in perspective.
Drawing pens (25) A drawing pen is an essential tool for the graphic designer.
They have tubular nibs which ensures that they write with an even line. They use either Indian ink or various differently coloured inks developed specially for use in these pens. The barrel and nib units can be purchased separately or in sets. This set (25) has a barrel and four nib units. *Drawing instruments* A set of drawing instruments is another essential for the graphic designer. This small set (26) includes all the attachments necessary for basic technical drawing. It includes two sizes of spring bow compass, which can be adjusted to a high degree of accuracy, dividers, small radius compass, ruling pens and extension bar for drawing larger circles.

113

Surfaces for the designer

Papers for design work are readily available in handy sizes — mainly the metricated 'A' sizes. Most types of paper come in several different sizes — for example the A2 pad of detail paper *(1)*, A3 block of layout paper *(3)*, A2 and A4 size pads of tracing paper *(2, 5)*, an A4 block of cartridge paper *(4)*, and an A4 pad of graph paper *(6)*. It is important that the designer can use not only the correct type but also a suitable size of paper.

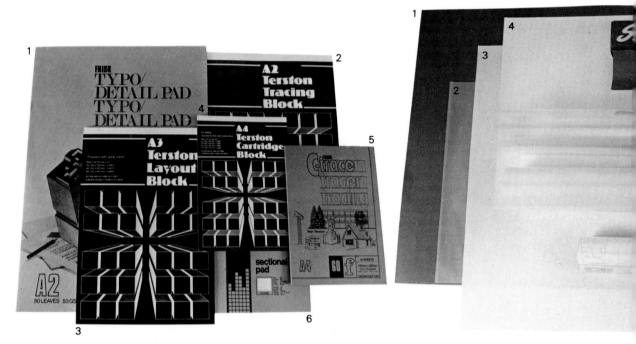

Cutting implements
Surgical scalpels *(1, 2)* are used for fine cutting. The interchangeable blades are suitable for different types of cutting. The pocket knife *(4)* has a retractable blade while the parallel cutter *(5)* has two blades and cuts in parallel lines. Scissors *(6)* are an obvious essential for design work. The craft knife *(7)* has a larger blade than the scalpel for cutting thicker materials such as stencils or board. Its extra blades can be used for scoring or routing. The trimming knife *(8)* which also takes various blades is a heavy duty instrument for all types of cutting. Replacement blades for these knives are available in packets.

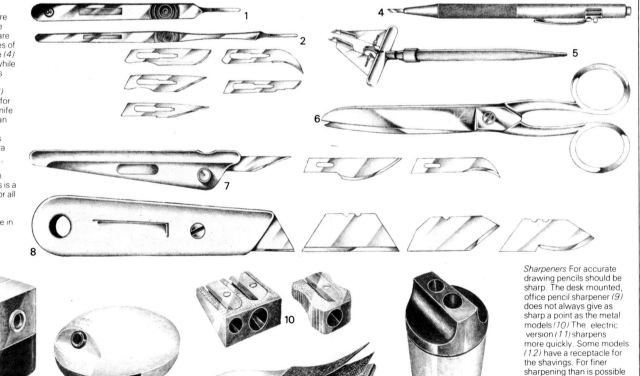

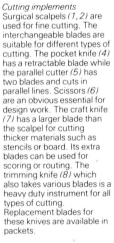

Sharpeners For accurate drawing pencils should be sharp. The desk mounted, office pencil sharpener *(9)* does not always give as sharp a point as the metal models *(10)* The electric version *(11)* sharpens more quickly. Some models *(12)* have a receptacle for the shavings. For finer sharpening than is possible with a conventional sharpener a sandpaper block *(13)* is useful.

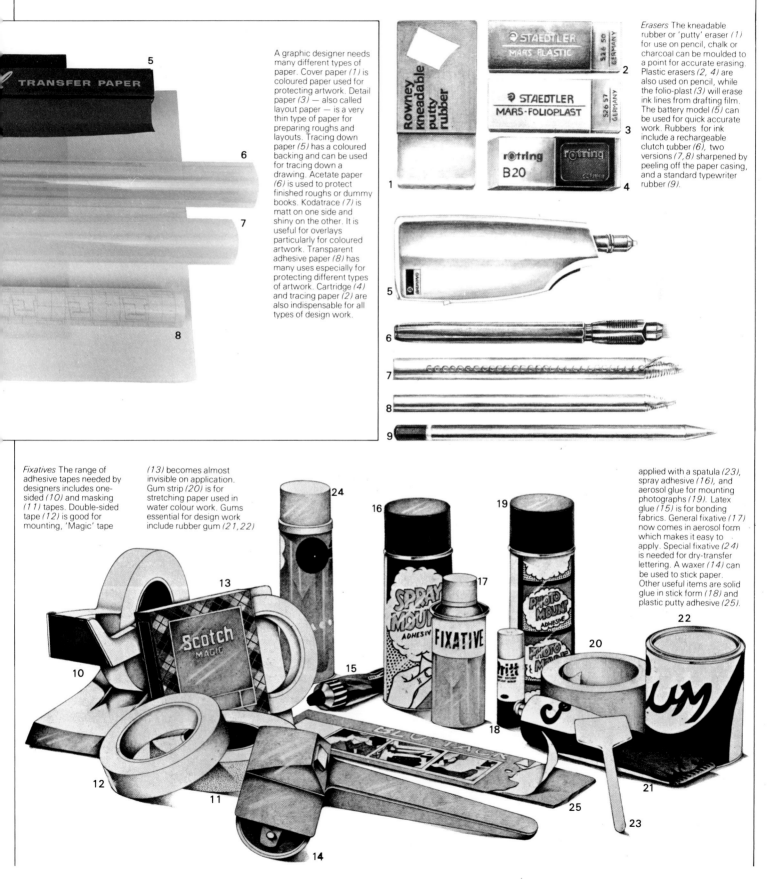

A graphic designer needs many different types of paper. Cover paper (1) is coloured paper used for protecting artwork. Detail paper (3) — also called layout paper — is a very thin type of paper for preparing roughs and layouts. Tracing down paper (5) has a coloured backing and can be used for tracing down a drawing. Acetate paper (6) is used to protect finished roughs or dummy books. Kodatrace (7) is matt on one side and shiny on the other. It is useful for overlays particularly for coloured artwork. Transparent adhesive paper (8) has many uses especially for protecting different types of artwork. Cartridge (4) and tracing paper (2) are also indispensable for all types of design work.

Erasers The kneadable rubber or 'putty' eraser (1) for use on pencil, chalk or charcoal can be moulded to a point for accurate erasing. Plastic erasers (2, 4) are also used on pencil, while the folio-plast (3) will erase ink lines from drafting film. The battery model (5) can be used for quick accurate work. Rubbers for ink include a rechargeable clutch rubber (6), two versions (7, 8) sharpened by peeling off the paper casing, and a standard typewriter rubber (9).

Fixatives The range of adhesive tapes needed by designers includes one-sided (10) and masking (11) tapes. Double-sided tape (12) is good for mounting, 'Magic' tape (13) becomes almost invisible on application. Gum strip (20) is for stretching paper used in water colour work. Gums essential for design work include rubber gum (21, 22).

applied with a spatula (23), spray adhesive (16), and aerosol glue for mounting photographs (19). Latex glue (15) is for bonding fabrics. General fixative (17) now comes in aerosol form which makes it easy to apply. Special fixative (24) is needed for dry-transfer lettering. A waxer (14) can be used to stick paper. Other useful items are solid glue in stick form (18) and plastic putty adhesive (25).

Drawing instruments For accurate drawing, precision instruments are needed and the compass and its related implements are indispensable to the designer. Spring bow compasses *(1, 2)* can be adjusted to a high degree of accuracy. They take many different attachments. The dividers *(3)* have an adjusting screw to ensure accuracy. This implement *(4)* is for drawing small radius circles.

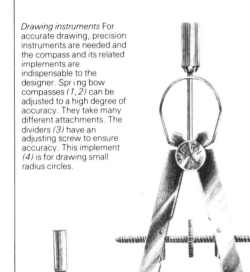

Compass attachments The compass becomes a very versatile tool when used in combination with different attachments. The lead *(6)* is one of the most frequently used. The ruling pen *(7)* draws with an even line. The cutter blade *(8)* attachment for stylo—tip pen *(9)* and an extension bar for large circles *(10)* further widen the uses of the compass.

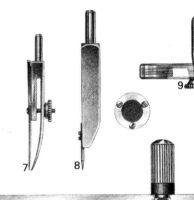

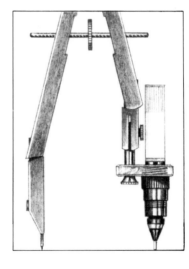

Left This device enables a stylo-tip pen to be attached to a spring-bow compass. This greatly increases the versatility of the instrument and its uses in design work.

Beam compass The beam compass *(11)* is for drawing circles or arcs larger than those which can be drawn with a normal compass. It is adjusted by moving the attachments along the central bar. An extension bar *(12)* is also available.
Proportional dividers These *(13)* are used for copying. drawings on a smaller or larger scale, they are used particularly by cartographers.
Dotting pen This device *(14)* draws dotted lines. It has a ruling pen which is raised and lowered at regular intervals by a wheel mechanism. Several dotting wheels are available to draw different broken lines.

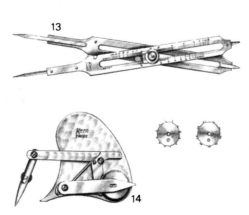

Ruling pens With a ruling pen the designer can draw a line of constant thickness in ink. The side view of two standard ruling pens *(15, 16)* shows where the ink is held between the two prongs of the nib. The screw is tightened to give the desired thickness of line. The graduated adjusting screw model *(17)* gives extra accuracy of adjustment. The border *(18)* has a swivel which opens to facilitate cleaning. The railroad pen *(19)* has a double nib attachment for drawing parallel lines. Ruling pens are also called drawing or bow pens. Although ink is the main medium used in these pens, paint can also be used if it is thinned down to the same consistency as ink

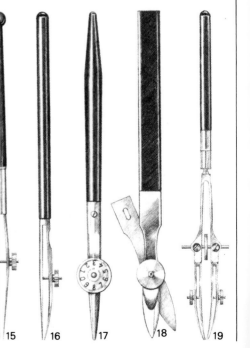

Instant transfer lettering
Manufacturers of instant transfer products supply a catalogue with examples of the wide range of lettering styles, typefaces, sizes, colours and effects available. Each has a reference number, which the designer uses to order the selected item. This makes the process quicker, and helps avoid errors.

Right Typeface layout page *(1)* showing the name of the typeface and the various sizes and forms in which it can be obtained. On this sheet of adhesive lettering *(2)* letters and numbers are arranged alphabetically.

Right Part of the very wide range of different instant transfer sheets available to the designer. These include: various standard typefaces in a range of point sizes, fount references and colours; specialized alphabets such as Greek, Hebrew or Arabic; Roman and non-Roman numerals; architectural and technical symbols; illustrations; textures and tones; rules and borders; lines and transfer tapes; colour surfaces such as Vinyl and PVC.

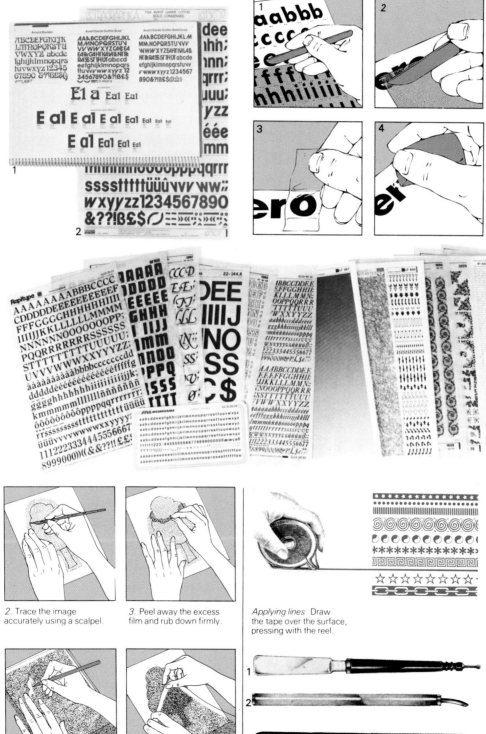

Left Applying instant dry transfer lettering. Select the required point size and typeface. Peel off the backing sheet. Position the letter on the art surface and press down *(1)*. Large letters must be pressed firmly into contact before transfer. Rub the back of the sheet with a spatula or pencil *(2)* until the letter is transferred. After transfer the letter may be more firmly secured by burnishing There are two main methods of correction. Place a strip of clear adhesive tape or masking tape over the letter to be corrected *(3)*. When the tape is peeled off the letter will lift off. Alternatively corrections can be made with a soft eraser *(4)*.

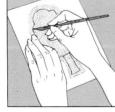

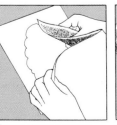

Letratone 1. Lay the film on the image and cut a rough outline.

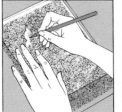

2. Trace the image accurately using a scalpel.

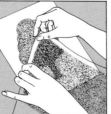

3. Peel away the excess film and rub down firmly.

Texture sheets 1. Lay the sheet print side down on the image.

2. Trace the image on the back of the sheet and rub down.

3. Peel off the sheet leaving the texture pattern on the image.

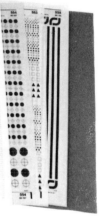

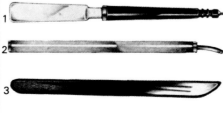

Applying lines Draw the tape over the surface, pressing with the reel.

Left Instant transfer tapes are designed for rapid, repetitive application of lines, symbols and borders.

Below *Storage cabinet* Filing or cataloguing systems make selection convenient and easy and keep the transfer sheets in good condition.

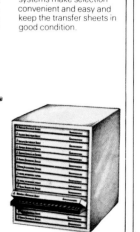

Above *Burnishers 1.* American model with adjustable spring and ball tip. *2.* Round-headed burnisher. *3.* Flat-tipped style.

Light boxes A light box is a necessary piece of equipment for any design studio. The light box provides uniform and colour balanced light diffusion over the viewing surface. This is necessary for checking the sharpness of transparencies and negatives, for checking colour separation and, in conjunction with a suitable overhead light, for colour correction. The exploded view *(2)* shows the light source, usually fluorescent, and the opalized perspex or acrylic diffuser through which the light passes before reaching the glass surface. Light boxes come in different sizes and models including table top *(1)*, wall mounted *(4)* portable *(5)* versions. A larger lighted surface is available on a light table *(3)*, which can be adjusted for angle.

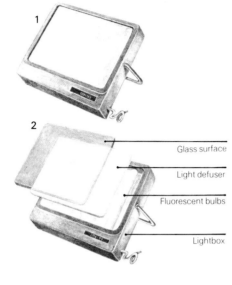
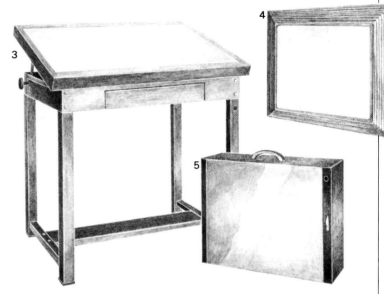

Glass surface

Light defuser

Fluorescent bulbs

Lightbox

Visualizer This machine is invaluable to the designer who wants to enlarge or reduce an image to an exact size. The image is placed on the copyboard. The designer looks down on to the viewing screen. The image is lit from above — or from below in the case of a transparency — and is projected through the lens. The degree of enlargement or reduction is achieved by turning two handles — one moves the copy board up and down, the other adjusts the lens. The image is projected on to the tracing paper placed on the glass viewing screen. It can then be traced off to an exact size. Although a visualizer is a fairly expensive machine it is a worthwhile investment for any designer or illustrator who has to work to very accurate sizes.

Folding hood

Viewing area

Lighting switches

Lighting bulbs

Lens

Copyboard

Stand

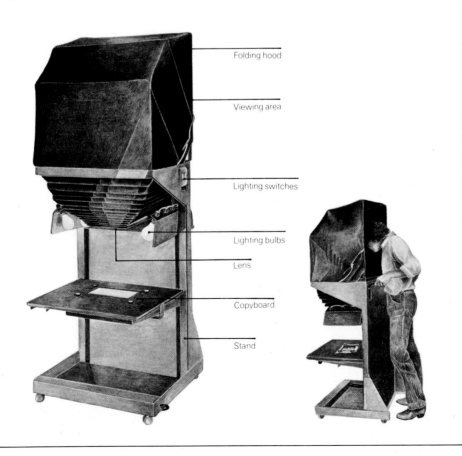

Magnifying glasses These are another essential for the graphic designer to check details, especially on work which is to be enlarged in reproduction. The numerous models available include the adjustable table-top *(6)* folding *(7, 8)* and hand *(9)* models. A special glass *(10)* is used for viewing transparencies. The repeat glass *(11)* is useful for repeating patterns to show how the finished design will look. It is used particularly in fabric and wallpaper design.

Guillotine The guillotine *(1)* will cut paper or card accurately and cleanly. For safety it must have a guard around the blade.

Miscellaneous equipment Glassine bags *(2)* made of paper with a glazed finish on both sides are useful for keeping artwork. Different sizes of polythene transparency holders *(3)* help protect transparencies. Petroleum spirit *(4)* cleans gum and grease off most surfaces.

Lights Good light is an absolute essential for any designer. The lamp *(1)* is highly adjustable. Its heavy base makes it very stable. It gives a good beam of light and has a long reach. It can be free-standing, screwed to a table *(2)* wall-mounted *(3)* or clamped to a table *(4)*.

The reading lamp *(5)* gives a smaller beam of light and is less flexible. The fluorescent lamp *(6)* gives an evenly distributed light over a larger area.

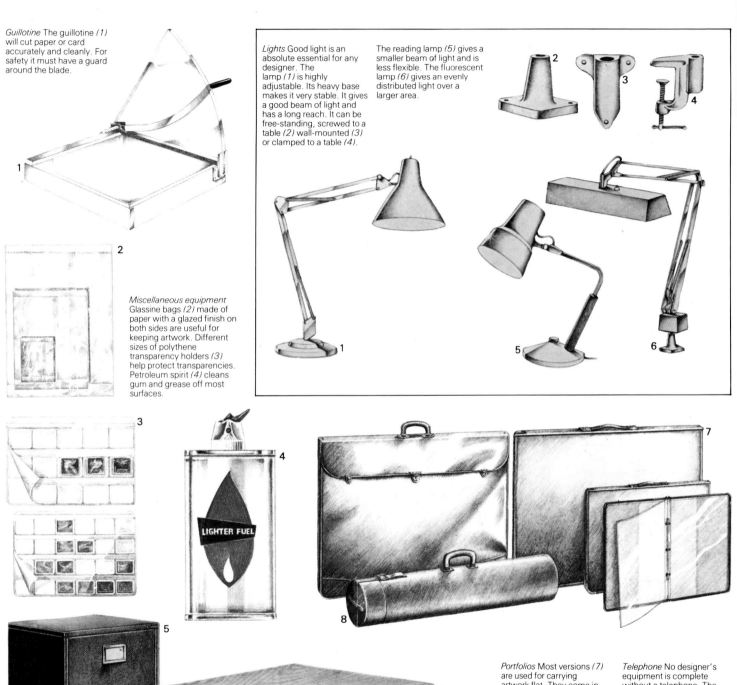

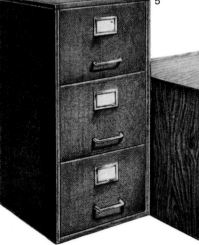

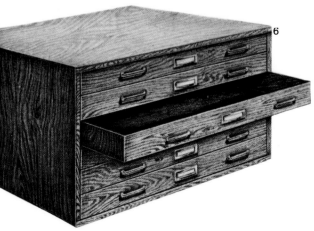

Portfolios Most versions *(7)* are used for carrying artwork flat. They come in different sizes and many are fitted with transparent leaves made of polythene which are a practical way of displaying work. A tubular model *(8)* is less cumbersome and can be used for work which can be rolled up.

Telephone No designer's equipment is complete without a telephone. The designer has tight deadlines and schedules to meet and therefore must be able to keep in close touch with clients, reproduction houses, printers, artists and photographers.

Chests and cabinets Today's designer is a far cry from the artist with his head in the clouds. A filing cabinet *(5)* is as necessary for the designer as it is for any office worker to keep papers in order. A large chest *(6)* is useful for storing artwork flat.

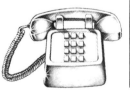

CHAPTER SEVEN

COPYING AND PHOTOPRINTING

A wide range of reprographic equipment is an essential feature of any modern design studio for, without it, it would be impossible for graphic artists to produce work to the high standards expected today. At one end of the scale is the simple photocopier; at the other are advanced and extremely versatile machines capable of producing a variety of sophisticated results, such as miniaturized reproductions. Progress in this field is continual; innovations and developments are constantly being made both to make the designer's job easier and to increase the quality of the end product even further.

Photocopying processes One of the most useful methods of reproduction is the photocopying process. A wide variety of machines can be used, ranging from the simple, easy-to-operate models designed for office purposes, to more advanced machines. The full range of equipment can be used for a variety of functions throughout the design process. These include the copying of all types of drawings, sample text settings and illustrations – as component elements, say, for making up dummy books – and copying complete documents for circulation and approval.

The designer uses photocopying in two main ways. The first is the straightforward duplication of documents and information for wider circulation and general distribution. This is the standard use of most basic equipment. The designer, however, is likely to require reproductions of a higher quality than that provided by the average machine.

The most suitable machine for the studio is one capable of producing prints to A3 size; this is the equivalent of two facing pages of A4 format, one of the sizes most frequently used in design. Even if the final document is designed for A4 format, this larger capacity is useful. This is because the preparatory drawings may well involve proof correction marks and instructions outside the finished size. These must be included on the copy.

The designer also has a more specialized requirement for photocopying equipment. This is the production of a clear, sharp copy of an illustration or text as a component of a design.

The principal problem here is that the artist may wish to incorporate different types of illustrative material within a single spread of two facing pages. This may mean combining artwork and photographs, or originals of many different forms – line, halftone, monochrome or coloured. They may be on paper or on a transparent material; moreover, they are unlikely to be precisely the size the designer needs. At present, there is no single machine capable of producing a satisfactorily sharp copy in such circumstances, or of coping with varying sizes. The designer, therefore, may have to use three or more different photocopying systems to produce the desired result.

There are two basic types of photocopying process. The thermal process uses a paper

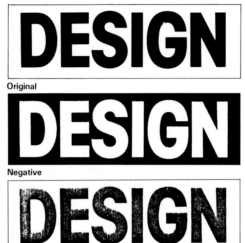

Original

Negative

Copy

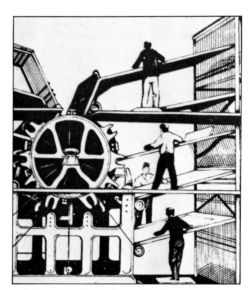

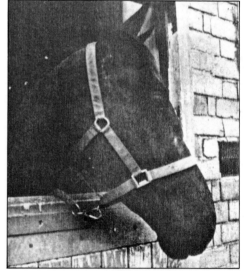

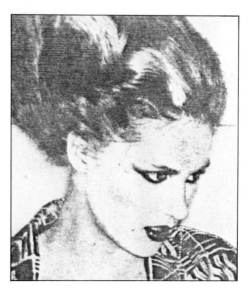

Left There are two main photocopying techniques. The thermal process involves a negative stage, as in the copy of the word DESIGN **(left)**. The more popular electrostatic technique does not use a negative and will print on to any paper. The electrostatic photocopying machine can be put to a wide variety of uses — from copying black and white photographs **(top right)** to showing reproductions of four colour artwork with no overlays **(middle right)**. It rapidly becomes evident that where the originals have sharp, well-defined edges with solid black areas as in the ink line drawing **(below left)** or even reproduction galley proofs **(bottom right)** and letters **(bottom centre)**, the photocopy itself is very good. On the other hand, the more tonal and linear detail there is in the original, the lower will be the quality of the copy — as with the screened PMT of an original colour transparency **(below)** and the magazine reproduction **(bottom left)**.

experts in their various that no illustrator or l can afford to be withou ded into two sections fo: stration and Design, tex a wealth of fascinating ssary technical detail. ion is introduced by a c he many types and uses o owed by a detailed examir lable, from traditional st innovations. The subje t media, ink, painting, l nical illustration. The book is introduced by a ts development, with cha; materials, designing for

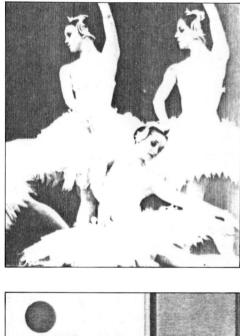

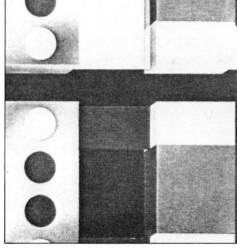

negative of the subject to be produced; this must be made on a proprietary brand of coated paper. The same type of paper is also used for the print itself.

The alternative method is the electrostatic technique. This does not require a negative. It will print on to any paper, including coloured and tracing papers, as well as on to plastic surfaces, such as polyester and cellophane. This flexibility is extremely useful; for instance, electrostatic copies are ideally suited for use in making up dummies, while the method can also be employed to produce overhead projector slides.

Three formats – A4, A3 and foolscap – are available; A3 equipment is probably the most useful. Japanese equipment produces particularly good halftone reproduction, probably because many Japanese manufacturers are also specialists in photographic equipment.

Colour electrostatic photocopying equipment is also available, but on a limited scale; only one British manufacturer, for instance, makes such equipment at the present time. Colour prints can be made from both paper originals and transparencies to A4 format. If 35mm transparencies need to be copied, they can either be enlarged singly to almost A4 size, or a maximum of eight transparencies can be copied same size on an A4 sheet.

Some types of monochrome equipment will produce copies reduced in size from the original at set reduction ratios. They can also be used to collate the finished copies, if desired.

Same size copies If high quality reproduction is not imperative, the electrostatic process can also be used to produce lithographic printing plates, though only at the same size as the original. Same size copies, however, are usually obtained by the dyeline process, one of the oldest systems of document copying.

Recently, there have been several innovations and developments in dyeline technique. The method depends on a transparent original being placed in contact with sensitized paper and exposed to ultra-violet light. In the past, the process involved using ammonia, which evaporated, making working conditions unpleasant, if not actually dangerous. Recent improvements in equipment have reduced this problem, while alternatives to ammonia have also been introduced.

Since the dyeline process can use transparent materials, it is particularly suitable for copying, say, engineering or architectural drawings made upon tracing paper or polyester. The range of sizes obtainable extends up to A0.

A variety of papers are suitable, as well as other surfaces. The most commonly used paper gives a dark blue copy on a white background, while good black copy can be obtained by using the appropriate paper. The present range of suitable materials also includes gloss-surfaced cards which can be used for high-quality 'pre-

stige' presentations; this has gone a long way to overcoming the traditional design objection to dyeline as producing unpleasant, cheap-looking results.

Coloured surfaces can also be used, as well as dimensionally-stable transparent materials. Whatever the surface, further dyeline copies can be taken from the copies originally produced.

The main disadvantage of the dyeline process is that it is not entirely light fast. This means that dyeline prints must not be exposed to strong sunlight for any sustained period or the image will deteriorate.

Photographic document copying processes
Standard copying equipment can produce copies of typesetting suitable for making preliminary checks, but they are not adequate for more than this. The designer needs clear, precisely defined reproduction and, to obtain this, the technique of photographic copying is normally used.

This method produces high quality prints which can be used in the same way as original artwork for reproduction purposes. A further advantage is that copies can be made as they are required within the studio. This makes it possible to experiment with effects, creating them to suit a specific design; it also allows the designer to make on-the-spot alterations and correct any mistakes.

Photocopying systems employ either a transparent negative or a paper equivalent; recently, however, there has been a trend away from the use of film negatives. Both types, however, allow the print to be increased or reduced in size from the original, a facility not available with standard copying equipment.

One of the most popular systems is the Photo Mechanical Transfer (PMT) machine. It has several major advantages. It is cheaper to use than conventional photographic systems, and does not require a darkroom for processing. It produces an excellent quality line origination and consequently it is often used for phototypesetting. It can reproduce halftones using a regular dot screen, a line screen or a random screen (see p 122). The resultant halftones are adequate for low budget work, although the quality does not match that of halftones made by a photoengraver.

Colour simulation PMT origination can also be used for colour simulation. This gives a design the appearance of colour, without having to go to the extent of full colour proofing.

The subject is first printed on to a film base material. This is then processed to produce a colour simulation known as a colour key. Dyes are used to develop the image in one of several stock colours, and, since both the colours and the film base are transparent, they can be superimposed. This means that it is possible to create the illusion of two or more colours printing in line or halftone. Combinations of line and halftone in colour may also be simulated; so

millimetres, depending on the kind of typesetting equipment being used. This calculation is worked out in terms of the piece of metal upon which the character sits. Within this dimension, the nature of the design can vary considerably. If, for instance, the x height – the overall height of the body of the type – is large in relation to the ascenders (the parts rising above the body) and descenders (the parts below it), the design will appear relatively large. In consequence, the type is known as a large appearing face. Conversely, a type with a small x height and large ascenders and descenders is known as small appearing.

Of the two measurment systems, the point system is the oldest. Before its introduction in France in the early eighteenth century, each individual typecaster could choose whatever size to type suited him personally. The point system was designed to end this confusion. It is based upon division of the inch (in mainland

The Photo Mechanical Transfer (PMT) Machine **(left)** is an extremely versatile process camera; it can change black to white and vice versa *(1, 4)*, convert colour to black and white *(2)* and reverse left to right *(5)*. The machine will also produce screens. In this instance, a pencil drawing *(3)* has been put through a mezzo screen *(6)*. Lettering and artwork can be converted into instant transfer (autotype) of any colour *(7)*. Finally, yet another use of the PMT machine is in the production of cells. In this technique artwork — for example the title of a book — is printed on to a clear film so that it can be manoeuvred on the layout. *(8.)*

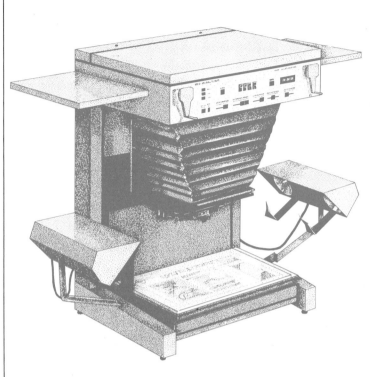

1△

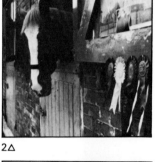

2△

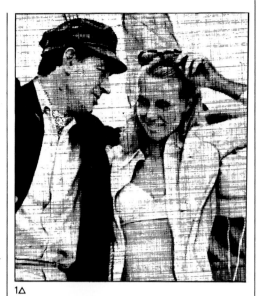

3△

4△

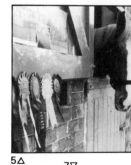

5△   7▽

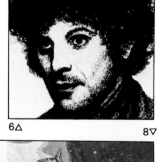

6△   8▽

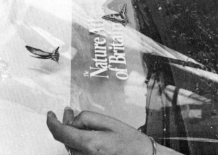

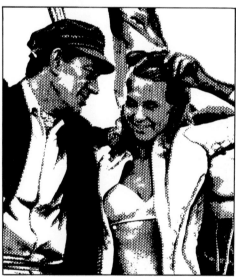

1△

4△   7▽

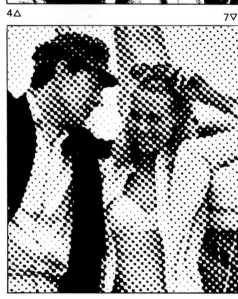

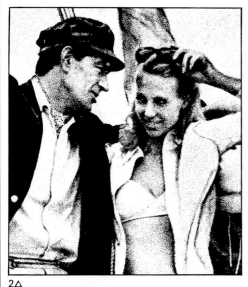

2△

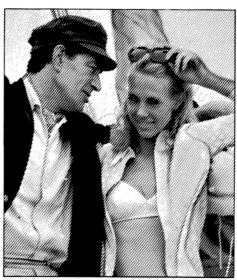

3△

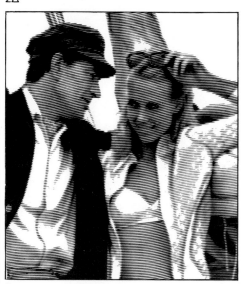

5△

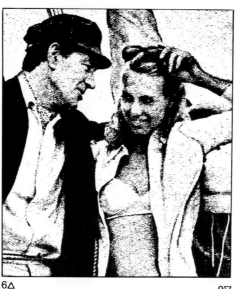

8▽ 6△

can duotones and even four colour effects outside the standard process printing colours.

The colour key technique also allows colours to be applied to adhesive surfaces. This means that the designer can produce a dry transfer in a single copy. This is particularly useful in advertising, for package designs, where the simulated image can be applied to almost any potential packaging material.

A sophisticated version of the dyeline technique, known as the Safir SC process, can be used to check the final appearance of a piece of artwork without incurring the expense of colour proofing. This system employs film base images of the artwork at its final size. These activate a photo-sensitive coating on a white polyester base. After exposure to light, dye adheres to the exposed areas and successive coatings or layers of colour can be built up. This process is especially useful for such purposes as cartography, in which it may be necessary to experiment with several colour effects.

Microfiche This is an area of specialized photographic copying which has developed rapidly in recent years. Basically, the system uses photographic techniques to miniaturize documents. This helps to save both storage space and postage costs. It is possible to produce microfiche direct from computer data banks; this enables information to be up-dated rapidly. Microfiche cards containing 270 pages equivalent to A4 are readily available in full colour in an A6 format.

Facsimile copiers These machines, first introduced in the 1970s, are a recent development in copying. They provide an instant electronic link between the studio and, say, the typesetter, as the system instantly transmits information from one to the other. Essentially this is an extension of the wire service transmission system used in the newspaper industry for many years.

All types of drawing can thus be circulated for confirmation or instruction, and this can considerably accelerate the design process. Facsimile copiers are available for A3 and A4 formats. One drawback, however, is the fact that equipment produced by different manufacturers is not always compatible, particularly as regards running speeds.

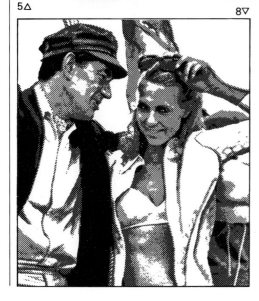

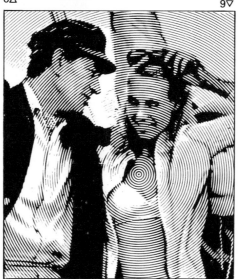

9▽

CHAPTER EIGHT

DESIGN AND TYPOGRAPHY

Designing for print is one of the most stimulating challenges any designer can face. However, there are several fundamental problems to be taken into consideration – the two most important being the varying width of the actual alphabetic characters and the difficulties of word spacing. Without some understanding of both problems, the end product may well fail the twin tests of attractiveness and legibility.

The problem with alphabetic characters is that they vary in width according to how they are produced. On a manual typewriter, for instance, all the characters have to be fitted into a single line width, so the alphabet is therefore designed with exaggeratedly wide serifs on letters such as 'i' and 'l'. This helps to reduce the amount of white space, which would otherwise tend to fragment the appearance of the type-written text. On the other hand, most electric typewriters use a system of three different character widths. Not only does this allow a greater variety of letterform design, but it also means that results approximating to type can be achieved. Most typesetting machines, for their part, use a system of nine different character widths to ensure optically even spacing between words.

Word spacing itself presents similar problems. These are of fairly ancient origin, for the convention of varying inter-word spacing developed

¹ lal	² lal	³ lll	⁴ lll
aba	aba	aea	aea
olo	olo	lkl	lkl
aaa	aaa	oao	oao

Above In designing for print the spacing of letters is an important factor. Each character must have some space on both sides — but too much space makes the appearance of the type fragment. In serif type faces (2, 4) spacing is regulated by the projections to the right of the type body; in sans serif faces (1, 3) lateral spacing is important.

Below The uneven letter size and spacing on the early Christian capital (1) makes it very hard to read — a difficulty overcome in the more precise Roman lettering (2). The even spacing of the characters on a standard typewriter (3) can be clearly contrasted with the varying letter widths on a sheet of dry transfer lettering (4).

long before the invention of printing and typesetting. In medieval Europe, scribes aimed at making the facing pages in their books appear symmetrical. This led them to insist that the right-hand margin should be vertically aligned; such an alignment could often be achieved only by abbreviating many words. To cope with this, a considerable number of signs extra to the 26 letters of the conventional alphabet were invented. Known as contractions, they were used to take the place of frequently abbreviated words.

The first printers, too, observed these conventions, though the use of contractions was soon abandoned. The alignment of the margin, however, was dictated by the demands of the letterpress printing process. In letterpress, every letter of type has to be held under tension within a rigid rectangular frame called a forme. A system of four different width spaces is sufficient to obtain this. When type is set with the right-hand margin aligned vertically, this is achieved by distributing approximately equal amounts of space between each of the words in the line.

This process is often referred to as justified typesetting; technically, however, this is a misleading use of the term. Strictly speaking, it refers to the process of making sure that all the lines of type on a page are the same length. If even a single line of type is short, the entire page will collapse if the forme is lifted, thus involving resetting it completely.

This convention persisted into the twentieth century, until technological developments made its observance no longer strictly necessary. With the advent of the so-called Modern Movement in type design during the 1920s and 1930s, both it and the convention of varied word-spaced composition were called into question. Instead, the members of this school advocated the use of constantly equal amounts of word space. This results in one ragged margin, which is usually placed on the right.

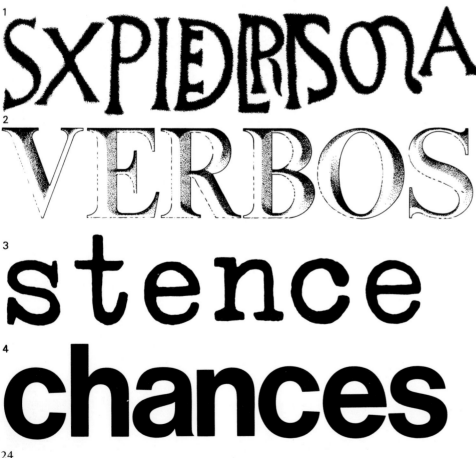

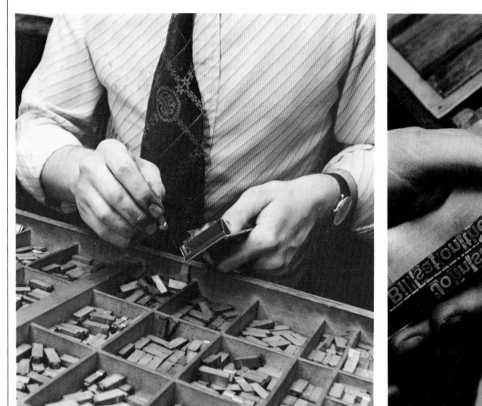

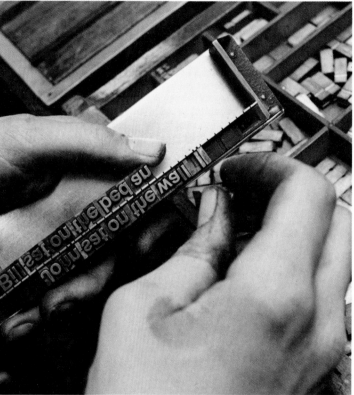

Composing type in letterpress
Type is spaced while it is being set. In hand-setting type is taken from the case **(above left)** and placed in the composing stick **(above right)**. The stick is set to the required line length. In order that the type does not fall out of the forme **(right)** when it is assembled from the individual lines, each line must be the same length. To do this, the right hand margin is aligned vertically and the words in the line spaced out. A system of four different line spaces has proved sufficient for this. This process is called justifying. The spaces between the words should be as even as possible. The same processes are carried out mechanically when the setting is done by machine.

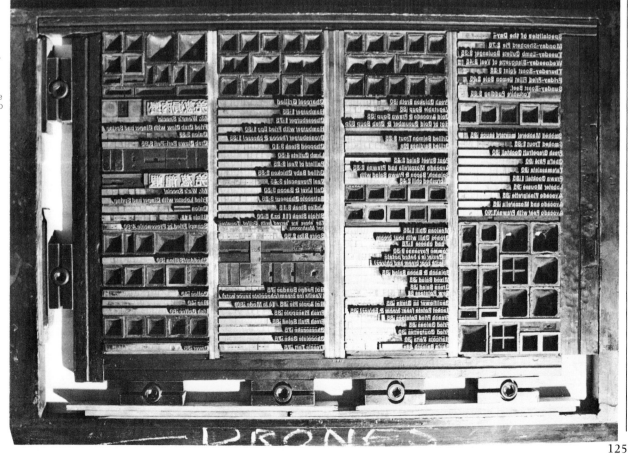

Type size Letterpress type has the part required to print raised in relief. The space remaining in the interior of the characters was, in the days of hand-cast type, produced by individual punches, each cut to the precise form needed. These tools were known as counterpunches; the term 'counters' is still used to describe the white, non-printing areas within a piece of type, irrespective of whether the type is produced in hot metal, film or any other form of composition.

Type size is measured in either points or millimetres, depending on the kind of type-setting equipment being used. This calculation is worked out in terms of the piece of metal upon which the character sits. Within this dimension, the nature of the design can vary considerably. If, for instance, the x height – the overall height of the body of the type – is large in relation to the ascenders (the parts rising above the body) and descenders (the parts below it); the design will

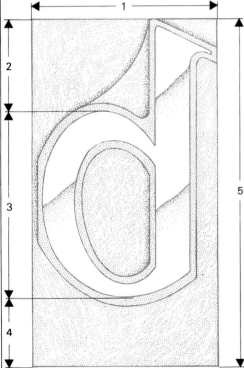

Typographical dimensions For calculating the dimensions of a piece of set copy the width and height of the character are important **(above)**. Character height is measured in points. The width of the character, measured across the page, is also calculated in points. These are called set points, often abbreviated to set. In order to work out the length of a line it is vital to know the set width of the characters. The piece of type **(right)** is a rectangular piece of metal with the printing surface uppermost. This surface is called the face and the block is termed the body.

1 Width (units of set)
2 Ascender
3 'x' height
4 Beard (space for descender)
5 Body (point size)
6 Front
7 Foot
8 Nick
9 Height (to paper)
10 Back
11 Shoulder

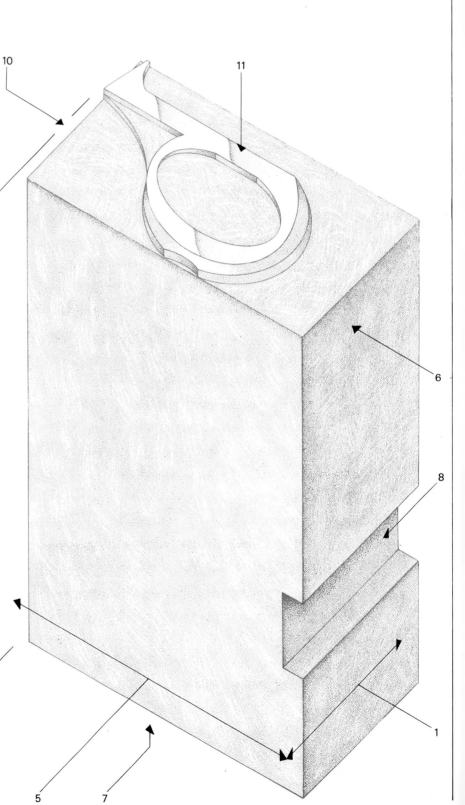

appear relatively large. In consequence, the type is known as a large appearing face. Conversely, a type with a small x height and large ascenders and descenders is known as small appearing.

Of the two measurement systems, the point system is the oldest. Before its introduction in France in the early eighteenth century, each individual typecaster could choose whatever size of type suited him personally. The point system was designed to end this confusion. It is based upon division of the inch (in mainland Europe, its pre-metric equivalent) into 72 subdivisions.

In the USA, the Anglo-American point system is still universal, but in the UK the position has become more complicated with the introduction of metrication. In Europe, metrication and the point section co-exist; the European point size is slightly bigger than the Anglo-American one.

The consequences of this are twofold. Typographic designers can either adopt a co-ordinated system of measurement on a metric basis; or, alternatively, they can work in points for type setting and metrics for illustrations and paper. Essentially, the choice is governed by the system of measurement adopted by the companies involved in producing the work. This is especially important, since it is becoming increasingly rare for all printing functions to be carried out within one unit. Frequently, typesetting is produced by one company, illustrations prepared and blocks or plates made by a second and the actual printing and binding carried out by a third.

In the Anglo-American system, the other main term used in printing measurement is the pica or pica em. Picas are twelve point units devised to measure the lengths of lines of type, as individual points are obviously too cumbersome for the purpose. The European equivalent is the *Didot*, named after the French typographer Firmin Didot (1764–1836) who refined a system first devised by his compatriot Pierre Simon Fournier. In France and Germany, the equivalent of the pica is the *cicero*; in Italy, it is the *riga tipografica* (*riga*); and in Holland it is the *augustijn* (*aug*). There is no relationship between the two systems; nor does the Didot relate to the metric system. It is now being gradually replaced by metrication for this reason.

Right This chart shows the differences in type body sizes between the Anglo-American and European point systems.

Far right The depth scale shows the number of lines needed to fill a given depth. The scale is calibrated for many different type sizes.

Point sizes

Even though the art of printing spread swiftly through Europe in the years following its initial development in Germany, it was not until the early eighteenth century that an attempt was made to standardize a system of type measurement. This happened in France, when Pierre Fournier proposed a standard unit of measurement of typesetting which he called the point. Before this time, the measurement of the metal type might vary — even by as little as a thousandth of an inch — so that the type cast by one foundry could not be used in combination with the type cast by another.

Fournier's innovations were developed by his fellow countryman Firmin Didot to produce a European standard, but Britain and American went their separate ways. There are now two point systems in operation — the Anglo-American and the European systems. The two differ in the basic standard of measurement used to determine the body size of a piece of type. The Anglo-American system works with a 12 point measurement of 0.166in — one point being 0.013833in. The European 12 point

measures 0.1776in — one point is 0.0148in. The unit of 12 points is called a pica in the Anglo-American system and a cicero in the European. The two systems do not relate to each other, but now the metric system seems likely to replace them both in time.

The term pica itself originates in the early days of printing. The term is said to come from the type size conventionally used for pocket breviaries in England — a type size which William Caxton christened 'pies'.

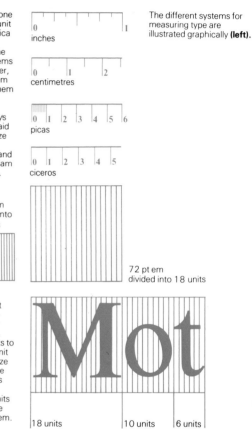

inches

centimetres

picas

ciceros

The different systems for measuring type are illustrated graphically **(left)**.

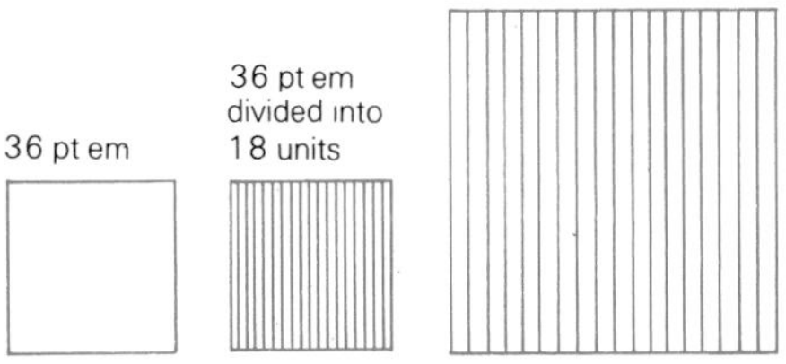

36 pt em

36 pt em divided into 18 units

72 pt em divided into 18 units

Above and **right** The unit system is used on photo-typesetting machines for measuring and counting. There are usually 18 units to the em. The size of the unit varies according to the size of the type **(above)**. In the world Mot **(right)** the *M* is 18 units wide, the *o* 10 units wide and the *t* 6 units wide. The spacing can be finely adjusted in this sytem.

18 units   10 units   6 units

Bodytype sizes

Point size	Lines to the inch	Anglo-American	Didot	Point size	Lines to the inch	Anglo-American (in decimals of inch)	Didot
3	24	.0415	.0444	8	9	.1107	.1184
3½	20.6	.0484	.0518	9	8	.1245	.1332
4	18	.0553	.0592	10	7.2	.1383	.1480
4¼	16.9	.0588	.0629	11	6.6	.1522	.1628
4½	16.	.0623	.0666	12	6	.1660	.1776
4¾	15.2	.0657		13	5.5	.1798	.1924
5	14.4	.0692	.0740	14	5.1	.1937	.2072
5¼	13.7	.0726	.0777	16	4.5	.2213	.2369
5½	13.1	.0761	.0814	18	4	.2490	.2665
6	12	.0830	.0888	20	3.6	.2767	.2961
6½	11.1	.0899	.0962	22	3.3	.3043	.3257
7	10.3	.0968	.1036	24	3	.3320	.3553
7½	9.6	.1037	.1110				

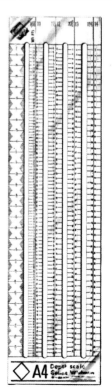

A4 Depth scale

Type families For the first 400 years of type's existence, its form was largely dependent upon the mechanical constraints of the printing processes of the times. Only in the nineteenth century did printing technology become sufficiently advanced to allow fancy and whimsy to play a significant part in type design. Today, there are literally thousands of different typefaces in existence; this prolixity can present the designer with what sometimes seems to be a bewildering array of choice.

As has been seen, the first printers based their conventions for typographic layout upon manuscript models, so it is hardly surprising that the earliest type designs were based upon the

Right *Type families* There is a vast array of type faces available today which the graphic designer can use. However, care should be taken when using the same typeface from different typesetters as the faces may vary considerably.

handwriting of the time. In Germany, where printing from moveable type originated, the local handwriting was what is known as Gothic, black letter or textura and type followed this in style. The letterform itself is written in such a way that the curved forms of the alphabet are difficult to produce and, in consequence, they tend to be reduced to a minimum. The result is not easily legible, though the visual effect is extremely distinctive.

When printing was introduced to Italy in the latter half of the fifteenth century, however, the type that developed there assumed a pronouncedly different form. The local handwriting used in Italy for formal documents is known as Chancery Italic; it has a much lighter and more legible appearance than German Gothic and so has had a profound influence on the development of type design. Some of the types developed at this time are still in use today in the form of versions adapted for mechanical compositions between the wars. Bembo is one leading example.

These earliest types are known as Old Style. They can be identified by the robust form of the serif – a small line used to complete the main stroke of a letter – which is triangular in form. The chief reason for this was that at the time of their introduction the surface of the paper used for printing was coarse and very uneven – so much so in fact that it was necessary to dampen it before printing to make it pliable enough to obtain a clear impression. Also, since printing presses were then made of wood, they could only exert pressure over a comparatively small area. Thus, the impact on to the paper could not be controlled with the delicacy required to obtain a lighter appearance. The other distinguishing feature of the Old Style types is the diagonal emphasis given to the thicker parts of curved strokes. This is derived from the manuscript models upon which this family of types was based.

Over the succeeding centuries, type assumed forms which were less influenced by handwriting. The processes of refining the mechanics of printing – and its associated materials, such as paper, ink and type – eventually resulted in the creation of a separate identity for printers' type. This thus came to be conceived quite independently of manuscript forms.

It is ironic that one of the most celebrated type designers to contribute to this development was himself a writing master. This was John Baskerville (1706–75), a Birmingham (UK) manufacturer who, in later life, made a significant contribution to the development of type design through the improvements he brought to the making of paper, type and ink. Baskerville's types are classic examples of a category known as Transitional. In these, there is a tendency to a lighter colour than that of Old Style, while the emphasis of the curved strokes tends to be perpendicular and the serifs more horizontal than diagonal.

Such improvements, however, did not easily

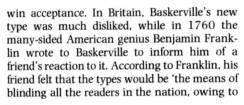

win acceptance. In Britain, Baskerville's new type was much disliked, while in 1760 the many-sided American genius Benjamin Franklin wrote to Baskerville to inform him of a friend's reaction to it. According to Franklin, his friend felt that the types would be 'the means of blinding all the readers in the nation, owing to

the thin and narrow strokes of the letters.' His comment on a type sample was to complain of 'Baskerville' pains of the eyes, though this particular type was, in fact, the product of a different designer, but in the same style.

The brilliance of which Franklin's friend complained was just as much the result of Baskerville's experiments with paper and ink, as well as with type. He invested considerable amounts of time and money in working out how to improve the surface of paper by pressing it between hot plates to give it a high gloss. Similar experiments produced an improved ink, which was much blacker than its predecessors. Though Baskerville's paper surface approximated to what is today known as wove, it excited the comment on its introduction that it was 'so glossy and of such a perfect polish that one supposes the paper made of silk rather than linen.'

Developments now followed relatively swiftly and, by 1798, yet another type style – the so-called Modern style – had been introduced. This was the work of the Italian printer and typeface designer Giambattista Bodoni (1740–1813). His type is characterized by maximum contrast between thick and thin strokes. The serifs are fine horizontal hair lines, while ascenders and descenders are both extended. In devising his type, Bodoni was clearly influenced by the prevailing artistic vogue for Classical Greece and Rome, demonstrated in both architecture and painting.

The next great step forward came with the Industrial Revolution of the nineteenth century.

Above This poster by Herbert Bayer for the Kandinsky exhibition in 1926 shows the ideas of the Bauhaus in practice particularly in the clarity of the typeface and relationship between the image and lettering.

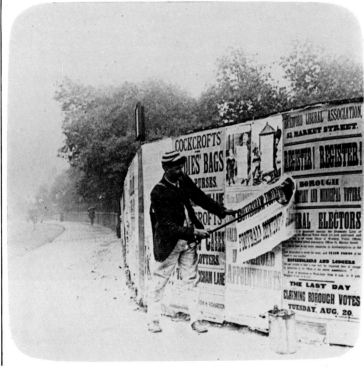

Left This early photograph shows a bill poster in Bradford. Bill posting has been a major advertising technique since the very earliest posters were hung on the walls of Paris during the French Revolution.

Main Categories in Typeface Design

Gothic
Also called black letter and, in Germany, Fraktur, this typeface family developed from manuscript writing. The vertical strokes are stressed.

𝔄𝔅ℭ𝔇𝔈 abcdefghijk

Old English

Old Face
In this typeface family there is little difference between the thick and thin strokes. The face is reasonably light and frequently has sloping serifs.

ABCDE abcdefgh

Bembo

Transitional
This group of typefaces falls between old face and modern face. There is less serif bracketing than in old face.

ABCDE abcdefghi

Baskerville Old Face

Modern Face
This family has thinner cross strokes than old face from which it was developed. The vertical strokes are stressed and the serifs hairline.

ABCDEF abcdefghi

Bodoni

Egyptian
This typeface group has an even-thickness form. The serifs are normally unbracketed and appear slab-like. Some of the condensed forms are known as Italian.

ABCDEF abcdefg

Rockwell

Fat Face
This cannot be used as a face for text setting. It was developed from modern face — the letters are much wider because the thick strokes are very broad.

ABCDE abcdef

Carousel

Sans Serif
This group of typefaces has no serifs. This category of typefaces is a relatively recent development.

ABCDEF abcdefgh

Helvetica

Technological advance, such as the introduction of mechanical type composition in the late 1880s, combined with market demand – particularly in the advertising field – to produce still more forms of type. These forms were designed to 'speak' more aggressively, both on hoardings and the printed page. They are bold and black, with the serif carrying as much weight as the other parts of the letter and thus are known as Slab Serif or Egyptian types. In extreme cases, the serifs are exaggerated to a point when they become gross and the design illegible: this type sub-family has the unflattering name of Fat Face.

It was as a result of this search for ever more striking types that designers came to realize that the silhouette of a letterform cannot be made infinitely bold. This is because, at a certain point, the counters become so reduced that the letterform becomes illegible. It was as a consequence of this that the first Roman types without serifs were introduced.

Initially, these Sans Serif or Grotesque types were used as poster faces, but before long they were also employed as jobbing faces, that is for general printing. They particularly appealed to the designers of the Modern Movement, who

used them to produce vibrant and sensitive results. In this they followed principles laid down by Jan Tschichold (1902–1974) one of the most energetic and influential typographers of his time, who in 1931 became a lecturer to the Munich Master Printers' School. His book *Die Neue Typographie* (The New Typography) has acted as a focus for several generations of typographers, many of whom are still working today. The geometric Sans Serif letterforms devised by the German *Bauhaus* school and the *De Stijl* movement in Holland were also extremely influential; a classic example of the former is Paul Renner's Futura (1928). The most significant British Sans Serif types were those designed by Edward Johnson for the London underground (subway) system (1918) and by Eric Gill for Monotype (1928).

Selecting faces Historical models have not been the sole sources for type design. The changing conditions of print production have continuously prompted the development of type designs suited to the technology of their times. At the beginning of the twentieth century, the first mechanical typesetting machines (Linotype and Monotype) came into full-scale use and thus the types pre-dating this were accordingly remodelled. The differing characteristics of the two systems influenced the re-design; hot metal Linotype machines produce each complete line of type as a single piece of metal, whereas the Monotype system produces a line formed of individual types and spaces combined to make up the required line.

Because of these different characteristics, Linotype equipment proved to be better suited to newspaper production, where the type has to be handled rapidly. Monotype, on the other hand, is more suitable for jobbing and book work. In consequence, the two systems developed different capabilities, with Monotype tending to develop a reputation for greater typographic elegance. This was largely attributable to the influence of the British typographer Stanley Morison (1889–1967), who oversaw the type development programme.

Morison's Times New Roman, commissioned by *The Times* newspaper in 1931, is probably the most significant example of a type designed to meet mechanical requirements. Although resembling an Old Style face, the exaggeratedly large x height was designed to give the maximum amount of legibility however small the size. Other types designed during this century, however, are extremely difficult to classify chronologically and are thus generally grouped under the title Twentieth Century. These include, for example, Perpetua, Joanna and the type in which this book is set – Monotype Photina 747.

Another factor that has to be taken into consideration in type selection is the particular process to be employed. In general, it should be remembered that the earliest types were orig-

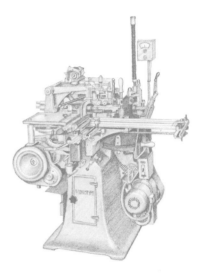

Above This Monotype machine produces a line of type formed from individual types and spaces. With this machine individual characters and words can be corrected.

Below This Linotype machine casts type in complete lines. For correction purposes whole lines have to be taken out and replaced.

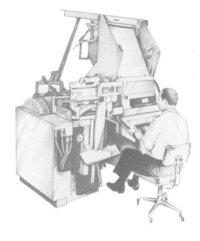

Below The Times New Roman type face created by Stanley Morison gives a high degree of legibility. This is achieved partly because of the exaggeratedly large x height.

abcd

THE TIMES

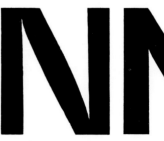

Above There is a clearly visible difference between these two letters. Both have been set using photocomposition. The Helvetica face (**right**) has even strokes, while the Univers (**left**) has deep indentations into the bottom of the strokes. These are necessary because the spaces tend to fill in during the printing process.

inally designed for printing by letterpress on uncoated paper, such as cartridge. Since then, however, paper has generally become more and more smooth and the impression ever lighter. This means that some types can appear fragile and spindly if printed on a glossy art paper. Modern faces, such as Bodoni or Walbaum, look more mellow and robust if printed by letterpress on cartridge paper. Typesetting equipment can also influence the appearance of a particular type design; photo-typesetters, for instance, often produce lighter results than the equivalent in hot metal.

Such effects – the properties of light and photographic processing in photo-setting and ink on paper, particularly in lithographic printing – have been taken into account by some type designers when conceiving a new typeface. Univers, designed by Adrian Frutiger in 1957, is probably the most prominent example demonstrating this approach.

A further technical constraint is whether numerous pages are required to have type reversed – that is, for the type to appear white on a coloured background. In such cases, it is unwise to select a type with fine lines as an integral part of the design; a Modern face or a

light weight of type, for instance, may well prove unsuitable. This is because the image area tends to be reduced by surplus ink and it may well disappear in part as a result. In four-colour reproduction, the gravure process can have the same detrimental effect upon the same range of types.

The choice of typeface can also be influenced by aesthetic considerations. A historical manuscript, for instance, can be set in an historically suitable type, while an industrial catalogue might be set in a Sans Serif or Egyptian face to give it a sober and unpretentious appearance. Sans Serif is similarly suitable for a reading book for young children, since, particularly in the case of 'a' and 'g', the characters closely resemble today's handwriting. In addition, the outline of the letterform is not obscured by the presence of serifs.

If, on the other hand, the job is a novel, a serified typeface, such as Baskerville, is probably a better choice. In the case of reference books containing complex typography, such as tables and bibliographies, a typeface with a wide range of variations in weight and italic is likely to be required. Garamond and Bembo are two leading examples. For manuscript containing mathematical formulae, Times is the most comprehensive choice. The typesetting is best done on Monotype equipment in this case.

The two closely related factors of colour and leading are the final influences on the choice of typeface. Colour is the term typographers use to describe the general tonal value of the text after setting; each typeface produces its own colour. This is further influenced by the leading – the amount of space added between each line. The name is a traditional one, dating back to the days of handset letterpress composition, when fillets of metal, known as leads, were used to space the lines further apart. The equivalent term in photocomposition is line feed.

Typesetting methods There are two basic forms of type origination – direct or by means of conversion to produce a suitable matrix. The oldest direct method is hand setting. The first types were individually cast and subsequently assembled by hand by the compositor into a form corresponding to the author's text. Type is still produced in limited quantities for use in this way by type founders; type suitable for hand composition is therefore known as founder's type.

Above left The changes in leading, space, weight and colour and the use of rules have a major effect on the visual impact of the printed product. The designer must bear such factors in mind when specifying instructions for the typesetter.

There are literally hundreds of breeds of horse in the world and their number and composition is constantly changing. There are many reasons for this; a breed can die out because the environment changes, for instance, or because it is no longer useful to man. The latter is now happening to many of the breeds of heavy horses, whose work is now frequently done by machines.

This decline, however, has been partly compensated for by growth in other parts of the horse world. With the increase in the number of people riding for pleasure in the last twenty years, many countries have started stud books for riding horses to meet growing demand.

The breeds of the world can be divided into hot-bloods, cold-bloods, warm-bloods and ponies. Hot-bloods are pure-bred, fiery, pedigree horses – the English Thoroughbred is a good example. Cold-bloods are the heavy horses, the work horses of the world. The warm-bloods are lighter animals, usually **riding horses, which frequently have both cold-bloods and hot-bloods among their ancestors. Ponies are the small breeds – those which are under 14.2 hands in height – and are the particular favourites of children.**

In this chapter, a breed is defined as one that has a stud book. There are two main types. Many stud books are opened, that is, stock is registered in the breed stud book on condition that the parents are approved by the relevant

There are literally hundreds of breeds of horse in the world and their number and composition is constantly changing. There are many reasons for this; a breed can die out because the environment changes, for instance, or because it is no longer useful to man. The latter is now happening to many of the breeds of heavy horses, whose work is now frequently done by machines.

This decline, however, has been partly compensated for by growth in other parts of the horse world. With the increase in the number of people riding for pleasure in the last twenty years, many countries have started stud books for riding horses to meet growing demand.

The breeds of the world can be divided into hot-bloods, cold-bloods, warm-bloods and ponies. Hot-bloods are pure-bred, fiery, pedigree horses – the English Thoroughbred is a good example. Cold-bloods are the heavy horses, the work horses of the world. The warm-bloods are lighter animals, usually riding horses, which frequently have both cold-bloods and hot-bloods among their ancestors. Ponies are the small breeds – those which are under 14.2 hands in height – and are the particular favourites of children.

In this chapter, a breed is defined as one that has a stud book. There are two main types. Many stud books are opened, that is, stock is registered in the breed stud book on condition that the parents are approved by the relevant breed society and are of pedigree stock themselves. The stallion and mare concerned need not necessarily be both of the same breed. The Hanover-

Left The tonal values of the text are important for how it will look and read. The text **(far left)** has been set in Univers light **(top)** medium **(middle)** and bold **(bottom)**. This contrasts with the second text **(left)** which has been set in the same type face with progressively less leading (or spacing) towards the bottom. The graphic designer should know how to achieve and use such typographic effects.

Venetian Centaur

ABCDEFGHIJK
abcdefghijklmnop

Old Face Bembo

ABCDEFGHIJK
abcdefghijklmno

Old Face Garamond

ABCDEFGHIJKL
abcdefghijklmnopq

Transitional Baskerville

ABCDEFGHIJK
abcdefghijklmno

Transitional Bell

ABCDEFGHIJK
abcdefghijklmnop

Modern Bodoni

ABCDEFGHIJKL
abcdefghijklmnop

Extra light extra condensed

Univers

Light extra condensed

Univers

Light condensed

Univers

Univers

Light

Univers

Univers

Medium extra condensed

Univers

Medium condensed

Univers

Univers

Medium

Univers

Univers

Medium expanded

Univers

20th Century Times New Roman

ABCDEFGHIJK
abcdefghijklmnop

Classification and recognition of typefaces The design of different typefaces has evolved over the centuries with the development of printing technology. The Venetian typeface, Centaur, retains more traces of the fifteenth century calligraphic origins of type than most other Old Style typefaces such as Bembo and Garamond which can be recognized by their triangular serifs and the diagonal emphasis given to thicker parts of curved strokes. Transitional typefaces tend to make the curved strokes vertical and the serifs horizontal. Modern faces, like Bodoni, have a strong vertical stress and hairline serifs. Twentieth century faces, such as Times New Roman were specifically designed to meet mechanical requirements. The distinguishing features of this group vary enormously. Sans serif typefaces, initially used for bold poster display, are now commonly used when a clear, unpretentious effect is desired.

20th Century Perpetua

ABCDEFGHIJKL
abcdefghijklmnopq

Geometrical Sans Serif Gill Sans

ABCDEFGHIJKLM
abcdefghijklmnopq

Grotesque Sans Serif Grotesque

ABCDEFGHIJKLM
abcdefghijklmnopq

Grotesque Sans Serif Univers

ABCDEFGHIJKL
abcdefghijklmno

Left The Univers typeface, a simple, classic face designed by Adrian Frutiger in 1957, is one of the most complete attempts to produce a series of letters of different weights and outlines. The flexibility of this range makes it one of the most widely used typefaces today.

Bold condensed

Univers

Univers

Bold

Univers

Univers

Bold expanded

Univers

Extra bold

Univers

Univers

Extra bold expanded

Univers

Ultra bold expanded

Univers

Hot metal Hot metal composition became the norm with the advent of mechanical typesetting at the beginning of this century. These machines assemble the matrices required for each letter in a line of text and make a casting from them in molten metal. It is these castings which are used to print the text – hence the name hot metal. The principal manufacturers are Monotype in the UK and Linotype in America. Other types of hot metal composition equipment, employed chiefly for the production of newspaper headings, are made by Ludlow and Intertype.

Hot metal composition imposes certain constraints on typography. For instance, the compositor cannot reduce the inter-character spacing or inter-line spacing. For this reason, kerned characters have been developed for some combinations of letters – a kerning letter is one in which some part of the design overhangs the body of the type and rests upon the body of a neighbouring letter or space. They are commonly used in mathematical setting. The mechanical constraints of the systems also limit the type sizes available for body text to a maximum of 14 point.

Photo-composition These constraints do not apply to photo-composition. Here, because the individual characters are projected as light on to photographic film, the physical limitations are considerably more flexible. It is possible, for instance, to set text closer together than the original sample alphabet indicates, though this freedom should be used with discretion. Although many typefaces may be set comparatively closer than their hot metal equivalents, there are some types, such as Univers, which were specifically designed to be set with wider spaced letters. Consequently they tend to read better when set as the designer intended.

Another facility of photo-setting is the ability to distort the appearance of type by introducing prisms into the light path. Depending on the nature of the prism, type can be condensed, expanded or inclined to form an italic as required; this does away with the need to re-draw each character independently. A third is the comparative ease with which matrices for variants, and even complete alphabets, can be produced.

The great advantage of photo-composition, however, is that the type it produces can be used as a matrix for processes such as lithography, gravure and screen printing without going through an intermediary photographic stage. A further plus is that a wider range of type sizes is available than in hot metal. Some comparatively simple machines provide a range from five point to 48 point in four alphabets as a standard specification. The range from 48 point upwards is usually catered for by the headliner type of equipment. This can set sizes up to 288 point (51mm).

Strike-on systems and typewriters Headline ma-chines are comparatively cheap and are often used with 'strike-on' equipment, such as the IBM Composer or the Adressograph Multigraph Varityper. These are essentially sophisticated electric typewriters, with interchangeable typing heads ('golf balls') for each alphabet. They can also be programmed to produce text with varied inter-word space to achieve vertically aligned margins on the right. These strike-on systems thus have many of the attributes of

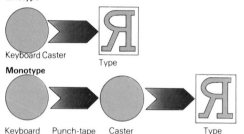

Linotype
Keyboard Caster   Type

Monotype
Keyboard   Punch-tape   Caster   Type

Above The Linotype machine combines keyboard and caster. Monotype uses two machines for these stages.

Right In computer setting the characters are revealed as steps on a grid when enlarged.

typesetting, though the quality of the output does not match that of hot metal or photo-composition.

Nevertheless, if typographic quality is not a critical factor and if costs have to be minimized, the standard manual typewriter is perfectly capable of producing acceptable results if sensitively used. Moreover, if printing is done lithographically from photosensitized plates, an alphabet size approximating to typographic

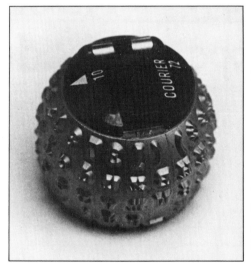

Above The 'golf ball', an interchangeable head producing letters in a particular typeface, can be used on a number of sophisticated electric typewriters to produce a form of typesetting. Such systems can vary word spacing to justify text on both left and right hand margins. This method of setting is relatively cheap but its quality is variable.

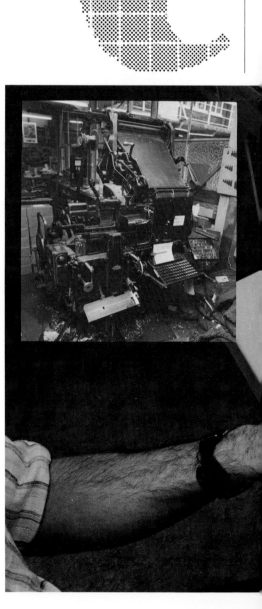

Right The remarkable technological development of typesetting systems over the present century is starkly contrasted here. The Linotype machine **(above),** which has a keyboard but which automatically casts type in the one machine, is a relatively primitive mechanical device when compared with the Linotron which uses a computer and other electronic equipment to produce film setting.

The form typography is to take
The form typography is to take
The form typography is to take
The form typography is to take
The form typography is to take

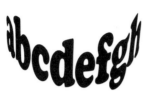

Univers Univers Univers

Photo-composition or film setting is a much more flexible method than hot metal composition. Character spacing, for example, can be varied to a fraction of a millimetre and letters can be elongated or contracted at will.

equivalents can be obtained by simply reducing the typing photographically at the plate-making stage. This technique has been adopted on more than one occasion where cost was not the critical factor, but simply because the designer believed that the typewritten format was the appropriate one.

Electronic typesetting At the opposite extreme of mechanical sophistication are electronic editing and typesetting systems. These use computers to sift and edit data, frequently in association with cathode ray tube (CRT) typesetting machines which produce as many as 8000 characters per second or up to 300 lines of typesetting per minute. If, say, a trade directory is being updated, an entire page can be typeset in as little as 17 seconds.

Technological progress means that these systems are constantly increasing in number. The first generation of videotex/Teletext systems, for instance, is now coming into daily use. These systems are today only in their infancy, but they are likely to develop rapidly into a new communications medium complimentary to radio, television and the press.

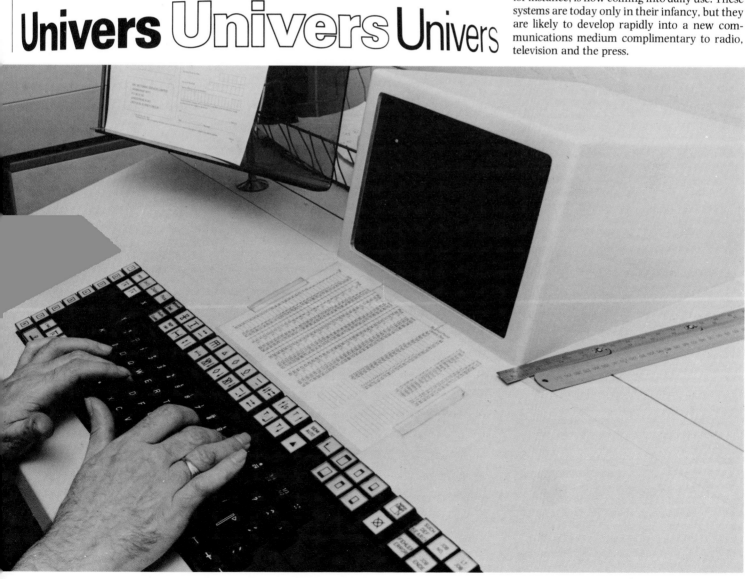

Preparing manuscript Whatever typeface or typesetting system is chosen, all copy has to be first prepared by the designer before the printer starts work. First read the manuscript; without an understanding of its contents, no designer can establish a suitable typographic structure. This entails deciding on the size and position of headings, sub-headings, references, footnotes and so on, which, in turn, may involve additional sub-editing after the design is formalized.

It is almost impossible to establish a clear typographic structure if the text is not type-written and it is usually essential for it to be typed to the same approximate line length as the final form. This can save considerable amounts of time and money, particularly if film setting is used. With this process, even minor corrections can be very costly when the type has been set. Retyping to the line length can also serve to confirm the proposed typographic structure; more significantly, it enables the designer to make an accurate estimate of the number of lines required for a particular manuscript in a specific form. From this, the number of pages required can also be calculated.

Casting-off The methods by which the length of a manuscript can be established are at best only approximations. In any cast-off, it is therefore advisable to round up any calculations and, better still, to allow five to ten per cent extra to the estimate. This extra allowance depends upon the complexity of the manuscript and the number of words per line once it is set in type. Problems can arise here where lines are short; if this happens, the number of hyphenated words, or exaggerated white spaces arising from the necessity to carry words over to the next line, is increased.

If the manuscript is typed upon a manual typewriter, the business of casting-off is made much easier because each typewritten letter occupies the same amount of space. This may be either 10, 11 or 12 characters per inch; the distance involved can easily be measured with a suitable inch scale. If the text is typed upon a variable character width machine, the count must then be made manually.

In either case, an approximation must be made of an average line, each inter-word space counting as a single character. This figure is then multiplied by the total number of lines of manuscript to give the number of characters involved. This figure can be used to estimate the cost of setting.

Following this, the designer establishes the amount of space the manuscript will fill. This will obviously vary, according to the typeface chosen. Normally, however, this is where budgetary considerations come into play; it is only very rarely that a designer is asked to increase the amount of space a manuscript may occupy. Usually, therefore, the task is to select the correct balance of layout, type, typesize and heading

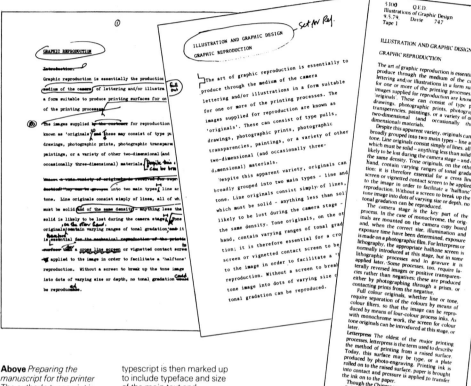

Above *Preparing the manuscript for the printer* The author's typescript is read and then any errors or alterations marked by the book's editor. Next the copy is retyped to the number of characters per line specified by the designer. The final typescript is then marked up to include typeface and size of the main text and headings. Line spaces should also be indicated where necessary. This mark-up **(below)** contains all information for the printer.

Number of Roman lower case letters per line					
Measure 12 pt.ems	6D	8D	Measure 12 pt.ems	9D	10D
15	40	32·3	21	38·5	33·1
16	42·7	34·4	22	40·4	34·7
17	45·3	36·6	23	42·2	36·2
18	48	38·7	24	44	37·8
19	50·7	40·9	25	45·9	39·4
20	53·3	43	26	47·7	41
21	56	45·2	27	49·6	42·5
22	58·7	47·3	28	51·4	44·1
23	61·3	49·5	29	53·2	45·7
24	64	51·6	30	55·1	47·3

Above This Monotype card, used by designers when hot metal was the most common form of setting, very conveniently had its own fitting table attached. This considerably helped the designer to cast off more quickly.

which will condense the manuscript into a predetermined number of pages.

The way this is calculated is by referring to the sample alphabet, in the appropriate size, provided by either the printer or the manufacturer of the typesetting equipment. Particular care must be taken to refer to the correct sample, especially when the manufacturer produces both hot metal and photo-composition equipment. This is because the same typeface may vary in appearing size when converted from one form of typesetting equipment to another.

Some manufacturers – Monotype is a leading example – produce a special set of tables covering their complete range of typefaces to aid in calculating text lengths. Each typeface has a reference ('factor') number – this same number may, in fact, be appropriate for several typefaces. The numbers can be read against the proposed line length to indicate the average number of characters per line.

Some alphabet sample sheets also contain simplified casting-off tables. These are simpler to use on the whole than the factor method; they are also particularly useful as they serve as samples from which accurate layouts can be derived. Yet another form of sample serves to give both an approximate number of characters per line as well as a sample text set in a variety of different leadings.

It is only through the use of samples such as these that a designer can judge the visual appearance of what, on the surface, may seem to be only minor amendments to a specification; these may well seem insignificant in theory, but they can have a considerable effect on the

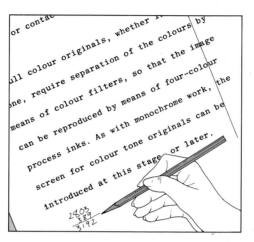

Casting off copy using copy fitting tables 1. A line is drawn by the copy's shortest line and the line's characters are counted. This is multiplied by the number of lines on the page. The number of characters in the ragged lines is calculated and added on.

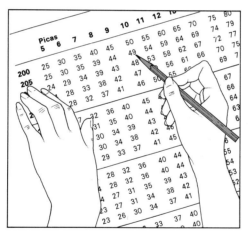

3. This figure is then read against the desired pica measure to get an exact line character count.

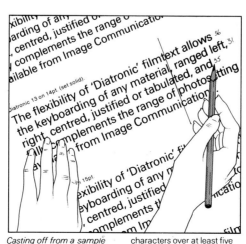

Casting off from a sample 1. Using a typesetter's specimen or a piece of copy in the desired typeface and size, count the number of characters over at least five lines. Divide this number by the lines counted to obtain the average number of characters per line.

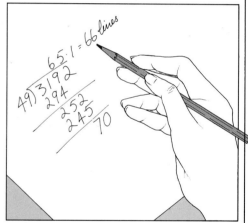

2. Having calculated the number of characters in the entire text, a factor figure is read from the table for the typeface, style and size, in which the designer has chosen to set the text.

4. This figure is divided into the total number of characters in the text to give the text's total line count. This figure will not be absolutely accurate because character widths vary, but it gives a very good working guide.

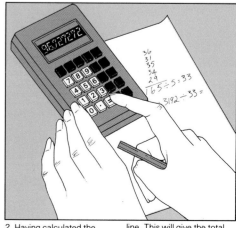

2. Having calculated the total number of characters in the copy, divide that number by the average number of characters per line. This will give the total number of lines the copy will occupy when set.

general colour of the page.

Layout The type of layout varies according to whether the design is purely typographic or whether illustrations are also involved. In the former case, the designer's task is to determine the types of heading involved and to find a satisfactory way of displaying any required emphasis in the text. This can be done in several ways; methods include capitalization, a change of type fount, a change of type size, use of interline space or indentation, or combinations of all these.

Layout is also governed by the number of lines per page and this is obviously affected by the combination of type size and leading. If, for instance, the designer thinks that the proposed typeface in the intended size may be uncomfortable to read, additional interline space may be added in the form of leading. Such a decision will have the effect of reducing the number of lines per page, which, in turn, will have a significant effect upon the number of pages required. It is also important to make an allowance for the blank spaces imposed by the typographic style to cover such details as sub-headings and paragraphing. This is likely to vary from job to job, but it is inevitable that it will add to the total number of lines.

There are two easy ways of measuring the number of lines per page. The first is to use a typescale, though this is likely not to contain all the increments that may be required. A full range of theses can be read off another variety of typescale, called a line counter. When using such an instrument, always measure from the same point – preferably the base line – against the type.

Illustrations present their own separate problems. The main aim should be to position them as closely as possible to the related text. It is also important to achieve consistency in design so as to balance illustrations and text.

There are literally hundreds of breeds of horse in the world and their number and composition is constantly changing. There are many reasons for this; a breed can die out because the environment changes, for instance, or because it is no longer useful to man. The latter is now happening to many of the breeds of

There are literally hundreds of breeds of horse in the world and their number and composition is constantly changing. There are many reasons for this; a breed can die out because the environment changes, for instance, or because it is no longer useful to man. The latter is now happening to many of the breeds of heavy horses, whose work is now frequently done by machines.

There are literally hundreds of breeds of horse in the world and their number and composition is constantly changing. There are many reasons for this; a breed can die out because the environment changes, for instance, or because it is no longer useful to man. The latter is now happening to many of the breeds of heavy horses, whose work is now frequently done by machines.

Above and **right** The layout of a page can vary considerably depending on the nature of the material and how the designer sees its function can best be served. The five examples here use the same block of type set in a chosen typeface, but show how the page can be filled out by using the type in different sizes, weights and leadings and by varying the width of the measures.

There are literally hundreds of breeds of horse in the world and their number and composition is constantly changing. There are many reasons for this; a breed can die out because the environment changes, for instance, or because it is no longer useful to man. The latter is now happening to many of the breeds of heavy horses, whose work is now frequently done by machines.

This decline, however, has been partly compensated for by growth in other parts of the horse world. With the increase in the number of people riding for pleasure in the last twenty years, many countries have started stud books for riding horses to meet growing demand.

The breeds of the world can be divided into hot-

There are literally hundreds of breeds of horse in the world and their number and composition is constantly changing. There are many reasons for this; a breed can die out because the environment changes, for instance, or because it is no longer useful to man. The latter is now happening to many of the breeds of heavy horses, whose work is now frequently done by machines.

There are literally hundreds of breeds of horse in the world and their number and composition is constantly changing. There are many reasons for this; a breed can die out because the environment changes, for instance, or because it is no longer useful to man. The latter is now happening to many of the breeds of

There are many reasons for this; a breed can die out because the environment changes, for instance, or because it is no longer useful to man. The latter is now happening to many of the breeds of

x height

Left In drawing up a grid there must be one line of reference from which all measurements can be taken. This x height on the top line of the grid is, in fact, the height of the letter x in whatever typeface has been chosen.

Right *Film make-up 1.* Along with the corrected galleys the designer sends a rough paste-up as a guide to positioning. *2.* Corrections are stripped into the film galleys. *3.* The strips of film are then made up into pages in reverse on a large board according to the layout design.

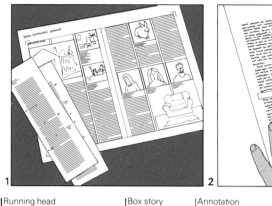

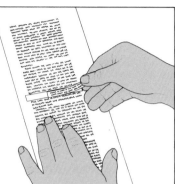

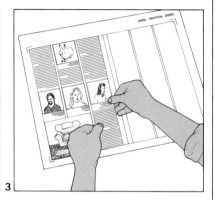

Below This page labels all the components that might be included in the design and make-up of a page.

| Sub heading | Running head | Box story | Annotation | Cross head |

Chapter heading

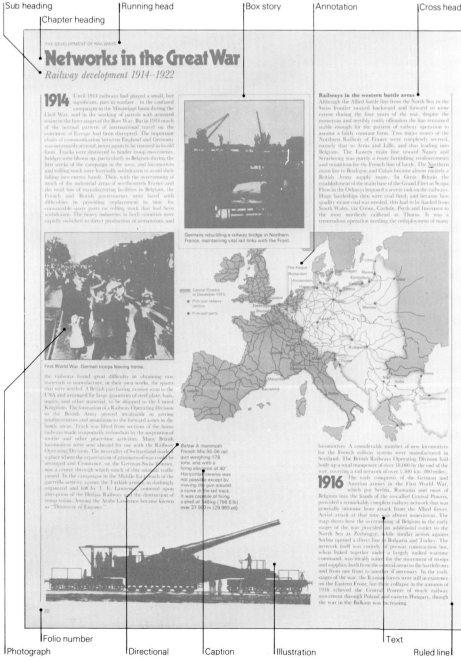

THE DEVELOPMENT OF RAILWAYS

Networks in the Great War
Railway development 1914–1922

1914 Until 1914 railways had played a small, but significant, part in warfare – in the confused campaigns in the Mississippi basin during the Civil War, and in the working of patrols with armored trains in the later stages of the Boer War. But in 1914 much of the normal pattern of international travel on the continent of Europe had been disrupted. The important chain of communication between England and Germany was necessarily severed, never again to be restored in its old form. Tracks were destroyed to hinder troop movements, bridges were blown up, particularly in Belgium during the first weeks of the campaign in the west, and locomotives and rolling stock were hurriedly withdrawn to avoid their falling into enemy hands. Then, with the overrunning of much of the industrial areas of northeastern France and the total loss of manufacturing facilities in Belgium, the French and British governments were faced with difficulties in providing replacement in time for consumable spare parts on rolling stock that had been withdrawn. The heavy industries in both countries were rapidly switched to direct production of armaments, and

Germans rebuilding a railway bridge in Northern France, maintaining vital rail links with the Front.

First World War. German troops leaving home.

the railways found great difficulty in obtaining raw materials to manufacture, in their own works, the spares that were needed. A British purchasing mission went to the USA and arranged for large quantities of steel plate, bars, ingots, and other material, to be shipped to the United Kingdom. The formation of a Railway Operating Division in the British Army proved invaluable in getting reinforcements and munitions to the forward zones in the hostile areas. Track was lifted from sections of the home railways made temporarily redundant by the suspension of tourist and other peacetime activities. Many British locomotives were sent abroad for use with the Railway Operating Division. The neutrality of Switzerland made a place where the repatriation of prisoners-of-war could be arranged and Constance, on the German-Swiss frontier, was a center through which much of this unusual traffic passed. In the campaigns in the Middle East much of the guerrilla activity against the Turkish armies, so dashingly organized and led by T. E. Lawrence, centered upon disruption of the Hedjaz Railway and the destruction of troop trains. Among the Arabs Lawrence became known as "Destroyer of Engines."

Below A mammoth French Mle 93–06 rail gun weighing 178 tons, and with a firing elevation of 40°. Horizontal traverse was not possible except by moving the gun around a curve in the rail track. It was capable of firing a shell of 348kg (766.5 lb) over 27,500 m (29,965 yd)

Railways in the western battle areas
Although the Allied battle line from the North Sea to the Swiss frontier swayed backward and forward to some extent during the four years of the war, despite the numerous and terribly costly offensives the line remained stable enough for the pattern of railway operation to assume a fairly constant form. Two major routes of the Northern Railway of France were completely severed, namely that to Arras and Lille, and that leading into Belgium. The Eastern main line toward Nancy and Strasbourg was purely a route furnishing reinforcements and munitions for the French line of battle. The Northern main line to Boulogne and Calais became almost entirely a British Army supply route. In Great Britain the establishment of the main base of the Grand Fleet at Scapa Flow in the Orkneys imposed a severe task on the railways. Huge battleships then were coal fired, and because best quality steam coal was needed, this had to be hauled from South Wales, via Crewe, Carlisle, Perth and Inverness to the most northerly railhead at Thurso. It was a tremendous operation needing the redeployment of many

locomotives. A considerable number of new locomotives for the French railways were manufactured in Scotland. The British Railways Operating Division had built up a total manpower of over 18,000 by the end of the war, covering a rail network of over 1,300 km (800 miles).

1916 The early conquests of the German and Austrian armies in the First World War, which put Serbia, Romania and most of Belgium into the hands of the so-called Central Powers, provided a remarkably complete railway network that was generally immune from attack from the Allied forces. Aerial attack at that time was almost nonexistent. The map shows how the overrunning of Belgium in the early stages of the war provided an additional outlet to the North Sea at Zeebrugge; while similar action against Serbia opened a direct line to Bulgaria and Turkey. The network itself was entirely of prewar construction but, when linked together under a largely unified wartime command, was ideally suited for the movement of troops and supplies, both from the central areas to the battlefronts and from one front to another if necessary. In the early stages of the war, the Russian forces were still in existence on the Eastern Front; but their collapse in the autumn of 1916 relieved the Central Powers of much railway movement through Poland and eastern Hungary, though the war in the Balkans was increasing

| Photograph | Folio number | Directional | Caption | Illustration | Text | Ruled line |

Grids All layouts should be designed on a purpose-planned double page spread. This plan is known as a grid: it should show all the features common to all pages, such as the maximum number of lines per column, text and illustration areas, position of headings, folios and so on. It serves as a reference both for the designer and the various craftsmen involved in production.

The use of a grid helps to minimize the amount of time required to prepare drawings; it also helps minimize the errors which might occur if each double page was drawn up individually. It is best if the master drawing of the grid is made on a transparent sheet, as this can then be used to check that the plate-maker or compositor have made up the spread correctly. This is done by simply laying the grid over a proof. The best material to use is one that is robust, dimensionally stable and accepts fine lines in ink readily. Polyester film is one of the most suitable.

In addition to this, it is a good idea to print the grid on to a card or board if a considerable number of pages are involved. This can be used as a base for pasting-up typesetting and illustration proofs prior to printing. This type of grid is best printed in a pale blue ink, as this will not be reproduced by the photo-engraver.

Type and illustration Type and illustrations can either be imposed (assembled) by the compositor, or, if prepared separately, by the designer or an independent art work team. If the printer imposes the job, he will assemble either hot metal type with blocks (if the work is to be printed by letterpress); if the printing process is lithography, screen process or gravure, he will impose film. The design team, on the other hand, will probably work with paper. Their product is known as artwork – reproduction drawings suitable for a photo-engraver's camera. It is best to use a stout white card as a base, while the adhesive used to stick the art work in position should not cockle the paper. Rubber cement, proprietary adhesive sprays or a waxing machine can be used.

Line illustrations can be drawn directly on to the art work. Alternatively, if the drawing is complicated, they can be prepared at a larger size, reduced photographically and then pasted up. A third possibility is to prepare all the art work, including all the typesetting, at a larger scale than the final product and then reduce it. If the final size required is not larger than A4, then a scale of one to one-and-a-half – known in the studio as 'half-up' – will probably be adequate.

It is best, however, not to include halftone illustrations in the paste up, unless quality is not the ultimate factor. If the resultant loss of quality is acceptable, cost is critical, or a coarse appearance is preferred, then halftones can be used in the form of screened PMTs (see p. 121). With the right equipment, these can be produced in the studio.

The best quality halftones are undoubtedly those prepared by a photo-engraver. In this case, the engraver produces either letterpress blocks or photographic film, from which lithographic plates, gravure cylinders or screen process stencils can be made. This means that the position of the illustration must be clearly indicated by means of external corner marks drawn in fine black ink line on the layout, while the precise dimension of the final size has to be indicated on

Below *Type specifications*
When the printer is doing the page make-up of an entire book it is vital to provide him, at the outset, with all the type specifications for the job. This must include information not only on how the text should be set but also about headings, running heads and folios.

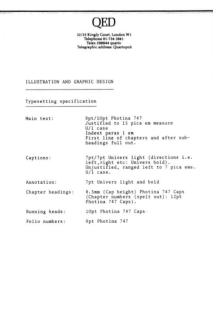

In the second quarter of the fourteenth century, illustration broke free from text illumination and panel painting became the rage. The church, state and laity continued to commission both well into the fifteenth century. Artists even acted as propagandists – Uccello, for example, painting for Cosimo de Medici a somewhat one-sided version of the 'battle of San Romano'.

The mid-fifteenth century brought new discoveries in oil painting techniques. Vasari (1511–74), the Italian artist and biographer of painters, credits the brothers Van Eyck with many of them, but it is now known that they were in existence centuries before. The earliest oil painting extant today comes from thirteenth-century Norway. What is certain, however, is that Jan Van Eyck (active 1422, d.1441) perfected an oil medium which revolutionized Flemish painting. It was later taken up by the Italians.

With the invention of movable type and the development of the printing press, illustration moved in two directions – namely works for reproduction and narrative painting. From about 1660, there was an increasing middle-class demand for both.

Scientific progress in glass and lens making during the sixteenth century also influenced artistic developments. The construction of the Camera Obscura by Erasmus Reinhold (1511–1553) for use in solar observation is one major example, for artists later took to the use of the invention to study and more closely observe the subjects of some of their drawings. Both Vermeer (1632–75) and Canaletto (1697–1768) used it to produce closer-to-life paintings. Vermeer's 'Lady with a Guitar' for instance, clearly shows the effect of such study in contour drawing around the folds of the dress.

By the mid-sixteenth century, copper engraving rivalled woodcut as a means of artistic reproduction and in the seventeenth century came the final break with the traditions of Gothic and Renaissance in pictorial art. On the painting front, oils reigned supreme. The decorative title page became a vehicle for engravers, who produced emblematic and allegorical designs, and this attracted many painters to

QED

32/33 Kingly Court, London W1
Telephone 01-734 3941
Telex 298844 quarto
Telegraphic address: Quartopub

ILLUSTRATION AND GRAPHIC DESIGN

Typesetting specification

Main text:	9pt/10pt Photina 747 Justified to 15 pica em measure U/1 case Indent paras 1 em First line of chapters and after sub- headings full out.
Captions:	7pt/7pt Univers light (directions i.e. left,right etc: Univers bold). Unjustified, ranged left to 7 pica ems. U/1 case.
Annotation:	7pt Univers light and bold
Chapter headings:	8.5mm (Cap height) Photina 747 Caps (Chapter numbers (spelt out): 12pt Photina 747 Caps).
Running heads:	10pt Photina 747 Caps
Folio numbers:	9pt Photina 747

Directors: Alastair Campbell/Edward Kinsey/Laurence F Orbach (USA)
QED Publishing Ltd Registered in England: no 1160378 VAT no. 242 2882 76

Above This galley proof has been marked up for literal corrections and author's alterations. This is the editor's job and the marks should be legible and neat, so as to be perfectly comprehensible to the typesetter. The designer must also look carefully at the galley proofs for such errors as damaged type, non-alignment of margins and other features which are ultimately the designer's responsibility.

Top right *Proof correction* When marking up proofs it is essential to use the customary proof correction marks. In most countries these systems have been standardized and published for example in Britain by the British Standards Institution. The named mathematical symbols are used when correcting technical matter. To avoid any misunderstandings with the printer these proof correction marks must be strictly adhered to and clearly marked, since corrections at page proof stage are extremely expensive.

Proof correction marks

Instruction to printer	Textual mark	Marginal mark
Delete	typeface groups	d/
Delete and close up	typeface groups	⌒/
Delete and leave space	typeface / groups	#
Leave as printed	typeface / groups	stet
Insert new matter	/ groups	typeface /
Change to capital letters	typeface groups	caps
Change to small capitals	typeface groups	s.c.
Change to lower case	(TYPEFACE) groups	l.c.
Change to bold	typeface groups	bold
Change to italics	typeface groups	ital.
Underline	typeface groups	insert rule
Change to roman	(typeface groups)	rom
(Wrong fount) replace by character of correct fount	typeface groups	w.f.
Invert type	typeface groups	⊙
Replace damaged type	typeface group	X
Close up	typeface group s	⌒
Insert space	typeface groups	#
Make space equal	typeface groups used	eq #
Space between lines	typeface groups	< 3pts #
Reduce space	typeface / groups	less #
Transpose	used groups typeface	trs
Move to right	typeface groups	冂

Instruction to printer	Textual mark	Marginal mark
Indent 1 em	☐typeface groups	☐ʎ
Take words (or letters) to beginning of following line	The height and the width	take over
Take words (or letters) to end of preceding line	The height and the width	take back
Raise (or lower line)	typeface groups	⊤
Correct vertical alignment	// typeface // groups	//
Straighten line	typeface groups	=
Push down space	typeface groups	⊥
Figure (or abbreviation) to be spelt out in full	12 point twelve pt	spell out
Substitute separate letters	phœnix	oe /
Use diphthong (or ligature)	manoeuvre	œ̂
No fresh paragraph	are called set points. The dimension of	run on
Begin new paragraph	are called set points. The dimension of	n.p.
Insert punctuation mark indicated	typeface groups/	ʎ
Substitute punctuation mark indicated	typeface groups/	o/
Insert em rule	typeface/groups	em ʎ.
Insert parentheses or square brackets	/typeface groups/	(/)/
Insert hyphen	typeface/groups	1—1
Insert single quotes	/Monotype/	ʻ ʼ
Refer to appropriate authority	15 point Bembo	?
Substitute superior character	childrens playground	ʔ

an overlay attached to the photograph itself. Any other instructions, such as requests for retouching, trimming and so on, should also be indicated on the overlay.

Ordering typesetting Typesetting is extremely costly, so it pays to get it right the first time. Bear in mind that more than one operator will be responsible for setting the type and that a separate team within the compositors will be responsible for the imposition, if this is undertaken by them. For this reason, it is wise to confine the type mark-up to the manuscript and layout instructions, such as positioning on the page, to the layouts themselves.

As far as typesetting is concerned, the compositor needs to know which founts are required and general stylistic instructions. Such information should be attached to the manuscript for permanent reference. On the manuscript itself, the exact words, lines, headings or paragraphs to be capitalized, italicized, set in a bold face or a different size must be clearly indicated. However, it is a mistake to make such instructions so dense that they become difficult to follow; in such a case, it is better to use a coding system based on numerals or letters and keyed to a master sheet.

Proofs Just as manuscript should be marked up correctly, so must proofs. These represent the last chance to get everthing right, so they must be scrutinized with meticulous care. Designers should always use the accepted marks when making any form of correction.

The first proof supplied by a compositor is known as a galley proof. This is simply the text set to the correct line lengths in one long continuous column. After this has been corrected for literal errors and any author's corrections have been incorporated, the galley is paginated and a second proof supplied in page form. This should include proofs of the illustrations. Alternatively the typesetter can supply photographic prints, known as bromides, from the galleys. These are pasted down to form a camera-ready paste-up.

Illustrations fall into two categories – black-and-white and colour. If a book, say, is totally black-and-white, it is not normal for separate illustrative proofs to be supplied, unless requested by the designer. Colour proofs, however, are essential. These can be of two types – two colour (black plus an additional colour) and four colour (the full colour process). In the case of two colour, the first proof may be of the two plates proofed in black only, with the second colour proofed on a translucent paper. With four colour, the first proof will usually be what is referred to as a 'scatter proof', that is, every illustration will be fully proofed but in a random sequence.

CHAPTER NINE

DESIGN PROCEDURES

All designs – whether for books, newspapers, magazines, advertisements or any of the thousands of related fields – start from the same basic premise. This is the realization that the task of any design is to communicate information in the clearest possible way to its audience. Its success or failure thus depends on a number of basic considerations and these remain the same whatever the job.

One of these considerations is obviously the person or persons commissioning the work. It is extremely rare for a designer to work without a commission and, even if the initial idea comes from him or her, it is almost certain to go through various modifications before it is finalized. The second basic factor is the outside audience at whom the design is ultimately aimed. A whole string of consequences follow from this: is information, for instance, the main aim of the design, or pure decoration? If the former, the solution may well be diagrammatic or typographic; the latter, however, may well call for an image or images to dominate the design, with little or no text at all.

Briefings

The first stage in virtually any job is the briefing between designer and client, art director, or whoever the person may be. This is the time that the required concept must be established, together with other vital factors, such as the budget for the job and the schedule allowed for it.

Briefings differ according to whether the designer is a freelance, who may have been asked to tender with others for the particular commission, or whether he or she works 'in house' – that is, on the permanent strength of the company. Often the freelance designer finds himself or herself given a greater degree of freedom than the staff designer. In the case of a book project, for example, the latter may well find that the size of the book, art work budget, number of pictures, amount of colour and the production system to be used have been established in advance. The former, on the other hand, may well be given greater financial freedom, provided that the people commissioning the design agree with the proposed overall budget figure.

It is important, therefore, for all designers to be able to budget accurately; in the freelance designer's case, it is vital. One golden rule is never to accept a commission if the time allowed and the budget are both inadequate. It is essential, for instance, for the designer to build in a realistic costing for his or her own time – a mark-up of three times the notional basic hourly rate is sometimes used. This takes account of basic salary, overheads and profit. Otherwise at the end of the day the job may leave the designer out of pocket. Once a budget has been established, it must be observed.

Another vital attribute for any designer is the

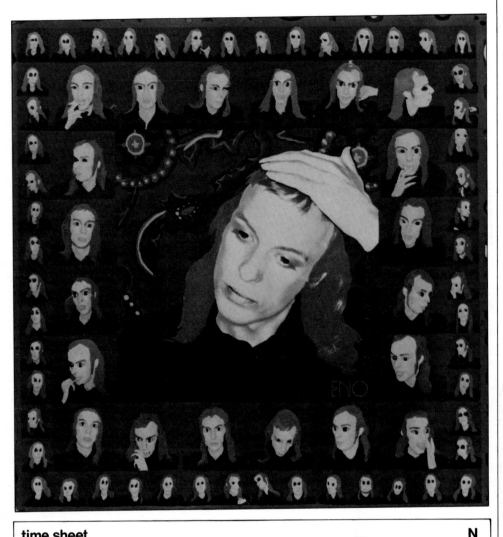

time sheet   name _____ **N**
                                          date _____

job no.	stage	drawing number/description	time										daily totals		stage	plan of work	
			9	10	11	12	1	2	3	4	5	T	O/T	Briefing	**A** Inception	2.1
															B Feasibility	
														Sketch plan	**C** Outline proposals	2.2
															D Scheme design	2.3
														Working	**E** Detail design	2.4
														drawings	**F** Production information	
															G Bill of quantities	
														Supervision	**H** Tender action	2.5
															J Project planning	
															K Operations on site	
															L Completion	
														Administration	**M** Feed-back	Ad
										productive total						

additional services
Sites and buildings	4.1
Feasibility studies	4.2
Development plans	4.3
Layouts, roads and sewers	4.4
Development studies	4.5
Special drawings	4.6
Negotiations	4.7
Changes in instruction	4.8
Delays in building	4.9

Prints	
Administration	
Holidays	
Studies	
Sickness	

special services
Town planning	5.1
Garden and landscape design	5.2
Interior design	5.3
Shop fitting and exhibition work	5.4
Furniture and fittings	5.5
Building systems and components	5.6
Quantities and surveying	5.7
Litigation	5.8
Consultancy	5.9

daily total

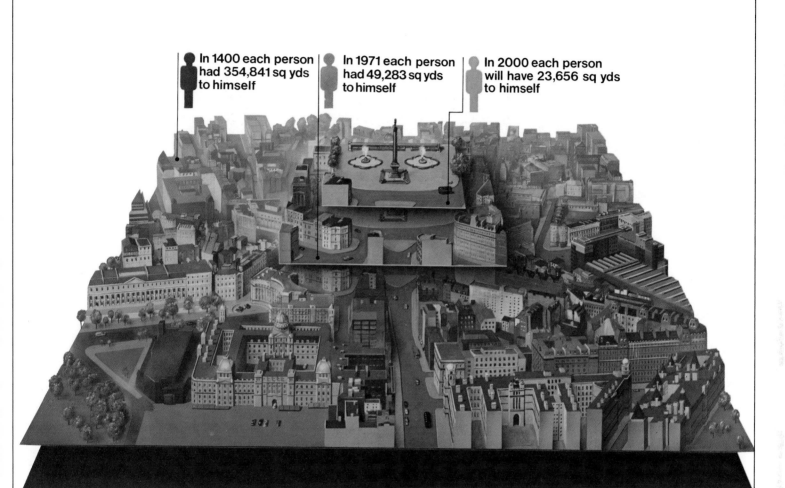

In 1400 each person had 354,841 sq yds to himself

In 1971 each person had 49,283 sq yds to himself

In 2000 each person will have 23,656 sq yds to himself

Figures in millions

Above left This LP cover is an example of a highly decorative design.

Below left This piece of typography shows a purely functional design. Here the necessary data is given in the clearest possible form.

Right This is an example of a design with a primarily informational function which has been combined with a decorative element to help convey the immediacy of the statistics. A more conventional method of display — typography or a simple bar diagram — would have less appeal for the reader.

2000 7,500
1950 2,517   **1971** 3,670
1900 1,650
1850 1,240
1800 900
1750 850
1700 800
1650 750
1600 700
1550 650
1500 600
1450 550
1400 500

ability to inspire the client with confidence, especially as the client may be authorizing the designer to spend large sums of money. To a large extent, this depends on who is present at the briefing; if the briefing is with an art director, say, the designer will be able to use more specialized language than if non-technical people are present. But the language the designer uses must be tailored to the understanding of the people listening to him at the presentation; it is a great mistake to be too technical. It is also an error to present a pre-conceived idea and then to stick to it rigidly. Such an emphasis may well cost a designer the commission; the rule here is to expect everything and anything to be fired at you from all sides until some kind of composite picture evolves.

There are, however, things the designer can do to bring about the right decision from his or her point of view. It is always a good idea to bring along some samples of previous work in order to assist explanation of ideas that may be difficult to relate verbally. Other essential equipment is a note pad, calculator and a cassette recorder, in case complex technical details have to be noted for future reference. Above all, this is the time to ask all the questions the designer considers necessary, so that the next stage of the commission can be tackled with confidence. If copy is involved, for instance, it is essential to find out who is going to supply it. It is always a good idea to prepare a list of questions covering all eventualities in advance of the briefing even though some of these questions may be irrelevant once the exact nature of the job has been established. Unasked questions can lead to problems later; no client likes to be contacted a day or so after the initial briefing with questions the meeting was designed to answer.

Having established all the basic facts, the designer then has to make the decision as to whether to accept the commission or not. This is his or her responsibility alone – but it is better to make it now rather than let the client down at a later stage. Remember, too, that from this moment the client is paying for the job; he will be justifiably annoyed if, once accepted, the designer fails to fulfil his or her part of the bargain.

Basically, what is happening at this stage is that the designer is selling himself or herself to the client. Nothing should be left undone to create the right impression. This precept even applies to dress; this, too, plays an important role in overall presentation.

Roughs

The stage after the very first briefing is the production of a rough version of the design. This can take a variety of forms – from an outline rough, giving an indication of a basic idea, to a finished rough. Again, the level required varies according to the demands of the client or whoever is being shown the finalized version. A rough for an art director, say, need not be

necessarily as full as one being prepared for a marketing manager. The rough can be drawn with almost anything; pencils and felt-tipped pens are common choices. The former is the better choice for detailed work, particularly if typography plays an important part in the composition.

Whatever the subject, the rough must utilize the basic principles of design. If it is decided to treat the subject typographically, the designer's decisions fall into several key areas. The first of these is the disposition of the type; by altering the spacing, it is possible to increase the emphasis of a key word or line, even if the type is the same size throughout. Changing to capitals produces the same result. Alternatively, the weight and size of the type can be varied, an extra colour used, or the key phrases set in italics or bold type.

If the solution is visual, then the basic question is to decide how many images are to be used. The subject may suggest the use of a single strong central image or a montage of different views. In addition, the designer has to decide what types of image to use – artwork, photographs or a mixture of the two – and whether they should be full colour, two colour, black and white or similarly mixed.

The basic principle behind each course of action is the same. The designer is trying to think of something new to say and the solution lies entirely in the imagination. Graphic design is first and foremost the art of visual communication, but, as one celebrated graphic designer put it, designers are also in the 'novelty business' and designs should reflect this fact. One of the purposes of the preliminary rough is to create a talking point – it should never be considered as the last word. For instance, there is no need to specify the extra central image to be used and supply the final transparency at this

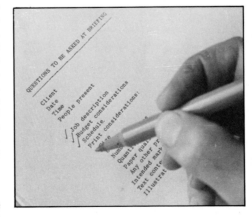

The briefing session between designer and client is of paramount importance. It is at this initial meeting that the client explains as fully as possible what image the design is to convey, and it is at this meeting that the designer must clarify any points he or she does not understand. All relevant details should be noted down by the designer during the session and it is usually a good idea to prepare a list of questions to ensure that, at the time, no important point is forgotten.

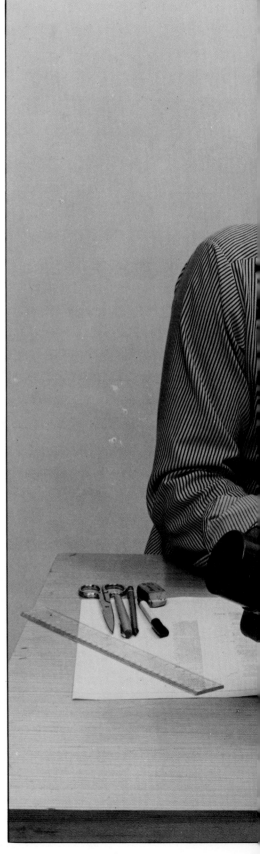

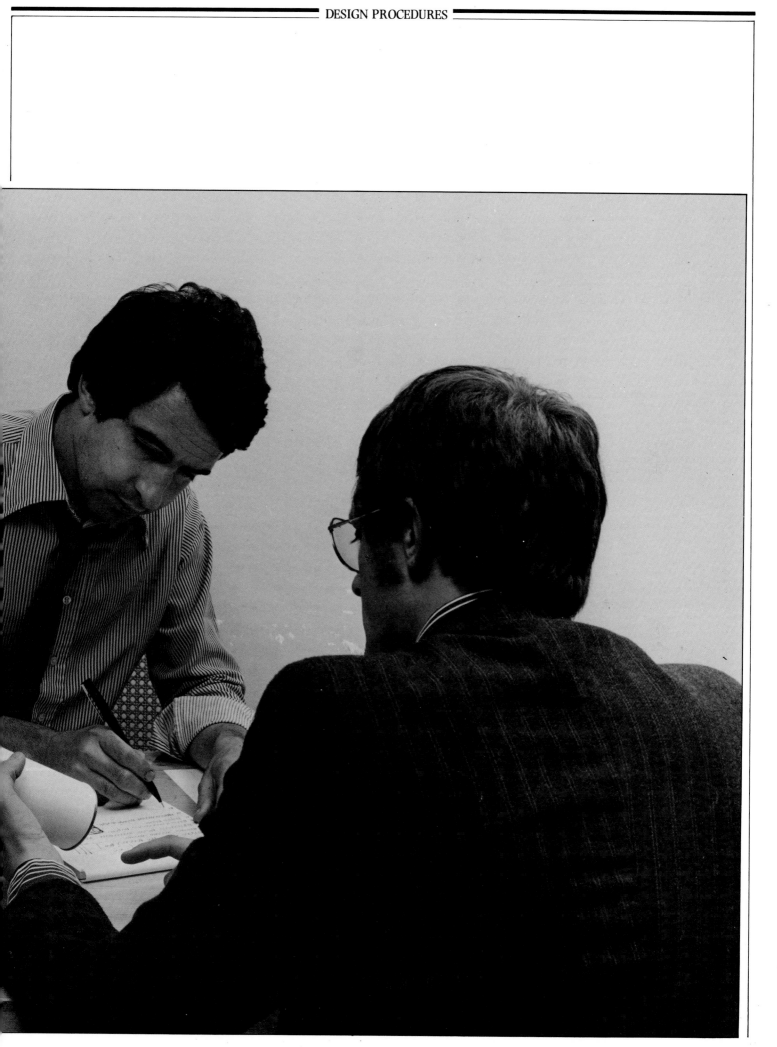

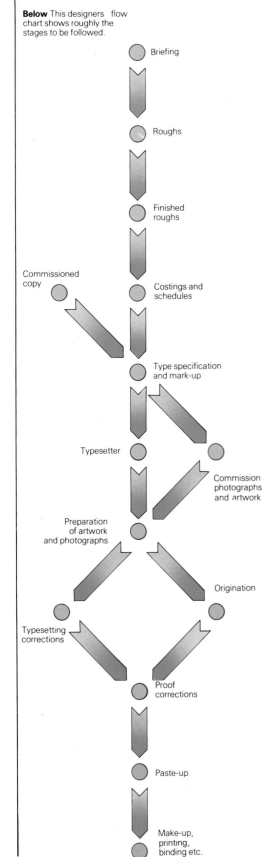

Below This designers flow chart shows roughly the stages to be followed.

Briefing

Roughs

Finished roughs

Commissioned copy

Costings and schedules

Type specification and mark-up

Typesetter

Commission photographs and artwork

Preparation of artwork and photographs

Origination

Typesetting corrections

Proof corrections

Paste-up

Make-up, printing, binding etc.

stage. What is important is to establish that there is a central image at all and the broad subject area of that image. Similarly in a typographical design, there is no need to establish the exact fount to be used, but the rough should certainly show headings, sub headings and the projected area the text type will occupy.

All this can be extremely time-consuming, especially as the designer may wish to present two or three alternative versions of these first thoughts. Here again, the problems of time and cost effectiveness come into play. The ideal to aim at is, of course, perfection, but, at the same time, there comes a point at which a halt must be called. This is particularly the case when making a preliminary rough, which may well have to be altered at least once, if not several times. It is usually a good idea at the initial briefing to tell the client how many and what standard of roughs he will be seeing.

A finished rough, on the other hand, must reflect the final product accurately. Though the images still need not be exact, they must show what the final art work or photographs will look like; the images on the rough should therefore be quite elaborate renderings, coloured if applicable. It is also sound practice to bring examples of the illustrator's or photographer's work to the approval meeting, so the client can get a clear idea of what style and standard the end product will eventually be.

Again, demands can vary. It is obvious that the design should be as attractive and professional as possible. The finished rough should be mounted on black card, protected with an acetate covering and given a black or coloured surround. Remember that the client may well wish to use it for purposes of display and even perhaps for photography. In some cases, all typesetting – headlines, copy, captions and so on – must be 'live' or real; in others, dummy type and dry-transfered (Letraset, Letter-Press etc) headings can be used. If 'live' type is to be used the designer must establish an effective liaison with the writer, so that the text reflects the illustrative treatment and is ready when required. In the second, it is obviously a good idea for the headings to be live if possible.

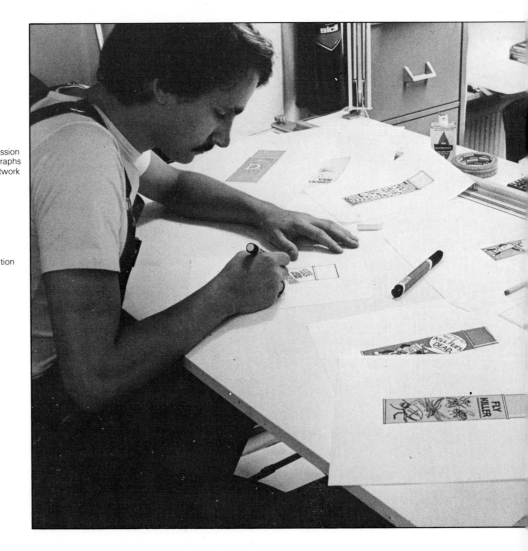

Right The designer, when presenting roughs to his client, should attempt to provide as wide a variety of alternative designs as possible. These must, however, be within the client's brief if, for example, he specifies a typographical design. They should also be as detailed as time and expense will allow.

Below The preliminary roughs with which the designer starts should be of an exploratory nature. If he or she is working 'in house', consultation with the art director after this stage may help to establish by elimination of some of the ideas the direction the design should take.

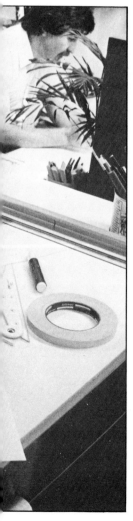

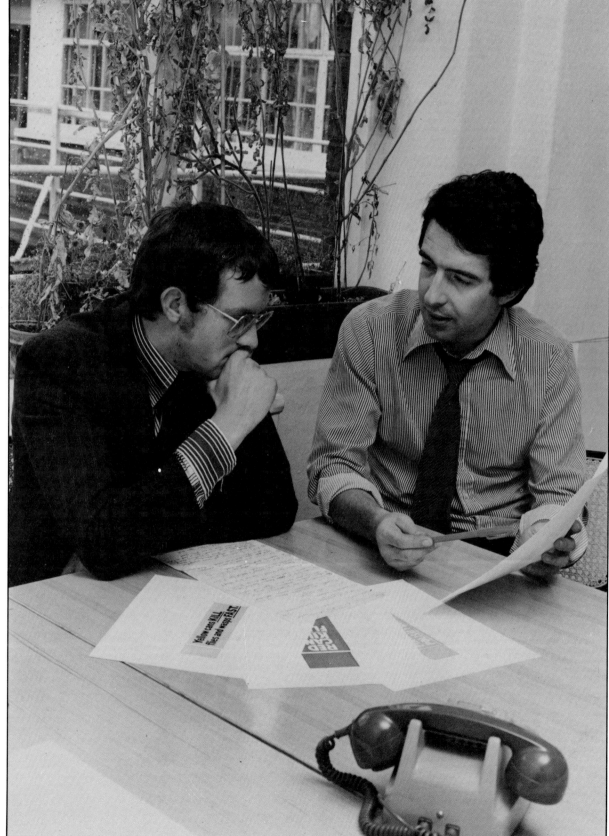

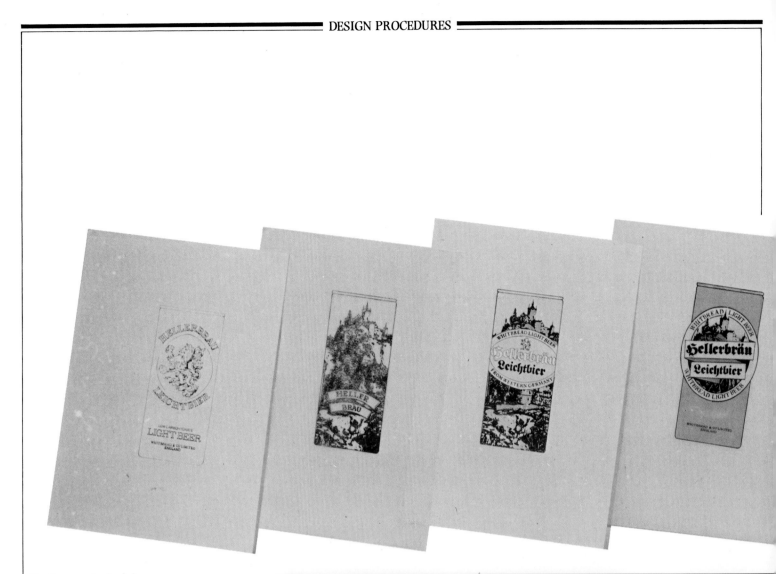

Costings and schedules

At the costing and schedule stage the designer may well be asked to provide printing estimates for the final job. The first decision is what paper is to be used; for this purpose it is a good idea to have samples at the approval meeting. The next step is to establish what type of printer the job requires: a large, traditional book printer, for instance, may not be able to turn a rush job around quickly, while a trade printer, though extremely quick, will be very expensive. A small printer may not be able to bind a booklet, and this, of course, will increase the cost of the job if it has to be sent outside for binding. The size of the run – the number of copies required – also influences the choice of printer.

Whatever type of printer is chosen, the people concerned will want as much information as possible about the job, unless it is so simple that they can work from a typewritten specification. The best guide is to produce a detailed layout, with all the basic information that both the designer and printer may need marked on it.

The designer must decide exactly how the job is to be handled from a technical point of view, unless this is predetermined by a production department. It is his or her decision, for instance, whether typesetting and origination (colour separations etc) is handled as a joint package or split up between two companies, with the illustrations going to a reproduction house for origination. The latter is standard practice for books and magazines. The type of printing process must also be specified; the printer must also know whether he will be required to do the

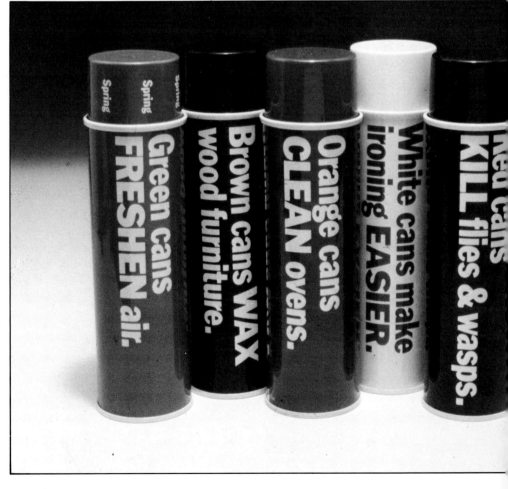

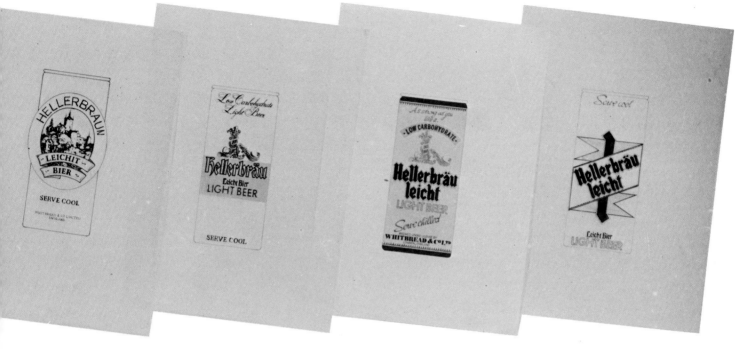

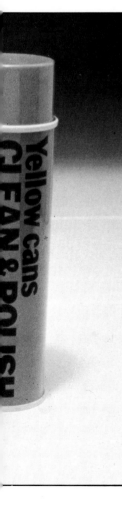

Above This series of roughs for Heldenbrau beer shows how remarkably different in conception and design each rough can be for a single subject. This series of designs was created by Michael Peters & Partners Ltd., London.

Left The final products are accurately represented in these finished roughs. The designer had finally decided to treat the subject typographically. In this way he was able to produce a 'brand image' for a variety of household products. The design style also has the advantage of being applicable to other forms of packaging the client may want to use.

make up (in lithography and gravure this means putting the type and colour-separated illustration film together as one piece), or whether a camera-ready paste-up of the type will be supplied. Where art work is concerned, a sample should be provided, showing any special requirements – the overlaying of a tint for example – so that an accurate costing can be made.

A minimum of three quotations should be obtained, so that the various prices can be compared. The designer has obviously to balance cost with quality; the aim is to achieve the highest possible standard – and maintain it overall – at the lowest possible price.

The printer will also supply a timetable, showing how long he estimates his part of the job will take. The designer must accommodate this in the master schedule which is now drawn up. This shows the key dates for every stage of the production process – from approval of the final rough to passing the final proofs for press.

Grids

For production purposes the designer must first decide whether it is a 'one off' job – such as a wall chart which requires no printed grid – or whether it requires consistency, as in the case of folded leaflets or jobs where pages must be turned. This applies particularly to books.

The purpose of a grid is to retain this consistency throughout the job. Primarily it should show type widths, picture areas, trim size, folds, gutters, column depths, margins and so on. It is important that this information is as complete as possible, since designers, illustrators, photographers, editors and printers will all be working

from it. The grid, however, should not be regarded as a straitjacket; if an idea demands it, quite a few of the dimensions above can be ignored.

The way a grid is produced depends on the number of pages or folds involved and the type of printing process selected. Printed grids are common in large jobs – books for example. Otherwise pencil grids are adequate, but, in either case, accuracy is of prime importance.

If the grid is printed, it is advisable to have two versions prepared – one on transparent layout paper and the other on board. The first can be used for tracing-off purposes and also to check the fit of illustrations, although this will need an accurate grid on film because tracing/detail paper is dimensionally unstable. The second type of grid is designed for paste-up, whether this is camera-ready or otherwise. This lessens the chance of inaccuracy at the paste-up stage.

Commissioning words

Commissioning words is normally the responsibility of an editor rather than the designer, but sometimes the latter, too, needs to commission words. In all cases, the designer should specify the total number of words required and, if the design is sufficiently advanced, the number of lines and the measure to which they should be typed. This is by far the most efficient method, as it lessens the problems that can arise with cutting and resetting. However, it can impose some degree of rigidity on the design at a relatively early stage.

Sometimes the copy supplied is 'final'. This means that it cannot be changed or cut and so it

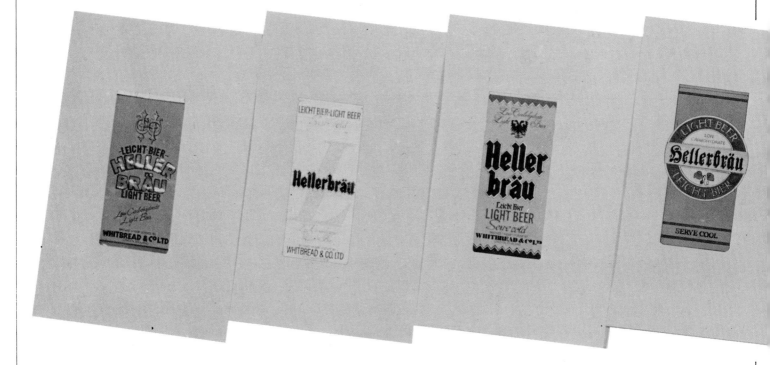

is the crucial determining factor in the design. More frequently, however, the designer asks the editor to cut, fill, add and even rewrite if the need arises. Whatever the job, the editor or copy-writer, and the designer must collaborate; neither process can be carried out in isolation. This is especially important if captioning is involved, though this is normally done at a later stage.

Photographs

Normally designers use two types of photo-graph – commissioned photographs, taken specially for the job, and existing stock pictures, held in photograph libraries and museums and obtained through picture research. If a photo-graph is commissioned, the brief given to the photographer must be as full as possible; this may well necessitate the client being present at the briefing. The photographer, too, should be selected on the basis of the job in hand; most photographers specialize in a subject area, such as fashion, food and travel, and they also specialize in the format they use.

The first decisions to be made are what format is required – either large or small – and whether the photographs are to be colour, black and white, or a mixture of the two. The exact type of picture needed should be described as clearly as possible, particularly in terms of atmosphere and mood. Economic constraints must also be taken into consideration. It is normal practice for a photographer to charge a day rate, plus expenses. These can include travel costs, the hire of models and so on. This is particularly important if special effects are required, which

may involve the hire of a studio and props.

The photographer can supply the designer with either prints or transparencies, so it should be specified which of the two are required. It is normal for more than one shot of the subject to be presented, unless large format is involved. This gives the designer a degree of choice.

Stock pictures are usually obtained from a picture library, agency or museum photography department by a researcher working from a brief prepared by the designer and, if necessary, from the copy. The brief should specify the total number of pictures, subject areas and projected cost; the selection should be as wide as possible within the subject area. The time taken to obtain pictures must also be taken into account, particularly if an international selection is required.

It is essential to specify what reproduction rights are needed at the earliest possible stage, so that the costs can be balanced against the budget. This normally means specifying exactly in what form, size, and country the photographs will appear, so that reproduction fees can be calculated. These are usually payable upon publication. Borrowed pictures should be returned as quickly as possible after use; otherwise holding fees can be charged.

As far as museums are concerned, the photographic department can sell the designer the pictures – taking them specially or printing them from existing negatives – or provide them on loan. In the latter case, it is vital to take care of the originals; replacement fees can be extremely high, especially if the picture is a rare one.

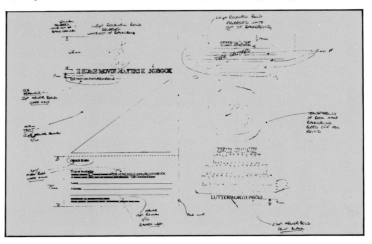

Left When the designer is working with a printer it is necessary to produce a marked-up layout showing all the information the latter may need. This includes type sizes of headings, running heads, folios etc as well as the positioning of such material if the printer is doing the page make-up.

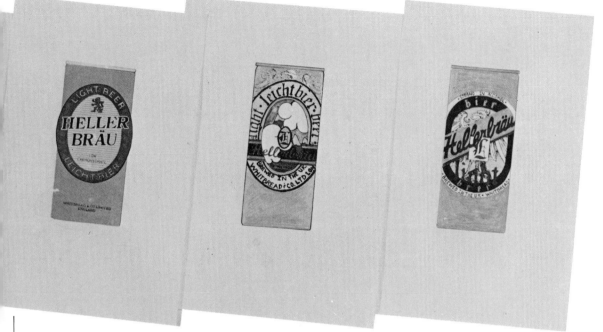

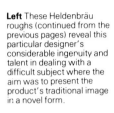

Left These Heldenbräu roughs (continued from the previous pages) reveal this particular designer's considerable ingenuity and talent in dealing with a difficult subject where the aim was to present the product's traditional image in a novel form.

Below This design, which the client finally chose, uses the German imperial eagle as a symbol of the beer's long-established reputation and strength. The overall impact is, however, striking and modern.

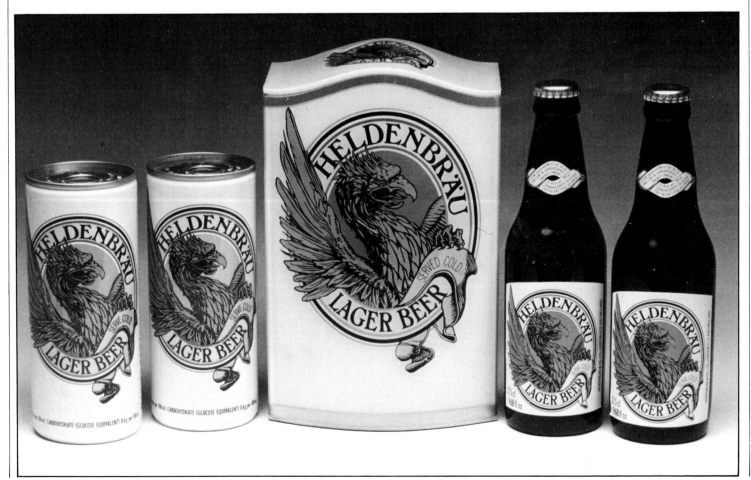

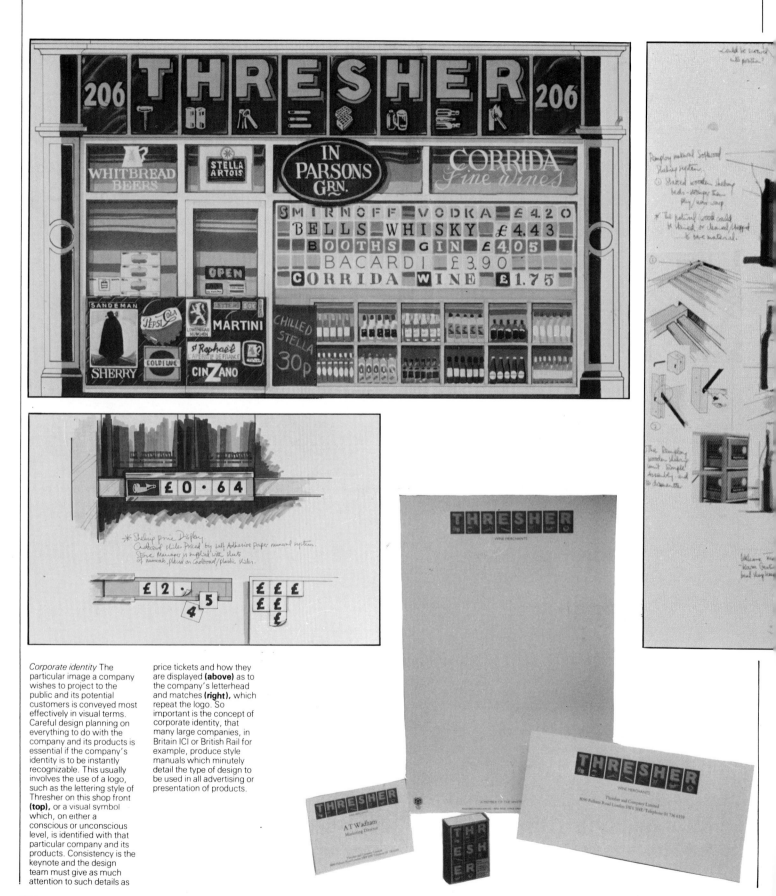

Corporate identity The particular image a company wishes to project to the public and its potential customers is conveyed most effectively in visual terms. Careful design planning on everything to do with the company and its products is essential if the company's identity is to be instantly recognizable. This usually involves the use of a logo, such as the lettering style of Thresher on this shop front **(top)**, or a visual symbol which, on either a conscious or unconscious level, is identified with that particular company and its products. Consistency is the keynote and the design team must give as much attention to such details as price tickets and how they are displayed **(above)** as to the company's letterhead and matches **(right)**, which repeat the logo. So important is the concept of corporate identity, that many large companies, in Britain ICI or British Rail for example, produce style manuals which minutely detail the type of design to be used in all advertising or presentation of products.

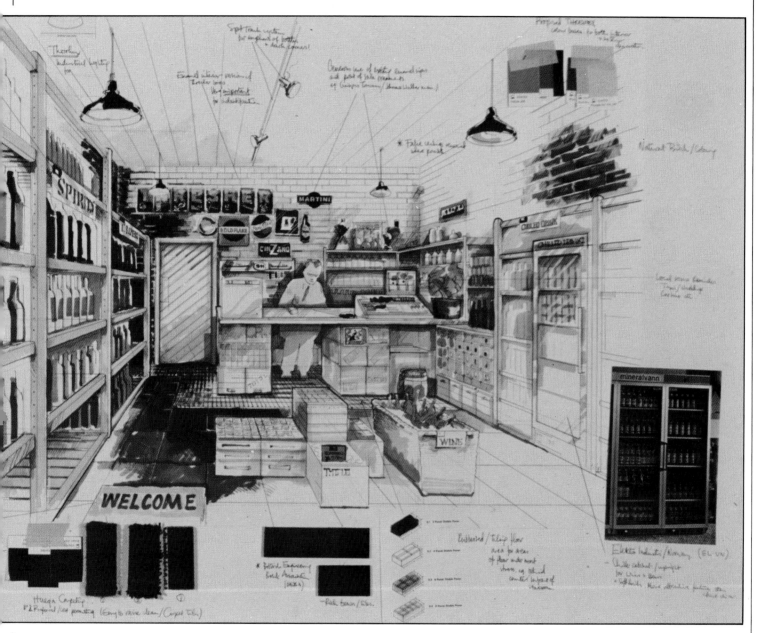

Above The shop's interior poses a more difficult problem for the designer. The company's logo is repeated but, like the shop's exterior, it must be used to blend harmoniously with the logos or symbols of the products it sells (Pepsi Cola, Martini etc). Simplicity and a careful choice of colours, which subtly reinforce Thresher's 'identity' are the key factors here.

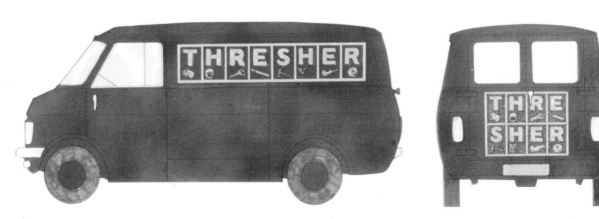

Right The design of the company's delivery vans repeats the logo and the colour which forms the logo's background.

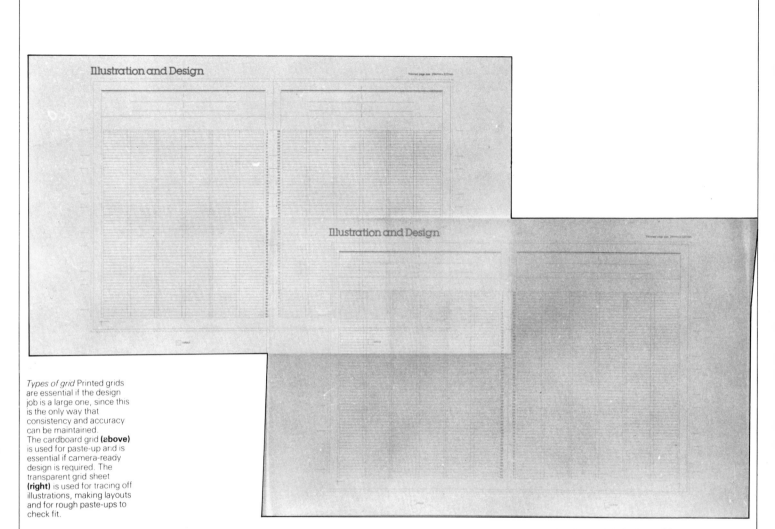

Illustration and Design

Illustration and Design

Types of grid Printed grids are essential if the design job is a large one, since this is the only way that consistency and accuracy can be maintained. The cardboard grid **(above)** is used for paste-up and is essential if camera-ready design is required. The transparent grid sheet **(right)** is used for tracing off illustrations, making layouts and for rough paste-ups to check fit.

Picture agencies frequently supply duplicated transparencies; these are usually not as sharp as the originals, so they should be carefully checked for acceptability.

Commissioning illustrations
The designer must consider that, like photographers, every illustrator specializes – either in subject area or an individual style of their own. Both these considerations must be born in mind at the commissioning stage; the designer must know, for example, whether a functional, realistic or decorative style is required and choose and brief the illustrator.

Other things, such as cost (illustrators are normally asked to quote a total for a job, based on an hourly rate) must also be established. Colour requirements will influence this, so it is important to be clear whether full colour, specially mixed colours, or black and white is required. Because cost is such an important factor – illustration can be far more expensive than photography – this must be balanced against quality. Any sub-standard work should be rejected, in which case a rejection fee (established in advance) is usually paid. It is also vital to establish very clear deadlines for delivery of the material, preferably well in advance of the

date at which the work is actually required to allow time for the inevitable alterations.

The actual artwork itself is frequently drawn at a larger size than the one at which it will finally print. Half up ($\times$ 1.5) or twice up ($\times$ 2) are both usual. Use of this technique can help cut costs at the separation stage because it reduces the number of camera shots and can also make the printed version look crisper and tighter. Many illustrators, however, stipulate that their work must be used same size and either draw to this or, possibly, even smaller. This is because their technique depends on same size reproduction or enlargement. It is best to ask for a pencil rough first in order to ensure that all the elements required are present. For the final version, art board or paper can be used; the latter is better for scanning at the reproduction stage because the surface is more flexible.

The designer's responsibilities do not end when the accepted illustration is passed for press. It is also necessary to establish who actually owns the illustration, as opposed to the copyright. It is generally accepted by illustrators that, unless it is stipulated that their client is buying the physical work, the original remains the property of the illustrator after its initial use and that he or she retains the copyright. Unless

this is clearly established, problems can arise – for instance if the artwork is re-used for another purpose. With photography, on the other hand, ownership may be sold outright.

Copy preparation
The copy is cast off, it is checked for fit and adjusted, if necessary, by the editor. It is then marked-up by the designer and sent for setting. If it is decided that the copy should be set in position on page, a detailed layout is necessary. Either a page or a galley proof is returned; this should be corrected for misprints (called literals) and any further necessary changes made.

Design processes
Once the designer has progressed through these preliminary stages, the task of assembling the design can begin. All the photographs, artwork and copy should now be in the designer's hands, ready to be prepared for eventual printing.

Selecting photographs
Meanwhile the appropriate photographs can be selected. Photographers often supply bracketed shots – that is, different ex-

posures of the same subject – so it is important to know which density will reproduce best. The only real guide to this is experience, though the better the exposure the better the colour|is.

Transparencies should be viewed on a colour-corrected light box (a light box with the right colour temperature). In addition, many transparencies have a colour scale along one side. This indicates whether the transparency has retained its colour over a period of time and thus is an important guide, especially in the reproduction of fine art. It is also useful for the reproduction house, which can then match up the separation with the original.

Sometimes the designer is faced with the problem of colour being paramount in the design, but only black and white photographs being available. The way around this is to use combinations of colours from the four-colour process with the black and white original to produce duotones, three colour, sepia, three, two and one colour tints and so on. This is done by the reproduction house. Use of four colour naturally means that the combinations of colour must fall within the limits of the process; one of the most frequently used combinations is black plus one other colour.

Library photographs and transparencies

Left The basic grid shows all the essential elements of the book's design. It must show type widths, column depths, picture areas, margins and so on. The information must be complete and accurate since not only the design team will be working from it, but also everyone connected with the job, especially editors, illustrators and printers. The design of illustrated books is frequently done in double pages which are called 'spreads'.

The series of designed spreads **(below)** shows the limitations within which the designer must work.

should be carefully checked with a magnifying glass for sharpness and for blemishes, such as scratches. Blemished pictures frequently need retouching and this is normally done by a specialized studio. If this is decided on, permission must be obtained first, or a duplicate made. Retouching can be taken to greater extremes, of course, if portions of the photograph are considered undesirable.

Sizing pictures

The first step when doing the sizing of pictures is to work out the dimensions involved. These should be clearly marked on a transparent overlay on to which a rough outline of what area of the original the final image will occupy is traced. This serves as a check for the reproduction house on any of the designer's special requirements, such as cropping (cutting away a part of the image). It is especially important with transparencies, which are often removed from their mounts for separation.

The next step is to calculate the percentage reduction. This is a way of saving money by grouping images of the same size on a single board. It is also extremely useful because the controls of reproduction cameras are marked in percentages, rather than sizes. Same size is

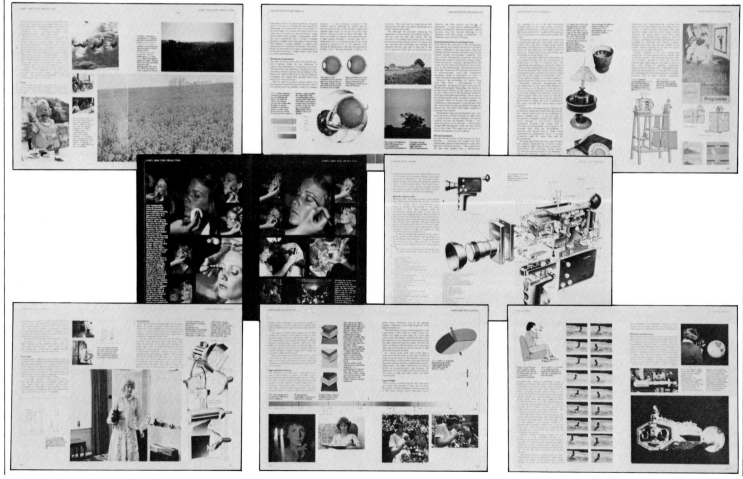

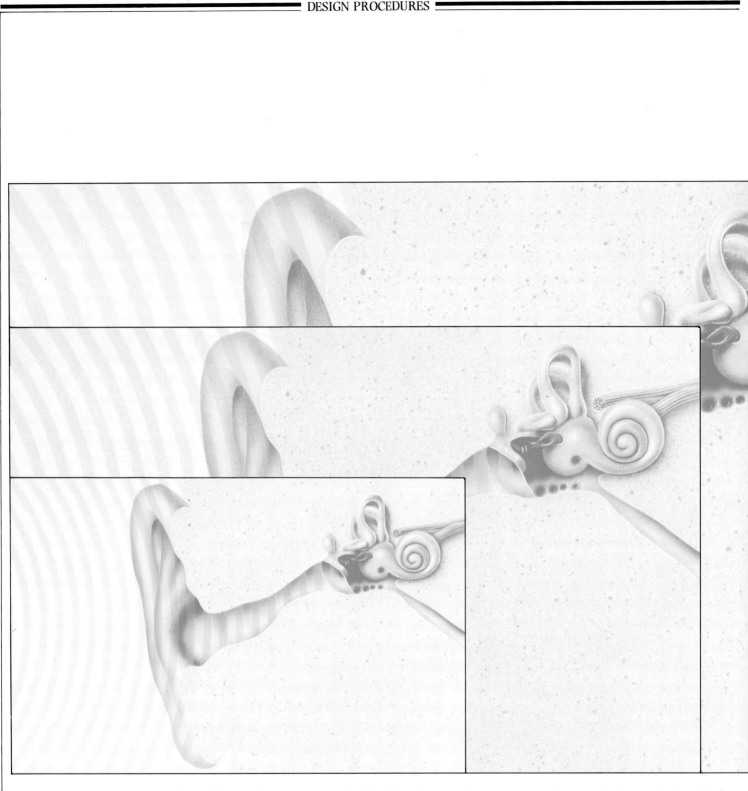

100%, while a reduction in size from 60mm square to 40mm would mean a percentage reduction of 66%. This figure should be marked on both layout and overlay.

It should also be specified whether the image is to be squared up, cut out, or 'cut into' another image. A squared up image sits on the page as it is, with its edges square. In a cut out the background is removed. With transparencies, it is best to select those in which a subject with a fairly simple outline is set against one with a white or pale background. Otherwise the final image may have dark edges. With black and white, unwanted areas should be painted out with process white. 'Cut into' means that the pictures overlap. The originator should be given very clear instructions, specifying which picture is cut into which, plus a special layout showing

their positions with all the dimensions marked.

Preparing artwork

The method of preparation of flat four colour artwork is the same for reproduction as for transparencies. Complications, however, arise if it is necessary to have a line overlay – for type labels, say – printing in a different colour. This is something that has to be done separately from the normal reproduction process. A drafting film overlay is taped over the art work, with registration marks (see colour correction) added to show where it fits. The additions are drawn or pasted down on the film.

Mechanical tints can be used to make black and white art work – maps drawn in line, for instance – appear in colour. Tints can be selected from the standard printers' colour chart if

process colours are being used; alternatively, they can be specified as combinations of specially-mixed colours.

Tints are laid over artwork in two ways. The first is to use one overlay with key lines defining the various tinted areas – in other words, all the colours required are shown on one overlay. The second is to use a different overlay for each colour. The former is a more convenient method than the latter, but it is more expensive.

Colour correction

Proofs returned for colour correction from the reproduction house take two forms. Either the illustrations are proofed exactly as they would appear in the final printed version, or they are proofed at the correct size but in random order. This is known as a scatter proof.

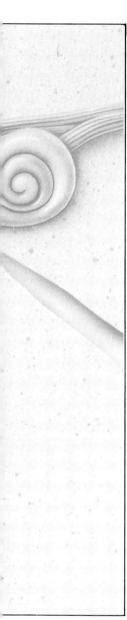

Left The size of the actual artwork to be reproduced can vary. Illustrators may produce work which is the same size as it will be printed . However, many designers prefer the artwork to be larger, either half-up or twice-up since this can make the printed version crisper.

Right The selection of transparencies should be made only after they have been carefully viewed on a light box. Examination of individual transparencies through a special magnifying glass will reveal any defects or inadequacies in the quality of the photograph.

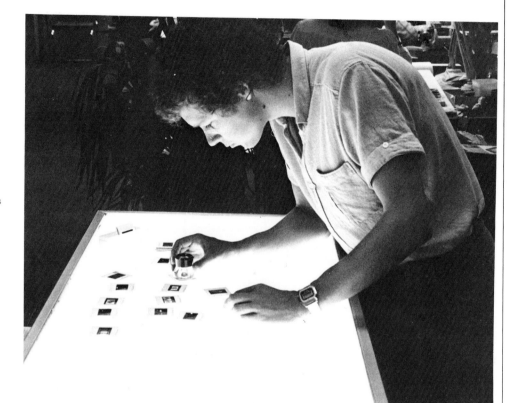

Below Before the transparency goes off for reproduction certain details must be marked on a transparent overlay. The dimensions of the image to be reproduced must be indicated, as well as a rough outline of that image since the designer may want to crop out some areas on the transparency. Other information should include the the percentage reduction if this is relevant, and the frame number, since transparencies are often removed from their mounts.

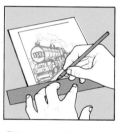 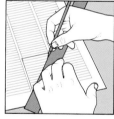 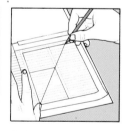

Fitting a picture 1. On a transparent overlay the picture area is squared up.

2. Using this overlay a diagonal line is drawn on the layout across the area into which the picture must fit.

3. This indicates how much of the picture area can be fitted into the allotted space.

4. The areas of the picture to be cropped, if any, are shaded out on the overlay and the layout dimensions indicated.

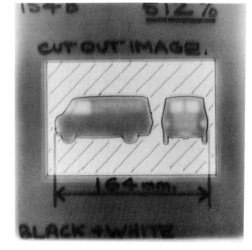

The most crucial task is to check the colour against the original and correct it, if necessary. Colour cannot be added directly; if a proof is lacking in magenta, say, this can be corrected by decreasing the proportions of cyan and possibly yellow. It is also possible to add colour by etching out the dot on the film negative although this will add to the cost because a new positive will have to be made. If there is too much of a colour, on the other hand, this can easily be etched out to a 10% maximum limit. The inking of the proofing press can also affect the colour. This can be corrected during printing, but all pictures will be affected as the process cannot be selective.

Proofs should also be checked for blemishes and register and fit now and at the actual printing stage. Scratches, acid stains or broken screens may necessitate remaking the illustration. Fit is more critical at the printing stage, but it should still be specified on the proof for the printer's benefit. If the colours in all the illustrations on the sheet are in the right position, they are in perfect register. If any are out of position, they are out of register and must be marked for correction accordingly. This is checked against the registration marks on the proof. If the colours of individual illustrations on any one sheet do not register, then the fit is incorrect.

Finally, it is vital to check that the pictures are the right way round and not reversed. If this happens, the picture has to be 'flopped' or 'flipped'. This is not just a simple case of turning the separated film upside down; a new contact has to be made so that the emulsion is on the underside of the film.

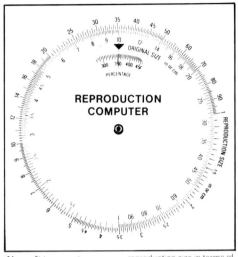

REPRODUCTION
COMPUTER

Above This percentage calculator can be used to indicate the required reproduction size in terms of percentage enlargement or reduction.

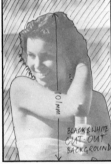

Below If the image is to be cut out or squared up and tones are to be used this must be clearly indicated on the overlay.

Below right Here a black and white picture is cut-into another black and white which has been overlayed with a tone.

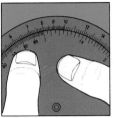
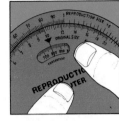

Calculating the percentage enlargement 1. In this example, a reproduction size of 80cm is required. The original size is, however, 10cm..

2. By sliding the disc so that these numbers meet, a percentage enlargement of 800 per cent is indicated. A calculator can also be used for this.

Paste-up
The paste-up takes two forms depending on on what the printer is contracted to supply. If he is to produce a page proof, the galley proof is pasted up to act only as a positional guide. If, on the other hand, a camera-ready paste-up is to be supplied – this is placed directly under the camera and shot to produce final film – reproduction pulls (repro) are used. Film setting pulls are called bromides or P.M.T. prints; hot metal ones are called barytas.

The first method allows for more correction than the second, but corrections at this stage are extremely expensive. The second gives the designer more flexibility; corrections, for example, can be set as single words or lines. These, known as patches, are stripped into place manually.

Everything that will appear on the text film – body text, captions, headlines, folios and rules (if boxes, for example, are a design feature) – must be included on the paste-up. The thicknesses and length of rules must be specified. Accuracy is extremely important; something positioned in the wrong place will appear wrongly positioned on the film.

With a positional paste-up, pictures and type can appear on the same board. With camera-ready paste-up, type only should appear, since the illustrations would have to be masked out for the film to be made. Type must not lift or curl at the corners so it must be stuck down securely using a suitable spray adhesive or rubber solution. These allow type to be removed and repositioned without damage. Small pieces of type such as labels can be secured with double-sided tape.

If any type is to print in a separate colour, this must be specified on the paste-up. Alternatively, an overlay can be used.

Printing
The printer first marries up the text film with the illustration film to produce either a final page proof or a blueprint, often called an ozalid. Text and illustration can now be seen together, just as they will print.

This is the last stage at which corrections can be made, but these are almost prohibitively

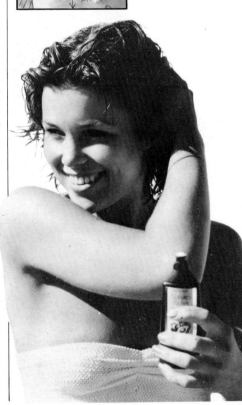

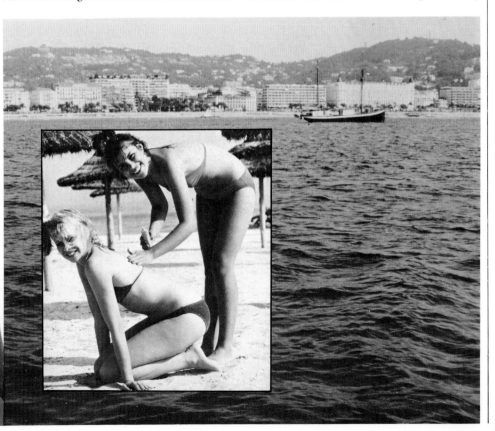

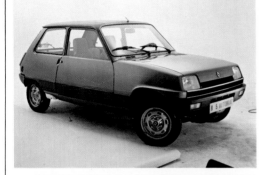

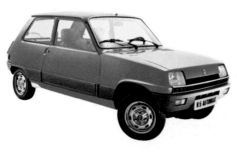

Photo retouching and photo composition (**left, below**) With these techniques it is possible to achieve effects using photographic techniques which hitherto would have been achieved using illustration. Invented in the late 1960s the techniques only became commercially viable using a special laboratory. The original colour of the car (**far left**) was changed using 'photo-composition'. This process adds colour using water-based dyes and removes it using chemical bleaches. Very subtle effects can be achieved. A retouching artist then effects the other changes — removing the back sticker, taking out the windscreen reflections and brightening the radiator. (**left**). The surreal but not obviously faked bottle/apple image (**below**) comes from combining two separate pictures (**far below, left, right**) and using very accurate masks to block out unwanted areas on the transparency.

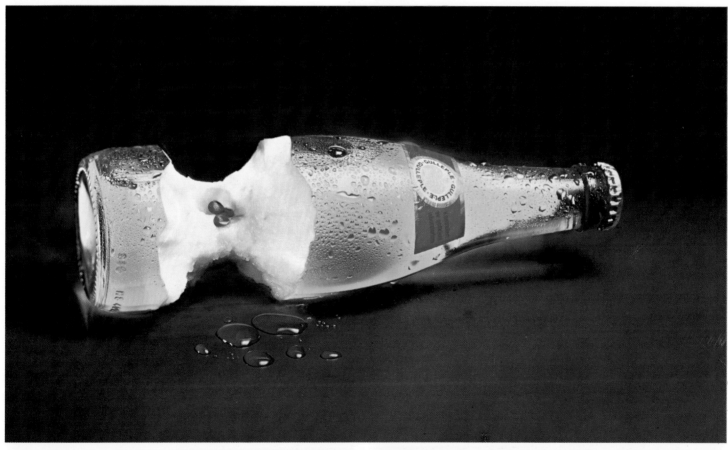

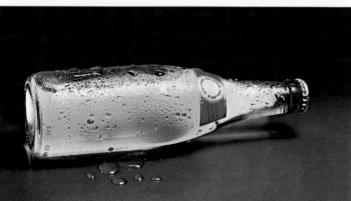

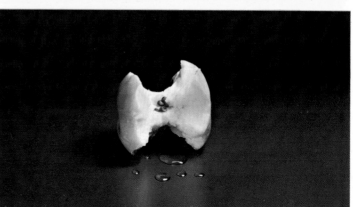

Process camera (**bottom left**) Also called a copy or graphic arts camera, it is used for photographing the original preparatory to making the printing plate. The original is held against the copyholder or copyboard by a vacuum. Moving the lens and the copyboard controls the degree of enlargement or reduction. A control panel adjusts exposure times, lights, filters etc. The camera produces a negative and can be used for black and white as well as colour work.

Right Electronic scanner The electronic scanner is gradually replacing the process camera. It is technically much more sophisticated and produces ready screened colour separations in one step without an intermediate contact screen stage. The original, which can be film or paper but must be flexible, is placed on a drum which revolves (**below**). The scanning is carried out with by a laser. The original is placed directly on the drum and the scanning produces screened film. The machine will enlarge and reduce; it also produces sharper separations with smoother gradations between tones than is possible by other methods. The scanner operator can also 'dial in' changes in colour or hue. The machine will take colour or black and white originals. It is slightly versatile and the technology is still developing fast.

Dot etching (**bottom right**) This form of correction is done by hand. The area is masked off and the correction made using bleach to lessen the intensity of the dots.

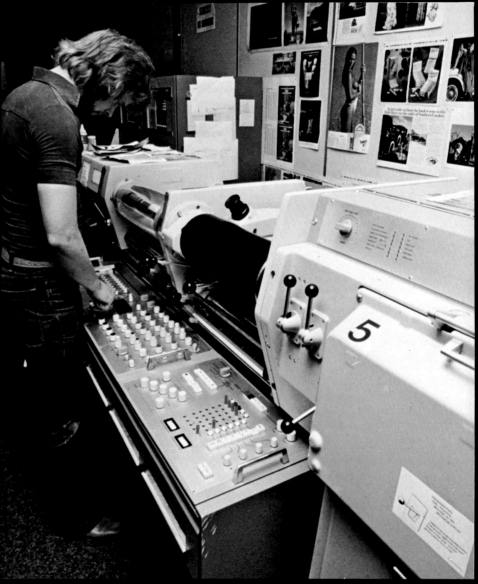

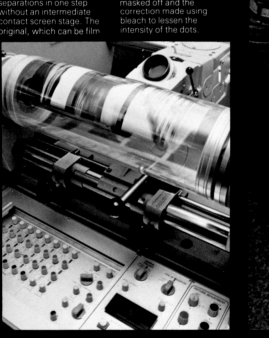

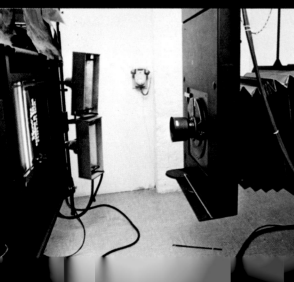

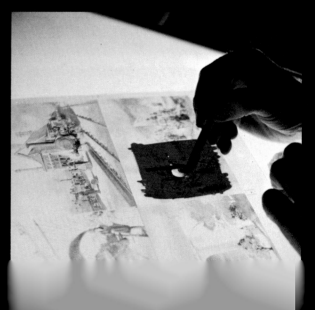

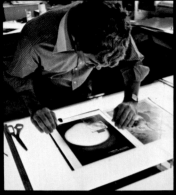
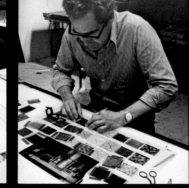
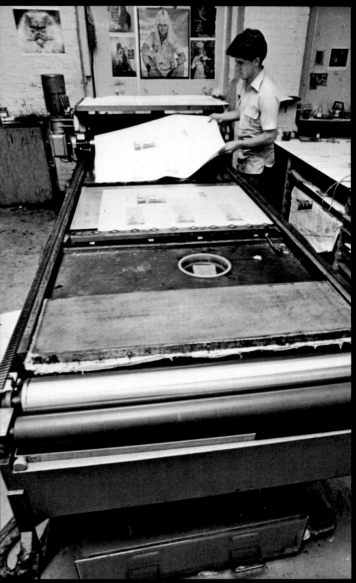

Combining text and image
Film negatives are used at the 'planning' stage when text and image are combined **(above: left, right).** A positive is then prepared. To prepare the plate the film is placed on top of the plate and exposed under ultra-violet light **(right).** The image thereby transfers to the plate. The densitometer **(below right)** is used at various stages in the origination process. Here the operator is checking that the colour is correct. Proofs are pulled using a proofing press **(far right).** The dye transfer method is a quicker way to proof colour material. For this a special gelatin coated paper is needed. Each colour is separately laminated on to light sensitive gelatin coated film **(below left).** The film is treated so that it only absorbs one colour. Dry powder dye is sprinkled on **(below centre)** and the dye transfers to the paper. The finished proof is laminated. This is also called 'Cromalin'.

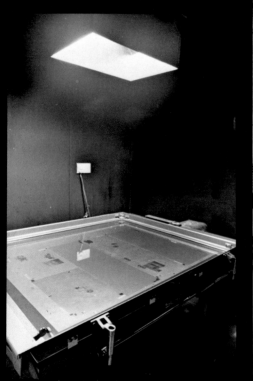

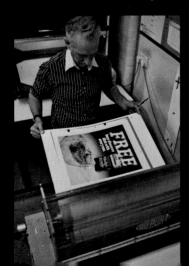
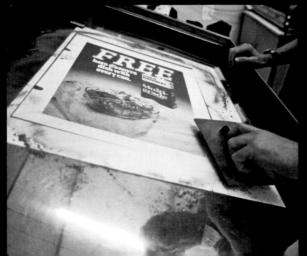
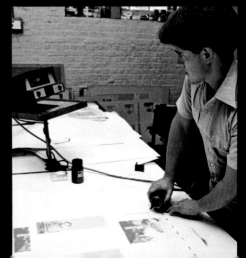

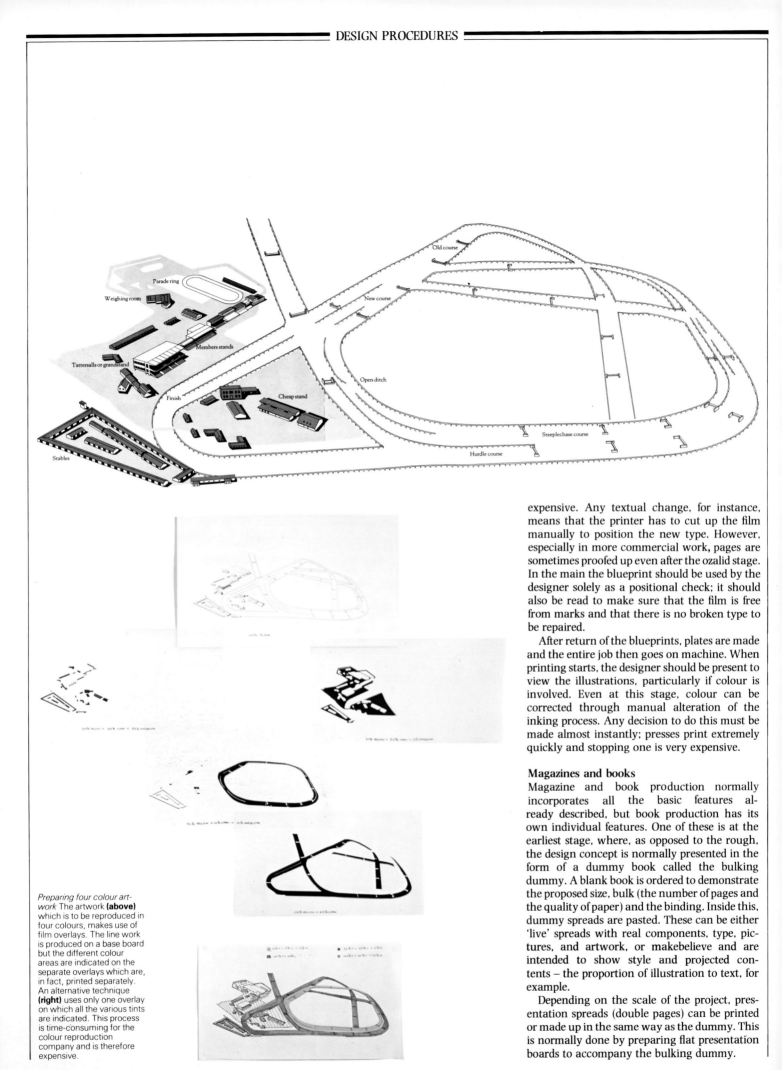

Preparing four colour art-work The artwork **(above)** which is to be reproduced in four colours, makes use of film overlays. The line work is produced on a base board but the different colour areas are indicated on the separate overlays which are, in fact, printed separately. An alternative technique **(right)** uses only one overlay on which all the various tints are indicated. This process is time-consuming for the colour reproduction company and is therefore expensive.

expensive. Any textual change, for instance, means that the printer has to cut up the film manually to position the new type. However, especially in more commercial work, pages are sometimes proofed up even after the ozalid stage. In the main the blueprint should be used by the designer solely as a positional check; it should also be read to make sure that the film is free from marks and that there is no broken type to be repaired.

After return of the blueprints, plates are made and the entire job then goes on machine. When printing starts, the designer should be present to view the illustrations, particularly if colour is involved. Even at this stage, colour can be corrected through manual alteration of the inking process. Any decision to do this must be made almost instantly; presses print extremely quickly and stopping one is very expensive.

Magazines and books

Magazine and book production normally incorporates all the basic features already described, but book production has its own individual features. One of these is at the earliest stage, where, as opposed to the rough, the design concept is normally presented in the form of a dummy book called the bulking dummy. A blank book is ordered to demonstrate the proposed size, bulk (the number of pages and the quality of paper) and the binding. Inside this, dummy spreads are pasted. These can be either 'live' spreads with real components, type, pictures, and artwork, or makebelieve and are intended to show style and projected contents – the proportion of illustration to text, for example.

Depending on the scale of the project, presentation spreads (double pages) can be printed or made up in the same way as the dummy. This is normally done by preparing flat presentation boards to accompany the bulking dummy.

Right *Checking colour proofs* Scatter proofs which are printed the correct size but in random order must be closely checked for colour accuracy, for blemishes and spots and for fit and register. It is also essential to ensure that the pictures are the right way round and not reversed since this is difficult to correct at a later stage.

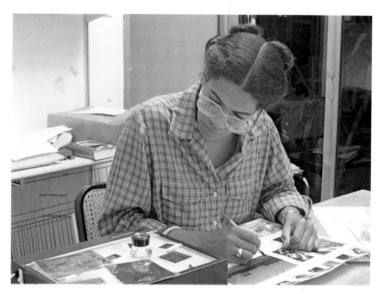

Jackets

These are perhaps just as – if not more – important than the actual inside of the book, as they have to convey its content and quality instantly to the prospective buyer. Rough jackets are usually covered with self-adhesive film laminate to give the impression of actual lamination; background tints should be carefully matched against available trade colours and a 'swatch' (piece) of the colour concerned provided for comparison.

Flat plans

Books are probably the most complex job a designer has to put together, so they must be planned carefully in advance. The way to do this is to draw up a flat plan, showing the chapter breakdown, the number of pages devoted to the index, preliminary pages, where colour falls, and so on. The most complex flat plans are called flow charts which give an idea of what will appear on every page of the book. These are pages drawn in miniature showing type and illustration on every page, and are more for sales purposes.

Binding and budgetary considerations also have to be taken into consideration, especially when planning the colour distribution. Books are normally bound in 16 page sections, so the designer has to work in multiples of eight. Most colour work is done in totals of 32 pages. One of the commonest colour combinations for printing is 'four back two' – that is, every four colour spread is followed by one in two colour.

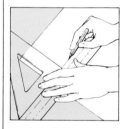

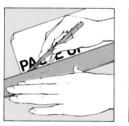

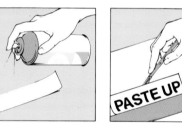

Making a paste-up
1. Positions and lines are marked on the board as on a grid.

2. It is helpful if the type to be pasted up is cut square. This makes it easier to line it up correctly.

3. The type is lightly sprayed with a special adhesive so that it can be repositioned if necessary.

4. The line up of type must be parallel. A T square or parallel motion table is used to ensure this.

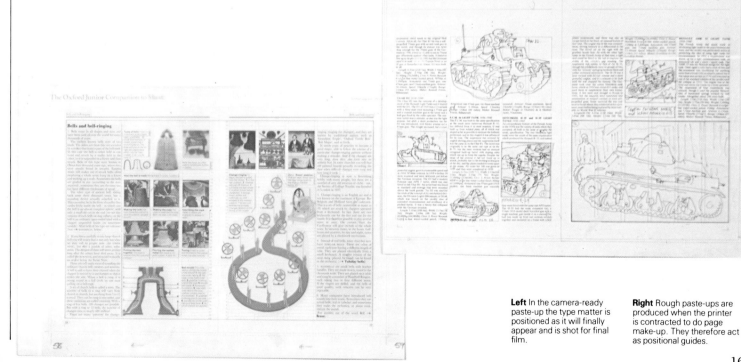

Left In the camera-ready paste-up the type matter is positioned as it will finally appear and is shot for final film.

Right Rough paste-ups are produced when the printer is contracted to do page make-up. They therefore act as positional guides.

CHAPTER TEN

DESIGN AND PHOTOGRAPHY

The designer's involvement with photography takes many forms. When a product is being photographed for advertising purposes, for instance, a photographer often finds himself working to a measured drawing produced by the designer; if the shot required is a complex one, the designer's presence may indeed be required throughout the entire shooting session. This is necessary because changes may have to be made in the layout of a page, for example, if it is discovered that the various elements comprising the shot simply cannot be made to fit the original drawing.

The designer's task here is to control the inevitable compromises which arise in the transformation from concept to finished photograph. At the opposite end of the spectrum, however, the designer's job is simply one of selecting pictures from a mass of stock material; this frequently involves bending to the required purpose pictures which have not been specially commissioned and which may range from the excellent to the barely discernible.

Photographs serve two separate functions in the context of printed reproduction. The relationship between them is the same as the one existing between technical drawing and illustration. In the first case, the image is required simply to document the reality presented to the camera; in the second, the special attributes of photography are used to further an editorial or promotional concept. The first relies almost solely upon the craft skills of the photographer and his or her experience in recording a sharply-defined, evenly-lit and correctly-exposed image. The second, however, depends

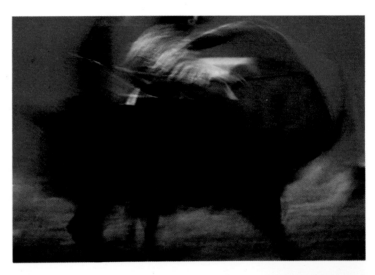

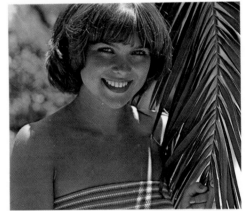

The shot of the bull-fighter **(left)** shows one of the ways a photographer can make the familiar unfamiliar and one way in which action can be conveyed. The close up of the bull and matador was taken on a 1 second exposure. The resulting blur which conveys the feeling of action is still recognizable because of the strong colours and the simple nature of the subject. Fashion photography, as in the shot **(below)** is a popular area of photography. The tractor **(right)** is a large object in a large format. In all design work involving photography the photographer should be briefed on the precise effect desired and the format in which the image will appear.

upon close communication between photographer and designer, and in particular, upon the designer's understanding of the mechanisms of photography and photographic reproduction.

This is not to suggest that the designer should constantly harbour ambitions to become his or her own photographer. Nevertheless, the selective perception which the designer brings to bear upon the typographic and illustrative aspects of design must inevitably lead to the conclusion that there is no such thing as a 'standard' photograph of any subject. It also leads to the awareness that the many possible variations of technique and attitude offer rich opportunities in a wide and under-exploited field.

Photography for reproduction Whether colour

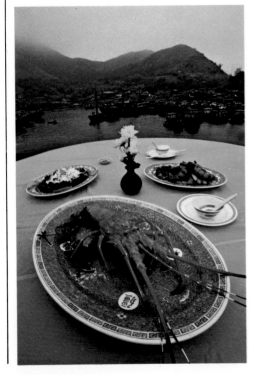

Food photography makes special demands on the photographer. In this photograph taken in Hong Kong **(left)** a wide angle (20mm) lens gave a combination of depth of field and sharp focus while a graduated filter ensured that the picturesque setting did not dominate the shot.

Technical photography also raises particular problems for the photographer and designer. For example, in the picture of the workings of a watch **(right)** it was important to make sure that there were no untoward shadows so that the detail could be seen clearly.

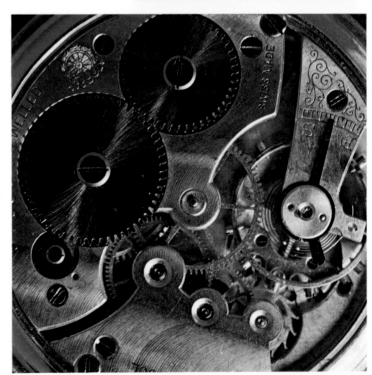

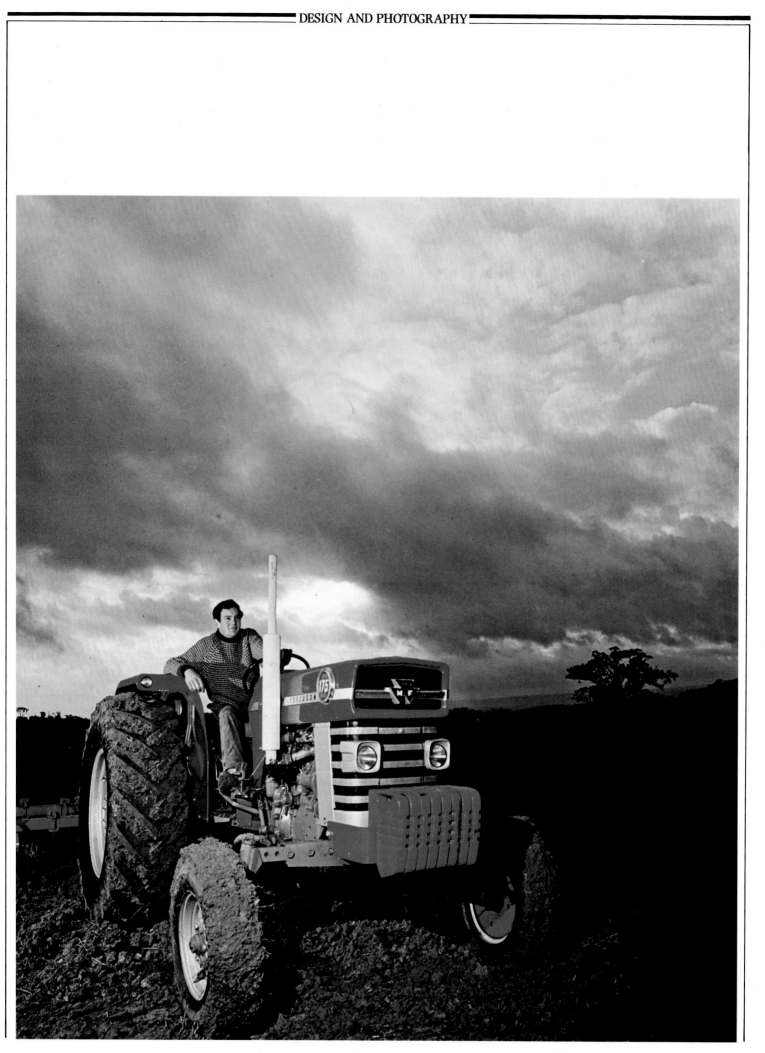

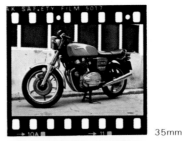

2¼ square   35mm   5 x 4

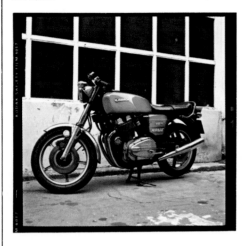

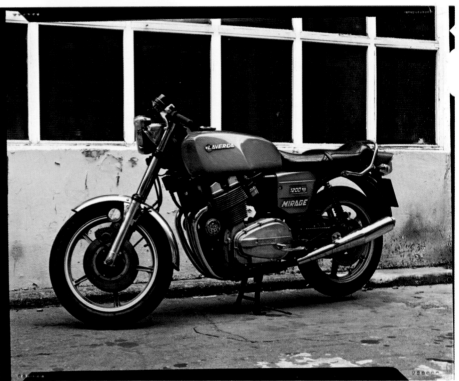

or monochrome, a photograph must have a number of qualities if it is to reproduce correctly. The basic requirement concerns what is termed the reproduction ratio. In theory, a photographic original can be enlarged to an enormous extent and yet remain intelligible. On the cinema screen, for example, the 35mm format film original may be subject to an enlargement of more than 30,000 per cent; however, the degradation of the image this involves usually goes unnoticed because of its almost constant movement and the distance between the viewer and the screen. On the printed page, however, the same original is without the benefit of movement and distance and so it begins to look blurred and give an impression of lack of colour saturation at an enlargement of 1000 per cent.

In the context of book and magazine production, the enlargement ratio for a 35mm transparency ranges typically between 100 per cent (same size) and 1500 per cent. At an enlargement of 875 per cent a 35mm transparency would cover this entire page, though a 4in × 5 in (100mm × 125mm) transparency would require only 220 per cent enlargement, and an 8in × 10in (200mm × 250mm) only 110 per cent (slightly more than same size). Since the grain structure – and hence the resolving power of the film emulsion – is the same regardless of format, the larger sizes obviously considerably improve the clarity of the printed reproduction.

Colour film types Reversal ('slide' or 'transparency') and negative films use the same principles as black-and-white film. The differences between them lie in the colour film's multi-layer construction and in the processing sequence.

Reversal and negative films both contain three layers of light-sensitive emulsion – a blue-sensitive layer forming a yellow dye, green-sensitive forming magenta and red-sensitive forming cyan. Combinations of the final processed dye layers can approximate most colours, with the exception of fluorescent ones. An important part of this process depends on the choice of the right type of colour film for the

35mm   2¼ square   5 x 4

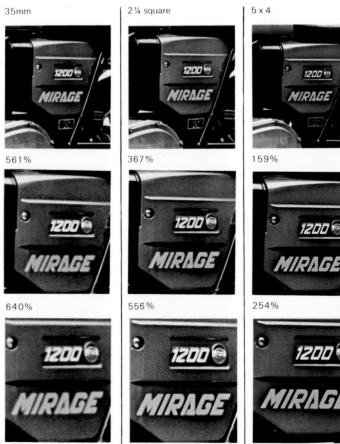

561%   367%   159%

640%   556%   254%

1200%   737%   333%

Enlargement
In most design work photographs have to be enlarged. It is vital that the designer takes into account the effect of enlargement on the original picture. The greater the degree of enlargement the less clear the detail and the more grainy the resulting image. These photographs of the same scene were taken with different film sizes to produce different image sizes — 2¼ in square **(above left)**, 35mm **(top centre)**, 5 x 4in **(above)**. These show the effect of the film size on the original produced. Enlarging sections of the different pictures demonstrates the effect of increasing enlargement on the image. The grain structure is the same regardless of the size of the film. This means that the larger the original the clearer the image on the enlargement: the 35mm is the least clear **(far left)** and the 5 x 4in **(left)** clearest. For work on magazines and books it is usual to enlarge a 35mm transparency by between 100 and 1500 per cent.

conditions in which the shot is being taken. 'Daylight' and 'artificial' light types must be used when appropriate. True colour rendering may also be seriously affected by inadequate care in storage, incorrect processing, or by exposure to a subject lit by an incompatible light source.

All reversal film is fundamentally of the same type, the main division being between the substantive varieties, such as Ektachrome, and the non-substantive, like Kodachrome. Substantive films can be processed by the user with chemicals supplied by the film manufacturer, since all the dye layers are present in the film structure, ready to be developed by chemical action. Non-substantive films, usually sold either process-paid or with a pre-paid envelope, have to be returned to the manufacturer after exposure, as they need a much longer and more critical processing treatment during which the dye layers are introduced into the film.

The capabilities of the two types of film are broadly similar, except that the non-substantive types cannot be subjected to special development. An example of this is when substantive film is 'pushed' in its first developer to gain speed. A film rated at 200 ASA, for instance, can be uprated to 400 or even 800 ASA – this is 'pushing' one and two stops respectively. The penalties are a resulting loss of picture quality, with increased graininess and contrast as well as degraded colour rendering. This is sometimes acceptable where additional lighting on the subject was either not available or desirable. Conversely, film which has been deliberately or accidentally over-exposed by a known amount, can be given a shorter first development – being 'pulled', usually by one stop (to 100 ASA in this instance).

The manufacture of reversal colour film is an

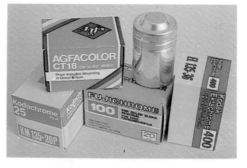

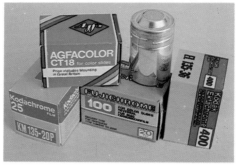

Different types of film give varied results. The shot was taken on a grey background. The result with Agfacolor **(top left)** gives strong colours, the grey is rendered almost as blue-green. Using Fujicolor **(top right)** gives a good match for the grey and sharp colour contrasts. Kodachrome **(bottom left)** gives reasonable colour contrast and warm colours with a red bias. Ektachrome **(bottom right)** gives a slight blue bias and cool colours. It is therefore important for the designer to choose the appropriate type of film to achieve the desired results.

Colour temperature
Colour temperature is measured in degrees Kelvin and expresses the colour quality or content — of a light source. The picture **(below)** was taken in overcast light while the sections of the same scene **(right)** illustrates how the colour temperature changes as the sun becomes lower in the sky.
As the colour temperature drops the hues become warmer. The average colour temperature for daylight is between 5,000 and 6,000K; while for a normal light bulb it is between 2,400 and 2,800K.

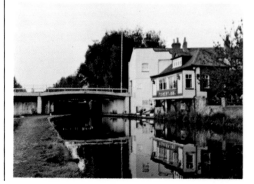

4 000 K 5000 K 6000 K

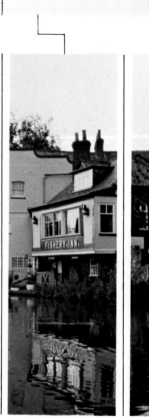

extremely exacting process, and the reaction of films from different production batches to the same subject may well not be identical. For this reason, film boxes are stamped with an expiry date and a batch code so that films required for one shooting session can be matched together. Sheet film can also vary in ASA rating, and a warning slip to this effect is included in individual boxes. In all cases, film should be processed as soon as possible after exposure.

Negative colour film is comparatively rarely used for reproduction purposes, but prints obtained from negatives are often made up into dummy packs and books for presentation. Large-format colour prints can be sent for reproduction to be treated in the same way as full-colour flat artwork. Negative duplicating film is used to make master originals in the mass-production of transparencies for audio-visual use. In this case the machinery and processes are substantially the same as those used for mass-duplicating feature films for cinema release.

Colour printing systems There are two distinct methods by which positive colour prints can be

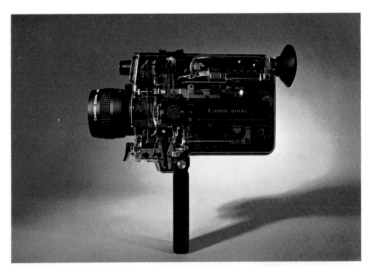

Coloured lights can be used to achieve unusual visual effects. For this picture of a camera **(left)** different coloured lights were placed on either side of the camera. The reason for this was that the image was to be used for a book jacket where colour is important.

Below The two pictures of the sky were taken in Hong Kong at sunset. The first was taken without any filter and shows the difference in brightness between the sea and sky. In the second a graduated filter took out some of the brightness of the sky, giving the sea and sky the same tone. This helps concentrate attention on the horizon. A 20mm lens was used.

Below This shot taken from Battery Park New York at sunset with an automatic exposure camera shows what spectacular colour effects can be achieved using long exposures. The light was so dim that the camera set itself an exposure of 45 seconds.

With exposures of over about 10 seconds the film becomes unable to respond normally. This results in the unusual colour effects seen here.

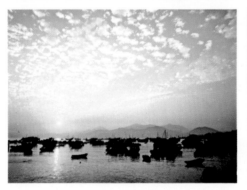

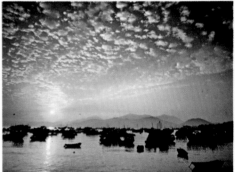

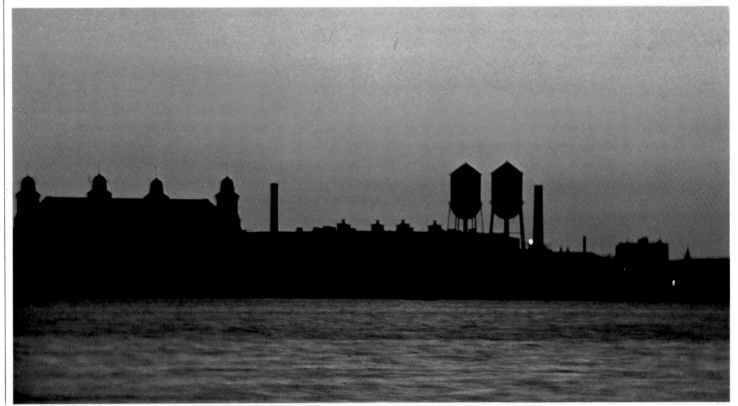

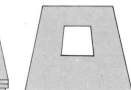

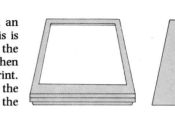

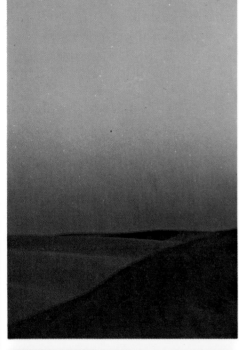

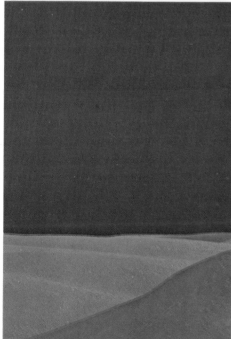

These shots show the results of using filters. In the first **(top)** no filter was used. The second **(above)** was taken using a polarizing filter which flattens contrasts and reflections. For the third **(right)** two transparencies were combined in a duplicating machine to give a very unusual result. Such effects can be useful to the graphic designer.

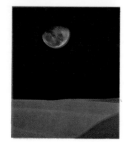

produced from transparencies. In the first, an intermediate copy negative is required; this is usually obtained by contact-printing from the original transparency. The new negative is then used to make what is known as a 'C-type' print. The second, more direct, method allows the transparency to be projected directly on to the printing paper.

Once again, there are two systems in common use. In the first, Ektachrome paper is processed very much like a reversal film, with the dye layers being introduced during processing; the second, Cibachrome, is a 'dye-destruction' process in which the coloured dye layers are incorporated in the paper structure during manufacture and the unwanted areas of colour are destroyed during printing and processing. In both systems, underexposure at the printing stage produces a dark print, and overexposure a light one. Areas of paper unexposed during printing, such as print rebates, will appear totally black. Both processes employ the same filtration system of cyan, magenta and yellow filters above the film carrier. This is used to neutralize any colour bias in the paper or, to a limited extent, in the transparency.

Further modifications to the print may be made by using the conventional 'dodging' and 'burning-in' techniques of black-and-white printing. Since this is a direct process, however, the effect of 'burning-in', for example, will be to lighten the treated area. Colour balance may also be altered locally by shading the printing paper with an appropriate filter.

The principal negative printing process uses the same filter mechanisms as the reversal methods. Its one filtered exposure allows similar controls and corrections.

The results produced by all these processes are superficially indistinguishable. The dye-destruction process is the most stable – resisting fading when the material is on display in daylight – but tends, in common with all direct methods, to yield high contrast prints. This means that if the original transparency already shows excessive contrast, direct processing may fail to produce an acceptable end product. Special papers can also be used to make black-and-white prints from both transparency and negative originals.

Film formats and equipment The choice of format is usually a compromise between cost and definition. The expense involved in using the larger formats – in terms of equipment, film, processing, lighting and studio space required, and often the photographer's fees – are proportionately greater than for the more portable small ones. It is obviously extremely important to match the format to the printed application wherever possible.

The sub-miniature format, using 16mm film, has been employed for reproduction, but the extreme degree of enlargement required makes it suitable for use only in an emergency. The 110

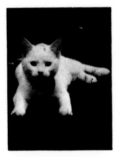

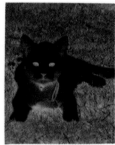

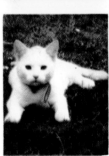

Colour printing There are two methods of making colour prints from transparencies. The direct method **(above left)** prints a positive image directly on to reversal paper so that no intermediate negative is required, as is the case with the indirect method **(above right)**. The direct method is easier to control and maintains detail better.

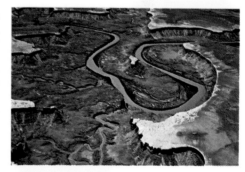

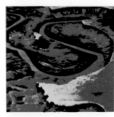

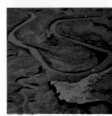

These visually very different results were obtained from the same transparency using a colour synthesizer, a machine used mainly for TV effects work. In the orange and violet shots **(left)** the synthesizer's three colour controls were used at their extremes. The synthesizer is used in a darkened room, the synthesized image displayed on a screen and rephotographed at a slow speed. Such effects can be useful for the graphic designer.

and 126 size pocket cameras come into the same category; the latter suffers more from low-quality camera optics than from the format (24mm square). The following are the systems in current use.

The 35mm system The 35mm system, especially the single-lens reflex, producing a frame size of 24mm × 36mm, now dominates all other formats. This is the case even when considerable degrees of enlargement are required, as the system is far more flexible than any of its competitors. This not only enables the photographer to work at high speed when necessary; it also means that he or she can snatch the opportunity of a completely fortuitous shot with comparative ease. A wide range of film emulsions is also available and their low cost similarly encourages experiment and intensive subject coverage.

The freedom this gives the photographer to produce a large quantity of photographs in a short space of time is obviously good 'insurance', and theoretically increases the likelihood of obtaining the desired result. However, even the rapid-action motor-drive of the 35mm camera – firing the shutter and moving the film forward at up to five frames a second – is no substitute for the perception needed to take the picture at exactly the right moment.

Finished transparencies must be handled with great care. Individual unmounted frames for reproduction should be sealed in transparent bags; complete unmounted films in their protective sleeving can be cut up while still in the sleeving and placed in cardboard mounts. Mounted transparencies processed by the film manufacturer are particularly vulnerable to dust and abrasion and should therefore be sealed in bags. Glass-mounted transparencies are intended for projection only – the film should be removed from the mount and protected as above.

The 120 system Cameras using 120 rollfilm fall into three groups. The largest of these produces 2¼in × 2¼in (60mm × 60mm) images; it is further subdivided into single-lens reflex camera types, such as the Hasselblad, and twin-lens reflexes like the Mamiyaflex and Rollei.

The advantages of this square format often fail to be fully employed in reproduction, since most reproduced images seem to call for a rectangular shape. To counter this, two additional formats

Left, above Two single-lens reflex cameras. With the single-lens system, the camera operator views through the taking lens and can see the actual image to be photographed. The most common single-lens reflex camera is the 35mm, such as the Olympus **(above)**. The Hasselblad **(left)** produces a square picture, 2¼in x 2¼in (6cm x 6cm). Both cameras can be equipped with interchangeable lenses.

Left The 2½in twin-lens reflex camera combines two lens units. The upper lens is used for viewing images produced on a viewfinder screen by a mirror set at 45° within the camera body. These images are laterally-reversed. The lower lens is the taking lens, equipped with a shutter and diaphragm.

Left Typical motor drive camera. Most modern 35mm cameras are equipped with a self-contained battery-powered drive mechanism. Motor drive allows the operator to select and control the number of frames taken per second — within limits — and permits continuous filming or intermittent action.

Left The 6cm x 7cm Pentax is essentially an enlarged version of the standard 35mm camera. It uses 120 rollfilm and produces larger, rectangular images, which are more versatile and popular than the square format. The camera has built-in metering, and can be used with interchangeable lenses.

using this film have recently been revived. The first, the so-called 'ideal format', measures 60mm × 45mm, and the other, larger, size is 60mm × 70mm. Relatively few cameras of this format are yet in use, but it is likely that both these sizes – especially the former – will be extremely significant in the future.

Though nearly four times the area of the 35mm frame, 60mm × 60mm transparencies should be protected in exactly the same way.

Smaller formats Three other formats in current use are 4in × 5in (100mm × 125mm), 7in × 5in (175mm × 125mm) and 8in × 10in (200mm × 250mm). The smallest of these includes some portable equipment – the 4in × 5in view camera, was the standard for press photography for many years – but they are normally used only in the studio. There, conditions can be controlled in conjunction with powerful lighting equipment and interchangeable backgrounds.

Image shapes can be manipulated and depth of field controlled by using the built-in movements of lens and film planes. The film used is supplied in packs of single sheets, to be loaded into double-sided, light-tight holders as required. The holder, or 'dark slide', displaces the

Right This sequence of shots was taken using a motor drive unit which was set to take three frames per second. These shots of a hawk-eagle in flight show it being trained to fly to its handler's arm and the effectiveness of using a motor-drive unit for action pictures and the range of pictures which can be taken in a short period of time — a particularly relevant factor for the designer.

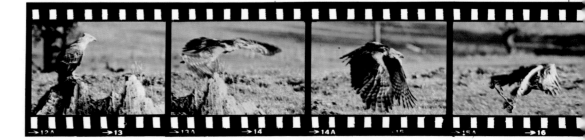

Below The monorail camera is an extremely versatile view camera, designed to adapt to a wide range of shooting situations — from landscapes to close-up magnifications. It consists of interchangeable lens units and film planes, with a moving bellows system, mounted on a rail on the tripod. The camera can use three film sizes — including Polaroid. **Right** Sectional drawings of a monorail camera showing interchangeable units.

camera's focusing screen when the composition has been confirmed, and a movable sheath is slid back ready for the exposure to be made. In the 4in × 5in format, holders are available for 120 size rollfilm, and, in the USA, for a pack of up to 16 sheets of film. A Polaroid film holder can also be fitted to allow a preview of the finished photograph. Since the film is produced in single sheets, test exposures can be made and processed during the course of a shooting session. This means that such crucial factors as composition, colour balance and rendering, and exposure, can be checked before the final shot is taken.

Use of these formats also allows a scaled tracing of the required composition to be taped directly to the focusing screen. Changes in the arrangement of the subject which conflict, say,

with accompanying areas of type or fall outside the page area, can be immediately seen.

Film sensitivity

All general-purpose camera films are panchromatic; they react to all colours in the visible spectrum, though not to the same degree in each case. This wide range of sensitivity is usually considered desirable, but, in certain cases, filtration may become necessary. This happens if certain areas of colour need either to be distinguished more clearly from the ones surrounding them, or need to be eliminated completely.

A common example is when a yellow filter on the camera lens is used to enhance the appearance of white clouds in a clear blue sky by reducing the amount of blue light reaching the film. The sky area consequently appears darker

Parallel effects
These pictures show the effect which can be gained using the camera movements. The first shot **(right)** is taken straight on and the sides of the can appear parallel. In the perspective shot **(below left)** the top of the can is visible but the sides taper towards the base. To take the third shot **(below right)** the bellows of the camera were adjusted to gain the effect of the first shot — the parallel sides — with the top perspective of the second. This effect can be used in many types of graphic design work.

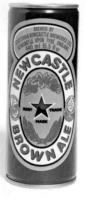

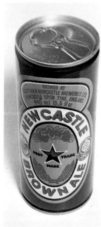

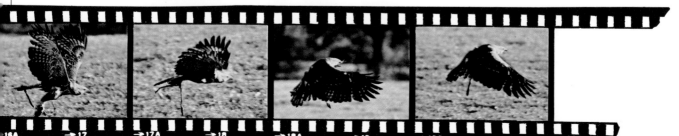

on the resulting print, providing a greater contrast to the white clouds. Conversely, a blue stain on a document, for example, can be weakened or eradicated in a photographic copy by the use of a blue filter of the same hue as the stain.

One of the fundamental rules to remember when using either colour or black-and-white films is that an increase in film speed leads inevitably to a loss of quality in the final image. Fast films have larger grains of silver in their chemical structure than slow ones in order to gain speed; these granules can become obtrusive on enlargement. Camera films range in speed from 32 ASA to 1250 ASA, though this upper limit can be further extended, at the expense of definition, to about 3000 ASA by forced development. The so-called high-acutance developers used on slower films can improve apparent definition by increasing contrast locally.

The choice of film is largely influenced by the weather, the lighting available, the subject, the context and degree of enlargement in reproduction and the chosen format. Some purely mechanical factors, however, also have to be taken into consideration. A medium-speed film of 200 ASA in a 35mm camera, for example, needs an exposure of 1/125 sec at f11 under typical bright overcast conditions. With a 50mm lens focused on a subject 25ft from the camera, the depth of field will extend from 11ft 6in to infinity – focused at 3ft, it will extend from 2ft 8in to 3ft 5in. These limits may require manipulation to suit the demands of the individual photograph, but, inevitably, some of these are incompatible.

In the first example given above, several approaches are possible. If a greater depth of field is required than that attained at f11, the lens can be further stopped down to f22, but the shutter speed must be reset at 1/30 sec. At this speed,

however, subject or camera movement, or both, may degrade the image. Alternatively, a faster film can be used, reverting to the original shutter speed, but the resulting increase in grain size may prove unacceptable.

Changing to a lens of shorter focal length – a wide-angle lens, say – will give a greater depth of field than a normal lens at the same aperture, but will also reduce the subject size within the film frame. Moving closer to the subject with the wide-angle lens to regain the desired magnification results in a changed viewpoint and a possibly undesirable exaggerated perspective. Additional lighting on the subject would allow the required reduction in lens aperture, but this is often difficult to achieve on a large scale except inside the studio. The photographer is faced with similar, and generally more complex compromises in all but the simplest commissions.

Lenses, magnification, perspective and definition The 'normal' lens, for any given format, is held to approximate normal human vision. In fact, the image seen by the eye and transmitted to the brain is on many levels totally unlike any conceivable photographic reproduction. Our two eyes give us 'binocular' vision – the ability to perceive our surroundings in depth. Except at very small eye-to-subject distances, our automatic focusing system gives us the impression that everything in our field of vision is simultaneously in sharp focus. Our overall 'angle of

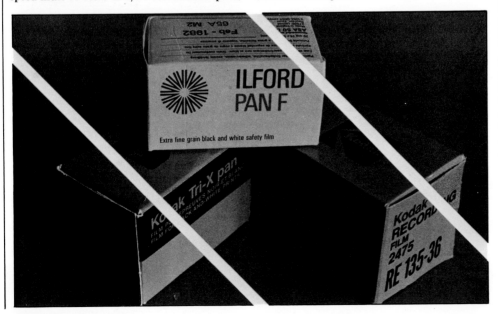

Below The graininess of a film affects the image it produces. The Ilford Pan F **(left)** is a fine grain ASA 50 film, the Kodak Tri-x **(centre)** is medium grain, ASA 400 film. Kodak recording film **(right)** with an ASA of up to 4000, is a high speed film for technical and scientific use.

view', at about 180°, is far more extensive than the 45° of the normal lens, but our area of sharp focus is minute by comparison. Try, for example, to stare fixedly at the word *eye* and attempt to read the next four lines of type without moving your gaze.

The 'normality' of the normal lens is nevertheless confirmed by any comparison between it and other lenses. Even an unsophisticated observer can soon identify photographs taken with extreme wide-angle or long-focus lenses. Close-up shooting with a wide-angle lens distorts the features of the face, for instance, while the apparent 'compression' of perspective induced by the extreme long-focus lens is a regular feature of sport and wildlife presentations.

This compression, although a powerful pictorial tool, is an illusion. The image a long-focus lens delivers to the film is simply a magnification of a small part of the same subject seen by the normal lens from the same viewpoint. Apart from the inherently shallow depth of field of the long-focus lens, perspective and size relationships between the various parts of the photographed subject are identical. These relationships are only disturbed if the viewpoint is changed as well as the lens in an attempt to maintain a constant image size for one object in the photograph. This is an effective device for falsifying or emphasising size relationships within the photograph.

The magnifying property of a lens is described by its focal length. In the 35mm format, a 50mm or 55mm lens is normal; 28mm or 35mm is wide-angle; and 90mm or 135mm is long-focus (usually – but incorrectly – called 'telephoto'). With larger formats, these figures increase – an 80mm lens is normal for 2¼in × 2¼in, 150mm for 4in × 5in, and so on.

Variable focal-length, or 'zoom' lenses can substitute for a number of fixed focal-length lenses in the 35mm format. The wide-angle zoom covers the range between 35mm and 85mm, and the long-focus equivalent from 70mm to 210mm. Maximum apertures are small compared with fixed focal-length lenses, and the large number of lens elements – up to 15 in some designs – can appreciably reduce contrast and definition, especially in bad lighting conditions. However, the ability of a zoom lens to deliver a precisely-framed image from almost any viewpoint greatly reduces the amount of cropping required for reproduction.

The range of commonly used focal length lenses is supplemented by the specialized lenses in use at the extreme ends of the scale. For instance, ultra-wide-angle lenses for 35mm cameras produce increasing degrees of linear distortion as the focal length decreases to around 6mm. One such lens is the 'fish-eye', which provides a circular image of everything in front of the camera and even slightly behind it. Horizontal lines towards the top and bottom of the subject are reproduced as sweeping curves.

Below These figures show the relative image size when different sized lenses are used.

15mm 50mm 105mm 200mm 400mm 800mm

Right The same sizes of lens are used here to show the difference in image size and the angles of view of the lenses.
Below left This wide-angle shot shows the characteristic curved distortion at the edges.
Below This shot was taken using a mirror lens which produces circular highlights around the edges.

800mm 3°
400mm 6°
200mm 12°
105mm 23°
50mm 46°
15mm 110°

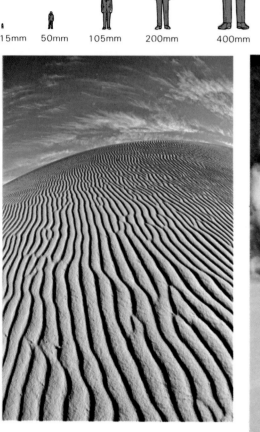

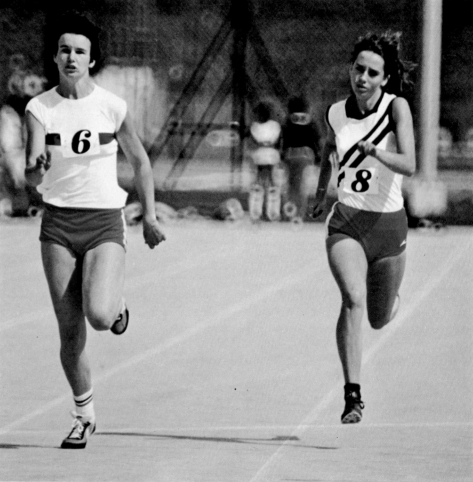

A heavily-corrected 15mm lens will give an acceptably 'real' image, but only if the principal plane of the subject lies parallel to the film plane.

By definition, a long-focus lens is as long physically as its focal length; a 600mm lens of this type is therefore extremely cumbersome, as it is as long as the average arm. Telephoto lenses, however, are shorter and mirror lenses even more so. The latter type has no conventional diaphragm, so exposure can only be varied by changing the shutter speed. The picture produced can be recognized by the circular 'doughnut' form out-of-focus highlights in the background. These are an effect of the small mirror in front of the lens.

All such lenses usually need to be supported by a heavy tripod to avoid camera shake. Results, however, can be disappointing if the distance between camera and subject is so great that the intervening atmospheric dust or heat haze degrades or distorts the image.

Special applications The lenses so far described in this chapter can cope with the vast majority of photographic tasks, but a different approach is

necessary for extreme close-up work. When the required magnification ratio approaches 1:1 (life-size), the camera lens must be moved further from the film plane than the ordinary focusing mechanism allows. A special focusing mount, extension tubes or bellows allow ratios of up to about 1:3 (three times life size).

Extra care has to be taken in lighting these subjects. Not only is the lens-to-subject distance so small that the lens itself may cast a shadow on the subject, but the lens-to-film distance is so great that an exposure reading taken from the subject may need modifying to allow for the fall-off in light reaching the film.

Even higher magnifications can be achieved

by removing the camera lens and coupling the body of the camera to a microscope. Images produced by an electron microscope (giving magnifications of several thousand times the original size) can be photographed directly from the instrument's own cathode-ray output tube.
Shutter speeds and action Photography is an instantaneous process and the photographer's usual aim is to ensure that, within reason, exposure duration is kept as short as possible. Lengthy hand-held exposures – longer than 1/30 sec – will certainly allow an unsupported camera, and possibly the subject, to move. Minute examination of results from some 35mm single-lens reflex cameras suggests that the

vibrations set up during the exposure by the camera itself have an effect on the sharpness of the image, and that the 'safe' lower limit for such an exposure should be raised to at least 1/125 sec. Paradoxically, it is often the noisier cameras which offend least, since the energy of vibration is expended in sound production rather than being absorbed into the camera body.

The shortest shutter opening on a conventional camera is usually 1/1000 or 1/2000 sec. Pictures of moving subjects, especially water, taken at these speeds, show a distinct 'frozen' quality. Even faster movement than this can be captured by electronic flash exposures. In this case, it is not the length of the shutter opening, which determines the appearance of the photograph, but the duration of the flash.

Slow shutter speeds also have a marked effect on the image. The extremely insensitive emulsions available to nineteenth century photographers forced them to take extremely long exposures – often of several minutes duration – even in bright conditions. Figures moving quickly through the field of view would simply fail to register or, pausing for a moment, produce an ill-defined blur on the photograph. The modern photographer, with infinitely faster film, is hard pressed to reproduce this effect. Shutter speeds are only fast or slow in the context of the subject. The classic example of a man on a bicycle exhibits several degrees of movement: his body remains relatively still, his legs move, but quite slowly, while the spokes of his wheels travel relatively quickly.

The blur produced by an excessively 'slow' shutter speed is in fact the most effective description of movement that photography can provide. However, the combination of flash and daylight exposure gives further opportunities in the recording of rapid movement.

Lighting More than any other variable, lighting controls what a photograph will actually look like. In comparison with the camera, the human eye is unreceptive to changes in lighting quality,

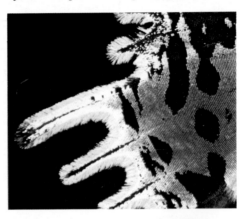

A medical Nikkor lens was used in these shots of a butterfly's wing **(above)** and of teeth **(below)**. This lens, designed for medical work, has a built-in ring flash which gives shadowless frontal illumination.

colour and direction.

Even in daylight conditions outside the studio, the photographer can still control lighting on a small scale. Direct strong sunlight, conventionally the ideal for photography, produces high contrast and hard shadows, but makeshift reflectors and diffusers can help to retain detail in the shadow areas and so bring the contrast range within acceptable limits. Indeed, when the sun is low in the sky, direct sunlight can be turned to advantage. With the sun directly behind the subject, a careful exposure reading of the shaded area will give a practically shadowless rendering of the subject, with an accompanying halo effect, against an overexposed sky. At the other end of the lighting scale, however, the photographer looking for sparkling contrast and deep shadows is virtually defenceless against totally diffused and dim conditions.

Artificial lighting seeks initially to imitate natural effects. A single high intensity light source forms the basis of most lighting set-ups; it may be used with reflectors and diffusers, and even with mirrors. Larger set-ups – and the conventions of portraiture – necessitate the use of subsidiary, or 'fill-in' lights at a lower intensity. These subsidiary lights all serve specific functions – to reduce the intensity of shadows or to produce additional highlights on the subject – but the unity of the photograph is disturbed if they begin to cast shadows of their own.

Continuous light sources Most studios have two kinds of light source. The first and most frequently used group consists of photoflood lamps.

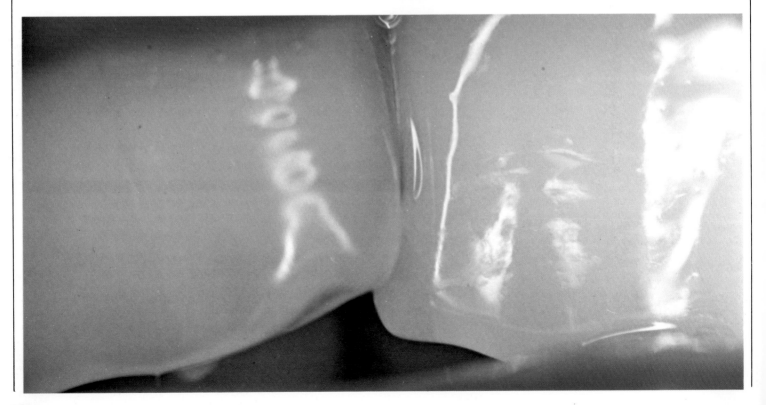

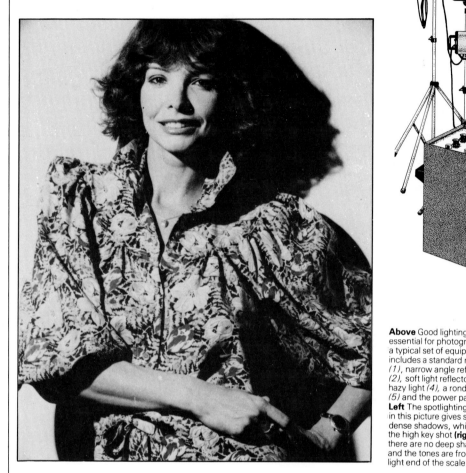

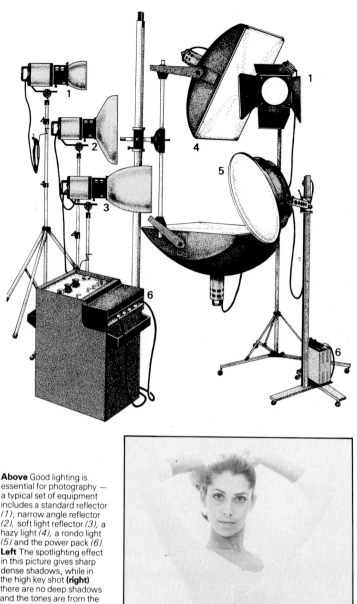

Above Good lighting is essential for photography — a typical set of equipment includes a standard reflector *(1)*, narrow angle reflector *(2)*, soft light reflector *(3)*, a hazy light *(4)*, a rondo light *(5)* and the power pack *(6)*. **Left** The spotlighting effect in this picture gives sharp dense shadows, while in the high key shot **(right)** there are no deep shadows and the tones are from the light end of the scale.

The basic photoflood is simply a domestic lamp designed to be 'over-run', that is, it gives an extremely high level of illumination but has a correspondingly short working life of two to three hours. There are several versions – a more refined one is more powerful and has an integral silvered reflector giving a relatively diffused light. This can be further softened by the use of reflectors and gauze, plastic or paper screens.

The second group includes spotlights and quartz-iodine lamps; the former are basically the same those used in the theatre. Both types produce a hard-edged pool of light which can be focused like the beam from a slide-projector. In a spotlight, the lamp is a halogen type, similar to that used in the projector. Accessory attachments enable this light to be accurately directed on to small areas of the subject.

All these sources can be used in conjunction with a control box which allows the lamps to be run at a much lower level when not actually required for a meter reading or an exposure. This greatly prolongs their life, but their designated colour temperature is only reached when at full power.

Electronic flash sources The average hand-held flashgun is not sufficiently powerful or versatile for studio use. Single studio flashguns, or 'heads', may be self-contained units, but more usually form offshoots of a single control console which may power as many as eight heads. The console shows the state of readiness of the individual heads, as well as housing the large capacitors which store the considerable electrical charge required. The lighting effect produced by a flash set-up can obviously not be ascertained by observation during a test firing, so each head is provided with a 'modelling light'. This continuous light, usually in the centre of the flash tube itself, gives a good approximation of the eventual result. Individual flash heads can usually be set to provide fractions of their full rated output, and attachments similar to those used on spotlights and photofloods are used to modify their effect.

Since conventional metering or flash-factor calculations are impossible with such an arrangement, a special meter provides the reading. Having been set to the ASA rating of the film in use, the quick-acting meter probe is placed at the subject position facing the main light source. A test firing of the heads produces a reading – often a direct indication of the f-stop to be used. With static subjects, a cumulative exposure can be made, firing the guns several times while the shutter remains open, until the total exposure reaches the required level.

When extremely large areas have to be lit,

several flash heads are often needed. The handling of these multiple sources is made more convenient by building them into a large mobile housing faced with a fabric or acrylic diffuser. The whole assembly is termed a 'fish-frier' and is used extensively to simulate daylight lighting conditions.

Unusual effects are obtainable with the ring-flash head. This was originally developed to aid the taking of close-ups, especially in medical photography. The flash tube encircles the camera lens-barrel, replacing the lens hood, and produces a virtually shadow-free result at close range. When used at portrait range, however, with the subject placed close to a flat background, an intense rim-shadow is cast all around the subject.

All these devices operate at very high voltages and generate a considerable amount of heat. Thus safety is a prime factor in their operation.

Studio effects In the controlled environment of the studio, reality can be subjected to many modifications. Such changes can be achieved optically within the camera, by filtration, by the use of scale models as substitutes for the real subject, by means of illusory backgrounds and by a range of special effects borrowed from stage and film techniques.

The staple item of studio furniture is a frame-

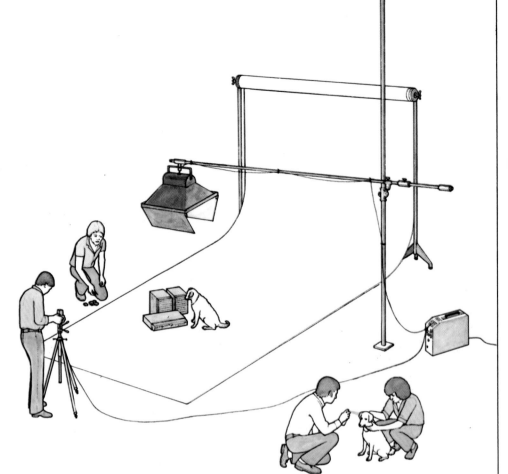

work supporting a 'sweep' – a wide roll of paper which is pulled down behind, and often under, the subject to be photographed. This paper, which may be up to twelve feet wide and in any of forty different colours, provides a seamless and unvarying background for a wide range of subjects.

When even this expanse proves insufficient, the walls themselves are used to form the background, the angle between them and the floor being concealed by a large timber or plaster coving. All surfaces are devoid of texture, and, to preserve their clinical appearance, are repainted before each new session. With the right lighting, the result is an impression of infinite space.

A neutral background may also be required for smaller-scale work – as in photography of glassware, for example. Such objects can be placed on a large light-box identical to the type used for viewing transparencies. The light produced is uniform, soft, and shadow-free, and can be easily balanced with other lights falling directly on the subjects. A refinement of this technique can be used to produce the impression that an object is floating in space. The subject is positioned on a large glass or acrylic sheet

Producing a design The first stage is the rough **(left).** This drawn version shows the basic elements of the design specifying the details. The idea behind the design was to show the progress in modern hi-fi equipment by using a pastiche of the HMV dog listening to some modern hi-fi. In the studio **(above)** the dog's ears had to be sprayed with black to make it resemble the original dog more closely. In order to get the dog's head at the right angle the handler tried calling its name, but a handful of dog biscuits proved more effective. Some 50 pictures were taken — three are shown **below left.** For the final design the edges of the shot were cropped out.

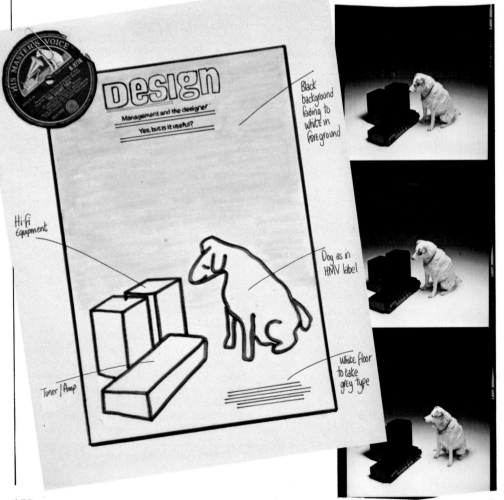

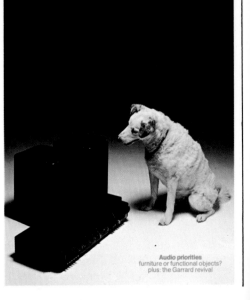

which, in turn, is supported at its extreme edges. The shot is then taken from above. In this process, careful masking of lights and potentially reflective studio equipment, often including the camera itself, is vital so that reflections in the supporting surface do not prejudice the illusion.

'Suspension' of a different kind is achieved by attaching the back of the subject to a rod which runs back towards, and is fixed to, the background. The rod is arranged to lie on the same axis as the camera and the subject. As long as it casts no shadow, it cannot be seen from the camera position.

More 'characterful' settings, such as those employed in food photography, are the preserve of the props specialists, who assist the photographer in the same way as their theatrical counterparts service the stage. Kitchen sets, for instance, are invariably built in the studio. Close-up shots may call for nothing more than a well-worn plank of timber to represent a country kitchen table, with dishes, cutlery and glassware chosen to complement the food being shown. Greater complexities arise when entire rooms have to be created on the studio floor. Once again, the same methods are used as in the theatre: large stage flats are suitably papered and painted and fitted with inset windows and doors, while carpets or tiles, domestic equipment and kitchen paraphernalia complete the scene. Any food on display will have been prepared in the studio's own separate kitchen by a professional home economist.

In such situations, it may be necessary to provide a naturalistic 'view' through a window to the outside world. Gauzes and distant backdrops with the addition of branches and foliage are often considered adequate but an even greater degree of realism can often be achieved through projection. With rear projection, the main problem is the large clear space required behind the projection screen. This is needed both to accommodate the projector and to allow it a sufficient 'throw' to produce a large image. Front projection, however, avoids this.

One simple front projection system uses a movie screen, a specially-treated mirror and a slide projector. The transparency forming the background is placed in the projector; this is positioned at right angles to the axis of the camera lens. The mirror, placed at 45° to this axis, and to that of the projector, redirects the image on to the highly-reflective background screen without affecting the view through the camera lens. Since the axes are perfectly aligned, the shadow cast by the foreground subject on the screen is invisible to the camera.

The subject is separately lit, so as to effectively remove any trace of the background image which may be projected on to it. Alternatively, backgrounds of this kind can be stripped in later by a retoucher where the foreground subject has a simple outline. The advantage of both pro-

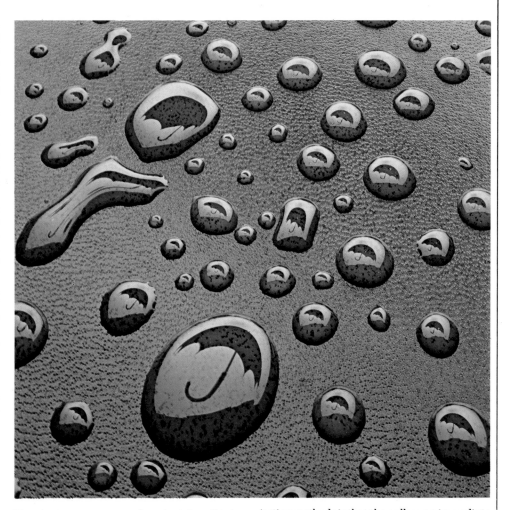

The magazine cover **(above)** is an example of concept photography. It was an attempt to illustrate rain. The drops of water are actually glycerine which is viscous and holds its shape. The 'umbrella' is a two-dimensional piece of black card stuck to the light. The visual effect in the second shot **(below)** was achieved by sticking the bottle to a base and photographing it on its side.

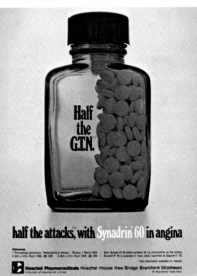

jection methods is that they allow an immediate inspection of the eventual result through the viewfinder.

Objects presented for photography in the studio may suffer from flaws which compromise the photograph. An armoury of equipment exists to retrieve such situations. An aerosol of dulling spray, for example, will deaden excessively strong highlights or reflections; a can of gloss varnish produces the opposite effect. A mist sprayer containing plain water will revive a tired lettuce and enhance the droplets on a cooled beer glass, while the beer itself often benefits from an enlivening burst of carbon-dioxide gas. But in spite of these aids, the camera cannot rescue a badly-made object. It is for this reason that such subjects as cardboard packs are carefully folded from flat blanks taken from the production line.

Climatic effects can be simulated in a suitably spacious and waterproof studio, using sprinkler hoses, wind machines and fog generated from dry ice (frozen carbon dioxide). Nevertheless, it is the simulation of natural lighting conditions which normally concerns the photographer, just as much as the re-creation of a credible reality in an artificial environment.

CHAPTER ELEVEN

REPRODUCTION AND PRINTING

The art of graphic reproduction is essentially to produce through the medium of the camera lettering and/or illustrations in a form suitable for one or more of the printing processes. The images supplied for reproduction are known as 'originals'. These can consist of type pulls, drawings, photographic prints, photographic transparencies, paintings, or other two and three-dimensional materials.

Despite this apparent variety, originals can be broadly grouped into two main types – line and tone. Line originals consist simply of lines, all of which must be solid – and of the same density – anything less than solid is likely to be lost during the camera stage. Tone originals, on the other hand, contain varying ranges of tonal gradation; it is therefore essential for a cross line screen or vignetted contact screen to be applied to the image in order to facilitate a 'halftone' reproduction. Without a screen to break up the tone image into dots of varying size or depth, no tonal gradation can be reproduced.

The camera stage is the key part of the process. In the case of monochrome, the originals are mounted on the camera copy board and, when the correct size, illumination and exposure time have been determined, exposure is made on a photographic film. For letterpress or lithography, the appropriate halftone screen is normally introduced at this stage, but in some lithographic processes and in gravure it is applied later. Some processes, too, require laterally reversed images or positive transparencies rather than negatives; these are produced either by photographing through a prism, or contacting prints from the negative.

Full colour originals, whether line or tone, require separation of the colours by means of colour filters, so that the image can be reproduced by means of four-colour process inks. As with monochrome work, the screen for colour tone originals can be introduced now or later.

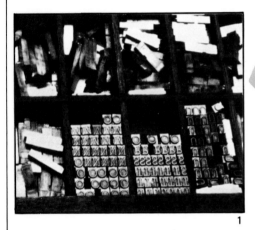

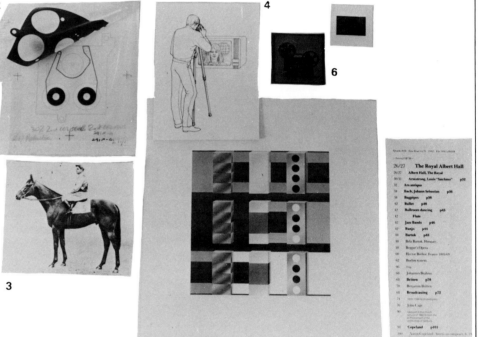

Below Four ways of making prints. In relief printing (1) paper is pressed on to inked, raised areas of wood or metal. For intaglio printing (2) lines are incised into a block and the paper absorbs the ink in the crevices. In planographic printing (3) the design is drawn in a grease which retains the ink. Screen prints (4) use stencils attached to a screen or mesh.

Above right Images for graphic reproduction are known as originals and can be prepared from various different forms of lettering and/or illustration. They include: lead type (1), artwork with transparent overlays (2), black and white photographic prints (3), line drawings (4), four colour artwork (5), photographic transparencies (6) and type pulls or repro (7).

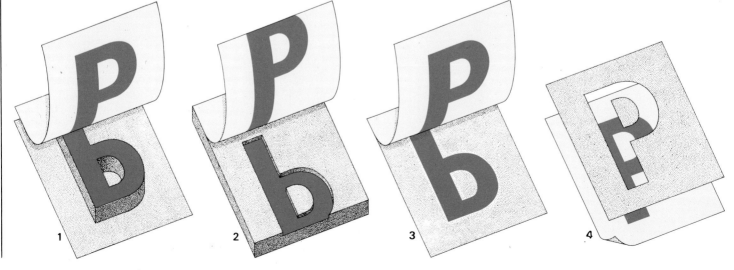

Letterpress

Letterpress is the oldest of the major printing processes, letterpress is the term used to describe the method of printing from a raised surface. Today, this surface may be type, or a plate produced by photo-engraving. Printing ink is rolled on to the raised surface, paper is brought into contact and pressure is applied to transfer the ink on to the paper.

Though the Chinese were practising a form of relief printing from wood blocks during the eighth and ninth centuries AD, letterpress printing as it is now known began in Europe in about 1450, when the German printer Johann Gutenberg first cast individual type characters which could be combined into words and used on the press. It is still the only process capable of printing from individual type characters, and is widely used for work in which type matter predominates and where it is important to have the ability to make late corrections – if necessary, on the press.

A letterpress printing surface may consist of type alone; alternatively the type can be combined with photo-engraved plates, which print illustrations in line or halftone. If an illustration is to be included, the line or halftone plate is produced separately, normally by a specialist firm of platemakers, and, after being mounted on a base material, is locked up in a framework, known as a forme. Plates may be made of zinc, magnesium, copper, or various types of plastic materials.

The metal type plate is first coated with a layer of light-sensitive material, usually a mixture of polyvinyl alcohol and dichromate salts. When dry, this coating is exposed to a powerful light source through a photographic negative of the original subject. The areas of coating struck by the light are hardened and made less soluble, thus forming an acid resist – that is, a material which will not dissolve in acid. Subsequent treatment in acid etches the non-image areas and leaves the protected areas in relief, forming the plate image.

Halftone plates on metal are produced in a similar way. The only difference is that the photographic negative is screened to break the subject up into a system of halftone dots of varying size in order to produce a range of tonal values on the final print.

Non-metallic (plastic) plates differ from metal ones only in the fact that the plastic material used is already light sensitive and therefore does not need preparatory treatment. Upon exposure to bright light under a negative, the plate will harden in the exposed areas and therefore become insoluble to a solvent. After exposure, the plate is 'washed out' in a solvent, leaving the printing area in relief.

Duplicates of a relief plate can be made by first making a mould or matrix on a hydraulic press.

Left An extract from Gutenberg's 42-line Bible. Gutenberg's printing types closely resembled hand-written Gothic script when cast in lines.
Below Three methods of letterpress printing. The platen press *(1)* is the simplest letterpress machine. The forme is held vertically and inked by rollers when the platen opens. When the platen is closed it presses the paper against the inked surface. The rotary press is a form of cylinder press which has a curved printing surface. The sheet-fed rotary press *(2)* can print single sheets in various sizes and at high speeds. In the flat bed cylinder press *(3)* the type forme lies on a flat bed and travels under the inking rollers. A rotating pressure cylinder presses the paper against the type.

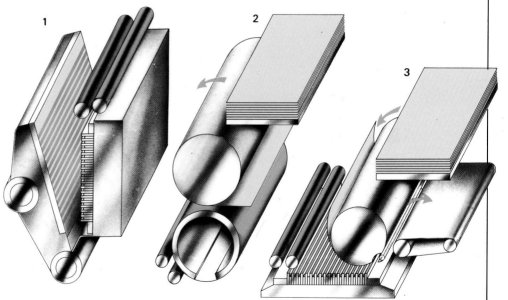

Platen press · Sheet fed rotary · Flatbed cylinder

Right The ten-feeder 'type revolving machine' patented by Richard M. Hoe of New York in 1845. This was the first successful rotary press, which used rotating impression cylinders and a central printing cylinder instead of moving flat beds of type. Hoe's press had four individually fed impression cylinders with separate inking systems. These surrounded a large central cylinder on which the type was locked. It could produce 8,000 sheets per hour, printed on one side. In later models the number of impression cylinders was increased.

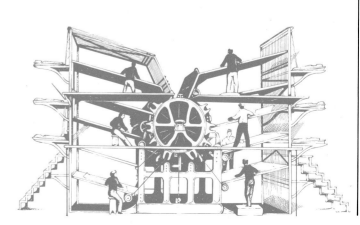

A fibrous board impregnated with a thermosetting resin is laid on the relief plate and heat and pressure applied. The resulting matrix can then be used on the same press with sheets of a thermoplastic material – PVC, for example – to produce duplicate plates. The flexibility of these plates means that they can be wrapped around a cylinder for rotary letterpress printing.

There are three main types of printing machines – Platen, Flat-bed, Cylinder and Rotary. Platen presses have been in use ever since Gutenberg's time. They are extremely versatile, being used to print a large range of work from very coarse printing on board to fine art printing. Two flat surfaces are brought together. The forme is placed vertically against the bed of the press and secured. The paper is held upon another flat surface which is then brought into contact with the inked forme under pressure. Various mechanical methods are employed to achieve this, the end result being the same.

In the flat-bed cylinder press, the forme is placed on the horizontal bed of the machine and the paper is carried across it on an impression cylinder. The return action of the cylinder mechanically lifts the impression and the inking rollers re-ink the forme ready for the next run. Impression can be varied within narrow limits by adjusting the thickness of the packing on the impression cylinder.

Flat-bed presses can be used for every type of printing, from rough work on coarse paper to the finest half-tone and colour work on coated paper. With modifications, the cylinder press is also used by carton manufacturers for cutting and creasing.

The two-colour cylinder press is an extended version of the single cylinder press. It carries two formes, two inking systems, and two impression cylinders. After printing on the first cylinder, the paper is automatically passed to the second, the result being a two-colour impression. The flat-

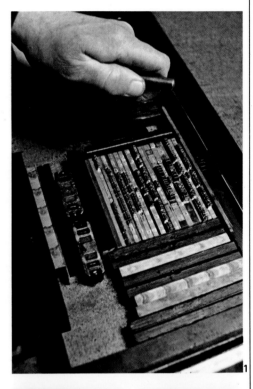

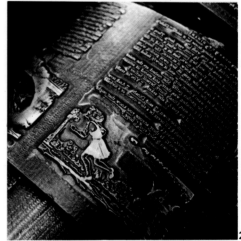

Left *A letterpress block* The design to be printed is etched or engraved on a metal plate so that it stands out in relief. Letterpress plates are usually made of zinc, magnesium or copper — of these, zinc is the cheapest and most common. The finished plate is mounted on a wood or metal block.

Right *An enlarged detail from a letterpress block* Letterpress is a relief printing process. This close-up of part of the halftone block above shows how the relief design is etched into the plate, using lines and tiny dots to build up the tonal effect. The dots are very small for the light areas, becoming larger for shadows and the dark parts of the image.

Letterpress
Letterpress or relief printing is the oldest form of printing using movable type. The first letterpress machines were platen or flat-bed presses, but most modern commercial letterpress takes place on web-fed rotary presses, such as those used for newspaper printing.

The type and illustrations to be reproduced are assembled in the chase by hand *(1)* or by mechanical composing systems such as the Monotype or Linotype setting machines. They are locked into place, together with leads and furniture for spacing.

To transfer the relief design from the flat forme to the printing cylinder a papier-mache mould, often called a flong, is made. This carries an accurate impression of the type and illustrations mounted on the forme. The mould is bent and coated with hot, liquid metal which hardens to create the curved printing plate *(2)*. The plate is mounted on the printing cylinder in the rotary press *(3)* and fitted into its correct position. To ensure that it will produce an even, clear impression, each part of the surface must be at the same level and exert an equal pressure. This is achieved by the process known as

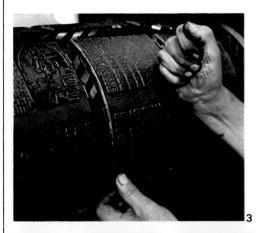

making ready (4, 5). The plates are raised (underlaying) or dressed from above (overlaying) to adjust the height and pressure finely.

The inking system in the rotary press involves numerous rollers which transfer the stiff printing ink from the duct to the type surface. The amount and consistency of the ink are very important, and can be regulated by the printer (6). The inking rollers apply the ink evenly over the relief surface of the cylinder plate.

The web-fed rotary press uses a continuous roll of paper. This is fed on to the impression cylinder of the machine (7) which carries it over the cylinder plate and presses it against the inked relief surface. The pressure transfers the ink to the paper to print the design.
After printing, the paper is conveyed to another part of the machine where it is folded and cut (8) so that it emerges ready for delivery. Modern rotary presses are capable of printing at very high speeds — over 25,000 copies an hour — and of producing long runs. This makes them particularly suitable for newspaper printing, which is the main modern commercial application of letterpress.

bed perfecting press is similar to the two colour cylinder press; in the perfecting press, however, the paper is turned over for the second printing. This type of press is widely used for book printing.

The rotary press operates on the principle of printing on every revolution of the impression cylinder; the flat-bed cylinder press, on the other hand, only prints on every other revolution. It is designed for high-speed, fine-register printing; its speed makes it possible to produce long-run high quality work extremely economically. As the printing surface for the rotary press has to be curved, special production methods are required. Though these are more costly than flat-bed printing surfaces, they can be readily altered as they are usually made from moulds of flat printing formes.

There are two main types of rotary press – sheet-fed and web-fed. The sheet-fed press is capable of speeds up to 6000 impressions per hour, and can operate on either the unit principle or the common impression principle. With the unit system, there is a separate unit for each colour to be printed – in three-colour printing there are three units and in four-colour printing, four.

With many of the modern multi-unit presses, it is possible to use some of the units independently of each other. This means that the press can be printing two different jobs simultaneously. If, for instance, the whole press consists of seven units, it can be printing a three colour and a four colour job at the same time.

In the common impression system, one impression cylinder is surrounded by up to five inking systems, all of which can print at one time. The plate cylinders are placed round the common impression cylinder. As the colours are all printed wet within a fraction of a second, very accurate ink control adjustment by the pressman is required.

As its name implies, the web-fed rotary press prints upon a continuous web of paper on both sides as the web passes from one cylinder to the other. In most high speed multi-colour rotaries, two or more plate cylinders are grouped around a common impression cylinder, with successive colours being printed almost simultaneously. Special inks and driers are used. These presses can operate at speeds of more than 500 metres per minute.

The wrap-around rotary press is a modern development of letterpress and prints from a one piece shallow relief plate fastened around a press cylinder. This system preserves the speed advantage of rotary printing and is ideal for general commercial printing, folding cartons, labels and business forms. The printing surfaces are usually produced on a plastic surface backed with a thin sheet of steel which allows it to be curved around a cylinder. The plate cylinder is often of a special magnetized type that will 'grip' the plate with no mechanical clamping device.

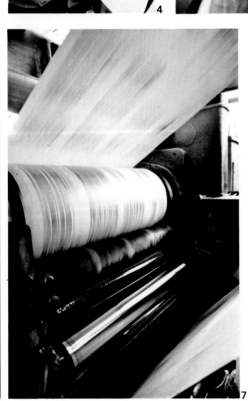

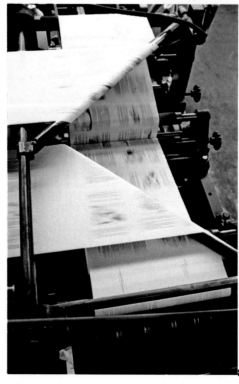

Lithography

The chief difference which distinguishes the lithographic printing process from letterpress is that, in lithography, the image areas on the plate do not stand up in relief. The process itself is based on the fact that grease and water do not readily mix; the image areas attract the greasy ink while the non-image areas repel it. Before each impression is made, a litho plate must be dampened and then inked.

Although lithographic printing was invented at the beginning of the nineteenth century by the German typographer Alois Senefelder, it is only fairly recently that the process has acquired the great commercial importance it has today. It is now the major printing process in common use, its applications ranging from the small office offset duplicating machine to the large installations used to produce magazines and newspapers.

The word lithography comes from two Greek words – *lithos*, meaning a stone, and *graphe*, a drawing. In the original process, the printing surface was made by drawing on a polished limestone surface with a greasy crayon. The stones were then incorporated into a flatbed printing press; modern litho presses, however, use the rotary principle. For this reason, litho printing surfaces must be made on thin, fairly strong, sheet material which can be wrapped round the curve of the cylinder. A great variety of materials are used, including zinc, aluminium, plastic, paper, and combinations of metals, such as copper and chromium. The greater majority of litho plates are produced on aluminium, as this material combines lightness, strength and excellent lithographic properties with relative cheapness.

The first step in litho platemaking is to apply a light-sensitive coating to the surface of the material being used. This can be done by placing the plate upon a machine called a whirler, to ensure the even application of the coating; alternatively, the coating can be wiped on with a sponge. However, it is now more usual for platemakers to purchase pre-prepared plates – these are known as 'pre-sensitive'.

All photomechanical methods of producing lithographic plates rely upon the principle of light affecting the coated surface. Depending on the type of light-sensitive coating used, they will either become more or less soluble in a particular solvent. After exposure, the more soluble areas can be washed away to leave a hard stencil of the image on the plate. The types of plates are known as 'negative-working' and 'positive working', depending on whether exposure is made through a negative or a positive.

Offset lithography is a planographic process of printing from a plane or flat surface, employing the principle that grease and water do not mix. The printing areas are on the same plane as the non-printing areas. The image, or printing area of the litho plate is made ink receptive, whilst the non-image areas remain non-receptive to ink. The printing surface first passes over water-bearing rollers, which dampen the non-image areas. The ink-bearing rollers then come into contact with the printing surface, depositing ink on to the image areas only – the remainder of the plate being damp will not receive the ink. The plate cylinder then comes into contact with the blanket cylinder, which has a rubber surface. An ink impression is left on the blanket, which in turn transfers the image to the paper. This is the reason for the use of the term offset lithography, as the paper does not come into contact with the printing plate.

The press itself operates on the rotary principle of making one impression with each revolution of the cylinder. The printing unit consists of three cylinders – plate, blanket, and impression. Offset presses are made in a number of sizes; these are usually designated by the maximum sheet size that can be handled. As with the letterpress printing press, litho presses may be sheet-fed or web-fed according to the type of work involved.

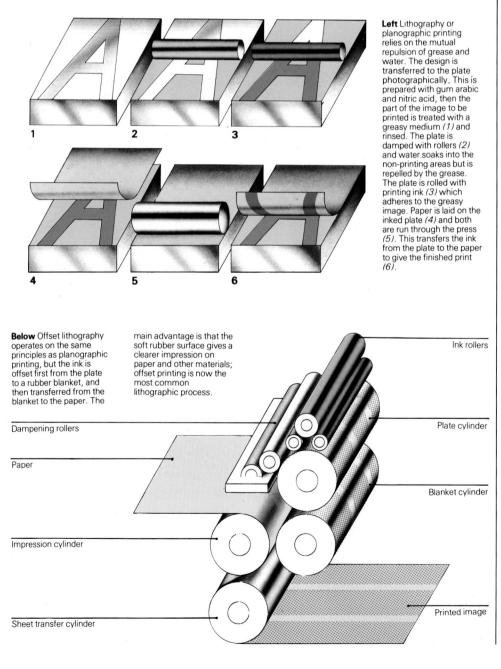

Left Lithography or planographic printing relies on the mutual repulsion of grease and water. The design is transferred to the plate photographically. This is prepared with gum arabic and nitric acid, then the part of the image to be printed is treated with a greasy medium (1) and rinsed. The plate is damped with rollers (2) and water soaks into the non-printing areas but is repelled by the grease. The plate is rolled with printing ink (3) which adheres to the greasy image. Paper is laid on the inked plate (4) and both are run through the press (5). This transfers the ink from the plate to the paper to give the finished print (6).

Below Offset lithography operates on the same principles as planographic printing, but the ink is offset first from the plate to a rubber blanket, and then transferred from the blanket to the paper. The main advantage is that the soft rubber surface gives a clearer impression on paper and other materials; offset printing is now the most common lithographic process.

Ink rollers

Dampening rollers

Paper

Plate cylinder

Blanket cylinder

Impression cylinder

Sheet transfer cylinder

Printed image

Offset duplicators There has been a rapid increase in the variety and number of small offset duplicating machines in the past decade. Because of their low cost per unit in production terms, the fact that they occupy the minimum floor space, their versatility, and their speed, these presses are in daily use in many establishments that used not to be called printers.

These machines are ideal for quick printing of office and plant forms, price lists, sales letters, minutes and so on. Handwriting, typewriting, and copy preparation are all faithfully reproduced on a paper direct image master. Pre-sensitized paper and metal offset plates are used to reproduce line and half-tone copy from prepared negatives/positives.

There are two general types of plate used for the offset duplicator – the paper direct image and the pre-sensitive plate. Direct image paper plates are made of non-sensitive material and can be written, typed and drawn upon. They are inexpensive and easy to produce, as they do not require any specialized equipment for their production. They are ideal for short run reproduction work. Pre-sensitized plates are made of aluminium, paper or plastic, coated with a light-sensitive material for the transferring of images photographically. The unexposed area of the plate becomes ink receptive, and thus forms the image.

Another, although not so frequently used, method of producing printing plates for offset duplicating is by electro-static means. The plate is first polarized and, upon exposure to light, the polarized areas are desensitized. The plate is then coated with a powder which adheres to the polarized areas to form the printing image. In contrast with the other types, this method of plate production requires specialized equipment.

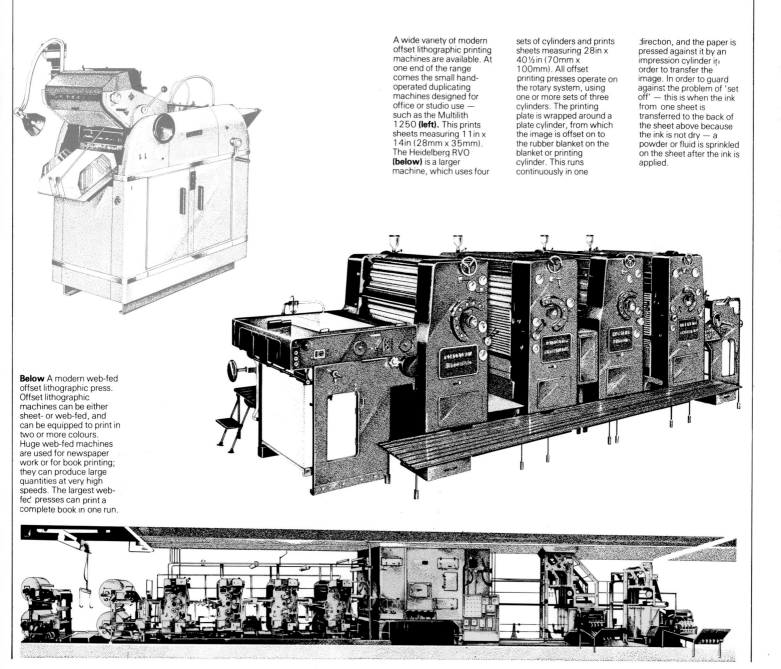

A wide variety of modern offset lithographic printing machines are available. At one end of the range comes the small hand-operated duplicating machines designed for office or studio use — such as the Multilith 1250 **(left).** This prints sheets measuring 11in x 14in (28mm x 35mm). The Heidelberg RVO **(below)** is a larger machine, which uses four sets of cylinders and prints sheets measuring 28in x 40½in (70mm x 100mm). All offset printing presses operate on the rotary system, using one or more sets of three cylinders. The printing plate is wrapped around a plate cylinder, from which the image is offset on to the rubber blanket on the blanket or printing cylinder. This runs continuously in one direction, and the paper is pressed against it by an impression cylinder in order to transfer the image. In order to guard against the problem of 'set off' — this is when the ink from one sheet is transferred to the back of the sheet above because the ink is not dry — a powder or fluid is sprinkled on the sheet after the ink is applied.

Below A modern web-fed offset lithographic press. Offset lithographic machines can be either sheet- or web-fed, and can be equipped to print in two or more colours. Huge web-fed machines are used for newspaper work or for book printing; they can produce large quantities at very high speeds. The largest web-fed presses can print a complete book in one run.

Right *Lithography*
Commercial lithography
normally takes place on an
offset press, printing from
photographic plates. The
plate can be made from
zinc, aluminium, stainless
steel or processed paper. It
is prepared by coating the
surface with a light-sensitive
photographic medium. This
is often done on a whirler
(1), which revolves as the
solution is applied, ensuring
that it spreads evenly over
the surface.

The plate is next placed in
contact with a photographic
negative of the image in
a vacuum frame *(2),* where
they are exposed to high
intensity light. After
exposure, the plate is
treated with an emulsion
developer which consists of
lacquer and gum-etch in a
solution of acid *(3).* This
dissolves the unexposed
coating, leaving gum on the
non-printing areas and
lacquer on the image.

After developing, the plate is
thoroughly rinsed with water
(4) and then coated with a
protective solution of gum
arabic. The finished plate is
mounted or wrapped
around the plate cylinder of
the offset press, and
clamped in place *(5).* In the
press it comes in contact
with two sets of rollers — for
dampening and inking. The
dampening rollers apply a
solution of water, gum
arabic and acid to the
surface of the plate; this
prepares the image and the
non-printing areas to retain
and repel the ink
respectively.

Lithographic inks *(6)* have a
greasy or fatty basis, so that
they are repelled by the
water on the non-image
areas of the plate. They are
normally very strong in
colour value, since relatively
small quantities are used,
compared with letterpress
ink, for example. The ink is
applied thinly and evenly
over the rollers *(7).* The inked
image is then transferred, or
offset, on to the rubber
blanket on the blanket
cylinder, which in turn
transfers the image to the
paper running over the
impression cylinder, to
produce the finished prints
(8).

The use of a rubber offset
blanket avoids damage to
the delicate lithographic
plate through contact with
an abrasive paper surface.
The rubber conforms to
irregular surfaces, making it
possible to print on a wide
variety of papers — from
newsprint to fine art paper.
Offset machines range from
small office duplicators to
large web-fed presses
which can produce an entire
book in a single run.

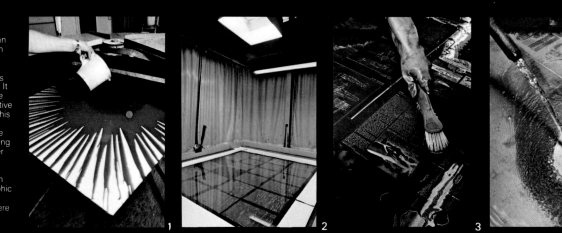

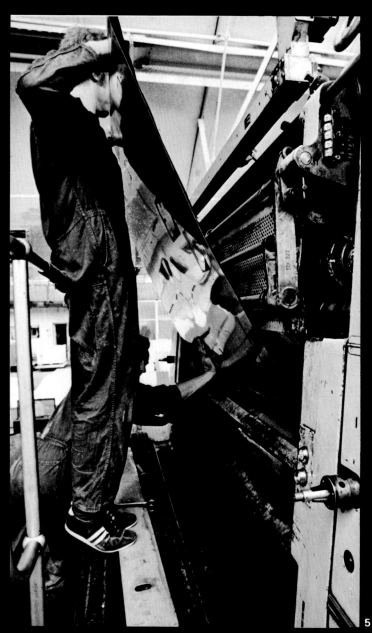

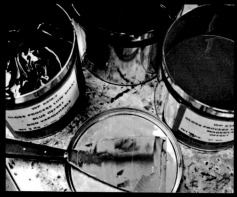

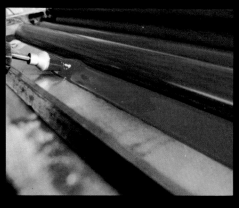

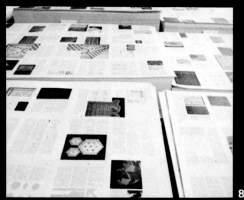

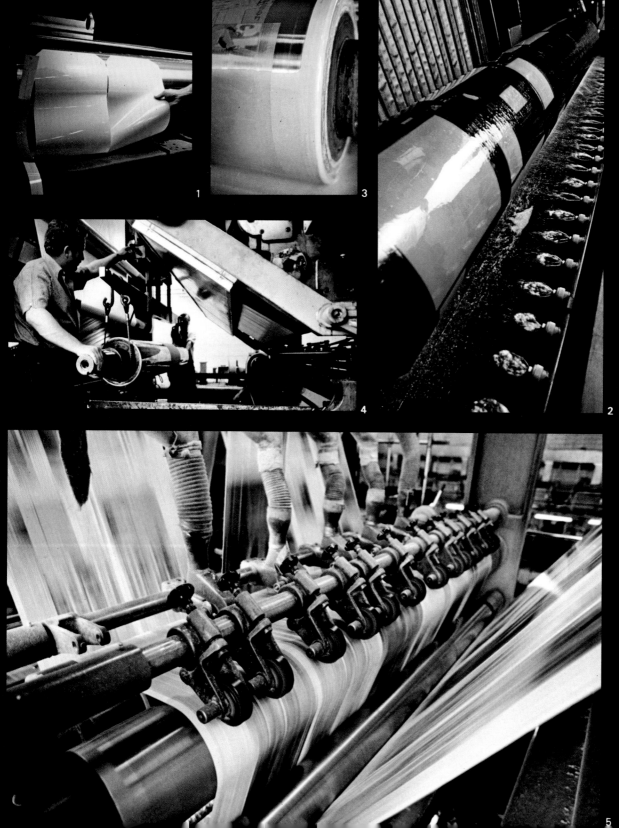

Left *Gravure printing*
Gravure is the method of intaglio printing used commercially for copying black and white or colour originals. It normally takes place on high-speed sheet-fed or web-fed (roto-gravure) presses.

The design to be printed is first etched on a cylindrical copper plate. The image is transferred by the use of a sensitized gelatin transfer medium known as carbon tissue. This is exposed to light in contact with the gravure screen, then the positives are exposed in contact with the carbon tissue, to harden the gelatin. The tissue is mounted on the cylinder (1) and when the paper backing is removed it is developed so that areas of gelatin remain as an acid resist.

The cylinder is etched in solutions of ferric chloride (2). The rate of penetration depends on the thickness of the gelatin resist. A graded etching is produced by using a series of solutions of progressively decreasing concentration. The process incises the lines of the design below the surface of the copper plate, so that they will retain the ink. At this stage a first proof is normally taken. Corrections in tone and colour may be made by rolling-up the cylinder with a stiff ink (3) and further local etching, in order to achieve a fine finish. When the etching has been perfected, the soft copper cylinder is normally 'chromed' in order to give it a more durable surface.

The finished cylinder is mounted in register on the rotogravure press (4) and locked into position below the impression cylinder. This is known as 'making ready'. The printing surface is inked by rotating the cylinder through a trough of printing ink. Excess ink is removed from the plate by a flexible blade known as a 'doctor' so that the non-image areas remain clear, but ink is held in the recesses of the design.

In web-fed gravure, the paper is fed through the press continuously (5). It passes between the etched plate cylinder and the impression cylinder, which has a hard rubber surface. This applies considerable pressure, which forces the ink from the etched lines of the cylinder on to the paper, and transfers the image.

A variety of surfaces can be used for gravure, including textiles, cellophane and vinyls. It is used commercially for packaging,

Gravure

The gravure process can be used very successfully to print on papers of various qualities ranging from newsprint to fine art. It is mainly used for printing magazines and packaging, but there are other applications, such as the production of decorative laminates, floor tiles, wall paper, postage stamps and fine art reproductions.

Gravure is an intaglio process – that is, the ink is transferred to the paper from very small cells of different depths which are recessed into the printing surface. Because the cells can be varied in depth, different amounts of ink may be transferred at different points. This depth ranges from about 0.001 mm in the highlight areas, to

Below Three types of gravure plate. In conventional gravure (1) the cells have equal surface areas but variable depths. Conventional gravure is used for short runs of high quality black and white or colour illustrations. In variable area — variable depth gravure (2) the size as well as the depth of the cells varies. This produces more durable tones, suitable for long run periodical printing. In direct transfer or variable area gravure (3) the image elements vary in area but not in depth, giving a limited number of tones. This is widely used for packaging and textile printing.

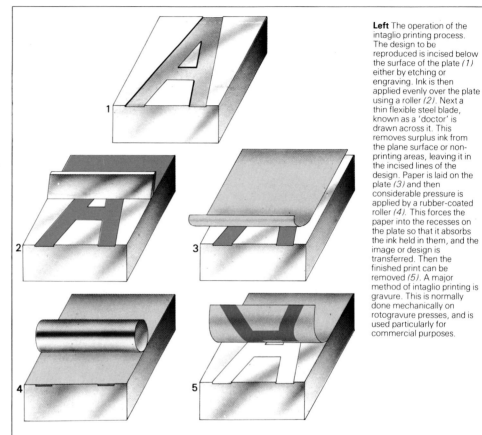

Left The operation of the intaglio printing process. The design to be reproduced is incised below the surface of the plate (1) either by etching or engraving. Ink is then applied evenly over the plate using a roller (2). Next a thin flexible steel blade, known as a 'doctor' is drawn across it. This removes surplus ink from the plane surface or non-printing areas, leaving it in the incised lines of the design. Paper is laid on the plate (3) and then considerable pressure is applied by a rubber-coated roller (4). This forces the paper into the recesses on the plate so that it absorbs the ink held in them, and the image or design is transferred. Then the finished print can be removed (5). A major method of intaglio printing is gravure. This is normally done mechanically on rotogravure presses, and is used particularly for commercial purposes.

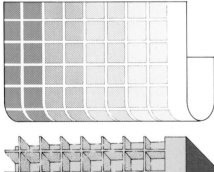

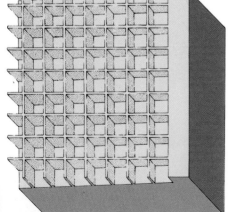

1 Conventional gravure

2 Variable area variable depth

3 Variable area direct transfer

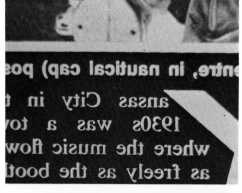

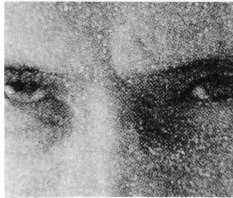

0.04 mm in the shadows.

There are three main types of cell structure, depending upon the method used to produce the printing surface. Conventional gravure consists of cells of equal surface areas but of varying depth. In invert halftone gravure, both the cell area and the cell depth varies according to tone; in the highlight, the cell becomes small and shallow, while in the shadow or dark area it becomes larger and deeper. This is particularly useful in colour reproduction.

In electro-mechanical engraving, a scanning head moves systematically across the subject to be reproduced. The signals from this are used to control the movement of a diamond stylus engraving head which cuts out cells in the form of inverted pyramids with varying depths and areas. Another method uses a laser beam to

Above left An enlarged detail of an intaglio plate. In gravure the plates are normally photo-engraved and printed on rotary presses. Gravure is unique in that all the copy, including pictures and type, is screened.
Left An enlarged detail from an intaglio reproduction printed in the *Sunday Times* magazine. Gravure printing involves a screening process in which the image is broken up into thousands of dots.

Photogravure printing can take place on sheet-fed rotary presses or on web-fed (rotogravure) presses. Sheet-fed presses **(below left)** are used for small editions or for high quality work — fine art reproductions, for example. Web-fed machines **(below)** can produce large quantities of prints at high speeds. This makes rotogravure particularly suitable for commercial purposes, such as magazine or packaging printing. Specially-equipped web-fed machines, with five or more units, are used with fast-drying ink for high-speed colour printing.

Sheet fed gravure

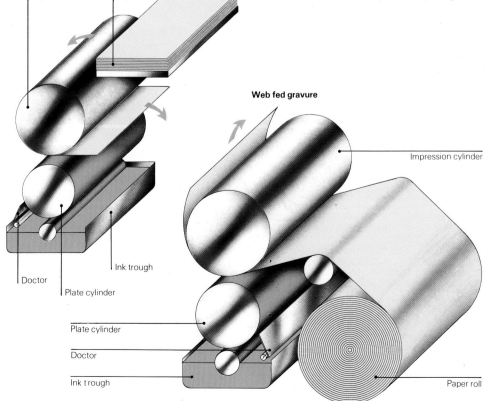

produce the printing surface; the laser decomposes the area it impinges upon according to the strength of the signal received from the scanning head.

The surface itself is normally made on highly-polished copper; this is often deposited as a thin skin by electroplating on a solid steel cylinder. As a precaution against the hard wear that can be expected on long print runs, this copper skin itself may be chromium plated after the cells have been formed.

If the printing surface is to be produced by traditional methods – that is, not by scanning – positives, rather than negatives, of both pictures and text are required. Carbon-tissue is used for this; the tissue is a light-sensitive paper coated with a pigment and dichromate suspended in gelatin.

The carbon-tissue is first screened to divide the printing area into small cells. This is done by placing the material under a gravure screen (composed of tiny opaque squares surrounded by clear lines) in a contact vacuum frame and exposing it to bright light. Next, the positives are mounted on a clear film base and are placed in contact with the carbon-tissue, again in a contact vacuum frame. There they are exposed to a diffused light. Where the tones are lighter the light passes through the positive freely. As a consequence the gelatin on the carbon-tissue becomes harder than where the light only reaches it weakly, that is from the darker areas of the positive. The screen lines remain the hardest.

The carbon-tissue is now ready to be mounted on the cylinder. This is done by slightly moistening the surface and then placing the gelatin in contact using a mangle-type machine. After mounting, the backing paper is removed and the cylinder 'developed' in warm water to wash away any soluble (unhardened) gelatin, leaving the hardened gelatin resist in place. When the gelatin has dried, various areas, such as the edges that need to be protected from etchant, are painted out with a bitumen-based varnish.

Ferric chloride ($FeCl_3$) is the mordant used for etching. The ferric chloride first penetrates the gelatin in the thinnest areas, where the printing tones will be darkest, and lastly the highlights, where the gelatin is thickest. When etching is completed, the bitumen varnish and the residual gelatin are removed and the cylinder dried again. It is then ready for printing.

Gravure is very suitable for high speed work. However, it is an expensive process and it is difficult to make changes easily. This makes it economic only for fairly long printing runs. Modern rotogravure presses can be run at very high speeds; for colour printing they have automatic register control, through the use of an electric eye which assures accuracy of colour reproduction. Sheet-fed gravure presses operate in much the same way as the web-fed presses, with one printing for each cylinder revolution.

Screen printing

Screen printing is printing from stencils to obtain repeat patterns is probably the oldest form of duplication used by man. The prehistoric cave dwellers of Gargas in Southern France, for instance, decorated their cave walls by using their hands as stencils, applying glue around the outline and sprinkling coloured earth on the wet glue. Thousands of years later, the rubricators of the Gutenberg Bible used stencilled outlines as guides upon which to place their colours.

Modern screen printing, formerly known as silkscreen, has evolved since 1918. It owes its popularity as a method of duplication to its low cost, the introduction of improved mesh materials, the use of photographic stencils and developments in ink technology. In the past it was often possible to identify screen prints by feeling the thickness of the ink on the sheet, but today the ink film thickness has been decreased considerably.

The printing screen consists of a piece of open weave silk, nylon, organdie or metal mesh, stretched very tightly over a wood or metal frame. This mesh serves to hold the portions of the stencil securely in place during printing. There are a number of non-photographic ways of making stencils for screen printing, involving work done by hand directly on the screen, but these are of relatively little importance in the commercial and industrial fields. Knife-cut stencils, however, are of very great value to the screen printer, as they can be cut directly from pencil layouts of artwork.

Progress in knife-cut laminate materials has, in the past, been confined almost entirely to the American development of solvent adhering stencil films, a great variety of which are now obtainable. The films consist of highly transparent, dimensionally stable plastic backing sheets, which resist certain inks and simplify the operation of cutting, striping and adhesion. Special films and matched solvents improve adhesion to the screen. The basic feature of all laminated knife-cut stencil films is the use of a backing sheet, which can be peeled away after the stencil has been fixed to the screen.

Either of two photographic methods – direct or indirect – can be used to produce photo-stencils. Direct photostencils are made by coating the screen mesh with a light-sensitive emulsion. After drying, the mesh is exposed to direct contact with a positive transparency, in a vacuum contact frame. Light-hardening of the emulsion occurs in the non-image areas, leaving soluble emulsion in the image details of the stencil. These areas are cleared by the action of hot or cold water. Indirect photostencils are prepared, exposed and washed out or developed before the stencil is fixed to the screen.

Screen process printing used to be called silkscreen; the term now in general use is screen process. In this, a stencil image is imposed on to

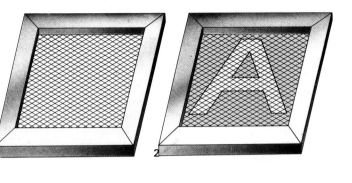

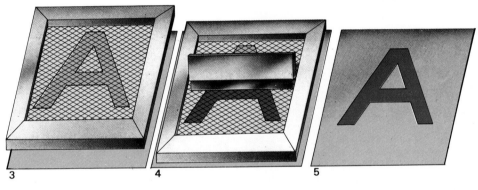

Left *Silkscreen printing* The simplest form of silkscreen uses a basic stencil. More sophisticated photo-stencil methods are used commercially. The screen is prepared by stretching a fine gauze over a wooden frame (1). The design is cut in a stencil, which is placed over the screen (2) so that certain areas are masked. The paper is positioned under the screen (3) and ink is drawn across it by a squeegee (4). The ink passes through the unblocked areas to produce the printed image (5).

Right In photographic silkscreen printing the stencil is prepared from a film positive. This often includes small flaws or 'pinholes' which are corrected manually by a process of retouching known as 'positive spotting' (1). The screen is coated with a light sensitive photographic emulsion (2).

Below The positive is placed under the pre-heated emulsified screen in a vacuum frame and exposed to ultra-violet light (3). When the screen is taken out it is washed with a cold water spray (4) to remove the emulsion from the image area.

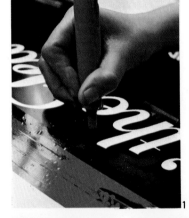

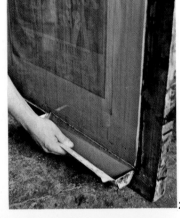

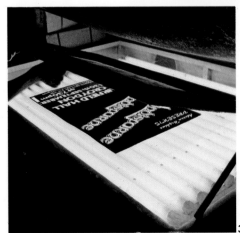

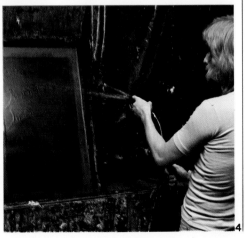

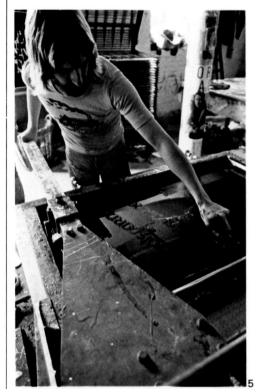

To remove any excess emulsion that may have built up the screen is scraped or swept (5). The paper to be printed is positioned accurately under the screen by aligning corresponding registration marks in the corners (6). When the screen and the paper have been assembled on the frame, the actual process of printing, known as 'pulling' the print, can take place. Printing ink is drawn across the screen with a rubber squeegee (7). The action of the squeegee presses the screen down slightly, and forces the ink through the unmasked areas of the mesh on to the paper. The wet print is removed carefully (8) and stacked with others on a drying rack (9) in front of a fan or blow heater, until it is dry. This popular method, using a photographic stencil, is ideal for producing sharp lettering and for reproducing pen and brush drawings. Prints can be made on a variety of surfaces, including wood, glass, metal, plastic and various fabrics.

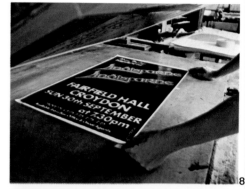

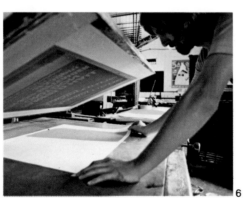

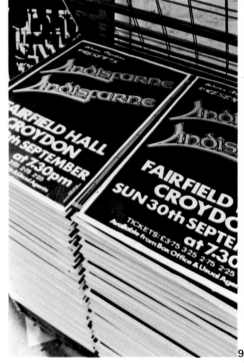

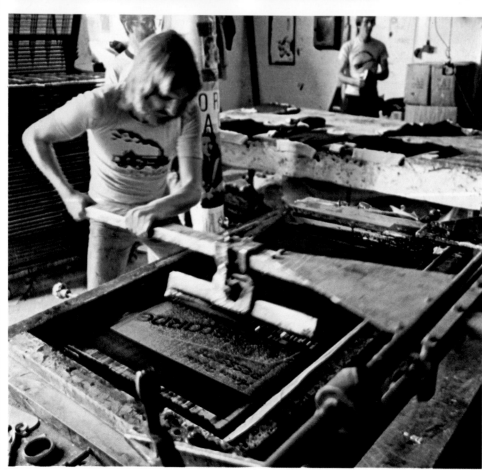

a screen mesh – the mesh consisting of a piece of open-weave silk, nylon, or metal – stretched over a frame. The design to be printed is either hand cut or photographically prepared. Ink is placed in the frame and forced through the mesh. The ink that penetrates the clear areas of the stencil forms the printing image.

The chief advantage of the process is its versatility; almost any surface – wood, glass, metal, plastic, fabrics, and so on – can be used for printing. One of its most important features is its ability to deposit a heavy film of ink, sometimes ten times as heavy as that of letterpress, on the image. The thickness may be controlled by the mesh of the silk, the ink itself, or various additives.

There are many types of presses manufactured for screen process printing – more often than not, equipment is specially designed to cover each and every requirement – but a high proportion is done by hand.

Collotype

The collotype process is a valuable method of reproduction, though it is not used on a large scale. Like litho, it is a planographic process, a film of gelatin carrying the actual image. It is the only process which can produce a high quality of black-and-white or colour continuous tone without the use of a screen.

A solution of gelatin, rendered light sensitive with potassium or ammonium dichromate, is poured over a thick sheet of plate glass which serves as a base. After drying, a photographic negative is placed in contact with the plate and exposed to light. The gelatin hardens in proportion to the amount of light passing through the negative and thus loses its property of absorbing moisture. The hardened portions are simultaneously made capable of accepting ink.

In common with lithography, the process depends on the antipathy between grease and water. The unexposed portions are kept moist with water and glycerine to enable them to repel the ink. The process is a gradation from the lightest tones of grey to the deepest black and the effects obtained are very comparable to an original photograph. The print produced can be identified under magnification, the half-tones being resolved into a very fine puckered grain. However, it is often necessary to examine various parts of the printed image in order to detect this typical puckered effect.

The stiffest inks are used for printing collotype, which, in turn, necessitates the use of well-sized paper. Special collotype cylinder machines similar to litho machines are used for printing. The process is a slow one – only about 1000 to 2000 copies can be taken from one plate – and it may take as long as two days to produce this number of impressions. However, collotype is capable of providing better colour prints than any other printing method; this justifies one of its chief uses – printing small runs of reproductions of paintings.

Flexography

The flexography process uses a very quick-drying fluid ink and is usually printed on a fast moving web. The basic principle is similar to that of letterpress; in flexography, however, the relief printing surfaces are made of flexible synthetic rubber, mounted round the press cylinder by using adhesives. The plates themselves are produced from a matrix which has been moulded from the flat engraved plates.

In this process, it is important that artwork is correctly prepared, as distortions take place when the rubbers are mounted on the cylinders. The natural stretch in one direction and the shrinkage in the other will cause a circle to distort into an oval. It is essential to make allowances for this at the preparatory stage.

Almost any material which will pass through the press as a web can be used. Highly absorbent paper should be avoided, however, as it tends to

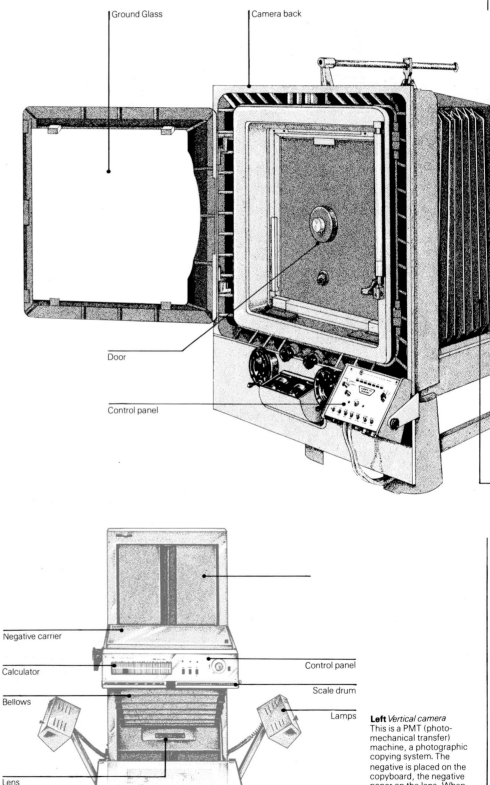

Ground Glass

Camera back

Door

Control panel

Negative carrier

Calculator

Bellows

Lens

Copy board

Control panel

Scale drum

Lamps

Glass

Left *Vertical camera*
This is a PMT (photo-mechanical transfer) machine, a photographic copying system. The negative is placed on the copyboard, the negative paper on the lens. When the negative is ready it is placed on to positive paper. The whole process which with earlier equipment would have taken about 1½ hours now takes about 10 minutes.

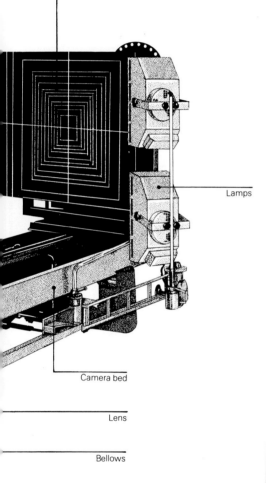

Copyboard

Lamps

Camera bed

Lens

Bellows

Above *Process camera*
The process camera, which is also called a copy or graphic arts camera, is used to produce negatives for plate or block making. The main parts of the camera are the copyholder or copyboard, lens and a film carrier. There are both vertical and horizontal versions, the horizontal can accommodate larger original and film sizes. Many also have transparency holders so that they can take both transmission and reflection originals. Those called darkroom cameras are partly in the darkroom and partly in the camera area, with the camera back or image plane being built into the darkroom wall. Originals can either be scanned directly by the lens or through a prism or mirror. The type and quality of light for such work is very important. The camera may have tungsten halogen, pulsed xenon, metal halide or fluorescent lights. The control panel adjusts the exposure, filters, and lights. The lens is coated and of a symmetrical design so as to eliminate distortion in the image. All lenses for process cameras are apochromatic — this means they are fully corrected for the visible spectrum. In colour separation work stable base films are best, continuous tone film is used for colour separations and masks. For line and halftone work a high contrast emulsion of silver halide in gelatin is recommended.

absorb so much ink as to make the process uneconomical. Nor is the process readily adaptable to the production of process work or screen tints. The liquid ink has a tendency to overflow the dots, making it difficult to get a clean cut half-tone.

Process camera

The process camera is a specialized type of camera which is used to produce negatives for plate or block-making. The main features of the camera are a copy holder, a lens, and a film carrier. They can be housed in either a vertical or horizontal camera.

The vertical camera has a vacuum or pressure type of copyholder. The copyholder of the larger format camera is approximately 600 mm × 900 mm; these proportions naturally govern the size of originals to be reproduced. The associated light sources, attached to the copyholder, may consist of tungsten halogen, pulsed xenon, metal halide or fluorescent lights. Depending upon the type of camera, originals can be viewed directly by the lens, or through a mirror or prism. The film carrier is a vacuum board which must be set square to the copyboard.

The horizontal camera has all the features of the vertical one. It is able to accommodate larger copy, and larger film sizes.

Ordinary photographic enlargers are sometimes used for colour separation of transparencies, but they can only be expected to give good register when they are strongly built, free from vibration, and equipped with colour-corrected lenses. Special vertical enlargers for this purpose came onto the market in about 1954; even more specialized forms of apparatus (sometimes called vertical projection cameras) have been developed since that date. The transparency holder is designed to take a colour transparency (or

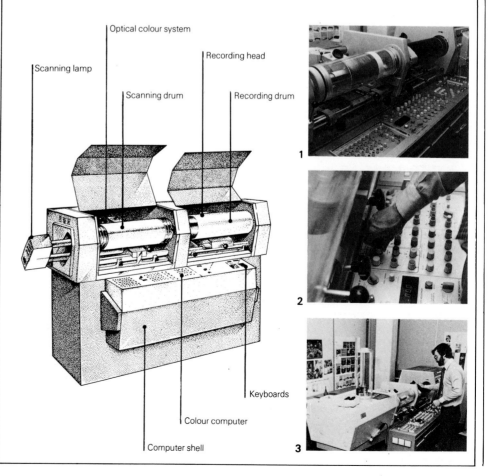

Electronic scanner This is a relatively recent development and technological advance. One machine can now carry out all the processes hitherto carried out by the process camera and screening processes. Most scanners will work with both colour reflection and colour transparency originals have a steplessly variable enlargement ratio and can also change contrast detail. The additional advantages of the scanner — apart from speed — are that four-colour separations are of a higher quality and that the reproduction remains much closer to the original. The scanner consists basically of two inter-connected rotating drums (1) and a colour control panel (2). This highly compact computer and laser operated machine needs only one operator (3).

Optical colour system

Scanning lamp

Recording head

Scanning drum

Recording drum

Keyboards

Colour computer

Computer shell

1

2

3

negative) from 35 mm size up to a maximum size of about 300 mm × 400 mm. Cameras and enlargers are provided with equipment to hold or support either a glass cross-line screen or vignetted contact screen.

Half-tone image formation It is impossible to print intermediate tones between black and white by lithography or letterpress because the ink film used is of uniform density. As a result, any originals having gradations of tone, such as a photograph, must be broken down into a series of dots which are so small that they cannot be resolved by the human eye at normal viewing distance. Instead, they are merged to create an optical illusion of continuous tone. The breakdown into dots is done at the camera stage by placing a screen in front of the film – either a conventional glass cross-line screen, or, more frequently, a vignetted contact screen.

In essence, a conventional halftone screen consists of two sheets of plate glass on which parallel lines are etched and filled in with black pigment. After this, the sheets are sealed together so that the rulings intersect at right angles to form an overall lattice pattern of opaque lines enclosing square-shaped windows.

Normally the opaque lines and the transparent apertures on a halftone screen are of approximately the same width, and for monochrome work the rulings usually run at an angle of 45°. This gives a dot formation which is less obvious to the eye.

Nearly all process cameras incorporate equipment for gauging the screen distance from the film – usually a matter of a few millimetres. During photography, the image projected by the lens passes through the tiny windows of the screen to produce the series of dots required on the film. These vary in size according to the degree of light reflected from the original. Since highlights in an original reflect plenty of light, the resulting negative will be predominately opaque in these parts, with the eventual printing surface peeping through as small transparent dots. On the other hand, the reflections coming from deep shadows will be very weak, showing up on the photographic negative as fairly large transparent areas relieved by small, opaque, non-printing areas. On photographic positives, the black and white will be reversed.

This simple principle applies proportionately to all the intermediate tones. Thus, an illusion of grey in a finished print is the result of the arrangement of jet black dots of different sizes at exactly the same distance from each other, reckoning from their centres.

Under magnification, a halftone print will show the shadows as large black dots, crowding out sparse amounts of white paper. The highlight dots, on the other hand, are smaller, and leave plenty of white paper uncovered. In effect, the massing of colour is diluted by the paper visible to the eye; in this way it creates differing tone values.

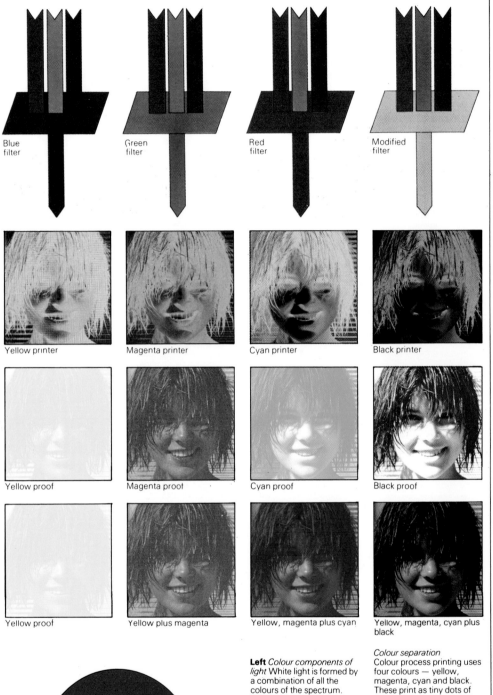

Blue filter   Green filter   Red filter   Modified filter

Yellow printer   Magenta printer   Cyan printer   Black printer

Yellow proof   Magenta proof   Cyan proof   Black proof

Yellow proof   Yellow plus magenta   Yellow, magenta plus cyan   Yellow, magenta, cyan plus black

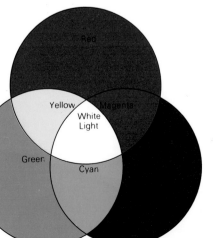

Left *Colour components of light* White light is formed by a combination of all the colours of the spectrum. These can be broken down into three main colour sectors — red, green and blue. Since these colours are added together or overlapped to create white light, they are known as 'additive' primaries. If one of the primary colours is taken away, a different colour is produced. Hence the combination of red and green, without blue, makes yellow, red and blue with green removed produce magenta, and green and blue minus red give cyan. The three colours made in this way — magenta, yellow and cyan — are known as 'subtractive' primaries.

Colour separation Colour process printing uses four colours — yellow, magenta, cyan and black. These print as tiny dots of solid colour, which combine to give the full colour range of the original. The copy is broken down into the process colours by photographic or electronic colour separation. In separation **(above)** the original copy is photographed four times using coloured filters, to produce a different separation negative for each colour. For example, a blue filter creates a separation negative which prints in yellow, and a green filter produces a magenta proof. The separation negatives are photographed again through a special screen.

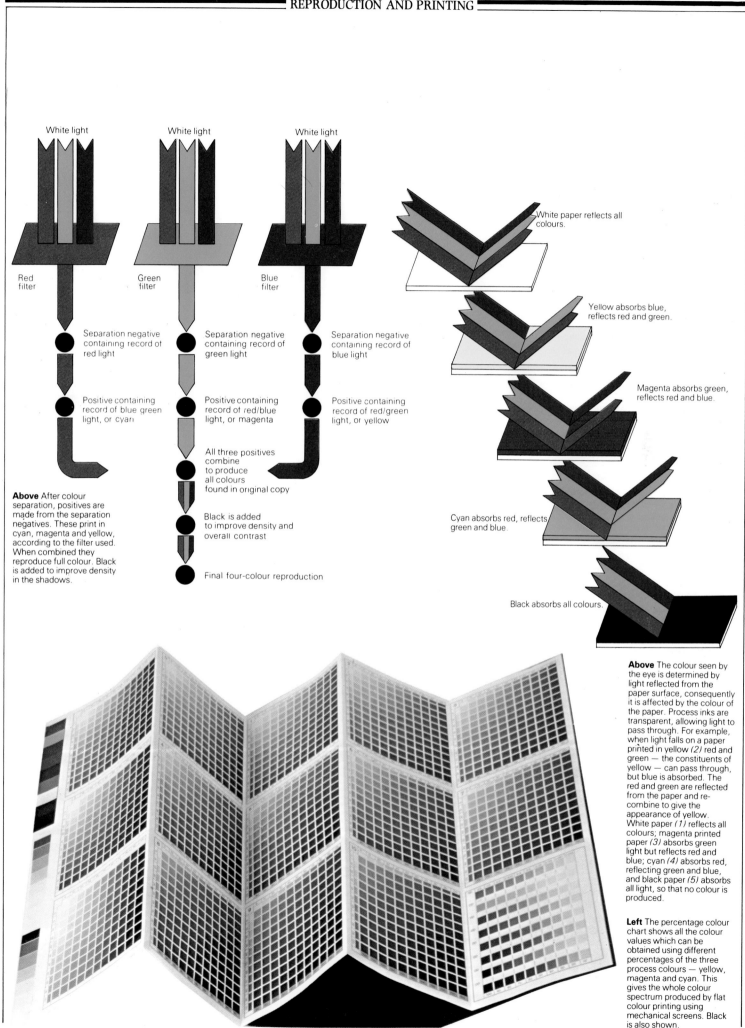

White light

White light

White light

Red filter

Green filter

Blue filter

Separation negative containing record of red light

Separation negative containing record of green light

Separation negative containing record of blue light

Positive containing record of blue green light, or cyan

Positive containing record of red/blue light, or magenta

Positive containing record of red/green light, or yellow

All three positives combine to produce all colours found in original copy

Black is added to improve density and overall contrast

Final four-colour reproduction

Above After colour separation, positives are made from the separation negatives. These print in cyan, magenta and yellow, according to the filter used. When combined they reproduce full colour. Black is added to improve density in the shadows.

White paper reflects all colours.

Yellow absorbs blue, reflects red and green.

Magenta absorbs green, reflects red and blue.

Cyan absorbs red, reflects green and blue.

Black absorbs all colours.

Above The colour seen by the eye is determined by light reflected from the paper surface, consequently it is affected by the colour of the paper. Process inks are transparent, allowing light to pass through. For example, when light falls on a paper printed in yellow (2) red and green — the constituents of yellow — can pass through, but blue is absorbed. The red and green are reflected from the paper and re-combine to give the appearance of yellow. White paper (1) reflects all colours; magenta printed paper (3) absorbs green light but reflects red and blue; cyan (4) absorbs red, reflecting green and blue, and black paper (5) absorbs all light, so that no colour is produced.

Left The percentage colour chart shows all the colour values which can be obtained using different percentages of the three process colours — yellow, magenta and cyan. This gives the whole colour spectrum produced by flat colour printing using mechanical screens. Black is also shown.

Screen rulings vary between 22 and 70 lines to the centimetre, and are used according to production requirements. The screen ruling for letterpress is directly affected by the surface and quality of paper to be printed upon. For example, newsprint is only suitable for half-tone reproduction when a coarse screen – say 22 to 29 lines to the centimetre – is used. Fine art paper will produce a good reproduction using a screen as fine as 70 lines to the centimetre.

In offset lithography, on the other hand, the print is taken from a rubber blanket, so the paper surface influences the choice of screen ruling less than in the letterpress process. The most common screen rulings for photolithography are 48 and 53 lines to the centimetre, irrespective of whether a conventional or vignetted screen, is used. Occasionally, for fine quality reproduction, a 60 line screen will be used. Web offset newspapers usually use 40 lines to the centimetre.

In essence, a vignetted contact screen consists of a sheet of film carrying a formation of vignetted dots. In the case of a magenta contact screen, the dots are formed with optically clear magenta dye with a solid core that fades away towards the circumference. Magenta dye has two advantages. Firstly, it prevents light scatter, therefore producing a cleaner dot; secondly, the colour dye allows filters to be used for contrast control.

Grey contact screens are marketed for both monochrome and colour reproduction. Various rulings are available – extending from 20 to 100 lines to the centimetre. For effective use, a vacuum-backed camera is essential. This ensures that the film lies absolutely flat and in perfect contact with the superimposed screen, through which the image passes during exposure. As in the conventional process, the stronger reflections are given off by the highlight areas. These penetrate to a greater or lesser degree the vignetted fringe of the dots on the contact screen; whereas the weaker reflections from the shadows penetrate only the outer fringes of the vignette. Thus, dots of various sizes are obtained.

Photomechanical reproduction of colour
Originals for colour reproduction can be grouped into two main types. The first of these is line originals; such originals consist of solid areas of colour without intermediate tones. The second group comprises originals in which the subject is rendered in full continuous tone colour. These can consist of any form of hand-created art, such as water colour, oil or tempera paintings, full colour photoprints and colour transparencies.

Such full colour originals – as drawings, paintings and photographic prints have a backing, such as canvas or paper. These originals are referred to as flat-copy, and are reproduced by the light reflecting from the original, whereas colour transparencies are reproduced by the

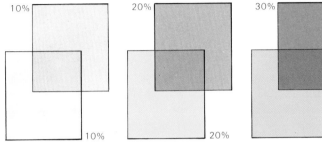

10% 20% 30% 40%

10% 20% 30% 40%

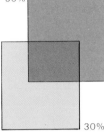
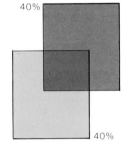

Above A range of tint blocks used for flat colour printing in black and white **(top)** and one colour **(bottom)**. Flat colour is used for the colour reproduction of black and white, line or continuous tone copy. A wide variety of effects is possible. Tints range **(left to right)** from 10%, which is very pale, to 100%, the darkest. They can also be superimposed. The colour of type must be chosen carefully. Positive type is clearest on a pale tint, where reverse type would be illegible. Reverse type is best for dark tints.

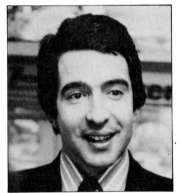
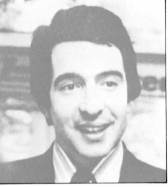

1 Black and white halftone

2 Second colour halftone

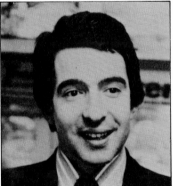

3 20% tint of second colour

4 Second colour tint over black and white halftone

Left Various effects can be produced by combining black and white and colour tints. In a normal black and white halftone (1) the subject appears in shades of black and white. In a colour tone (2) black is replaced by a second colour and the image appears in shades of colour and white. The colour tint (3) is chosen from a range of percentage blocks. Finally the black and white halftone is combined with the second colour to create a flat tint halftone, (4), where the subject appears in shades of black, white and colour.

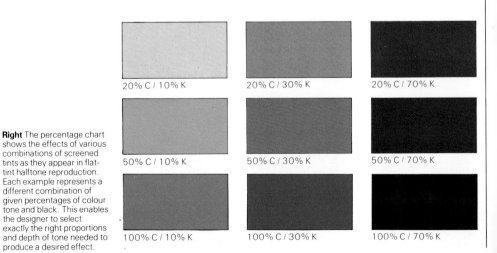

20% C / 10% K   20% C / 30% K   20% C / 70% K

50% C / 10% K   50% C / 30% K   50% C / 70% K

100% C / 10% K   100% C / 30% K   100% C / 70% K

Right The percentage chart shows the effects of various combinations of screened tints as they appear in flat-tint halftone reproduction. Each example represents a different combination of given percentages of colour tone and black. This enables the designer to select exactly the right proportions and depth of tone needed to produce a desired effect.

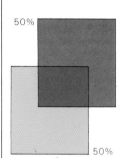
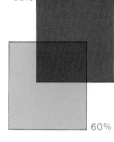

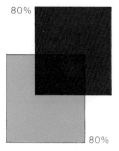
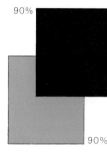
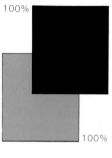

50% / 50% 60% / 60% 70% / 70% 80% / 80% 90% / 90% 100% / 100%

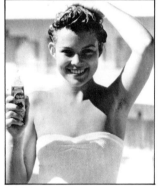

1 Black halftone

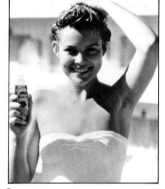

2 20% colour halftone over black

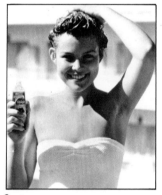

3 40% colour halftone over black

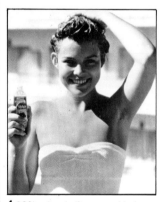

4 60% colour halftone over black

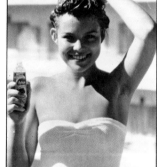

5 80% colour halftone over black

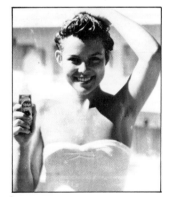

6 Full value colour halftone over black

The duotone **(above)** is a two-colour halftone, created from a normal black and white photograph. The photograph is taken twice; the first shot provides a black plate *(1)* which gives contrasts and darker tones. The second shot is for the colour plate and gives the middle tones of second colour. Then the plates are combined to create an image in a full range of tones. The best second colour for duotone is normally a pastel shade, which will not dominate the contrast. Various percentages of second colour tint can be used: 20% *(2)*, 40% *(3)*, 60% *(4)* and 80% *(5)* up to a full value colour halftone over black *(6)*.

Right *Pantone Colour and Black Selector* The Pantone colour matching system is based on eight basic colours, plus black and white. The selector is a colour swatchbook illustrating ninety different shades of these colours. It enables the designer to choose the colour wanted and indicate it to the printer by a reference number.

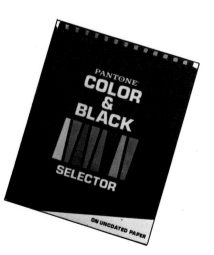

light being transmitted through the transparency.

A colour original can be reproduced with three printing inks – yellow, magenta and cyan – though black ink is usually added. This gives superior detail and shadow rendering. By mixing the yellow, magenta, and cyan pigments in the correct proportions, nearly all desired colours can be obtained. There is one major drawback, however. Unfortunately, the pigmented inks are by no means pure, that is they do not reflect or absorb all incidental light truly. This deficiency necessitates the use of various methods of colour correction.

Colour line illustrations As line originals appear as solid colours, there need be no restriction on the number of colours used. Each can be printed as a 'self-colour'. Depending on the way that the original is prepared, the separations of each colour may be very simple, or very complicated and costly.

If the original is prepared using the actual colours intended for the final printed version, difficulties may arise in reproduction. For example, some of the colours used may not be suitable for the photographic process used in colour separation. In addition, each colour will require an individual printing surface, so that when each colour is superimposed on the press, the illustration matches the original.

A more economic way of producing colour line is to use standard tri-chromatic colours to match the inks. This is particularly important if the line illustration is to be printed in a standard publication, where special inks cannot be used economically. This method does not restrict the designs to yellow, magenta, cyan and black, as might be supposed, because other colours can be created by overlapping solid colours; yellow and cyan, for instance, can be used to produce green. Even the shades of this can be varied by using different tints of the yellow and cyan.

The best and most economical way of presenting a colour line original for reproduction is to produce a representation of each respective colour on a transparent overlay with the black as a base. If the original is presented in colour, separation methods must be used.

Colour separation (line) Negatives from originals having coloured areas or lines can generally be made with a suitable panchromatic photographic emulsion and a range of colour filters. Areas which are to photograph black – that is, clear on the negative – require an emulsion that is insensitive to that colour, or a filter to absorb it. Coloured areas which are to photograph white – that is, dense on the negative – require an emulsion that is sensitive to the colour, with or without a filter transmitting it. Using these principles, it is possible to produce an emulsion-filter combination which will make a negative in which one colour is 'lost' and another 'retained'. Black, can never be 'lost'.

Generally, tri-chromatic colour filters are used, with the addition of one or two yellow filters. By viewing the artwork through each filter respectively, it soon becomes apparent which colours can be 'lost' and which can be retained. Areas which appear light tend to record with high density, while those that appear dark tend not to record.

The principle is best understood through an example – a cartoon strip, say, which has a base of black, the sky in blue, coats in red, ground in yellow. Here the best choice of filter and emulsion would probably be: **Red printer negative** – panchromatic emulsion, double filtered by successive exposures through blue and green filters. **Blue printer negative** – panchromatic emulsion and red filter. **Yellow printer negative** – panchromatic emulsion and blue filter. **Black printer negative** – panchromatic emulsion and no filter.

In this case, a great deal would depend upon the strength and purity of the colours in the original. Black cannot be eliminated from the colour negatives, but it is possible to mask the black out by superimposing a positive made from the black printer negative, or painting it out by hand.

If, however, the same original were prepared by overlaying the black drawing with transparent overlays – one for each colour area – but presented in black – there would be no need for colour separation at all, as each overlay could be photographed as it stood.

Colour separation (continuous tone originals). In the production of colour separations of continuous tone originals for letterpress, lithography, and gravure, it is normal for standard trichromatic inks to be used for printing. There may be the occasional deviation from this, but only in very exceptional circumstances.

In photographing a colour original for separating into its separate records of yellow, magenta and cyan components, it is necessary to photograph each respective negative through a colour filter which has been matched to the standard inks and also to the respective parts of the colour spectrum. The representation of the yellow component of the original requires a blue/violet filter for making the negative. The

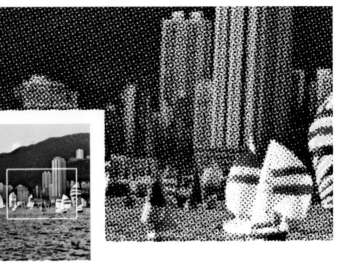

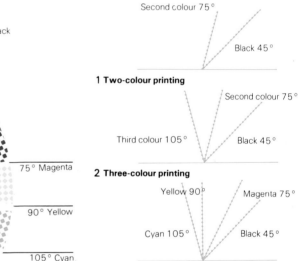

Left The section outlined in the colour print **(far left)** has been magnified to show the pattern of dots which creates the appearance of full colour in four-colour process printing.
Below For printing in two colours (1) the black screen is positioned at 45° — the least visible angle — the second colour at 75°. For three colours (2) a third screen is added at 105°. In four-colour printing (3) the black screen is angled at 45°, magenta at 75°, cyan at 105° and yellow, the lightest colour, at the most visible angle of 90°.
Below left The arrangement of colour screens in four-colour process printing, giving full colour reproduction.

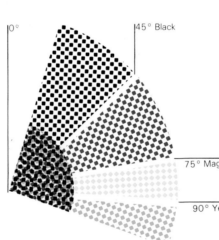

0°   45° Black

75° Magenta

90° Yellow

105° Cyan

Second colour 75°

Black 45°

1 Two-colour printing

Second colour 75°

Third colour 105°   Black 45°

2 Three-colour printing

Yellow 90°   Magenta 75°

Cyan 105°   Black 45°

3 Four-colour printing

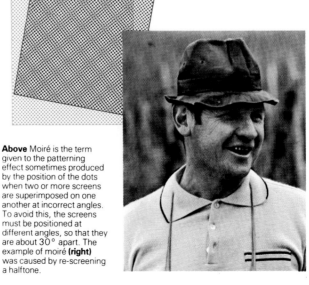

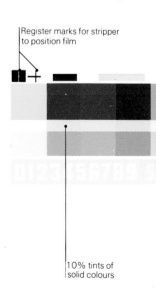

Above Moiré is the term given to the patterning effect sometimes produced by the position of the dots when two or more screens are superimposed on one another at incorrect angles. To avoid this, the screens must be positioned at different angles, so that they are about 30° apart. The example of moiré **(right)** was caused by re-screening a halftone.

Register marks for stripper to position film

10% tints of solid colours

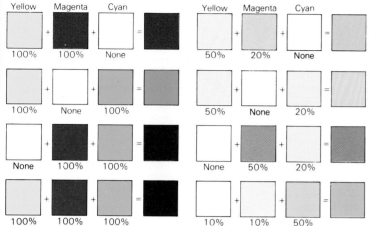

Yellow	Magenta	Cyan	
100%	100%	None	=
100%	None	100%	=
None	100%	100%	=
100%	100%	100%	=

Yellow	Magenta	Cyan	
50%	20%	None	=
50%	None	20%	=
None	50%	20%	=
10%	10%	50%	=

Left This chart shows the way in which the four process colours can be combined to give the appearance of flat colours in printing. The first four columns show various combinations of solid process colours. The columns on the right of the chart show percentage tints and combinations. The main use of process colours is in reproducing full colour continuous tone originals, but this technique enables the printer to reproduce black and white line copy in colour. It is used particularly for advertising, posters, magazine work and book jackets.

effect of this filter will be to absorb all wavelengths of light reflected from the yellow components. In visual appearance the yellow will appear dark, and thus will not record on the photographic emulsion, whereas the areas of blue will appear light and will record on the emulsion. Similarly a green filter is used for the magenta negative record, and for the cyan negative record, a red filter. To produce the black negative record, either no filter is used, or a combination of the blue/violet, green and red are used, according to the colour bias of the original.

Separation negatives There are various methods of producing the separation negatives for each of the main printing processes of lithography, letterpress and photogravure. The methods are referred to as indirect and direct.

Below A colour bar is included on most colour proofs. It is independent of the image being produced and functions as a standard or 'control' against which the printed colours can be measured. It is a simple, quick reference enabling the printer to estimate the accuracy of the colours, and regulate them. The bar shows the four process colours in various forms. The solid colours indicate the amount of ink the printer should lay down. Various percentage tints, overprints and slur guides are included, plus star targets. The bar provides a quick method of checking colour strength, but further measurements can be made with a densitometer. It normally includes such printing faults as poor trapping and dot gain. If there is not enough space for a full bar, a quality control (QC) strip can be used.
The example shown is that supplied by the Graphic Arts Technical Foundation.

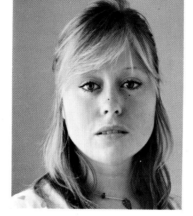

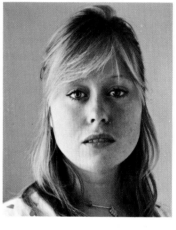

Far left This picture shows the effect of incorrectly printing a four-colour transparency. Cyan is printing as magenta and vice versa; black reproduces normally. The effect is the result of wrongly 'patching up' — the term given to the arrangement of coloured films in printing. **Left** A proof of the same transparency, this time printed so that the colours are arranged correctly.

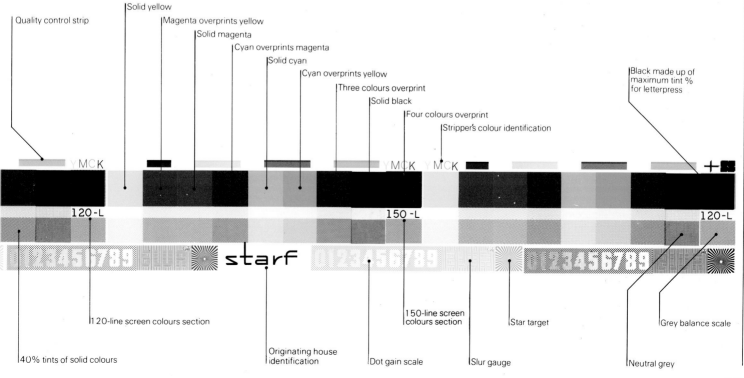

Quality control strip

Solid yellow

Magenta overprints yellow

Solid magenta

Cyan overprints magenta

Solid cyan

Cyan overprints yellow

Three colours overprint

Solid black

Four colours overprint

Stripper's colour identification

Black made up of maximum tint % for letterpress

120-line screen colours section

150-line screen colours section

Star target

Grey balance scale

40% tints of solid colours

Originating house identification

Dot gain scale

Slur gauge

Neutral grey

199

In the indirect method, the resulting negatives are in continuous tone (no half-tone screen) and are called continuous tone separation negatives. They are an accurate record of each of the primary colours. These separation negatives can then be transposed to produce positives. If they are to be used for lithography, it is at this stage that the screen can be introduced, and also colour correction. If the separations are to be used for photogravure, then continuous tone positives are produced and colour correction introduced. For letterpress, the continuous tone positives can be colour corrected and re-screened to negative.

In the direct method, the primary colours are separated and half-tone negatives produced in one photographic operation. This is done by placing the half-tone screen in the camera at the time of colour separation.

Colour correction Theoretically, each of the three inks – cyan, magenta and yellow – should satisfy the following requirements. Firstly, they should absorb completely one of the three spectrum colours which go to make up white light; secondly, they should transmit completely each of the other two spectrum primary colours. However, it is impossible in practice to produce perfect colour reproductions using the imperfect inks available, without resorting to a special method of correcting these imperfections in colour rendering.

Colour correction is the process of adjusting the separation negatives or positives to counteract these fundamental deficiencies. This can be done by skilled hand re-touching or by a process known as photographic masking. If the colour separation negatives or positives have been produced by the use of a colour scanner, then the necessary corrections are programmed into the scanner.

There are very many different approaches to methods of achieving colour correction, but the principal aim is either to increase density in certain areas of the negative/positive, or to reduce it. Taking the hand method first, organic dyes of differing strengths are used if the colour density needs increasing. If density is to be reduced, then reducers are employed. Similar results can also be achieved by photographic masking methods.

Another masking technique in use in colour reproduction is referred to as undercolour removal (UCR). The principal purpose of UCR is to remove unwanted colour from beneath the black printing areas. This is necessary because black does not filter away, and therefore is recorded on every colour. This means that every colour will be retained beneath the black unless removed.

If the speed of printing is such that each colour can be allowed to dry before the application of the next, then there is no particular need for UCR, although it helps achieve the economic use of inks. However, with the advent of fast printing

methods, each successive colour is very often overprinted upon the other before the previous one has dried. This means that excessive layers of unwanted wet ink are present in the black areas. This is when the use of UCR is of advantage.

To produce UCR negatives/positives, photographic masking is usually employed to remove the undercolour. The photographic mask is produced from the black separation negative/positive and superimposed upon the respective colour separation negative/positive.

Screened half-tone colour In making half-tone colour separation negatives/positives, each colour is photographed through the same screen, but there is normally a 30° difference in the angle of the screen for each individual colour. This angle, however, may be varied to suit the subject to be reproduced.

The changing of the angle is necessary to avoid each set of half-tone images clashing and so producing an objectionable colour effect, a periodic pattern known as a moiré. The result of altering the angle is that the small dots produced do not overlap; instead, they form a small rosette pattern, which can be clearly seen with a magnifying glass.

Suitability of colour originals Most types of original are suitable for half-tone reproduction if they are to be reproduced facsimile. If, however, an original is presented which has, say, an unwanted colour bias, it is not always possible to correct this. If the original is very flat (lacking contrast) it is possible to increase this slightly, but the quality of the reproduction will always be inferior to that of a perfect original. When using coloured photographs, always avoid those with a textured surface because the results will be similarly sub-standard.

It is always best to use colour transparencies whenever possible, but not all of these are suited for photomechanical reproduction. Many old transparencies lack sharpness and therefore will not reproduce to the high standards normally required. Reproduction houses usually lay down set standards and all designers and photographers should be aware of these.

For satisfactory reproduction a colour transparency should, within reasonable limits, satisfy the following conditions. Firstly, the density range should not be too great; secondly, the details should be clearly rendered both in the shadows and the highlights; thirdly, the definition of the image must be good enough to stand up successfully to the final enlargement; and finally the overall colour balance should be neutral, that is, there should be no general colour cast. Before any colour work is sent for reproduction it is vital that the originals are checked thoroughly. For all such checking a suitable type of light must be used. Nevertheless, no colour reproduction will be good quality unless the original is also high quality.

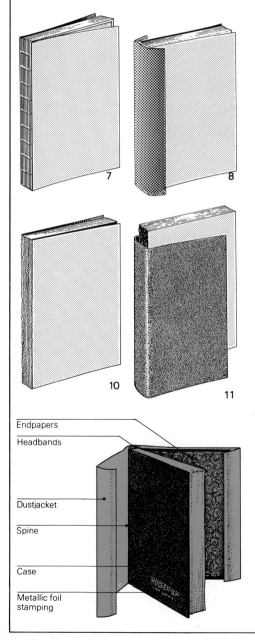

Bookbinding methods
There are four main methods of book binding. These vary according to the nature of the book being produced, and to the materials being used. Edition or case binding is used for hardcover books. Perfect binding is used for less expensive paperback or uncased books. Mechanical bindings are used on manuals and notebooks. Wire stitching is used for magazines and pamphlets.

Mechanical binding
A plastic gripper (1) slides tightly over the spine and holds the covers and pages together. In open-flat mechanical binding (2, 3, 4) holes are drilled through the covers and pages. They are then bound together with a wire or plastic coil, such as the wire-O (2), spiral (3), or plastic comb (4). This method allows the book to lie absolutely flat when opened, so it is idea for reference manuals.

Endpapers
Headbands
Dustjacket
Spine
Case
Metallic foil stamping

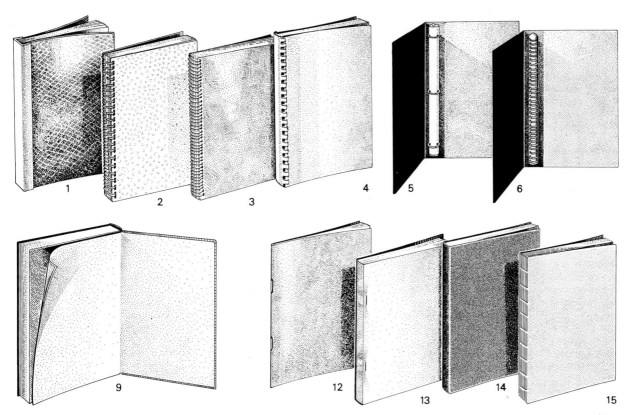

Ring binding This is another open-flat method. The loose-leaf post or ring binder (5) has two or four rings riveted to a stiff binder. These spring open to insert ready-drilled paper. The multiple ring binder (6) uses the same principle but has many rings.

Stitching This is a permanent form of binding. There are four main methods. Saddle-stitch binding (12), is the most common. The book is opened over a 'saddle' and it is stapled along the back fold. Side-wire stitching (13) is used for thicker magazines and pamphlets. Wire staples are inserted form the front, about ¼ in from the back edge, then clinched at the back. In thermoplastic binding (14) the pages are gathered in sections, trimmed on the back edge and bound with a hot plastic glue. In sewn thread binding (15) the pages are gathered in sections and sewn, then assembled in order and sewn again. This is the strongest stitched method.

Edition binding
This is the conventional method of hardcover book binding. It is the strongest form, but also the most expensive. The printed sheets are folded into sections of 16 or 32 pages, then collated and sewn by machine. The edges are trimmed and the sewn back edge coated with glue (7). This is then rounded on a special machine to give the characteristic rounded back, which allows the book to open easily. A strip of gauze is glued to the backbone so that it overlaps on each side (8). At the same time a cloth cover is prepared. Finally (9) the book and cover are placed on a casing-in machine which pastes the end-leaves and fits the cover.

Perfect binding The pages are folded and collated, then the spine edge is ground or roughened so that the binding glue will adhere strongly. A lining is placed over the backbone and the cover glued firmly in place (10). This form of binding is less expensive than edition binding, but also less durable. It is used particularly for paperback books (11).

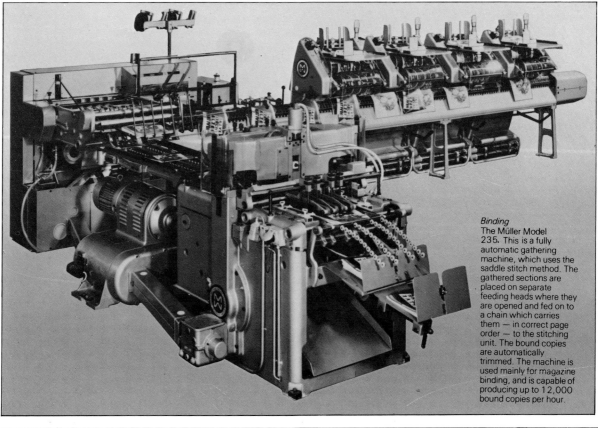

Binding
The Müller Model 235. This is a fully automatic gathering machine, which uses the saddle stitch method. The gathered sections are placed on separate feeding heads where they are opened and fed on to a chain which carries them — in correct page order — to the stitching unit. The bound copies are automatically trimmed. The machine is used mainly for magazine binding, and is capable of producing up to 12,000 bound copies per hour.

Imposition

It is probable that the term imposition derived from the continual use of the words 'in position'. In printing the term refers to the position of the printed sheet on a page.

Knowledge of how the printed sheets are to be folded is essential to ensure that the pages appear in the right order. It is also especially important in the positioning of illustrations and holds good whether the sheet is folded by hand or machine. In planning imposition, a sheet of paper is placed 'landscape' (the long edge towards the body) upon a table. It is then folded across the short side to bring the right edge to the left edge and then folded again to bring the top edge to the bottom. A folder of four leaves is thus obtained, with eight printing pages.

The folded section is then placed 'portrait' – the spine or the back to the left – with the pages

number 1 to 8 in correct order, and the whole sheet is then unfolded. The complete scheme of printed page layout can be seen on both sides of the sheet. Pages 1, 8, 4 and 5 are one side, with 4 and 5 upside down in relation to 1 and 8; pages 2, 7, 6 and 3 are on the other side, with 6 and 3 upside down in relation to 7 and 2. This is sheet work – so called because one sheet of paper is printed to produce a complete section. The forme containing the first and last pages is the 'outer', and the one with the second page the 'inner'.

In half-sheet work, where all the pages are imposed in one forme, a sheet twice the size of the finished copy is needed; however, only half of it is required to produce one complete section. In other words, sheet work gives one copy of the section, but needs two formes; half-sheet work produces two copies for each printed sheet, having one forme printed on both sides.

From this, it is easy to grasp the principles involved in the most frequently used imposition schemes for four, eight, sixteen and thirty-two pages respectively. Impositions of four, sixteen and sixty-four pages have the same layout as for the first four pages; eight page and thirty-two pages sections are similarly parallel.

One important factor which affects all such schemes is the difference between imposition for 'right' reading copy and that of the imposition layouts illustrated for compositors, who are dealing with 'wrong' reading materials. Mistakes can happen if the two contexts are confused, and, for all practical purposes, it is best to consider only the actual folding methods involved in the folding of the sheet. For this reason it is always preferable to obtain a 'dummy' of a section – before it is cut or trimmed – to ascertain the correct sequence for the page imposition.

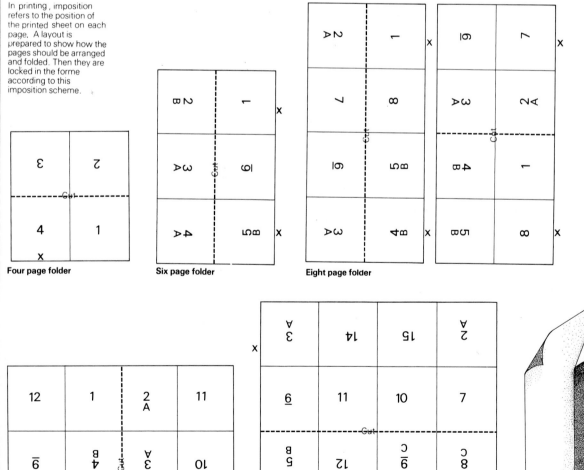

In printing, imposition refers to the position of the printed sheet on each page. A layout is prepared to show how the pages should be arranged and folded. Then they are locked in the forme according to this imposition scheme.

Four page folder

Six page folder

Eight page folder

Twelve page forme

Sixteen page forme

Left to right The most common impositions: four page folder (1); six pages (2); eight pages – work and turn (3); eight pages – work and tumble (4); twelve pages (5); sixteen pages (6).The numbers on the diagrams indicate the order of the pages when folded; the letters (A, B, C) show the folding sequence and the letter X indicates where the grippers are placed. The dotted lines show where the paper is cut. 'Work and turn' means that the sheets are turned over left to right after the first side is printed so that the same gripper edge is used for both sides. In 'work and tumble' the sheets are turned over so that the opposite edge becomes the gripper edge.

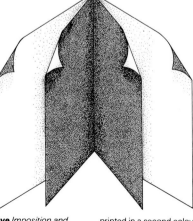

Above *Imposition and colour* In an eight page folder, the pages can be arranged to give the impression of two-colour printing, although in fact only one side of the sheet is printed in a second colour. Here, pages 1, 4, 5, 8 are on one side of the sheet, printed in two colours. Pages 2, 3, 6, 7, on the other side, print the first colour.

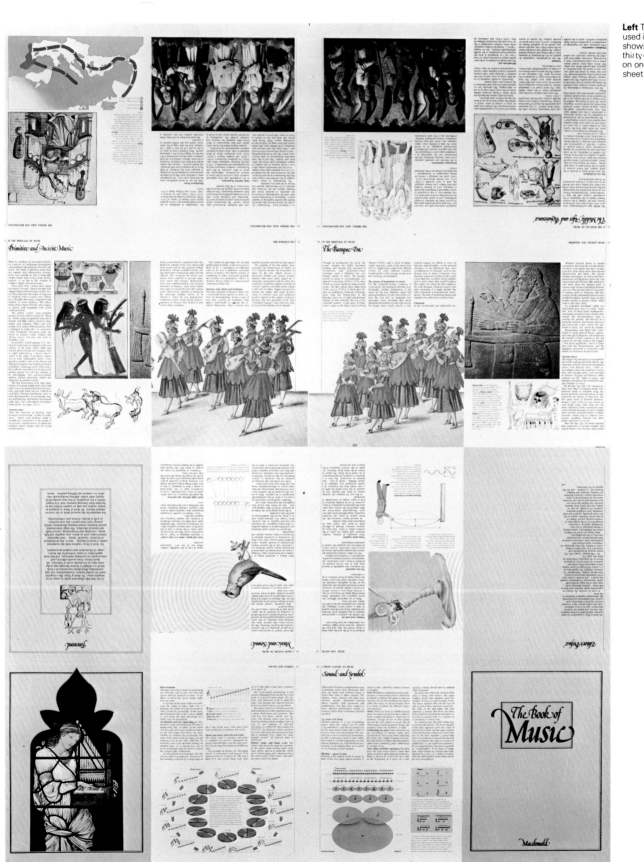

Left This typical imposition used in an actual book shows the page layout for a thirty-two page signature, on one side of the printed sheet.

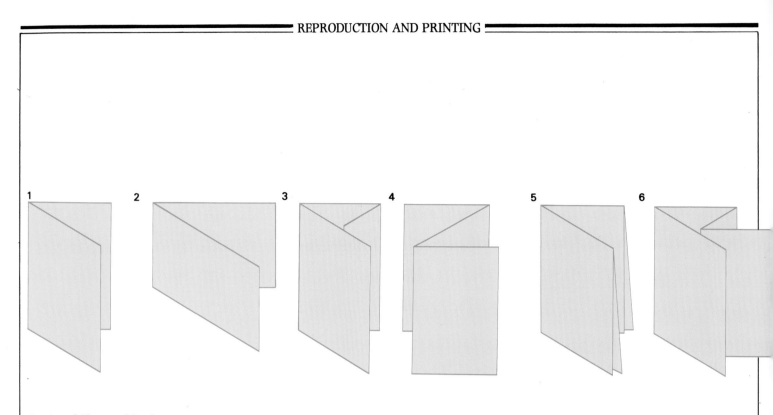

1 2 3 4 5 6

Scoring, folding and binding

The term score is used to define folding without breaking the fold. Scoring against the grain gives maximum folding endurance, although scoring with the grain provides a softer, smoother fold. There are several methods; which one is best will depend on the specific paper used, and the purpose of the fold. The most frequently used method of scoring employs a round face scoring ruler locked in a forme on a printing press. The width of the rule depends upon the thickness of the paper or board to be scored. A thicker paper needs a thicker rule to give a wider crease that will help to make a cleaner fold.

Folding is almost always done by machine; hand folding is prohibitively expensive on all but the shortest print runs. Two points worth noting are that thick papers – particularly cover papers – should not be used for folders of more than eight pages and that the actual folders must be planned with great care. When map folds and double folds are included, for instance, an allowance must be made for the fold-in and the inside page must be slightly smaller than the outside ones. The minimum margin should be at least 0.25mm; if smaller than this, any folding faults will be immediately obvious. This is particularly the case in complex jobs, where the paper may not always fold squarely.

Stitching and binding There are two methods of stitching – saddle stitch and side stitch, or stab stitch as it is often known. Saddle stitching is used for magazines and material less than 0.25mm in bulk. The folded sections are inserted (one placed inside the other), positioned on a 'saddle' beneath a mechanical head, and the staple is forced through the spine of the book. This method is the simplest and least expensive type of binding; when saddle stitched, the booklets will lie flat and stay open for ease of reading.

If the books are of greater bulk, side-stitching is used. The folded sections are gathered (placed one on top of the other) and the stitches forced through from first page to last, where they are clinched. The stitch is approximately 3mm from the spine so it is important to allow for a wide inside margin. The chief disadvantage of the

Above left to right *Folding methods* In single fold the paper is folded once, either lengthwise *(1)* or widthways *(2)* to give a four page folder. For a double fold two parallel folds are made, either regular (gate) *(3)* or accordion *(4)* to produce six pages. An eight page folder is made by folding the paper three times — either one parallel and one right angle fold *(5)*, two parallel folds *(6)*, or three accordion folds *(7)*. Twelve pages are made with one parallel and two right angle folds — regular *(8)* or accordion *(9)*. A sixteen page folder is made with one parallel and two right angle folds *(10)* or three parallel folds *(11)*.

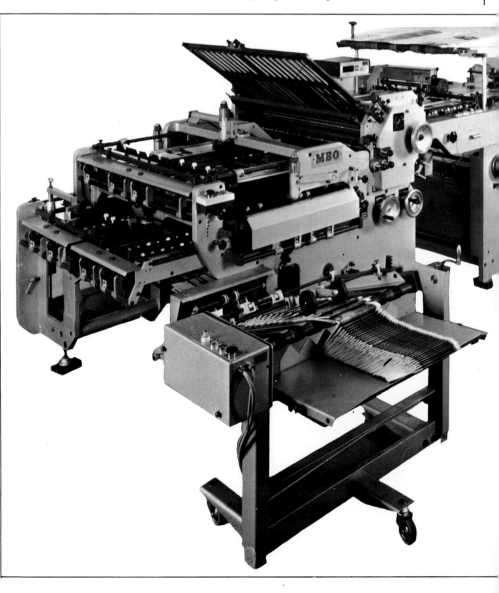

7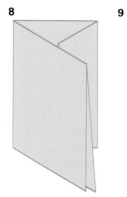

8 **9**

10 **11**

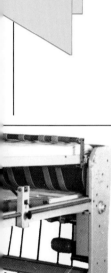

Today, folding is almost always done by machines such as the MBO Combi Folding machine Type K 76/4 **(left).** This machine is equipped with a continuous feeder system. It is used mainly for producing book sections and signatures of up to 32 pages, using a maximum sheet size of 30in x 44in. It also produces brochures, pamphlets and other general folders. The machine can be adapted for double stream work, folding two copies at once, and thus effectively doubling its output.

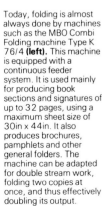

Above *Folding* There are two basic methods of paper folding. In parallel folding **(top)** the folds run parallel, either in concertina form or in a flat roll. Parallel folding is used mainly for leaflets. In right angle folding **(below)** each fold is made at right angles to another; normally pages are folded two, three or four times. This method is normally used for binding books and newspapers. Both methods can be done quickly and relatively cheaply by folding machines.

method is that side-stitched books cannot be opened flat.

There are many different types of binding in use, but probably the most common is perfect or threadless binding. In this, the gathered folded sections have the back fold trimmed off and the pages are glued by their back edges to the cover. Due allowance must be made for the trim at the backs and for the gutter margin.

Embossing To produce embossed images a set of moulds have to be made – one male and one female. These are usually of brass or steel; the choice of material depends very much on the type of paper or board that has to be embossed. The best results are obtained on a fairly soft type of paper or board.

Embossing can be done on a normal flatbed printing press, but, if high quality and fine detail is required, then it should be done on a special four pillar embossing press. This press will also heat the moulds and therefore give sharper detail. When heat is used, foils can be used to produce various colours.

Another method which gives the impression of embossing is achieved by taking the printed material while it is still wet and passing it through a special powder which will adhere to the wet ink. The sheet is then heated, causing the powder to fuse with the ink. When dry, this will give a raised image.

Translations One final problem that frequently faces designers is if foreign languages are involved in any stage of the process. If text is involved, for instance, the problems of translation must always be considered. As far as illustrations are concerned, lettering should not be superimposed upon them unless absolutely necessary, since changes here are very costly – new plates being required in each case. Equally, if the text matter is to be printed in various colours, plate changes will have to be made.

The way to keep cost to a minimum is to confine all text matter to the black printer, with no lettering over the illustrations unless black is used. Printing is then simply a matter of producing the total amount of, say, cyan, magenta and yellow required, and by remaking the black printer to overprint in the language required.

The paper-making process
One of the main constituents of paper is cellulose fibre. Today, this is normally obtained from wood, rag or old paper, which are sometimes combined. In the past, many other sources, such as grasses, bamboo or sugar cane, were used. The type of paper obtained is determined by the nature of the fibre used.

Softwoods *(1)* such as pine, spruce and fir, have a long fibre, which gives strength to the finished paper. Softwood timber is grown extensively in Scandinavia for pulp and paper making. Timber can be reduced to pulp by either chemical or mechanical processing. The latter is the simpler and more economical method, which produces weaker less permanent papers, such as those used for newspaper production.

Chemically produced pulp gives a much stronger, brighter and permanent high quality paper than groundwood pulp, but the yield is smaller, and the method consequently more expensive.

The pulp *(2)* normally arrives at the mill or factory in the form of bales of fibre. Before delivery it is washed, screened for impurities, bleached and finally beaten. This breaks down the fibres and releases a gelatinous substance which helps to bond them together.

At the mill, fillers, sizing and dyes are added. The most common additive is china clay *(3)*. This serves as a filler, to add bulk to the more costly cellulose; it also improves the colour and opacity of the paper and is used as a surface sizing for high gloss papers.

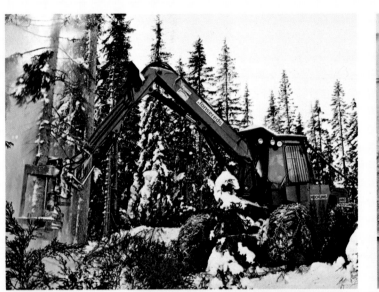

1

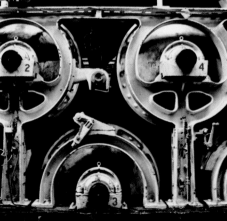

2△

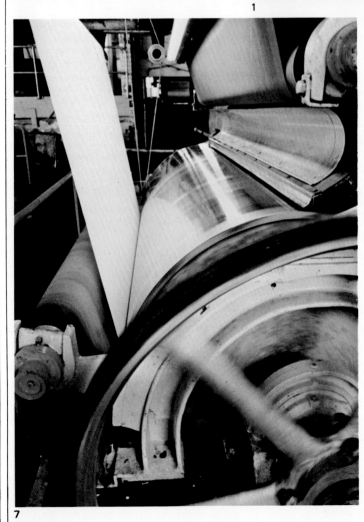

7

6△

8

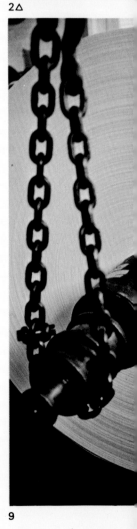

9

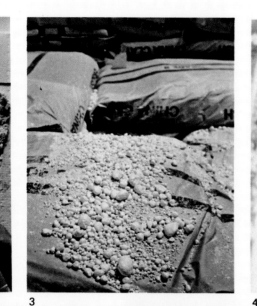

3

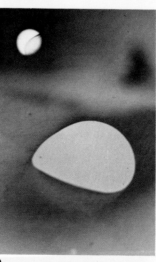

4

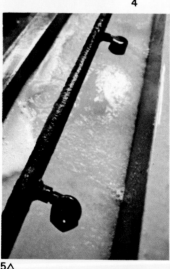

5△

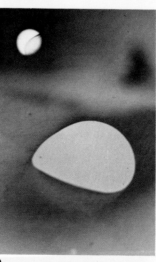

10

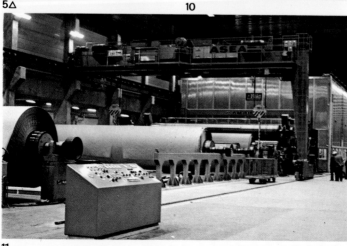

11

The pulp is further broken down in the pulper *(4)* where it is mixed with a given quantity of water to form a slurry called 'furnish'. This has a known consistency or percentage volume of fibre and water. After further mechanical and chemical treatment to break down the chemical structure of the fibres, the furnish is pumped to the 'wet end' of the system *(5)*. Here it is further diluted, then moved to the flow head or head-box, which feeds it on to an endless, moving wire. This conveys it through a series of presses, where most of the water is squeezed out.

It next moves to the drying section of the machine *(6)*. This consists of a series of many heated rollers. They are basically hollow metal cylinders through which steam passes *(7)*. The steam heats the surface of the cylinder so that the paper is dried as it passes over them. The heat cylinders are mounted on a frame *(8)* and surrounded with felts, over which the paper can move smoothly. At the end of the drying section the surface of the paper is further smoothed and finished by passing under heavy chilled iron rollers. These exert a heavy pressure to compress the surface fibres. This process is known as calendering, and the degree of smoothness of the paper is determined by the number of calenders or 'nips' the paper runs through — the more calenders, the higher the final gloss.

The finished paper is reeled up on bobbins *(9)* until the roll reaches the required size. Then it is removed, without interrupting the continuous web production process. Certain types of paper — particularly the more expensive, high quality grades — are treated with fluorescing agents to increase whiteness. At the end of the production line these are exposed to an ultra-violet lamp *(10)* to check the degree of fluorescence present.

The whole paper-making operation, from pulp to the finished paper, can be performed, as a continuous production process, by automatic machines, housed in one factory building or mill. The machine *(11)*, with its various component units, may be several hundred feet long. However, it can take less than two minutes for the pulp to pass from the head box at the 'wet end' until its emergence as a finished sheet of paper. The end product is a continuous sheet of paper, known as a web. This can be used at once, in reel form, for web-fed printing — for newspapers, for example — or transferred to another machine which cuts it into sheets for a sheet-fed press.

GLOSSARY

A

Accent A mark added to a letter in some languages to indicate a change in pronunciation, stress etc, eg acute é, grave è, cedilla ç.
Addendum Matter to be included in a book after the body has been set which is printed separately at the beginning or end of the text.
Airbrush (Aerograph) A small gun used to improve tonal value in retouching.
Albumen plate A lithographic plate with a light-sensitized albumen coating.
Albion press An iron, hand printing press introduced in the early 19th century by R.W. Cope and Company. It replaced the wooden screw press.
Align To arrange letters and words on the same horizontal or vertical line.
Ampersand The sign (&) for the word 'and'.
Aniline ink Cheaply made volatile printing ink which consists of a dye dissolved in methylated spirits, bound with a resin. It dries almost immediately.
Animal sized Describes paper which has been hardened or sized with animal glue or gelatine, by passing the finished sheet through a bath of glue.
Annotation A type label used on an illustration.
Antiqua Early type taken from scripts developed by the Italians Niccoli and Poggio, based on Northern Italian manuscripts of the 11th and 12th centuries. It is also the German name for ROMAN type.
Antiquarian The largest known size of hand-made paper, 53in × 31in.
Antique A rough surfaced finish to paper.
Antique laid A rough-surfaced laid paper. The term originally described paper made on moulds which had the chain wires laced direct to the supports of the mould.
Appendix Matter subordinate to the text of a work and printed immediately after it. It is planned from the beginning as an integral part of the text.
Aquatint An INTAGLIO process for reproducing illustrations which are normally tones, but often a combination of tones and etched lines.
Art paper After the paper has been made it is coated on one or both sides with casein, or glue, mixed with starch and china clay.
Ascender That part of a lower case letter that rises above the X-HEIGHT.
Asterisk The sign (*) usually used to indicate a footnote or give special emphasis.
Authors' proofs Marked proofs with literal typographical errors corrected by the printer's reader. The author reads them and makes any necessary alterations.

B

Back The part of a book nearest to the fold.
Back lining A paper or fabric strip fixed to the back of a book before casing in.
Back up To print the second side of a sheet of paper. Backed refers to the sheet when it has been backed up.
Banner A main headline across the full width of the page.
Baryta paper Paper coated with barium sulphate gelatine which is used for text impressions on photo-composing machines.
Base line The imaginary line on which the bases of capitals rest.
Bastard A letter foreign to the fount in which it is found. It is also an obsolete paper size 33in × 20in. Finally it describes any non-standard size paper.
Bastarda A cursive Gothic letter with pointed descenders and often looped ascenders used in the 15th century and introduced into England by William Caxton.
Batter Type which is damaged or worn and thus gives a defective impression.
Beard In Great Britain beard is the space on a type between the bottom of the X-HEIGHT and the upper edge of the shank or body. It is the area into which the descenders of the lower-case letters extend. In the USA it is the bevel between the face of a type character and the shoulder.
Bed The steel table of a printing press on which the forme is placed for printing.
Belly The front or NICK side of a type.
Benday prints A series of mechanical tints in the form of celluloid sheets which are used in blockmaking and lithography to add texture, shading and detail to line drawings.
Bevel The sloping surface of a type rising from the shoulder to the face.
Bible paper A very thin, tough, opaque paper used mostly for printing bibles and prayer books.
Bite The action of acid in the etching of a metal plate.
Blackletter A script with angular outlines developed in Germany which superseded the lighter ROMAN in the 12th century. The term is also applied to types developed from it. It is also known as Fraktur, Gothic, and Old English.
Blanket The sheet made of rexine or rubber etc used to cover the impression cylinder of a printing machine. It is also the similar sheet used to cover the flong when making a stereo mould from a forme.
Bleach-out The under-developed bromide print used as a basis for a line drawing. The bromide is bleached away after drawing.
Bleed That part of the image which extends beyond the trim-line of the page. Illustrations which spread to the edge of the page and allow no margins are described as bled-off.
Blind An impression made without foil or ink on the case of a book.
Block Firstly, a half-tone or line illustration which is engraved or etched on a zinc or copper plate, used in LETTERPRESS printing. Secondly, a metal stamp, usually of brass, used to impress a complete design on a book cover. Thirdly, to block means to emboss a book cover.
Blurb The description of a book or author printed on the jacket flap.
Board Heavy cardboard used in printing, particularly for covers.
Body Firstly, the shank of a type. Secondly, the main portion of a book, excluding the prelims and appendices.
Bold face Type which has a conspicuous black, heavy appearance, which is based on the same designs as its medium weight in the same fount.
Bolts The folded edges of a sheet or section of a book on three sides which will eventually be trimmed off.
Border A continuous decorative design arranged around matter on a page.
Box An item ruled off on all four sides usually with heavy rule or border.
Box wood Hard wood used as end grain blocks for wood engraving.
Brace A sign used to group lines or phrases, it appears as }.
Brackets see PARENTHESES.
Brass Lettering engraved on brass and used in blocking the case of a book.
Brass rules Strips of brass of type height used to print lines and simple borders.
Break up Means to separate the parts of a forme and distribute the type.
Bristol board Fine cardboard made in various qualities and thicknesses, usually of smooth finish, used for printing and drawing.
Broadside Old term for a sheet of paper printed on one side only.
Brochure A pamphlet or other unbound short work with stitched pages.
Bronzing Means to produce a gold or metallic effect by applying powder to a sheet which is printed with special ink.
Buffing The final polishing of a reproduction plate before etching.
Bulk The thickness of a book excluding its covers. It also refers to the thickness of a sheet of paper related to its weight.
Burin An engraving tool used by wood and metal engravers.
Burnisher A smooth, curved metal tool, used for removing rough spots from plates and half-tones.
Burr A rough edge left on a block by the rotating machine. It is also a characteristic of the surface of a dry-point plate.

C

Calender The calender is a column of usually five iron or steel rolls at the dry end of a paper making machine. When paper is passed under pressure through it the action closes the pores and smooths the surface.
Calligraphy The term comes from the Greek meaning beautiful handwriting. A calligrapher is a person who writes elegantly, especially a skilled transcriber of manuscripts.
Calotype A process made public in 1841 by W.H. Fox Talbot for producing negatives on silver iodide paper by developing with gallic acid. Positive copies were made afterwards by contact printing on silver chloride paper.
Cambridge India paper The trade name of a high quality BIBLE PAPER made at Bury, Lancashire, UK by J. R. Crompton & Bros. In 1945 it was selected for the airmail edition of *The Times*.
Cameo coated paper An American brand of dull-finished coated paper presenting a delicate surface, for printing half-tones etc. It gives a non-lustrous surface which provides a rich and soft background for artistic engravings.
Cancel To cut out and replace a wrongly printed leaf or leaves.
Canvas Heavy cotton binding cloth firmly woven. It is used for binding cheaper grades of books. It is also called DUCK.
Cap Abbreviation for CAPITAL LETTER, also for FOOLSCAP.
Capital letters, capitals. The name of the upper case letters. It derives from the inscriptional letters at the head, or capital, of Roman columns.
Caps and smalls Capital letters and small caps used with caps for initials, the small caps replace lower case.
Caption Strictly speaking, the caption is the descriptive matter printed as a headline above an illustration. It is usual, but incorrect, to refer to descriptive matter printed underneath an illustration as a caption.
Caret The symbol (/) used in proof correcting to indicate an insertion. This symbol was first used by scribes in the early 13th century.
Carolingian script A 9th century script developed for the Emperor Charlemagne's revision of grammars, bibles, church books etc.
Carriage The part of a printing machine on which the forme moves backwards and forwards during printing. It is also the similar part on a typewriter.
Cartouche The space on a map, enclosed by an elaborate drawing of human figures, plant life, animals or heraldic devices, in which the name or title is printed. The cartouche may also be in the form of a scroll with rolled ends and the title in the centre.
Cartridge paper A rough-surface printing paper, often tub-sized, and used for a variety of purposes, such as drawing, envelopes, jackets, offset printing, wrapping etc. Offset-cartridge may include ESPARTO.
Case Firstly, the case is a cover, made by hand or machine, consisting of two boards, a hollow, and binding material. The case is subsequently attached to the book, providing the style in common use by most British and American publishers. Hard-back books are correctly described as cased. Secondly, it is the compositor's case, a shallow box, divided into many compartments, in which individual letters, numerals and spaces are kept. The capitals are usually in a case set at an angle behind and above that for the other letters. Thus capitals are called upper-case letters, and the others lower case.
Cased book A fully bound book with a stiff case.
Casein A substance obtained from curdled milk. It is used as an adhesive in the manufacture of coated paper.
Casing in Means inserting the book into the case and pasting this down.
Cast coated paper An art paper with an exceptionally high finish, developed in America about 1950.
Caster The part of a Monotype composing system which casts the type.
Cast-off Calculation of how much space a given amount of copy will take in a given type size and measure, usually done by the printer.
Cast-up Calculation by the printer of the cost of setting up matter in type.
Centred Type which is placed in the centre of a sheet, or in the centre of a type measure.
Centre spread The centre opening of a section, ie two pages. It is also the centre opening of a folder in which type matter or blocks continue across the sheet.
Chain lines The vertical lines on laid paper, about 1in apart.
Chalking A printing fault caused by using an over-reduced ink or one unsuited to the paper, which causes the ink to soak into the paper leaving the pigment deposited on the surface.
Character A single sign, whether a letter, punctuation mark or space, cast in type.
Character count The number of characters in a piece of copy.
Charcoal paper A soft, rough-finished paper used for making illustrations with a charcoal crayon or pencil.
Chase A metal frame into which type and blocks are fitted to make one page. The type is held in place by FURNITURE and QUOINS.
Chiaroscuro The earliest form of colour printing from wood blocks which became popular in the 16th century in Italy, having been introduced from Germany. A key block in outline was first printed, and then the colours were printed from separate blocks in register. The colours were usually grey, brown and dull yellow.
China paper A thin hand-made paper of silky texture made from bamboo and used for proofing wood engravings. Its modern machine-made substitute is more accurately termed Japanese paper.
Chromo-paper Paper which is more heavily coated than art paper. The surface can be dull or glazed. It is used for colour lithography.
Chromograph An apparatus for reproducing multiple copies of, for example, plans or manuscripts using an aniline dye instead of ink.

The impressions are taken from a gelatinous substance to which the material to be copied has been transferred.

Chromium facing A deposit used to give a harder, more durable surface to a block, usually a stereo.

Chromolithography Lithographic printing in several colours. The term has been used since 1837.

Cicero A Continental unit for measuring the width or 'measure' of a line of type and the depth of a page. One Cicero = 4.511mm or 12 Didot points.

Clean proof A printer's proof which is free from errors.

Cliché The French word, also used elsewhere on the Continent, for a block, stereotype or electrotype.

Close up An instruction meaning to delete a space, ie bring characters together.

Club line A short line coming at the end of a paragraph, which should not occur at the top of a page in book work.

Clump The piece of metal used for spacing greater than six point thickness.

Coated paper A general term for art, chromo, enamel, and similar groups of paper on the surface of which a mineral, eg china clay, is applied after the body paper has been made. It is also known as 'surface paper'.

Collate To put the sections of a book in order. It also means to compare one copy of a printed and bound book with another copy of the same impression, or to describe the physical make-up of a book in terms of a standardized formula.

Collotype A planographic, photo-mechanical, non-screen printing process suitable for fine detail reproductions. Printing is done from a glass plate prepared by printing a negative on a gelatine film containing dichromate.

Colophon The colophon was the inscription formerly placed at the end of a book giving the title, printer's name, place and date of printing. In modern times it also refers, incorrectly, to a publisher's decorative device printed on the title page, the last page of text, or elsewhere.

Coloured edges The edges or top of a book which have been coloured with a brush-on fluid.

Colour guide The colour guide is the set of small marginal marks placed on each of the three negatives used in making blocks for colour printing, so that the printer can superimpose them in register when building up the picture. It also refers to the set of progressive proofs supplied by the plate and block-maker as a guide to the printer.

Colour key A process for reproducing coloured line drawings. A line block is made from the original drawing and pulls are taken from this, printed in light blue ink; on these the colours are drawn and etched, a separate sheet for each printing.

Colour separation This is used to give two or more colours on one sheet by separating type and blocks from the first setting into one forme for each colour.

Colour sequence The accepted order of letterpress printing. In four colours it is yellow, red, blue, black.

Column rule The light faced rule used to separate columns in newspaper.

Combination line and half tone A combined block used to reproduce photographs with superimposed letters, figures, diagrams etc.

Compose To set copy in type. This is done by the compositor or comp.

Composing stick A metal holder in which the compositor sets up type in words and lines.

Condensed face A type face having an elongated or narrow appearance.

Contact screen A half-tone screen made on a film base which has a graded dot pattern. It is used in direct contact with a film or plate to obtain a half-tone negative from a continuous tone original. Contact screens give better definition than the conventional glass screen.

Contents A page of a book listing the articles or chapters.

Continuous tone This term is used to refer to photographs or coloured originals in which the subject contains shades between the lightest and the darkest tones.

Copal A substance exuding from various tropical trees, used as a vehicle in making printing inks.

Copper engraving The impression taken from an engraved copper plate.

Copy Matter to be set in type by the printer. It can also refer to illustration for reproduction.

Counter The inside area of the type-face such as the centre of an 'o' or the space between the vertical strokes of an 'n'.

Counter-mark A watermark with the paper maker's initials, which is placed in the second half of the sheet opposite the normal watermark.

Cover The paper, board, cloth or leather to which the body of a book is secured by glue and thread.

Cover papers Papers for the covers of books, pamphlets etc, made from almost every kind of paper-making material and of endless variety in colour and finish.

Cover title The title of a book as stamped or lettered on the cover. This may be an abbreviation of the full title.

Cradle A bow-shaped steel rocker, with a toothed edge, used to roughen the surface of a copper mezzotint plate, so that an even and deep grain is given to the entire surface.

Crash finish A variety of paper having a surface like coarse linen.

Creasing is a linear identation made by machine in thick paper to provide a hinge. It is also a printing fault which produces deep creases, which may occur, especially when paper is not stored at the correct humidity.

Crop To trim a photograph or illustration. The crop is the part of the photograph or illustration to be eliminated.

Cropped A cropped book has had its margins unduly trimmed. They are said to bleed.

Cross-head Sub-section, paragraph heading or numeral printed across the page and centred in the body of text from which it is separated by one or more lines of space. It usually marks the first sub-division of a chapter.

Crown A standard size of printing paper 15in x 20in.

Cursive A running script. The letters are formed without raising the pen.

Cut edge The three edges of a book which are cut with a guillotine.

Cut flush Describes a book which has its cover and page edges quite even, the cutting being done after the cover has been attached. It is also known as 'trimmed-flush'.

Cyan ink The correct name for the shade of blue ink used in four-colour printing.

Cylinder press A printing press in which the forme is carried on a flat bed under a paper-bearing cylinder for an impression to be made at the point of contact.

D

Dabber An inking pad made of cotton, silk or leather.

Daguerreotype A method of making and fixing a photographic image. It was invented in 1833 by L.J.M. Daguerre.

Dash A punctuation mark (—), usually known as an em rule.

Dead matter Unused overmatter.

Deckle edge The rough uneven edge of handmade paper.

Deep-etch half-tone A half-tone plate from which the screen dots of any unwanted areas have been routed completely away so that these areas appear as plain paper on the printed sheet.

Deep-etching The removal, by etching, of the unwanted material on half-tone plates to give a white background.

Delete Instruction meaning to take out.

De luxe edition An edition of a work printed on higher-grade paper than the standard edition, often from specially cast type, and usually expensively bound and lavishly illustrated.

Demy A standard size of printing paper 17½in x 22½in.

Densitometer The instrument used to measure the quantitive colour of a colour transparency.

Descender That part of a lower case letter that falls below the X-HEIGHT.

Device A pictorial design of an heraldic or allegorical nature used as a printer's trademark.

Didot point The Continental unit of measurement for type established by the French typefounder, Firmin A. Didot in 1775. One Didot point equals 0.0148in; one English point equals 0.013837 in.

Die An intaglio engraved stamp used for impressing a design.

Die stamping A form of printing where all the characters are in relief.

Differential spacing The spacing of each character of type according to its individual width.

Display Printed matter, normally hand-set, to which prominence is given by size and position. This includes prelims, part and chapter titles, headings, advertisements.

Display type Larger type-faces designed for headings etc. In bookwork, type sizes above 14pt, requiring to be hand-set, are regarded as display type.

Dis, diss An abbreviation for DISTRIBUTE.

Distribute Means to return used type characters to the correct boxes in the case after being used in the forme.

Double column Two columns across each page.

Double-spread Two facing pages on which matter is continued directly across as if they were one page.

Dragon's blood Powdered resin used in the making of a line block to protect the shoulders of the etched areas in order to prevent undermining by subsequent etching.

Drawn on Describes a paper book cover which is attached by gluing it to the back.

Draw-out This means a letter or block accidentally displaced from the forme while it is in preparation or running on machine.

Drop folios Page numbers printed at the foot of each page.

Drop letter An initial letter covering two or three lines of text type.

Dry mounting The use of heat sensitive adhesives.

Dry point An engraving process in which a design is hand-cut directly on to a burnished copper plate with a steel or diamond point, no acid being used.

Drytransfer lettering A form of lettering which is transferred to the page by rubbing the letter off the back of a sheet. It is frequently used by designers and a wide range of type-faces and sizes is available.

Duck see CANVAS.

Duct The ink reservoir in a printing machine.

Dummy The prototype of a proposed book in the correct format, paper and bulk but with blank pages.

Duotone An illustration process in which the image is printed in two colours. Two negatives are made from a monochrome original, one for the darker shade with the greater detail, the other for the lighter flat tint.

Duplex half-tone Screen reproduction in two printings, generally black and a colour tone, intended to give the impression of a mellow one-colour picture.

Dutch mordant An etching fluid made up of 2 per cent potassium chlorate and 10 per cent hydrochloric acid, for use in aquatint and hard- or soft-ground etching.

Dutch paper Formerly limited to Van Gelder's hand-made paper, but now describes any deckle-edge paper produced in Holland.

E

Ear The advertising space or spaces beside the front-page title-line.

Echoppe An etching needle ground to a bevel used by the earliest etchers to obtain a swelling line in imitation of the burin.

Edges The three cut edges of a book.

Edition The whole number of copies of a work printed from the same set of type and issued at one time.

Eggshell finish A relatively rough finish imparted to drawing paper and notepaper by omitting calendering.

Egyptian A group of display types with heavy slab-serifs and little contrast in the thickness of strokes.

Electrotype A duplicate printing forme made in a galvanic bath by precipitating copper on a matrix.

Em This is a unit of linear measurement, usually 12 points or 4.5mm.

Embossing Relief printing or stamping in which dies are used to raise letters or a design above the surface of paper, cloth or leather.

En A measurement half the width of the em, used in casting off.

Enamel paper see COATED PAPER.

End-papers The leaves of paper at the front and end of a book which cover the inner sides of the boards and, with the linings, secure the book to its case or binding.

Engraving Any metal plate or wooden block on the surface of which a design or lettering has been cut or etched. It is also a print taken from such a plate.

En rule A dash (–) approximately half an em rule.

Enschede The most famous Dutch typefounding and printing concern. Established in Haarlem in 1703 by Izaac Enschedé.

Erratum An author's or printer's error, only discovered after the book has been printed. Its plural is errata.

Esparto A long, rough grass with fine, soft fibres. It grows in Southern Spain and North Africa and is used for making paper. The fibres assist stability during printing.

Estienne A firm of Parisian scholar-printers, founded in 1501 by Henri Estienne.

Estimating The calculation of the cost of work on a printing order done by the printer.

Etching The treatment with acid of a metal plate on which certain parts of the surface are protected by the application of a ground. It is also a print taken from the etched plate.

Even pages The left hand pages ie those with even numbers.

Even smalls Small caps used without capitals.

Expanded type Type with a flattened, oblong appearance.

F

Fabriano An Italian hand-made paper.

Face The printing surface of any type character. It also refers to the group or family to which any particular type design belongs.

Factor number A copy fitting number given for each composition size of many faces, developed by the Monotype Corporation. The factor number expresses an average character of a size of a face as a decimal part of a pica em, to 1/200 part.

Family A group of printing types in series with common characteristics in design but of different weights such as italic, bold, condensed, expanded etc.

Fashion boards Simple body boards lined on one side with a good rag cartridge paper, and with a thin paper on the other to prevent warping. They are used by artists when preparing original artwork.

Feathering A method of biting certain areas of a plate using drops of acid and controlling their movement with a feather.

Featherweight paper A light, bulky paper, preferably with a high Esparto content, made with little or no calendering.

Fecit In Latin 'he has made it'. This word used to be added to an artist's name on a drawing or engraving.

Feeder Apparatus for feeding and positioning paper sheets in printing presses, and in paper processing machines of various kinds.

Feint ruling Thin lines ruled on sheets as a writing guide. They are usually blue.

Felting The binding together of fibres in the wet pulp when making paper.

Fibre A plant cell, largely composed of cellulose; it is the basic element of paper-making material.

Figures Arabic figures eg 1, 2, 3 are most commonly used. Roman figures eg I, II, III are used for prelims, chapter heads, part headings etc.

Film-Klischee A process devised by Film-Klischee GmbH, Munich, for the making of half-tone blocks using the swelled gelatine principle. It was first used in Britain in 1957.

Filmsetting The process of using photographic film and a photo-composing machine for letterpress composition.

Fine line work This refers to maps etc composed of many fine lines. It is more costly than ordinary line work.

Fine rule A rule of hair-line thickness.

Finish The surface given to paper during manufacture.

Flat-bed Describes a press which has the printing forme on a plane surface, as distinct from a press with a curved printing surface. In a flat-bed cylinder press the forme is placed and moved to and fro under the cylinder, while the flat-bed web press prints from a flat forme on to an endless roll of paper.

Flexography A method of letterpress printing from rubber or flexible plates.

Flimsy Thin, tough, and semi-transparent bond paper used for planning by the layout department.

Flong The sheet of papier-mâché used to make a mould from a forme for casting a stereotype plate.

Flowers Type ornaments used to embellish, for example, page-borders, chapter headings, title pages to enliven printed matter.

Flush The cover of a book which is cut flush with the inside.

Flush paragraphs Paragraphs in which the first word is not indented but set flush with the vertical line of the text.

Fly A sheet which is folded once so that it makes four pages.

Fly-leaf Another term for end-papers.

Folded and collated copy The folded and collated copy of a work sent to the publisher for approval of printing before binding begins. It is also known as advance sheets.

Folded and gathered sheets Abbreviated to F and Gs. Sheets which are collated in order but not trimmed.

Folding The folding of flat printed sheets to book size. The number of pages in the folded sheet is always a multiple of four.

Folio In design and printing folio has several meanings. It is the book size formed when a sheet is folded once so that the pages are half the size of the sheet. To express the size clearly the paper size must also be stated, for example 'Crown folio'. Folio also means a leaf of paper numbered only on the front and, in loose usages of the term, a page number and the running headline of a page.

Folio at foot This means that the page number appears at the foot of a page.

Follow copy An instruction to the compositor indicating that the spelling and punctuation of a manuscript are to be followed, even if unorthodox, in preference to the house style.

Font A corruption of FOUNT.

Foolscap Standard size of printing paper 13½in x 17in.

Foot The margin at the bottom of a page; also the bottom edge of a book. It also means the undersurface of a type.

Footnotes Short explanatory notes, printed at the foot of the page or at the end of a book.

Fore-edge (pronounced 'forage') The outer-edge of a book parallel to the back.

Forward The binding of a book after sewing and before casing in.

Foreword Introductory remarks to a work or about its author and not written by the author.

Format The general appearance or style of a book including size, shape, paper quality, type face and binding.

Forme Type matter and blocks assembled into pages and locked up in a chase ready for printing.

Foul biting Accidental dots or other irregular areas bitten into a plate, caused by imperfect GROUNDS.

Founder's type Type cast by a type founder for hand composition.

Fount A complete supply of a type face in one size only.

Foxed The term is applied to book pages discoloured by damp which has affected impurities in the paper.

Fraktur A German BLACK-LETTER type face believed to have originated in Augsburg in 1510.

French fold A sheet printed on one side only and then folded into a section with the bolts uncut; the insides are blank.

French folio Thin, smooth, sized paper.

Frontispiece An illustration facing the title-page of a book.

Fugitive colours Colours or inks which are not permanent, and change or fade when exposed to light.

Full point A full stop.

Furniture Pieces of wood and metal, less than type height, fitted around type and blocks to hold them in the forme. They are used to make margins or fill blank areas on a page.

G

Galley An open sided shallow tray in which lines of type are held so that they can be moved about in the printing shop; pulls taken at this stage are known as galley pulls or galleys.

Gathering Placing the sections of a book in the correct order for binding.

Gilt edges, gilt top The three edges, or top of a book which are covered with gold leaf and rubbed down. This prevents the absorption of dust.

Gloss ink A printing ink consisting of a synthetic resin base and drying oils. These inks dry quickly, without penetration, and are suitable for use on coated papers.

Glued back only This refers to a paper cover which is glued to the back of a book only, leaving the sides loose.

Glued or pasted down to ends A paper cover glued at back, with each side also glued or pasted to the first and last leaves of the book.

Gold blocking The stamping of a design on a book cover using gold leaf and a heated die or block.

Gothic Another name for BLACKLETTER.

Gouache Opaque watercolour for which the pigments are mixed with white lead, bone ash or chalk.

Grain direction The direction in which the majority of fibres lie in a sheet of paper.

Graining The process by which a lithographic plate is given a moisture-retaining surface. The process uses abrasive powder and either glass or steel marbles. Mechanical agitation produces the required surface.

Graphite A crystalline, naturally occurring allotropic form of carbon made up of hexagonal laminas. It can also be produced by heating anthracite in an electric furnace.

Graver see BURIN.

Gravure A printing process in which the image is etched into a plate. The plate is inked, then wiped clean, thus leaving the ink in the image. It then prints off on to the paper.

Grid A measuring guide used by designers to help ensure consistency. The grid shows type widths, picture areas, trim sizes, margins etc and is used particularly where the work has more than one page.

Gripper edge The edge which is caught by the grippers as a sheet of paper is fed into a cylinder press.

Grippers On job presses grippers are the iron fingers attached to the platen to keep the sheet in place and take it off the type after the impression. On cylinder presses, grippers are the short curved metal fingers attached to an operating rod which grip the sheet and carry it round the impression.

Ground A thin coating made from pitch, gum-mastic, asphaltum and beeswax which protects the non-image-bearing parts of an etching plate from the action of the acid.

G.S.M., grams per square metre A unit of measurement for paper used in printing.

Guards Narrow strips of linen or paper to which the inner margins of single plates are pasted before sewing them with the sections of a book.

Guillotine A machine for cutting a large number of sheets of paper accurately.

Gutter A term used in imposition for the space made up of the fore-edges of pages plus the trim, where these edges fall internally in the forme.

H

Hair-line rule The thinnest of printers' brass rules.

Hair-lines The thin strokes of a type face.

Hair space The thinnest metal space between type.

Halation The spreading of light around the highlights of an image.

Half-bound A book with its back and corners bound in one material, the sides in another.

Half-title The title of a book as printed on the leaf preceding the title-page.

Half-tone Process by which continuous tone is simulated by a pattern of dots of varying size. A half-tone block is a zinc or copper printing plate prepared by this process.

Half-tone screen A sheet of glass bearing a network of lines ruled at right angles. The screen is used to translate the subject of a half-tone illustration into dots.

Hand-composition Setting type by hand.

Hand press A printing press in which the forme is inked, the paper is fed and removed, and the pressure is applied by hand.

Hand set Type matter which has been composed letter by letter in a STICK.

Hanging-indent An indented setting where the first line of each paragraph is set full-out to the column measure and the remaining lines indented 1 em.

Hard size Paper which contains the maximum amount of size.

Hardware A term for equipment — used in computer typesetting it includes keyboards, magnetic tape printers, tape punch units etc.

Head The margin at the top of a page.

Headband A cotton or silk cord sewn to the top of the back of a book.

Headline It is mainly the title of a book as printed at the top of every page of text; also known as a 'page head'. Variants of this — title on the verso pages, chapter title on the recto — are referred to as 'running heads'.

Heidelberg An automatic printing press made by the Schnellpressenfabrik A.G., Heidelberg. The first machine was built in 1914.

Height to paper The overall height of printing plates and type in letterpress printing.

Hollow The strip of brown paper placed in the centre of a case to stiffen the spine.

Hot metal General term for composing machines casting type from molten metal.

Hot-pressed Paper glazed by heated metal plates.

House corrections Alterations made to proofs or script by the publisher or printer, as distinct from those made by the author.

House style The style of spelling, punctuation and spacing used in a printing or publishing house to ensure consistent treatment of copy during typesetting.

I

Image The subject to be reproduced as an illustration on a printing press.

Imperfection A book which has been incorrectly bound.

Imperial A size of printing and drawing paper, 22in x 30in.

Impose To arrange pages of type in a forme so that when the sheet is folded the text will read continuously.

Imposing stone see STONE.

Impression Firstly, all copies of a book printed at one time from the same type or plates. It also refers to the pressure applied to a frame of type by the cylinder or platen.

Imprimatur Latin meaning 'let it be printed'. In early books it was a statement to show that permission to print the work had been given by the appropriate authority.

Imprint The printer's imprint is the name of the printer and the place of printing. It is required by law if the paper or book is meant to be published. The publisher's imprint is the name of the publisher with place and date of publication.

Incanabula A printers' term for printed matter produced before 1500.

Indentation Any setting

short of the column measure.
India paper A very thin but strong opaque paper, made from rags and used for printing bibles and dictionaries.
Inferior figures Small letters or figures printed at the foot of ordinary letters and cast partly below the base line, for example in chemical formulae such as H_2O.
Initial A large capital often found at the beginning of a chapter. It is sometimes raised above the first line but more usually dropped to a depth of two or three lines below it.
Inkers The rollers on a printing press which apply ink to the type and block surfaces.
Inset A sheet or part of a sheet placed inside another which is not part of the book's normal pagination.
Intaglio A printing image below the surface of the plate.
Interlaying Placing sheets of paper between a printing plate and its block or mount.
Interleaved Firstly refers to a book which has blank leaves between the printed pages for entering notes by hand. It also refers to a book with thin tissue inserted to prevent the illustrations and text from rubbing. Thirdly it means a plate which has a thin leaf bearing a descriptive caption pasted to its inner margin.
Intertype An American composing machine similar to the Linotype.
I.P.H. The abbreviation for impressions per hour.
Italic Type with sloping letters — *a, b, c* etc. It is indicated in MS by a single underline.

J

Jacket The paper wrapper in which a book is sold.
Japanese paper A thin, tough and highly absorbent paper of silky texture used for artist's proofs.
Jobbing work Small everyday printing such as display cards, letter-headings, labels, handbills and other printing — as distinct from bookwork.
Joint The flexible part of a case between the boarded side and the spine.
Justification Spacing of words and letters exactly to ensure that each line of text finishes at the same point — or, in printing terminology, 'makes the measure'.

K

Keep standing This mean to keep type made up ready for possible reprints.
Kern The part of a letter which overhangs the shank. An italic '*f*' is kerned on both sides.
Key The block, plate or stone containing the main outlines of the design. It acts as a guide for the position and registration of the other colours.
Keyboard The rows of keys for composing in typesetting machines. On a Monotype system the keyboard is similar to a typewriter.
Kiss impression The ink is deposited on the paper by the lightest possible surface contact and not impressed into it. This technique is necessary when printing on coated papers.
Klischograph A German electronic photo-engraving machine which produces a plastic, zinc, copper or magnesium half-tone plate.
Knocking up The adjustment on one or two edges of a pile of sheets so that they can be cut squarely.
Kraft paper Strong brown paper made from sulphate pulp. It is often used for packing books.

L

Laid paper Paper which shows the wire marks of the mould or dandy roll used in manufacture.
Lampblack Pure carbon deposit. It was formerly the most important black pigment used in manufacturing printing inks.
Lay down A term for placing on stone ready for imposition, an alternative for IMPOSE.
Lay edges The two edges of a sheet which are placed flush with the side and front lay gauges or marks on a printing machine to ensure that the sheet will be removed properly by the grippers, and have uniform margins when printed.
Layout An outline or sketch which gives the general appearance of the printed page, indicating the relationship between text and illustration.
Lead The main story in a newspaper or the opening paragraph of any news story.
Lead (pronounced 'led'). The strips of type metal or brass of varying thickness and less than type height which are used to space out headings and text.
Leaded Type which is set with leads between the lines.
Leader A group of dots, usually three (. . .). It sometimes appears as (. . . . . .) in forms etc.
Leader line A line on an image keyed in to annotation.
Leaf Firstly, leaf refers to newly formed sheets of paper before they are dried and finished. A leaf is also each of the folios which result when a sheet of paper is folded. Each side of a leaf is called a page.
Leave edge The opposite edge to the gripper edge.
Legend Correctly, legend is the name for the descriptive matter printed below an illustration. The custom of printing and publishing houses is to prefer the term 'caption'. CAPTION is more often, but incorrectly, used.
Legibility The cumulative effect of printed matter on the human eye.
Letterpress The main printing process. The image is raised and inked to produce an impression. Letterpress also refers to the text of a book, including line illustrations but excluding PLATES.
Letterspacing The insertion of space between the letters of a word to improve the appearance of a line of type. Lower case words do not need to be letterspaced.
Lifted matter Type matter already set which is taken out of one job to be used in another.
Ligatures Tied letters in type, which are cast on one body, such as ff
Light face The opposite of BOLD FACE.
Limp binding A form of binding using a flexible cover eg paper, cloth or leather, and no board stiffener.
Line and half tone An illustration process in which line and half-tone negatives are combined, printed on to a plate and etched as a unit.
Line block A printing plate made of zinc or copper consisting of solid areas and lines. It is reproduced directly from a line drawing without tones. It is mounted on a wooden block to type height.
Linecaster This is the generic term for all keyboard-operated slug-casting composing machines, Linotype or Intertype.
Lino-cut A relief printing surface of linoleum on which the background to the design is cut away with a knife, gouge or engraving tool.
Lino film A photo-composing machine built by the Mergenthaler Linotype Company of New York, first demonstrated in 1954.
Linotron A high-speed photocomposing machine which uses the cathode ray tube as part of its fast setting technique.
Linotype The first key-board operated composing machine to employ the principle of the circulating matrix and cast type in solid lines or slugs. It was invented by the German/American engineer Ottmar Mergenthaler and first used in 1886.
Literal A mistake in setting type which does not involve more than a letter-for-letter correction. It includes wrong founts and battered letters.
Lithography Abbreviated form litho. Printing from a dampened, flat surface using greasy ink, based on the principle of the mutual repulsion of oil and water. The original printing surface was a porous stone but later a grained zinc plate took its place.
Live matter A forme of type which awaits printing, stereo-typing or electro-typing.
Locked up When all the type and blocks are fitted into a chase to make up the forme, quoins are used to 'lock up' that is to hold all the type, blocks and furniture rigidly in place so that nothing falls out of the forme.
Logotype A word or several letters cast as one unit.
Long-bodied type Type cast on bodies larger than normal such as 10 point or 12 point.
Lower-case The small letters in a fount of type.
Ludlow Machine which casts display sizes of type on a slug from hand-assembled matrices.
Line engraving An INTAGLIO method of engraving lines on a copper plate using a burin. It superseded the wood-cut for book illustration in the 16th century and reached its peak in France in the 18th century.
Line gauge The printer's rule. It is calibrated in picas and is 72 picas long (11.952in):
Linen finish The embossing process which makes paper or book cloth resemble woven linen.
Line up When two lines of type, or a line of type and a block, touch the same imaginary horizontal line.
Lining The first lining is a strip of mull glued down the back of the book, which projects round the sides in forwarding. The second is a strip of stiff brown paper glued over the first lining. In flexiback lining a strip of linen is applied by machine and a second lining is not necessary.

M

Machine-made paper The continuous web of paper made on cylinder machines.
Machine proof A proof taken when corrections marked on the galley proof and page proof have been made and the forme is on the printing machine. Machine proofs provide the final opportunity for correcting mistakes before the final printing.
Magenta ink The name of the shade of red established as one of the standard four-colour letterpress printing inks.
Make-up Refers firstly to the sheet indicating the placing of the various items on a page, and secondly to the actual assembling of the page.
Making ready In letterpress printing the surface on which the paper rests has to be built up in places to give an overall evenness of impression. This is called making ready; the build-up backing is known as make ready. Make ready is not necessary in gravure or litho.
Manuscript Literally, a work written by hand. It refers either to a book written before the invention of printing or the written or typed work which an author submits for publication.
Marbling Decorative paper used for binding books, and sometimes the book edges. It is done by dipping the sheet in a bath of colours floating on a surface of gum. The colours do not mix but can be combined into patterns with the use of a comb, and transfer readily to the paper surface.
Margins The blank areas on a printed page which surround the matter.
Marked proof The proof, usually on galleys, supplied to the author for correction. It contains the corrections and queries made by the printer's reader.
Mark up To mark up is to specify every detail needed for the compositor to set the copy. The mark up is copy with instructions on it.
Mat abbreviation of MATRIX
Matrix Firstly, a metal die from which a single type is cast. It also refers to the impression in papier-mâché taken from a page of type for stereotyping and the stereotyper's flong after moulding.
Matt art A clay-coated printing paper with a dull finish.
Matter Either manuscript or copy to be printed, or type that is composed.
Measure The width of a setting, usually measured in pica ems.
Medallion An illustration printed on paper, pasted to the front of the case of a book.
Medium Has four meanings. Firstly, it is a standard size of printing paper (18in × 23in). It is also the liquid, usually linseed oil, in which the pigment of a printing ink is dispersed, an alternative name for Benday tint and the weight of type-face midway between light and bold.
Metallic ink A printing ink which produces an effect of gold, silver, copper or bronze.
Miehle A printing press from the Miehle Printing Press and Manufacturing Co., Chicago.
Mill brand The trade mark and brand name of the manufacturer.
Mill boards Strong grey or black boards of good quality used for the covers of books.
Misprint A typographical error.
Modern face A type face with vertical stress, strong stroke contrast and unbracketed fine serifs.
Moiré A printing fault where half-tones appear as a mechanical pattern of dots. In four-colour work this is minimized by photographing each colour at a separate angle.
Monotype Monotype is firstly the trade name for composing machines which cast single types. The system was invented by Tolbert Lanston of Ohio in 1887. Secondly, it refers to the process of making a painting on glass or metal and then taking an impression on paper. It is only possible to take one impression.
Montage Assembling portions of several drawings or photographs to form a single original.
Mordant An adhesive for fixing gold leaf. It is also any fluid used to etch lines on a printing plate.
Morocco Tanned goat-skin, which is finished by glazing or polishing and used in bookbinding.
Mortise A space cut out of a printing plate in order to insert type or another plate. It is also the process of cutting away metal from the non-printing areas at the sides of a type to permit closer setting.
Mottling An uneven impression, especially in flat areas. It is usually caused by using too much pressure, an unsuitable paper or an unsuitable ink.
Mould A flat impressed sheet made by beating or pressing flong on to type, for casting a stereo.
Mould-made paper A manufactured, imitation hand-made paper.
Mount The base — usually of wood, but sometimes

metal — used to support a printing plate and bring it type high.

Mull A coarse variety of muslin which forms the first lining of a case-bound book. It is also known as SCRIM.

Muller A metal, glass or stone block used in grinding inks and pigments.

Multiple tool A wood engraving tool for making several lines with one stroke.

Munsell colour system A system of colour measurement and notation which defines all colours in terms of hue, value and chroma. It was devised by A.H. Munsell of Massachusetts.

Mutton The term for an em quad.

N

Neck line The amount of white or leading under a running head.

Nick A groove on the body of a piece of type. The compositor places the type in his stick with the nick uppermost. This ensures that the type, although upside-down, will read from left to right.

Nickel facing A deposit applied to blocks (usually stereos) which gives a harder and longer-lasting surface.

Nipping Means pressing a book after sewing but before forwarding. This flattens the bolts and expels air from between the sheets.

Nonpareil The name for an old type size (approximately equal to 6pt). It is still used as an alternative term, particularly to indicate spacing.

Not A finish in high quality rag papers, which is midway between rough and hot pressed.

Nut An en quad.

O

Octavo A sheet of paper folded in half three times, to make eighths or sixteen pages. It also refers to a standard broadside divided into eight parts.

Offset lithography A method of lithography by which the image is not printed direct from the plate but 'offset' first on to a rubber covered cylinder, the blanket, which performs the printing operation.

Offside The part of the case which comes at the end of the book.

Old face Type form originating in the 16th century, characterized by diagonal stress and sloped, bracketed serifs.

Opacity The term used to describe non-transparency in printing papers.

Optical character recognition usually abbreviated to O.C.R. a device for the electronic scanning of copy and its conversion into photoset matter without keyboard operation.

Orthochromatic Refers to photographic materials sensitive to green and yellow as well as blue light.

Out of register This means that one or more colours in a sequence do not correspond exactly with the others in the same piece of printing.

Overlay Firstly, a transparent sheet used in the preparation of multi-colour artwork. Alternatively, it is a translucent sheet covering a piece of original artwork, on which instructions may be written.

Overmatter Matter set which does not come within the appropriate space.

Overprint Printing over an already printed area.

Overrun To transfer one or more words from the end of one line to the start of the next, eg to improve spacing, to 'make' a line etc.

Overs Paper issued beyond the bare requirements to allow for make-ready, spoils etc. It also refers to the quantity produced above the ordered number.

P

Page one side of a LEAF.

Page proofs Proofs of type which has been paginated and locked up in a chase. It refers to the secondary stage in proofing, after galley proofs and before machine proofs.

Pagination The term given

to numbering the pages of a book.

Palette knife A thin, flat, flexible steel knife used for mixing colours or inks.

Pallet Has three meanings. Firstly, it is a wooden storage device on which sheets of paper are stacked. Secondly, it is the brass finishing tool used for impressing straight lines on covers. It is also a small hand-tool in which letters are placed and heated to stamp the cover of a book.

Panchromatic Photographic material which is sensitive to all visible colours and to ultraviolet light.

Pantograph An instrument for copying a design. The copy can be same size, reduced or enlarged.

Parchment Goat or sheep-skin, scraped and dressed with lime and pumice and used for writing on.

Parentheses A punctuation mark or ornament, which appears as ( ). They are more usually called brackets.

Paring In hand binding, paring is thinning and chamfering the edges of leather to give a neat turn-in over the boards.

Paste-up A layout of a number of pages used to plan the positioning of blocks, captions and text.

Peculiars Type characters for non-standard accent-bearing letters used when setting certain foreign languages.

Perfector A press which prints both sides of the paper at a single pass. All letterpress rotaries and web-offset machines are perfectors.

Perforation Firstly, print perforation is obtained by printing with a slotted rule slightly above type high. Secondly, pin-hole perforation is obtained by punched holes eg postage stamps.

Period A punctuation mark, the full stop.

pH In printing this is a unit for measuring the acidity or alkalinity of a solution or material.

Photocomposition The production of display line and text by photographic means on film or paper. Photocomposing machines assemble lines of letters from various forms of photo-matrix. They are usually operated by tape, justified and hyphenated on a computer, originated from keyboarded tape-perforators.

Photogravure The process of printing from a photo-mechanically prepared surface, which holds the ink in recessed cells.

Photolithography A method of lithographic printing in which the image is transferred to the plate photographically and printed on a lithographic printing

machine. This is sometimes known as OFFSET.

Photopolymer plates Sensitized plastic plates on which negatives can be printed down; a relief printing surface is formed by a chemical wash-out. Photocomposed pages can thus be converted into letterpress printing surfaces, either by printing direct from the photopolymer plate or moulding from it to make stereoplates.

Photostat A facsimile copy of a document — typed, written, printed or drawn.

Pica The old name for 12pt. The pica em is the unit of measurement used in setting.

Pie Type which has been accidentally mixed.

Plank grain Plank refers to the grain of wood running parallel to the block, as in a wood-cut.

Plate Plate has four meanings. Firstly, it is an electro or stereo of set-up type. Secondly, it is a sheet of metal bearing a design, from which an impression is printed. It also describes a full page book illustration, printed separately from the text often on different paper. It is also a photographic plate; a whole plate measures 8½in × 6½in, a half plate measures 6½ × 4¾ in.

Plate mark The imprint of the bevel of the plate which is found on all INTAGLIO prints.

Platen press A printing press in which a flat plate, or platen, is lowered and pressed against a horizontal forme. The earliest hand-printing presses were platens.

Point The standard unit of type size. In the British/American system it is 0.01383in, or approximately 72 to the inch. The Continental (Didot) point is calculated differently.

Portrait An upright image or page.

Powderless etching on zinc or magnesium A process which gives a faithful reproduction, greater depth between the fine lines and a smooth, even shoulder. The plates print well, and are ideal for subsequent electro or stereotyping.

Preliminary matter, Prelims The pages preceding the body of a book. They usually consist of half-title, title, preface and contents.

Press proof The last proof to be read before printing, which authorizes printing.

Presswork The printing-off on to paper of matter set in type.

Process engraving The name given to several photo-mechanical methods of producing relief blocks or plates for printing illustrations.

Progressive proofs The proofs taken in colour printing as a guide to shade and registration. Each colour is shown separately and also imposed on the preceding colour.

Proof An impression obtained from an inked plate, stone, screen, block or type in order to check the progress and accuracy of the work. It is also called a pull.

Q

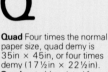

Quad Four times the normal paper size, quad demy is 35in × 45in, or four times demy (17½in × 22½in).

Quadrant abbreviated form **Quad** Pieces of blank metal under type height which are spacing. They come in sizes of multiple ems.

Quarter-bound A case bound book using a stronger material for the back than for the sides.

Quarto A piece of paper folded in half twice, making quarters or eight pages.

Quire The term for 24 sheets of paper or 1/20th of a ream.

Quires, quire stock (Printed sheet stock) The sheets of a book which are printed but not folded.

Quoins Two bars of metal which are held together by springs, but which can be forced apart using a square-sectioned key. As the key is turned the quoin opens; it presses against the furniture and the edge of the chase and holds the type and blocks rigidly in place.

R

Range Firstly, a form of setting in which lines of unequal length abut a margin at left or right. It is also an instruction to position the right or left-hand edge of a block vertically to the type above or below it.

Reader The reader is the person who reads and corrects the printer's proofs against the original manuscript.

Ream The name for 500 sheets of paper.

Recto The right-hand page of a book.

Register Refers to the correct alignment of pages with the margins in order. It is also the correct positioning of one colour on another in colour printing.

Register marks These are the crosses, triangles and other devices used in colour printing to position the paper correctly.

Register ribbon The strip of ribbon fastened at the back of a book for a book-marker.

Reglet A strip of wooden furniture 6, 12 or 24 points thick, for spacing.

Repoussage The process of hammering up the back of a metal plate in order to remove some of the engraved or etched work.

Reproduction proofs also called **Repro** High quality proofs on art paper, which can be used as artwork.

Resist An acid-resisting ground applied to a plate before etching.

Retroussage The term given to flicking a soft rag lightly over a wiped INTAGLIO plate, to draw out the ink slightly and give a softer line.

Revise A proof embodying the corrections made to the first proof by the author and/or reader.

Rivers The streaks of white spacing produced when spaces in consecutive lines of type coincide.

Rocker A tool used in mezzotint to prepare the plate surface.

Roman Ordinary vertical type as distinct from italic. It was based on the humanistic hand of Italian Renaissance scribes.

Rotary A reel or web-fed newspaper press which uses a cylindrical printing surface. The papers are delivered folded and counted, ready to be dispatched. When the printing is done on sheets it is called 'sheet-fed rotary'.

Roulette An engraving tool with a freely-running toothed wheel which makes a series of small indentations on the plate.

Round and back Refers to a concave appearance at the foredge of a book and a convex back with a projecting shoulder.

Router A machine which uses a rotating cutter to remove the superfluous parts of a wood or metal half-tone block.

Royal A size of printing paper 20in × 25in.

Rubrication The insertion of written initial letters and other decoration in early printed books.

Rules Metal strips, of type height, in various widths and lengths, used for printing lines.

Run The number of impressions taken from a forme at one time.

Running head The line of — usually small — type which repeats a chapter heading etc at the top of a page.

Run on An instruction to printer that text is continuous and no new paragraph is to be made. A run on chapter is one which does not begin on a new page.

Run round This refers to an illustration set in a page of text which has been indented to allow for it.

S

Saddle stitch A method of stitching brochures; they are opened over a saddle-shaped support and stitched through the back.

Sandbag A leather cushion packed with sand; the plate or block rests on it during engraving and can be easily turned for engraving curved lines.

Sans serif A type face without serifs which usually has no stroke contrast.

Scraper A tool with a three sided tapered blade, used for removing the unwanted burr in copper plate engraving or mezzotint.

Scraperboard Prepared board with a surface of gesso. It is first inked over and then scratched or scraped with a point or blade to give the effect of a white line engraving.

Scoring Refers to making a crease in paper or card so that it will not be damaged by folding.

Scorper A tool with slightly rounded edges used in wood engraving for clearing spaces.

Screen The number of dots per square inch on a half-tone process block; the lower the number, the coarser the reproduction will be.

Scrim see MULL.

Script A type-face designed to imitate handwriting.

Serif The small terminal stroke at the end of the main stroke of a letter.

Set Firstly, set refers to the width of a type body. Secondly, it is used as an instruction, as in 'set to 16 pica' or as a description, ie 'hand set'. It is also used in a special sense by 'Monotype' to describe the proportions or the em of a size of type.

Set close Describes type set with the minimum of space between the words and no extra space between sentences.

Set off The accidental transference of an image from one sheet to the back of the next impression. Alternatively, in lithography, it refers to an impression

taken from a key outline of a design which is powdered with a non-greasy dye while the ink is damp, then placed on the stone or plate and passed through the press. It acts as a guide for subsequent workings.

Set solid Refers to type set without leading.

Sewing Fastening together sections of a book using thread.

Shank The body of the type.

Sheet A single piece of paper.

Sheet fed A printing machine into which sheets are fed singly.

Sheet-work The sections of a book printed by backing up a sheet with a different forme from the front. The opposite of 'work and turn'.

Shoulder The projection down each side of a book's spine, obtained by rounding and backing.

Shoulder-notes The marginal notes at the top outer corners of a paragraph.

Show through The fault in which a printed impression on one side of the lead is visible on the other side through the paper.

Side head A subheading set flush left in the text.

Side notes Notes in the foredge margin or (rarely) in the gutter, outside the normal type area.

Signature The letter at the tail of the first page of each section in a book, running in alphabetical order, which serves as a guide to the binder in gathering. It also refers to the individual sections themselves.

Skiver The outer, grain side of sheets in which sheepskin has been split.

Slab serifs Square serifs which are almost as thick as the upright strokes on which they are placed, such as those in most 'Egyptian' type-faces.

Slip case An open-sided case to hold one or more books so that the spine is visible.

Slit This usually means cut (in half). It also means slit on a machine, or cut on the printing press by a rotary knife between impress cylinder and delivery.

Slug A metal bar on which separate types and spaces are cast as one piece, set on a Linotype, Intertype or Ludlow.

Slur An effect that results from movement between type and paper during impression.

Small capitals Capital letters which are smaller than the standard and usually aligned with the ordinary line of type ie SMALL CAPITALS. They are indicated by double underlining in MS.

Software A term used for computer programmes and general items. It also refers to paper and magnetic tape.

Sort One individual piece of type.

Space A non-printing graded unit for spacing out a line of type, classified into hair, thin, mid and thick.

Special sorts Type characters not normally included in a fount ie fractions, musical symbols etc.

Spine The centre of the case of a book which covers the back when it is cased in.

Spirex binding A form of binding in which a spiral wire holds the leaves together.

Spitstick A wood-engraving tool which is used to produce curved lines.

Split boards The boards used for library binding. They are made by pasting together a thick and thin board, leaving a split about 1½ in wide, into which endpapers and tapes are inserted.

Spoils Badly printed sheets, not included in delivery of a job.

Sprinkled edges The edges or top of a book speckled with splashes of coloured fluid.

Square The portion of the inside of a case to project beyond the cut edges of a book.

Square back A binding which is collated and sewn but not rounded and backed.

Star A typographical ornament, also an incorrect name for an asterisk.

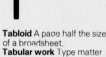

Stereo A flat plate made by stereotyping from type or blocks, usually applied to advertisements supplied in plate form.

Stet The Latin word meaning 'let it stand', written in the margin in proof corrections to cancel a previously marked correction.

Stick An open-sided metal box in which type is hand set.

Stipple or mechanical tint A mechanical method of obtaining a background where this is impossible to achieve by hand in the original. By adding a dot or design to the line block many different effects can be created. These areas are indicated with blue shading on the original.

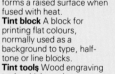

Stock The metal part of a printing roller, covered with composition. It is also a printer's term for paper etc to be used for printing.

Stone The stone, or, more correctly, imposing stone, is the smooth iron or steel surface on which the pages are assembled in a forme. It was originally made of marble, hence the name.

Stripping The removal of photographic emulsion from a support to assemble with others on another support.

Style see HOUSE STYLE.

Sub-head The heading for the division of a chapter.

Substance A term which refers to the weight of paper.

Subtitle A phrase, often explanatory, which follows the title of a book.

Supercalendered Refers to paper with a smooth surface, produced by rolling between metal calenders or rollers.

Super caster A Monotype machine which casts large sizes of type for headlines, rules, borders and leads.

Superior letters or figures The small letters or figures which are set at the top of normal characters eg 2^{10}.

Surface paper see COATED PAPER.

Swash letters OLD FACE italic types with calligraphic flourishes.

Swatch A colour specimen.

Swelled rule A rule which prints as a thick line in the centre, tapering at both ends.

T

Tabloid A page half the size of a broadsheet.

Tabular work Type matter set in columns.

Tail The bottom of a book, the margin at the bottom.

Tail-piece A design at the end of a section, chapter or book.

Thermographic printing The process in which freshly printed sheets are dusted with resinous powder which forms a raised surface when fused with heat.

Tint block A block for printing flat colours, normally used as a background to type, half-tone or line blocks.

Tint tools Wood engraving tools which produce an even line of varying thickness.

Tipped in Refers to an illustration printed on a single page and inserted separately in a book, by gumming or pasting one edge.

Title page The right hand page at the front of a book which bears the title, the names of author and publisher, the place of publication and other relevant information.

Titling A headline type, which is only available in capitals.

Tooling A method of impressing decorations and lettering on the covers of books by hand, using brass letters, pallets, rolls and dies.

Transitional Type forms invented in the mid 18th century which are neither OLD FACE nor MODERN. They include Fournier and Baskerville.

Transpose To transpose is to change the order of letters, words or lines.

Trimmed flush see CUT FLUSH.

TTS Abbreviation for **Teletypesetter** A machine in which a line-caster is operated by perforated tape.

Tying up This means using string to secure type which has been set and made up into pages, until it is surrounded by furniture.

Type A character cast on a rectangular piece of metal, used in letterpress printing.

Type-height The standard height for type and blocks, 0.918in.

Typescript A typed manuscript.

Typographer The person who designs and plans the typographical layout of a proposed printed work. This may include designing type-faces.

Typography The art of the typographer.

U

Undercutting This is the faulty etching of a block in which the metal is etched from the side, so that the strength of the block is weakened.

Upper-case The capital letters in a fount of type.

V

Vellum The skin of a calf, kid or lamb, which is treated to be used as a writing surface.

Verso The left-hand page of a book.

Vignette A small illustration or decoration without a border.

Volume A work published with its own title page and contained in covers.

W

Wash-drawing A drawing containing washes of tone in addition to areas of solid colour.

Washing-up The cleaning of ink from the forme or the printing press.

Watermark A distinctive design incorporated in paper during manufacture. It is visible when the sheet is held up to the light.

Web-offset An offset press working from a web or reel of paper.

Weight The degree of boldness of a type face. Univers type, for example, is made in light, medium, bold and extra bold; these are known as the different weights.

Wet-on-wet printing Colour printing in which the first colour of ink is still wet when the subsequent colours are printed.

Wire stitching A method of binding in which wire staples are passed through the back of the printed section.

Work and turn The method by which the matter for both sides of a sheet is set in one forme. One side of the sheet is printed, then turned over end for end and backed up from the same forme.

Wove paper Paper made on a roll of closely-woven, finely-textured wire, which leaves no marks on the paper surface.

Wrong fount The indication that a letter of the wrong size or fount has been set by mistake. It is abbreviated as w.f.

X

X-height The height of letters with neither ascenders or descenders, such as the letter x.

Z

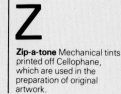

Zip-a-tone Mechanical tints printed off Cellophane, which are used in the preparation of original artwork.

Papers and sizes

Types of paper

It is important to choose the correct type of paper. Printing papers come in either coated or uncoated forms.

Uncoated papers

Offset cartridge paper is strong and rough-surfaced. It is made specially for use in offset lithography. Imitation art paper is made by mixing china clay with the paper pulp during manufacture. This gives the paper a smooth finish which resembles coated papers, although it is not of such high quality as the coated finish. Antique paper has a rough finish. It is bulky and mould-made. When the marks of the mould show, it is called 'antique laid'. If the mould marks do not show, the paper is called 'antique wove'. Machine finished papers are smooth on both sides. However, the surface is not as smooth as that of super-calendered paper, the surface of which has a high gloss finish, having been passed through calendered rollers. With machine-glazed paper one side is rough while the other is smooth and glossy.

Coated papers

Coated papers have a layer of china clay and adhesive applied to their surface. The finest surface of all is found on cast-coated paper. This is paper which has been previously machine-coated and then has a thick ink-absorbent coating laid on top. It is given a final polish by a heated glazing drum. With brush coated papers, the coating is applied by a revolving cylindrical brush. The coated paper is then drawn over a rubber apron and the coating smoothed by a series of oscillating flat brushes. The third main type of coating is called machine coating. This is a simpler process than the others, but does not give such a high quality result.

ISO A series — trimmed

A0	841 x 1189 (mm)	33.1 x 46.8 (inches)
A1	594 x 841	23.4 x 33.1
A2	420 x 594	16.5 x 23.4
A3	297 x 420	11.7 x 16.5
A4	210 x 297	8.3 x 11.7
A5	148 x 210	5.8 x 8.3
A6	105 x 148	4.1 x 5.8
A7	74 x 105	2.9 x 4.1
A8	52 x 74	2.1 x 2.9
A9	37 x 52	1.5 x 2.1
A10	26 x 37	1 x 1.5
RA0	860 x 1120	34.4 x 44.8
RA1	610 x 860	24.4 x 34.4
RA2	430 x 610	17.2 x 24.4

ISO A series (trimmed)

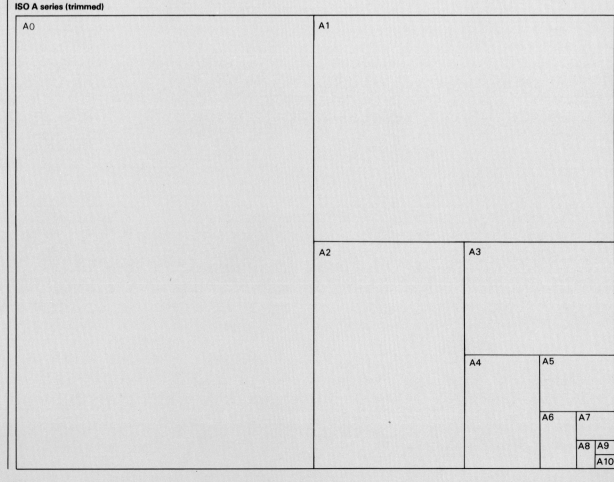

The 'A' series system of sizing paper was first adopted in Germany in 1922, where it is still referred to as 'DIN A'. The sizes were calculated in such a way that each size is made by dividing the size immediately above into two equal parts. the sizes are all the same geometrically, as they are made using the same diagonal. The basic size (A0) is one square metre in area. It is important to note that the 'A' series sizes refer to the *trimmed* sheet. The untrimmed sizes are known as 'RA'. About 26 countries have now officially adopted the 'A' system, and it is likely that this system will gradually replace the wide range of paper sizes still used in Great Britain and the USA.

Unlike the metricated 'A' series of paper sizes, the British and American systems refer to the untrimmed size. In Britain sizes are usually referred to by name, but as this can lead to confusion, both the name and the size should be given in any specification.

British — untrimmed

Crown	15 x 20 (inches)
Double crown	20 x 30
Quad crown	30 x 40
Demy	17½ x 22½
Small demy	15½ x 20
Double demy	22½ x 35
Quad demy	35 x 45
Foolscap	13½ x 17
Small foolscap	13¼ x 16½
Double foolscap	17 x 27
Quad foolscap	27 x 34
Imperial	22 x 30
Medium	18 x 23
Double medium	23 x 36
Post	15¼ x 19
Large Post	16½ x 21
Double large post	21 x 33
Royal	20 x 25
Double royal	25 x 40

American — untrimmed

Writings	16 x 21 (inches)
Basic size — writings	17 x 22
Writings	17 x 28
Writings	18 x 23
Writings	18 x 46
Writings	19 x 24
Basic size — covers	20 x 26
Covers	23 x 35
Printings	24 x 36
Basic size — offset, book	25 x 38
Covers	26 x 40
Printings	28 x 42
Printings	30½ x 41
Printings	32 x 44
Printings	33 x 44
Printings	35 x 45
Printings	36 x 48
Printings	38 x 50
Printings	38 x 52
Printings	41 x 54
Printings	44 x 64

German and Swiss — untrimmed

Vereinsdruck 1	500 x 760 (mm)
Vereinsdruck 2	550 x 840
Vereinsdruck 3	640 x 940
Vereinsdruck 4	700 x 1000
Normal A1	610 x 860

Regular paper subdivisions (British)

Subdivisions into 'thirds' (British)

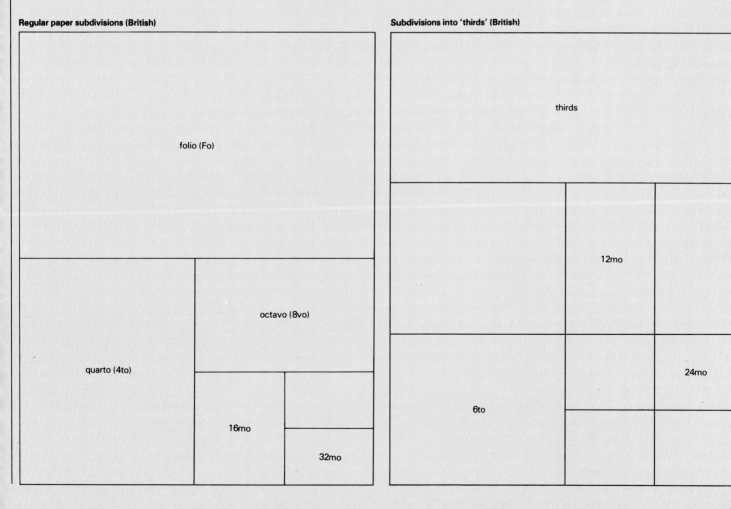

Manufacturers and suppliers, etc

United Kingdom

GENERAL SUPPLIERS

Acorn Art Shop, 28 Colquoun St., Glasgow.
Aitken, Dott & Son, 26 Castle St, Edinburgh.
Fred Aldus Ltd, 37 Lever St, Manchester.
Alexander of Newington, 58 South Clerk St, Edinburgh.
The Arts Centre, 71 Causeyside St, Paisley.
The Arts Centre, 583 Fishponds Rd, Fishponds, Bristol.
Art Repro, 8 De-la-Beche St, Swansea.
The Art Shop, 40 Castle St, Guildford.
The Art Shop, 54 Castle St, Trowbridge.
The Art Shop, Great Coleman St, Ipswich.
E. Bayliss Wright & Co, 21 Prince of Wales Rd, Norwich.
Binney & Smith, Ampthill Rd, Bedford.
The Blue Gallery, 16 Joy St, Barnstaple.
H. Blyth & Co, 53 Back George St, Manchester.
Brentwood Arts, 106 London Rd, Stockton Heath, Warrington.
Briggs Art and Book Shop, 15 Crouch St, Colchester.
Cannon Graphics Ltd, 14-18 Old St, London EC1.
The Chantry Studios, Pauls Row, High Wycombe.
C. J. Graphics Ltd, 4 Ganton St, London W1.
Joseph Colgrove Ltd, Lincoln House, Turl Street, Oxford.
Colyer & Southey Ltd, 17-18 Tooks Court, Cursitor St, London EC4.
Colyer Thorpe Ltd, 31 King Street, West 3, Manchester.
The Copy Shop, 95 Fore Street, Exeter.
Copystat (Cardiff) Ltd, Repro House, Park Lane, Cardiff.
L. Cornellison & Son, 22 Great Queen St, London WC2.
Cowling & Wilcox, 26 Broadwick St, London W1
Daler Board Co. Ltd, Wareham, Dorset.
J. Davey & Sons Ltd, 70 Bridge St, Manchester.
The Dollar Gallery, 22 West Burnside, Glasgow.
J. B. Duckett & Co Ltd, 74 Bradfield Rd, Sheffield.
DPP Graphics Ltd, 31 Aylesbury St, Bletchley, Milton Keynes.

Daley's Art & Graphic Materials 37 Great Horton Rd, Bradford, W. Yorks.
The Drawing Centre, 76 North St, Leeds.
The East Anglian Art Shop and Haste Gallery, 3 Great Coleman St, Ipswich.
E. P. Instruments Ltd, 23 Whitchurch Rd, Cardiff.
Eurographics, 18-20 Clevedon Terrace, Bristol.
Falcon Art Supplies Ltd, 26 George St, Prestwich.
Ivor Fields, 21 Stert St, Abingdon.
W. Frank Gadsby Ltd, 9 Bradford St, Walsall.
Geliot-Whitman Ltd, 22 Herschell St, London SE23.
Greyfriars Art Shop, 1 Greyfriars Place, Edinburgh.
Gordons Gallery, 152 Victoria Rd, Scarborough.
Handyman, 43 Tamworth St, Lichfield.
Harper and Tunstall, 13 Cannon Street, Birmingham; 16 Lynedoch Crescent Glasgow G3; Denington, Wellingborough.
H. D. Finch, 1 University St, Belfast.
Helix International Ltd, P.O. Box 15, Lye, Stourbridge.
E. Hopper & Co Ltd, 48 Market Place, Malton, Yorks.
International Graphics (Ireland) Ltd, 28 Merrion Square, Dublin 2.
Langford & Hill, 10 Warwick St, London W1.
Liverpool Fine Arts, 85a Bold St, Liverpool.
Llanelli Art Centre, 31 Market St, Llanelli.
Lomas & Baynes Ltd, 44 Canal Street, Manchester.
Mair & Son, 46 The Strand, Exmouth.
John Mathieson & Co, 48 Frederick St, Edinburgh.
Mawson Swan and Morgan Ltd, Alliance House, Grey Street, Newcastle-upon-Tyne.
Miller's Drawing Materials, 569 Sauchiehall St, Glasgow G3.
O'Sullivans, 66 Camden St, Dublin 2.
A. Perkin & Son, 2a Bletchington Rd, Hove, Sussex.
Reeves & Sons Ltd, Lincoln Rd, Enfield, Middx.
Reeves Art Materials, 178 Kensington High St, London W8.
C. Roberson & Co Ltd, 71 Parkway, London NW1.

George Rowney & Co Ltd, P.O. Box 10, Bracknell, Berks.
George Rowney & Co Ltd, 121 Percy St, London W1.
Studio 10, 10 Edleston Rd, Crewe.
Torbay Art and Craft Centre, 109 Union St, Torquay, Devon.
Trinity Galleries, Trinity St, Colchester, Essex.
Van der Velde Ltd., Blandford Street, Newcastle-upon-Tyne.
Warwick & Paulig Ltd, Legion Works, Kimberley Rd, London NW6. (drawing boards etc.)
Will D.O, 79 Victoria Rd, Farnborough, Hants.
Winsor & Newton Ltd, Wealdstone, Harrow. Middx.
Winsor & Newton Ltd, (showroom), 51 Rathbone Place, London W1.

PAINT
The Acrylic Paint Co, 28 Thornhill Rd, London N1.
Berol Ltd, Northway House, High Rd, Whetstone, London N20.
Brodie and Middleton, 79 Long Acre, London WC2.
John T. Keep & Sons Ltd, 15 Theobalds Rd, London WC1.
Spectrum Oil Colours, 51 Brighton Rd, Horsham, Sussex.
A. E. Tunley and Sons Ltd, 12/13 Gloucester St, Swindon, Wilts.

RAW CANVAS
Kantex (Fabrics Ltd), 22 Rathbone Place, London W1.
Russell and Chapple, 23 Monmouth St, London WC2.

PAINTING EQUIPMENT
Guanghwa Co, 7-9 Newport Place, London WC2. (bamboo brushes).
S.H. Cornell Ltd, 38 Lind Rd, Sutton, Surrey, (brushes).
J. F. Hill & Co, 1 Townsend Close, Cranfield, Beds. (brushes)
Lion Brush Works Ltd, Planet Place, Killingworth, Newcastle-upon-Tyne.
R. Morrall & Sons, Trafalgar Works, Trafalgar St, Sheffield, (palette knives).
Nailsworth Art Gallery, Fountain St, Nailsworth, Glos. (easels).

Team Valley Brush Co Ltd, Whickham Industrial Estate, Swalwell. Newcastle-upon-Tyne.

PAPERS
(wide range, unless otherwise stated)
H. Band & Co Ltd, Brent Way, High St, Brentford. (hand-made parchment and vellum).
Bowaters U.K. Paper Co Ltd, Sittingbourne Mill, Sittingbourne, Kent.
Culter Mills Paper Co. Ltd, Culter Mills, Peterculter, Aberdeen.
Falkiner Fine Papers Ltd, 4 Mart St, London WC2. (all types of hand-made papers).
Frank Grunfield Ltd, 32 Bedford Square, London WC1.
Green, Barcham & Co Ltd, Hayle Mill, Maidstone, Kent. (hand-made water colour and drawing papers).
Inveresk Group Ltd, Clan House, Tudor St, London EC4.
Paperchase, 216 Tottenham Court Rd, London W1.
G. F. Smith & Son (London) Ltd, 2 Leathermarket, London SE).
Wiggins Teape (Mill Sales) Ltd, P.O. Box 88, Gateway House, Basing View, Basingstoke, Hants.
Reed Paper & Board (U.K.) Ltd, Reed House, 82 Piccadilly, London W1.

DRAWING EQUIPMENT
(wide range, unless otherwise stated)
Berol Ltd, Northway House, High Rd, Whetstone, London N20. (pencils).
Copystat Cardiff Ltd, Repro House, Park Lane, Cardiff.
Cumberland Graphics Ltd, Bearwood Rd, Smethwick, Warley, W. Midlands.
His Nibs, 182 Drury Lane, London WC2. (pens and nibs).
Mentmore Manufacturing Co Ltd, Platignum House, Six Hills Way, Stevenage, Herts. (Platignum pens).
E. S. Perry Ltd, Osmiroid Works, Gosport, Hants. (Osmiroid pens).
Reece, Hartley & Co, Building One, GEC Estate, East Lane, Wembley, Middx. (Rotring pens)
Royal Sovereign & Staedtler Ltd, Glamorgan. (pencils).
Venus Esterbrook Ltd, Kings Lynn, Norfolk. (pencils).

AIRBRUSHES
The DeVilbiss Co Ltd, Ringwood Rd, West Howe, Bournemouth; 63 Blucher St, Birmingham; Glasgow Rd, Kirkintilloch; 12 Charlotte St, Manchester; Temple House, Temple Way, Bristol.

PRINTMAKING MATERIALS
Hunter, Penrose & Littlejohn, 7 Spa Rd, London SE16. (presses)
T. N. Lawrence & Son Ltd, Bleeding Heart Yard, Grenville St, London N1. (etching and wood engraving tools, woodblocks).
Henry Righton & Co Ltd, 70 Pentonville Rd, London N1. (copper sheets).
Selectasine Screen Printing Supplies, 22 Bulstrode St, London W1.
Sericol Group Ltd, 24 Parsons Green Lane, London SW6. (silkscreen).

DRY TRANSFER LETTERING
Chartpak Ltd. Station Rd, Didcot, Oxford.
Letraset U.K. Ltd, 195 Waterloo Road, London SE1.
Mecanorma Ltd. 10 School Rd, London NW10.

PHOTOCOPYING EQUIPMENT
Agfa-Gevaert Ltd, 27 Great West Rd, Brentford Middx.
I.B.M. (United Kingdom) Ltd, 40 Basinghall St, London EC2.
Mitsubishi Corporation, Bow Bells House, Bread St, London EC4.
Rank Xerox (UK) Ltd, Rank Xerox House, 338 Euston Rd, London NW1.
3M United Kingdom Ltd, 3M House, P.O. Box 1, Bracknell, Berks.

PHOTOGRAPHIC SUPPLIES
Wallace Heaton, 127 New Bond St, London W1.
Keith Johnson Photographic, Ramillies House, 1-2 Ramillies St, London W1; 11 Bennet Rd, Headingley, Leeds 6.
Kodak Ltd. P.O. Box 66, Kodak House, Station Road, Hemel Hempstead, Herts.
Leeds Camera Centre Ltd, Lovell House, North St, Leeds.
Pegasus House, 375 West George St, Glasgow G2.
Jas A. Pollock Ltd, 87 Great Victoria St, Belfast.
Hamilton Tait, 141 Bruntsfield Place, Edinburgh.

PRINTING EQUIPMENT
Heidelberg Graphic Equipment Ltd. 23 Eyot Gardens, London W6.
Linotype-Paul Ltd. Kingsbury Works, Kingsbury Rd, London NW9.
Monotype Corporation, Honeycrock Lane, Salfords, Redhill, Surrey.

SOCIETIES ETC OF INTEREST TO ILLUSTRATORS AND GRAPHIC DESIGNERS
The Association of Illustrators, 10 Barley Mow Passage, Chiswick, London W4.

Design Council, 28 Haymarket, London SW1.
Designers and Art Directors Association, Nash House, Carlton House Terrace, London SW1.
Institute of Incorporated Photographers, Amwell End, Ware, Herts.
International Council of Graphic Design, Warren House, St Pauls Cray Rd, Chislehurst, Kent.
National Graphical Association, Graphic House, 63-67 Bromham Rd, Bedford.
Society of Industrial Artists and Designers, 12 Carlton House Terrace, London SW1.
Society of Lithographic Artists, Designers, Engravers and Process Workers, 55 Clapham Common, South Side, London SW4.

United States

GENERAL SUPPLIERS

Aldy Graphic Supply Inc, 1115 Henn Avenue, Minneapolis.

Alvin & Co Inc, 1330 Blue Hills Avenue, Bloomfield, Conn 06002; Box 188, Windsor, Conn. 06095; 2418 Teagarden St, San Leandro, Calif. 94577.

Arthur Brown & Bro. Inc, 2 W. 46th St, New York, N.Y. 10036.

Theo. Alteneder & Sons, 1225 Spring Gardens St, Philadelphia, Pa. 19123.

Art Source Inc, 524 Central Way, Kirkland, Seattle, Washington.

Asel Art Supply Inc, 2701 Cedar Springs, Dallas, Texas.

Associated Graphic Design, 1752 S E Hawthorne Boulevard, Portland, Oregon.

Baders Art Supply, Clayton Store, 8007 Maryland, St Louis, Missouri.

Central Art Supply Co, 1126 Walnut, Philadelphia, Pa. 19123.

Charette Corporation, 212 East 54th St, New York, N.Y.; 31 Olympia Avenue, Wob. Boston.

Clinton Art Supplies, 126 N Labrea, Los Angeles, Calif.

Connoisseur Studio, Box 7187, Louisville, Ky. 40207.

Daniels, 2543 W 6th Street, Los Angeles, Calif.

Dixie Art Supplies Inc, 323 Magazine, New Orleans, Louisiana.

Dupont Graphic Arts Inc, 745-T Route 46, Parisippany, N.J. 07054.

Duro Art Supply Co Inc, 1832 Juneway Terrace, Chicago, Ill. 60626.

Faber Castell Corp, 41 Dickerson St, Newark, N.J. 07107.

Favor-Ruhl, 4863 Woodward, Detroit, Michigan.

The Fine Art Store, 8843 Clairemont Mesa Boulevard, San Diego, Calif.

Sam Flax, 55 E 55th St, New York, N.Y.

Smith J. Gordon Inc, 2808 Commerce Street, Dallas, Texas.

Gramercy Corp, 1145 A., W. Custer Place, Denver Col. 80223.

Grand Central Artists Materials Inc, 18 E 40 St, New York, N.Y.

M. Grumbacher Inc, 460 West 34th St, New York, N.Y. 10001.

Keufel & Esser, 20 T Whippany Road, Morristown, N.J. 07960.

Koh-i-Noor Rapidograph Inc, 100-T North Street, Bloomsbury, N.J.

Loew-Correll Inc, 131 W. Rugby Avenue, Palisades Park, N.J. 07650.

Lutz Superdyne Inc, 64 70th Street, Guttenberg, N.J. 107093.

Markal Co, 270 North Washtenaw Ave, Chicago, Ill.

The Morilla Co Inc, 43-01 21st St, Long Island City, N.Y. 11101.

Morris Art Supplies, 3141 Main, Kansas City, Kansas.

Morse Graphic Art Supply Co, 1938 Euclid, Cleveland, Ohio.

Multi-Graphic Market Ltd, 887 Spring Street NW, Atlanta, Georgia.

Nova Blue, 4017 East St, Fairfax, Va.

Pickett Industries, 17621 Von Karman Avenue, Irvine, Calif. 92713.

T-Square Miami Blueprint Co Inc, 636 SW 1 Ave, Miami, Florida.

F. Weber Co, Wayne & Windrim Aves, Philadelphia, Pa. 19144.

Winsor & Newton Inc, 555 Winsor Drive, Secaucus, N.J. 07094.

WS, 3425 Cahuenga Boulevard West, Hollywood, Los Angeles, Calif.

Yasutomo & Co, 24 California St, San Francisco, Calif. 94111.

PAINT

(wide range, unless otherwise stated)

Advance Process Supply Co, 400 N. Noble St, Chicago, Ill. 60622.

Bocour Artists Colors Inc, 1291 Rochester Rd, Troy, Mich. 48084.

Cooper Color Inc, 3006 Mercury Rd, Jacksonville, Florida 32207.

Danacolors Inc, 1833 Egbert Avenue, San Francisco, Cal. 94124. (bulletin, fluorescent)

Day-Glo Colour Corp, 4732 St Clair Avenue, Cleveland, Ohio 44103. (fluorescent)

Finke Co, 2226 Bertwynn Drive, Dayton, Ohio 45439. (oil).

Harold W. Mangelson & Sons Inc, 8200 J. St. Omaha, Nebra. 68127. (water colors).

Markal Co, 250 N. Wasltenaw Avenue, Chicago, Ill. 60612.

Masury & Son Inc, 1400 Severn St, Baltimore, Md. 20730.

Palmer Paint Products Inc, 1291 Rochester Rd, Troy, Mich. 48084.

Salis International, 4040 N. 29th Avenue, Hollywood, Florida 33020.

Sanford Corp, 2740 Washington Blvd., Bellwood, Ill. 60104.

R. Simmons Inc, 510 6th Avenue, N.Y. 10011. (water colors).

Skyline Distributing Co, 1609 12th Avenue N., Great Falls. Mont. 59403.

Spectronics Corp, 956-T Brush Hollow Road, Westbury, N.Y. (fluorescent).

BRUSHES

(wide range, unless otherwise stated)

Artistic Brush MFG Corp, 103 Central Avenue, Clifton, N.J. 07015.

Burnstone Enterprises, 7205B Lockport Place, Lorton, Va. 22079. (red sable).

Gyros Products Co Inc, 200 Park Avenue, New York, N.Y. 10003. (oil).

Hopper Koch Inc, Box 3249, N. Hollywood, Cal. 91609.

Hunt MFG Co, 1405 Locust St, Philadelphia, Pa 19102. (oil).

Marx Brush MFG Co Inc, 400 Commercial Avenue, Palisades Park, N.J. 07650. (red sable).

DRAWING MEDIA

Berol Corp. USA, Eagle Rd, Danbury, Conn. 06810. (carbon, charcoal pencils).

Binney & Smith Inc, 1100 Church Lane, Easton, Pa. 18042. (chalks).

Carters Ink Co, 275 Wyman St, Waltham, Mass. 02154.(pens).

Charvoz Carsen Corp, 5 Daniel Rd, Fairfield, N.J. 07006. (pens).

Eriksons Crafts Inc, 1101 N. Halstead, Hutchinson, Kans. 67501. (charcoal).

Fullerton Sales Co, 847 Air Way, Glendale, Cal. 91201 (charcoal).

General Pencil Co, 67 Fleet St, Jersey City, N.J. 07306. (pens, pencils).

Hanover Pen Corp, 501 Fame Avenue, Hanover, Pa. 17331. (wide range).

Koh-I-Noor Rapidograph Inc, 100 North St, Bloomsbury, N.J. (pens, pencils).

Pentel of America, 2715 Columbia St, Terrance, Calif 90503.(oil pastels).

Rich Art Color Co Inc, 109 Graham Lane, Lodi N.J. 07644. (charcoal).

J.S. Staedtler Inc, P.O. Box 787-T, Chatsworth, Calif.

Stanislaus South West, 1208 Viceroy, Dallas, Texas, 75247. (charcoal).

DRAWING BOARDS AND EQUIPMENT

Fairgate Rule Co, Cold Spring, New York, N.Y.

Keuffel & Esser Co, 20 Whippany Rd, Morristown, N.J. 07960.

Swanson, 803 Park Avenue, Murfreesboro, Tenn. 37130.

Tara Materials Inc, Industrial Park Drive, Lawrenceville, Ga 30245.

Wolsey Co. 15110 E. Nelson St, City of Industry, Cal. 91747.

CANVAS

Fredrix Artists Canvas, Box 646, Lawrenceville, Ga. 30245. (wide range).

Harold M. Pitman Co, 515 Secaucus Rd, Secaucus, N.J. (wide range).

Wolsey Co, 15110 E. Nelson St, City of Industry. Cal. 91747. (polymer).

AIRBRUSHES

Advance Process Supply Co, 400 N. Noble St, Chicago, Ill. 60622.

Badger Air-brush Co, 9128 W. Belmont Avenue, Franklin Park, Ill. 60131.

The DeVilbiss Co, 300 Phillips Avenue, Toledo, Ohio 43612.

Douglas & Sturgess, 730 Bryant St, San Francisco, Cal. 94107.

Paasche Airbrush Co, 1909 Diversey, Chicago, Ill. 60614.

World Air Brush MFG Co, 2171 N. California Avenue, Chicago, Ill. 60647.

X-Acto, 45-35 Van Dam St, Long Island City, N.Y. 11101.

PRINTMAKING

Graphic Chemical & Ink Co, 728 N. Yale Avenue, P.O. Box 27, Villa Park, Ill. 60181.

DRAWING OFFICE EQUIPMENT

Bishop Graphics Drafting Supply Center, 835 Stewart Drive, Sunnyvale, San Francisco, Calif.

Bruning Division, Addressograph Multigraph Corp., 1834 Walden Office Square, Schaumberg, Ill.

Hopper's Office Furniture, 3901 San Fernando Rd, Glendale, Los Angeles, Calif.

May Line Co, 627 N. Commerce St, Sheboygan, Wisconsin.

Vemco Corporation, Fair Oaks & Fillmore, Pasadena, Calif.

PAPERS (wide range unless otherwise stated)

American Pad & Paper Co, Box 1250, Holyoke, Mass. 01040.

Bee Paper Co Inc, 100 8th St, Passaic, N.J. 07055.

Cartis Paper Div, James River Corp., Paper Mill Rd, Newark, Dela. 19711. (litho).

Class Craft Div, Box 448, St. Louis, Mo. 63166.

Craft World Inc, Rt 27 & Hahn Rd, Westminster. Md. 21157.

Crescent Cardboard Co, 100 W. Willow Rd, Wheeling, Ill. 60090.

Fax Corp, 1 Rowan St, Danbury, Conn. 06810

GAF Corp 525 E Imperial Highway, Los Angeles, Calif. (tracing paper)

National Card, Mat & Board Co, 14455 Don Julian Rd, City of Industry, Cal. 91746.

Scott Paper Co, 30 Gaylord Street, South Hadley, Mass.

Special Papers Inc, 8 Sandfordtown Rd, W. Redding, Conn. 06896.

Steiner Paper Corp, 601 W. 26th St, New York, N.Y. 10001.

Strathmore Paper Co, S. Broad St, Westfield, Mass. 01085.

DRY TRANSFER LETTERING

Chartpak, 1 River Rd, Leeds, Mass. 01053.

Letraset Manufacturing Inc, 24 Empire Boulevard, Moonachie, N.J. 07074.

Martin Instrument Co, 13450 Farmington Rd, Livonia, Michigan, Ill. 48150.

Transfertech, 225 Park Ave S, New York 10003.

Zipatone Inc, 150 Fencl Lane, Hillside, Ill. 60162.

PHOTOCOPYING EQUIPMENT

Eastman Kodak Co, 343 State Street TR, Rochester, N.Y. 14650.

IBM, 360 Hamilton Place, White Plains, New York, N.Y. 10601.

Mitsubishi International Corp, 277 Park Ave, New York, N.Y. 10017.

3M Centre, St. Paul, Minnesota, 55101.

Xerox Corporation, Stanford, Conn. 06094.

PHOTOGRAPHIC SUPPLIERS

Bennett's Camera, 3363 Severn Ave, Metaine, New Orleans, Louisiana.

Adolph Gasser, 5733 Geary Blvd, San Francisco, Calif.

Claus Gelotte Inc, 284 Boylston St, Boston, Mass.

Mayfair Photo, 2817 Coney Island Ave, New York, N.Y.

Ron-Com Photo, 226 Massachusetts Ave NE, Washington DC.

Schaeffer Photo, 6520 W. Sunset Blvd, Los Angeles, Calif.

PRINTING EQUIPMENT

Mergan Thaler Linotype Co, 201 Old Country Road, Melville, New York, N.Y. 11747.

Monotype Graphic Systems Inc, 509 West Gulf Road, Arlington Heights, Ill. 60005.

SOCIETIES ETC OF INTEREST TO ILLUSTRATORS AND GRAPHIC DESIGNERS

Art Directors Club, 488 Madison Ave, New York, N.Y. 10022.

Graphic Arts International Union, 1900 L Street NW, Washington DC, 20036.

Lithographers and Photo Engravers International Union, 233 West 49 St, New York, N.Y. 10028.

Professional Photographers of America, 1090 Executive Way, Oak Leaf Common, Des Plaines, Ill. 60018.

Society of Illustrators, 128 East 63 St, New York, N.Y. 10021.

Society of Typographic Artists, 228 North La Salle St, Chicago, Ill. 60601.

INDEX

ACKNOWLEDGEMENTS

Numerals indicate page numbers

10 Lascaux: Snark International; Book of Hours: Bodleian Library, Oxford. **12** Uccello: Uffizi (Scala); Leonardo: Biblioteca Reale, Turin. **13** Toulouse-Lautrec: Musée d'Albi. **17** Photo: Peter Cogram. **18** Photo: Peter Cogram. **19** Maestro de Trionfo della Morte: Pisa, Cimitero Monumentale (Scala); Altimira: Scala; Dürer: reproduced by courtesy of the Trustees of the British Museum. **20** O'Keefe: The Museum of Modern Art, N.Y.; Toulouse-Lautrec: Musée d'Albi (Scala); Goodman: The Museum of Modern Art, Gift of Mr and Mrs Walter Bareiss; Photo: Michael Busselle. **21** Photo: Michael Busselle. **22** Michelangelo: British Museum; Leonardo: reproduced by Gracious Permission of Her Majesty Queen Elizabeth II (Windsor Castle, Royal Library); Rembrandt: Kupferstichkabinett, Staatliche Museen, W. Berlin; Altimira: Snark; Photos: Peter Cogram. **24** Turner: British Museum; Photo: Michael Freeman. **25** Bellows: Fogg Art Museum, Bequest of Meta and Paul J. Sachs; Daumier: Bibliothèque Nationale, Paris (Scala); Kollwitz: National Gallery of Art, Washington DC, Rosenwald Collection. **26** La Tour: reproduced by courtesy of the Trustees, National Gallery, London; Legros: British Museum; Muir: Sunday Times. **27** Degas: Hammer Foundation, LA, (Snark) ©S.P.A.D.E.M.; McCarver: artist's collection. **28** Ingres: Louvre (Snark). **29** Constable: Victoria and Albert Museum, Crown Copyright; Wood: Whitney Museum of American Art, NY; Dalley: artist's collection; Hogarth: Private Collection; Seurat: Yale University Art Gallery, Everett Meeks Fund. **30** Photo: Peter Cogram. **31** Boyd Harte, Davis, Hollyhead, Williams: artists' collections. **32** Rosa: Ecole de Beaux-Arts, Paris. **33** Bottecelli: British Museum; Leonardo: Biblioteca Reale, Turin. **34** Dürer: Kupferstichkabinett, Staatliche Museen, W. Berlin. **34-5** Leonardo: reproduced by Gracious Permission of Her Majesty Queen Elizabeth II (Windsor Castle, Royal Library); Dürer (top): Albertina, Vienna; Dürer (bottom): Metropolitan Museum of Art, Robert Lehmann Collection. **36** Rubens:Fitzwilliam Museum, Cambridge, UK. **37** Van Dyck: British Museum; Rembrandt: Metropolitan Museum of Art, Bequest of Mrs. H.O. Harvemeyer; Hogarth: British Museum; Rosa: British Museum; Rowlandson: J. Grego — *Rowlandson the Caricaturist,* Chatto and Windus, 1880. **38** Gibson: from *Sketches in Egypt,* Harper & Bros. 1899; May: British Museum; Du Maurier: *Punch.* **38-9** Rackham: British Museum; **39** Caran d'Ache: *3 ème Album,* E. Plon, Nourrit et Cie., 1893; Sullivan: British Museum. **40** Picasso: Galerie Louise Leiris, Paris ©S.P.A.D.E.M.; Van Gogh: British Museum; Matisse: British Museum © S.P.A.D.E.M. Grosz: *Ecce Homo,* Der Malik Verlag, Berlin, 1923. **41** Photo: Michael Busselle. **43** Niczewski: artist's collection; Gaudier-Brzeska: Victoria and Albert Museum, Crown Copyright. **44** Beardsley: from *Rape of the Lock,* 1896 (Mansell Collection); Ardizzone: collection of the artist; Glaser: for Hermann Hesse Calendar, collection of the artist; Brown: for *New Society;* Fraser: for *English Legends,* Batsford, 1950. **45** Sendak: from *Higglety Pigglety Pop! or there must be more to life,* Bodley Head, US: Harper and Row, 1967; Peake: for *Treasure Island,* Methuen (coll. Gilmore); Jacques: for *Radio Times* (artist's collection). **46** Dulac: British Museum; Glaser: for *New York Magazine.* **47** Hogarth: Private Collection, © Artist; Jak: © *Evening Standard.* **48** Holmes: for *Time* magazine; Baker: for Penguin Books; Masterman: collection of artist; Gray: for *Sunday Times;* French horn: from *The Book of Music* ©QED/Macdonald Educational Ltd. **49** Steadman: for *Weekend* magazine. **50** Sanderson: artist's collection. **51** Allen: artist's collection. Hogarth: from *Walking Tours of Old Boston,* © Boston Public Library, Dept. of Prints and Drawings. **52** MS Douce 135 f.4; MS Douce 93 f.100v: Bodleian Library, Oxford; Vermeer: The Greater London Council as Trustees of the Iveagh Bequest, Kenwood. **53** Van Eyck: Gemäldegalerie, Staatliche Museen, W. Berlin. **54** Blake, Thornton: Victoria and Albert Museum, Crown Copyright. **55** Degas: Burrell Collection, Glasgow Museum of Art © S.P.A.D.E.M.; Rowlandson and Pugin: *Microcosm of London,* 1809 (British Museum). **56** Larsson: National museum, Stockholm; Pyle: *Harper's* Dec. 1905, Delaware Art Museum, Howard Pyle Collection. **57** Colville: National Gallery of Canada, Ottawa; Rockwell: University Art Gallery, Nebraska, Gift of Nathan Gold. **58, 60** Photos: Peter Cogram. **63** Crabbe: courtesy of Young Artists; Sardet: courtesy of *Sunday Times;* Holmes: collection Sonny Mehta **65** Photos: Peter Cogram. **68** Bayley: from *The Tyger Voyage* by Richard Adams, Jonathan Cape Ltd.; Lee: from *Faeries;* Weaver: artist's collection. **69** Photos: Peter Cogram. **70** Brookes, Grimwood, Dalley: artists' collections. **71** Hardie, Norrington; artists' collections. **72** Photos: Peter Cogram. **74** Leonard: artist's collection. **75** Manham: for Penguin Books; Sanders: artist's collection. **77** Hiroshige: Victoria and Albert Museum, Crown Copyright. **78** Cooke: Private Collection. **78-86** Heale: artist's collection. **81** Martin: courtesy of Christie's Contemporary Art; Hockney: Private Collection, London. **82** Solly: courtesy of Christie's Contemporary Art. **83** Spencer: Private Collection, London; Proctor: Private Collection, London. **84** Toulouse-Lautrec: coll. Mlle. Marcelle Lender (Cooper-Bridgeman Library). **86** Pasmore: Christie's Contemporary Art. **87** Ford: Christie's Contemporary Art. **88** Uccello: reproduced by courtesy of The Trustees, National Gallery, London. **89-91** Agricola, Fludd, Dürer: Ann Ronan's Picture Library; Leonardo: Fotomas Index. **91** Dürer: Albertina, Vienna (Cooper Bridgeman Library); Brunel: Science Museum (Lund Humphries Ltd.). **93** Ford Motor Co. Ltd. **94** Photo: Peter Cogram. **96** Johnson: Fischer Fine Art, London; Black: *Sunday Times.* **97** Photo: Peter Cogram. **100** Photo: Peter Cogram. **101** *Sunday Times.* **104-5** Mary Evans Picture Library. **107** Mary Evans Picture Library; E.C. Kinsey; Book of Hours: Bodleian Library, Oxford (MS. Liturg. 41,ff 4ᵛ-5). **117** Photo: Peter Cogram. **125** Jon Wyand. **128-9** Photos: Peter Cogram. **130** Bayer: Private collection. **136** Alastair Campbell; Jon Wyand. **137** Peter Cogram. **141** Page from *The World Atlas of Railways* © Rand McNally/Intercontinental Books/Chris Milsom/Q.E.D. **145** QED for *Sunday Times.* **147** Photo: Peter Cogram. **149** Photo: Peter Cogram. **150-5** Michael Peters. **156** Peter Cogram. **158** From *The Book of Music* © Macdonald Educational/Q.E.D. **161** T.R.P. Slavin. **162-3** Jon Wyand. **165** Peter Cogram. **166** Michael Freeman. **167** Michael Busselle. **169** Photos: Jon Wyand, Peter Cogram. **170-1** Michael Freeman. **170** Roger Pring; Michael Busselle. **171** Dora Kinsey. **172** Michael Freeman. **173** Michael Busselle. **174-5** Jon Wyand. **175** Michael Freeman. **176** Michael Freeman. **177** Michael Busselle. **178-9** Michael Freeman. **179** Michael Busselle. **180** Peter Cogram. **182-3** Photos: John Wyand, Peter Cogram. **182** Michael Busselle. **186-7** Jon Wyand. **190-1** Jon Wyand. **193, 196** Michael Busselle. **198** Photos: E.C. Kinsey; Jon Wyand. **199** Michael Busselle. **203** QED/Macdonald Educational Ltd. **206-7** Photos: Jon Wyand; Tony Dumpleton.

QED would also like to extend special thanks to Geo. Rowney & Co. Ltd., the Moving Picture Company, and Keyth Rooney for their help.